The Tank Killers

A History of America's

World War II Tank Destroyer Force

Also by Harry Yeide

Steel Victory : The Heroic Story of America's
Independent Tank Battalions at War in Europe

The Tank Killers

A History of America's

World War II Tank Destroyer Force

Harry Yeide

CASEMATE

Havertown, PA

Published by
CASEMATE
2114 Darby Road, Havertown, PA
Phone: 610-853-9131

Typeset and design by
Savas Publishing & Consulting Group

ISBN 1-932033-26-2

First edition, first printing

Cataloging-in-Publication data is available
from the Library of Congress

Printed in the United States of America

To those who fought

An M3 on maneuvers in 1942. A larger gun shield was added in response to combat reports from the Philippines. *NA*

Contents

Maps

Illustrations

Preface

Yoke (Company B commander) to Yoke 10 (probable platoon commander): "What is your situation now and did you get anything?"

Yoke to Sugar 6 (battalion headquarters): "They have approximately five enemy vehicles knocked out. Situation is pretty good. . . ."

Sugar 6 to Yoke: "Did we get them?"

Yoke to Sugar 6: "The can-openers got some and we got some. . . . Five Mark IVs, two by our cans [and] three by TDs."

— Tactical radio logs of the 743d Tank Battalion, 15 January 1945

It was tanks that led me to tank destroyers (TDs). While researching *Steel Victory, The Heroic Story of America's Independent Tank Battalions at War in Europe* (Presidio Press, 2003), I frequently encountered this *other* presence: A doctrinal division between the tank and tank destroyer forces that left tankers poorly equipped to deal with heavy German panzers, references to tank destroyers in radio logs and after-action reports (AARs), a photograph of an M4 and an M10 fighting side by side in the streets of Aachen. Then a friend and colleague handed me a copy of Dr. Christopher R. Gabel's short work on tank destroyer doctrine, part of the U.S. Army Command and General Staff College's Leavenworth Papers series. I was hooked.

The tank destroyer was a bold—if some would say flawed—answer to the new challenge posed by the seemingly unstoppable blitzkrieg. The tank killers were in on the fighting from the start in both American theaters, from the losing battle against Japan in the Philippines and the Allied landings in North Africa. The history of the TD battalions is woven into that of the American fighting formations in World War II. This work examines their battle against Hitler's Germany, for it was the struggle against the panzers that determined the destiny of the Tank Destroyer Force. Other battalions fought in the Pacific under conditions bearing no relationship to those anticipated in tank destroyer doctrine.

The reader who would like to take a deeper dive into the experience of a tank destroyer outfit has but a few options. The Center for Northern Appalachian Studies of Saint Vincent College markets two fascinating oral histories of the 704th Tank Destroyer Battalion, *Men of the 704th* and *Reluctant Valor*. Calvin C. Boykin's history of the 814th Tank Destroyer Battalion, *Gare La Bête* (C&R Publications, 1995), and Harry Dunnagan's story of Company B, 813th Tank Destroyer Battalion, *A War to Win* (Royall Dutton Books, 1992), were also still commercially available as of this writing. A few other battalion histories, such as Tom Sherman's account of the 636th Tank Destroyer Battalion, *Seek, Strike, and Destroy*, have been printed by small outlets in limited runs and are difficult to find. Many histories published by the battalions themselves at the end of the war are now only to be found buried in archives and perhaps a few libraries. Lonnie Gill's *Tank Destroyer Forces, WWII* (Turner Publishing Company, 1992), published with the cooperation of the Tank Destroyer Association, pulls together a large number of stories and anecdotes from TD battalion veterans.

This account is intended to give the reader both a broad history of the Tank Destroyer Force and a representative look into the world of the men who fought in the TD battalions. It becomes increasingly selective as the story progresses from Oran to VE Day because of the rapidly expanding size of the conflict. Elements of only two tank destroyer battalions participated in the start of the North Africa campaign in November 1942. There were sixty-one in action in the European and Mediterranean theaters on 8 May 1945. I have selected material from each period that illustrates the experiences of the TD men in general or important unique events.

The selection of material also results in part from the quality of available records. This is the victory or revenge of the unheralded personnel who wrote the AARs and kept the operations journals during the war. Battalions that had good scribes are over-represented in this account. Peter Kopscak, former CO of the 602d Tank Destroyer Battalion, lamented in the outfit's informal history, penned by Bertrand J. Oliver in 1990, "If I had to do it over again, I would put a top individual to be the battalion historian, who would contact each unit daily and record all actions in detail. Too many entries in our battalion history simply state that the battalion command post moved from here to there. . . . Details of our primary battles were omitted."

I have taken some small liberties with texts drawn from the military records to correct grammatical errors and spelling mistakes, and to introduce some consistency in references to unit designators, equipment, dates, and numbers.

Harry Yeide
February 2004

Acknowledgments

I would like to thank my wife Nancy, who is first in my book and makes me better in every endeavor, including this one. Mil gracias, danke schön, and hvala lepo to my editor, Eric Hammel, who has taught me a thing or two about the craft. I am indebted to the assistance offered by many tank destroyer veterans, including Bill Harper and Randolph Mojsl of the 601st; John Pilon of the 609th; Noble Midkiff, Arthur Edson, and John Hudson of the 701st; Edward McClelland of the 773d; and William Zierdt and John Spence of the 805th. I am particularly indebted to John Hudson and Calvin C. Boykin Jr. (814th Tank Destroyer Battalion), who reviewed the manuscript and offered many helpful observations. Lieutenant Colonel Mark Reardon, U.S. Army, provided helpful material and comments. This work would not be as good if it were not for their contributions. All remaining errors are mine.

I am grateful to Calvin C. Boykin Jr. and Thomas Sherman (636th Tank Destroyer Battalion), who granted permission for the use of material drawn from their battalion histories. I would also like to thank the cheerful and efficient public servants at the National Archives and Records Administration's document, microfilm, still photo, and moving image reading rooms in College Park, Maryland. The taxpayer is getting a good deal.

Chapter One

Seek, Strike, and Destroy

The TD's motto, "Seek, Strike, Destroy," won out in a close
race with the laconic slogan, "Guns and Guts."

— "The Tank Killers," *Fortune*, November 1942.

The U.S. Army's Tank Destroyer Force in World War II must rate as
one of the most successful "failures" in American military history. The
tank killers contributed immensely to the success of American arms
under conditions ranging from North African desert to the Italian
mountains to north European forests and cities. They performed a
remarkably diverse range of jobs, with elements of the tank destroyer
battalions fulfilling the roles of antitank weapons, assault guns, artillery,
cavalry, and infantry. They often served at the very pointy end of the
spear. Yet the Army at the end of the war judged the concept of a distinct
Tank Destroyer Force to be so flawed that not a single tank destroyer
battalion existed after November 1946. The Tank Destroyer Force
existed one month short of five years.

Starved of resources by an isolationist and tight-fisted Congress, the
U.S. Army had allowed its tank force to fade into irrelevance after World
War I, and most serious thinking about fighting against tanks faded with

it. The Germans were brewing blitzkrieg while the U.S. Army dozed. In 1936, the Army's Command and General Staff School finally published—for instructional purposes—a manual entitled *Antitank Defense (Tentative)*, which anticipated the establishment of antitank companies in the infantry regiments and an antitank battalion at the divisional level. In 1937, the 2d Infantry Division conducted field tests that resulted in a recommendation that all infantry divisions be reorganized into a triangular—or three-regiment—configuration and establish an eight-gun antitank company in each regiment.[1] Brigadier General Lesley J. McNair was the chief of staff of the 2d Infantry Division and had been keenly interested in antitank defense for several years.[2] He was to have more influence than any other American officer over the evolution of the tank destroyer concept, as well as the way in which the infantry interacted with armor and antitank forces in general.

By 1939, an updated version of the U.S. Army's manual, now entitled *Antimechanized Defense (Tentative)*, advocated an antitank defense in depth, with divisional antitank battalions that were to be both motorized and supplied with a reconnaissance element so that they could mass quickly against armored thrusts. Yet while thinking was beginning to respond to the demands of the looming modern battlefield, the Army's organization and equipment were not. When the Germans overran Poland in 1939, the Army had neither antitank units nor an antitank gun in production. In 1940, a copy of the German 37mm antitank gun—already nearing obsolescence—was hurriedly produced.[3] McNair recognized this deficiency and in June 1940 told the War Department General Staff that the greatest problem confronting it was to find a way to stop armored divisions, and that a flat-trajectory gun heavier than either the 37mm or 75mm guns in use would be necessary for that purpose.[4]

Stunned by the Wehrmacht's romps through Poland and France, Congress found the money, and the Army recreated an Armored Force on 10 July 1940.[5] Induction of the National Guard and Reserves followed, along with implementation of a peacetime draft. The rapid German victories, meanwhile, raised fundamental questions about the soundness of a tank defense based primarily on antitank guns, which the highly respected French Army had tried without success. The fact that most American field artillery officers charged with antitank defense had never even seen a tank in action did not help matters.[6] Nor did the fact that antiaircraft artillery regiments had not yet practiced antitank fire.[7]

McNair, for one, kept the faith. In July 1940, he argued in a memo: "When the armored vehicle faces the antitank gun, the combat is essentially a fire action between a moving gun platform in plain view and a small, carefully concealed, stationary gun platform. The struggle is analogous to that between ships and shore guns, and there is no question that the shore guns are superior—so much so that ships do not accept such a contest. . . . If the gun outmatches the tank, then not only is the gun superior to the tank in antitank defense, but employing armored units against other armored units positively should be avoided whenever possible. The gun, supported properly by foot troops, should defeat hostile armored units by fire and free the friendly armored units for action against objectives which are vulnerable to them."[8]

McNair's arguments were to shape the Tank Destroyer and Armored Forces in fundamental ways. The U.S. Army was to enter the war believing that tanks should not fight tanks, and it selected its equipment on the basis of that doctrinal assumption.

In August 1940, McNair rejected passive antitank defense and first proposed the establishment of mobile antitank groups of three battalions each that would be able to rush to confront a mechanized attack. The next month, the War Department issued a training circular that directed that units concentrate their antitank guns in a mobile reserve and deploy a minimum in fixed initial positions.[9] In April 1941, U.S. Army Chief of Staff General George Marshall ordered his operations chief (G-3) to consider the creation of "highly mobile antitank-antiaircraft units as Corps and Army troops for use in meeting mechanized units." These elements would be in addition to organic antitank weapons.[10]

The Army, meanwhile, had become mired in a debate over who should manage antitank matters—the infantry or the field artillery (the newly created quasi-branch of armor was uninterested and was being told it should not fight tanks in any event)—and how. The Army authorized antitank companies to the infantry divisions in autumn of 1940. Nonetheless, the next spring McNair—by now the chief of staff at General Headquarters (GHQ)—was moved to complain, "It is beyond belief that so little could be done on the [antitank] question, in view of all that is happening abroad." He accused the Army of apathy.[11]

Marshall, in May 1941, moved to cut the Gordian knot; he ordered his G-3 to take charge of antitank development. The G-3, on Marshall's instructions, immediately established a Planning Branch under LtCol

Andrew D. Bruce. This staff, which was to form the core of the tank destroyer brain trust, reaffirmed the need for divisional antitank battalions.

The Army finally ordered the establishment of those units on 24 June—two days after Hitler's panzer spearheads rolled into the Soviet Union! The first battalions were a heterogeneous lot, but they typically consisted of three to five batteries withdrawn from the field artillery and equipped with 75mm, 37mm, or simulated guns.[12] As of the end that month, only a handful of antitank battalions existed: the 93d at Fort Meade, Maryland; the 94th at Fort Benning, Georgia; the 99th at Fort Lewis, Washington; and battalions 101 through 105, which had been inducted into Federal service during the mobilization of the National Guard in January and February of 1941.[13]

Also in June, GHQ launched the first of a series of large-scale maneuvers. In the first corps-versus-corps wargames, held in Tennessee, MajGen George Patton Jr. deployed his 2d Armored Division in highly successful cavalry-style slashing maneuver. The units opposing him, however, had virtually no antitank capability.[14] Indeed, after 10 July, when the 28th Infantry Division Antitank Battalion (provisional) was formed, the men exercised using 3/4-ton weapons carriers as prime movers, with towed "guns" made out of miscellaneous pieces of pipe, wood, and other materials.[15] And thousands of miles away in the real war, German antiaircraft and other artillery on the Egyptian-Libyan frontier that same month played a major role in the destruction of more than two hundred British tanks, which caught the attention of the War Department intelligence chief (G-2).[16]

The next round of maneuvers would be different. On 8 August, and in line with his proposal of one year earlier, McNair ordered Third Army to organize three regiment-sized provisional antitank groups. Each consisted of three antitank battalions (armed with 37mm and 75mm guns), a scout car reconnaissance platoon, three engineer platoons, and three rifle platoons. The groups were to be attached at the field-army level and were trained to execute an "offensive role," including vigorous reconnaissance, preemptive contact with enemy armor, and destruction of enemy tanks with massed gunfire.[17] This rough mix of components and doctrinal orientation would soon provide the foundation for the separate tank destroyer battalions.

The debates were not over, but the die was cast. McNair continued to champion a dramatic expansion of the antitank program.[18] On 18 August, the War Department released a detailed memorandum calling for the formation of two hundred twenty antitank battalions, fifty-five of which were to be organic to the divisions, fifty-five pooled at the corps and army levels, and one hundred ten allocated as GHQ assets. McNair praised the boldness of the proposal but withheld his concurrence because he objected to the War Department's plans to subordinate the antitank units to the Armored Force; to disperse some antitank battalions among divisions, corps, and armies; and to create two hundred twenty battalions, a number he judged excessive. McNair eventually had his way on almost every point.[19]

In September, Third Army faced Second Army in Louisiana in the largest field exercises in the nation's history. Two types of makeshift proto-tank destroyers were employed. The first consisted of a 3/4-ton truck with a railroad tie secured across the bed; a 37mm gun with its wheels removed was fixed to the tie and its split tail wired to the corners of the truck bed.[20] The second mounted a 75mm gun on a 1-1/2-ton truck.[21] Antitank guns—although mostly from the infantry's organic defenses—stymied Second Army's I Armored Corps at almost every turn, to McNair's obvious delight. The rules, however, now gave antitank weapons a tremendous advantage, and armor's difficulties derived in large part—as subsequent experience would show—from trying to operate with all-tank formations.[22] In other words, the maneuvers gave very little idea how American antitank elements might be expected to perform against *Germany's* combined-arms blitzkrieg.

On 7 October, Marshall approved the War Department's estimate for antitank battalion needs and suggested the immediate activation of sixty-three battalions. He also decided to rename the units "tank destroyers" for psychological reasons.[23]

The final phase of the GHQ maneuvers took place in North and South Carolina in November 1941 and pitted 865 tanks and armored cars from I Armored Corps against First Army's 764 mobile antitank guns and 3,557 other pieces of artillery. Men from the 1st Provisional Antitank Battalion—later the 601st Tank Destroyer Battalion—would remember the maneuvers for the cold and rain on some days and the dust on others, as well as the first-ever issue of C-rations.[24] First Army had received the three GHQ antitank groups and organized three more "Tank Attacker"

(TA) groups of its own. TA-1 included the 93d Antitank Battalion, which was outfitted with experimental self-propelled guns constructed from 75mm field pieces mounted on halftracks. In addition to the mix fielded by the antitank groups during the Louisiana maneuvers, it also had an antiaircraft element and observation planes. The tank forces suffered tremendous losses during the wargames. The 1st Armored Division was ruled destroyed, and 983 tanks were "knocked out," 91 percent by antitank guns. In the most startling incident, TA-1's self-propelled guns on 20 November charged the bivouac of the isolated 69th Armored Regiment and, taking full advantage of the rules, "annihilated" the formation.[25]

* * *

The Armored Force drew solid lessons from its failures and reorganized the armored divisions to provide more infantry for combined-arms operations, and to reduce the proportion of vulnerable light tanks. McNair and his supporters among antitank thinkers, on the other hand, concluded that they had solved the puzzle. On 27 November, the War Department ordered the activation of fifty-three tank destroyer battalions under GHQ control. On 3 December, it removed all existing antitank battalions from their parent arms, redesignated them tank destroyer battalions, and subordinated them to GHQ as well. Battalions originating in infantry divisions received unit numbers in the 600 series, while those from armored divisions and GHQ field artillery units were given designations in the 700s and 800s, respectively.[26]

Despite the subordination of the new tank destroyer units to GHQ, the Army initially associated the battalions with their parent divisions as they were activated in December. The 601st through the 609th, for example, were so designated on the basis of co-location with the 1st through the 9th Infantry divisions of the Regular Army. Those attached to the mobilized National Guard divisions were numbered 626th through 645th. These associations did not last long in most cases.[27]

The 27 November War Department directive also established a Tank Destroyer Tactical and Firing Center at Fort Meade, Maryland, to oversee the formulation of doctrine, draft field manuals, determine the organization of the separate battalions, and organize a common training program. Lieutenant Colonel Bruce of the Planning Branch assumed command, a job that would bring him two stars in nine short months.[28] With the reorganization of the War Department in March 1942, McNair became the commanding general of Army Ground Forces (AGF). Bruce's center became a separate Tank Destroyer Command, based at Camp Hood, Texas, joining armor, antiaircraft, and airborne as quasi-arms of the Army. Many officers nevertheless questioned whether tank destroyers merited such separate status, and the Armored Force lobbied to take control over training. In July, McNair acknowledged that the Tank Destroyer Command actually lacked command authority similar to that of the Armored Force, and he in August redesignated Bruce's operation a center again.[29]

At this time, there were roughly seventy tank destroyer battalions scattered around the country, all looking to the center to end widespread confusion over organization, tactics, and training. To meet this need, the center's powers to ensure uniform standards in all tank destroyer units and its physical training facilities expanded substantially in late 1942.[30]

Crafting A Tank Destroyer Doctrine

The Tank Destroyer Center/Command formulated a doctrine that embodied the lessons that the drafters thought they had learned in 1941. The doctrine also seemed to embody the character of center commander Bruce. "A.D." Bruce had graduated from Texas A&M in 1916 and shipped overseas as a provisional lieutenant. He rose to command a machine gun battalion in the 2d Infantry Division and fought in every one of its major engagements. Bruce's fighting style speaks for itself: He returned with the Distinguished Service Cross, the Legion of Honor, the Croix de Guerre with two palms and a star, and two or three other decorations. Bruce was a tall, rugged man who punctuated his conversation with energetic gestures. When he spoke of striking a blow, he would slam his fist into the palm of his other hand with a force that jarred the office. Bruce was impatient with bureaucracy and traditionalism.[31]

The tank destroyers would rely on mass, mobility, firepower, and aggressiveness to accomplish their mission. Indeed, the training notes written by the 93d Antitank (redesignated 893d Tank Destroyer)

Battalion—which had executed TA-1's fabled destruction of the 69th Armored Regiment during the Carolina maneuvers—became the interim guidance for new tank destroyer battalions while an official doctrine was under development.[32]

In a 1942 interview, Bruce described his vision. "The autocrat of the ground battle in this war has been the tank. With the tank destroyer we think we have its number. The destroyer's gun and mount don't have the tank's armor, but its crew commands greater speed, visibility, and maneuverability, and at least equal firepower. It can pick the time and place to deliver its punch and then hightail it to a new position to strike again. One good tank destroyer can be produced for materially less than the cost of a tank, and in far less time and with less critical materials. And by using tank destroyers to stop enemy tanks, you leave your own tanks free to dash through and spread hell among the enemy."[33]

The new doctrine was formalized in FM 18-5, *Tank Destroyer Field Manual: Organization and Tactics of Tank Destroyer Units*, distributed to formations as a draft in March 1942 and published in June. The manual proclaimed that the destruction of hostile tanks was the sole mission of the unit. It described the likely foe as a large and fast mass of tanks—most of them light—operating more or less independently of infantry and artillery. The prescription offered was:

> Tank destroyer units are employed offensively in large numbers, by rapid maneuver, and by surprise. . . . Offensive action allows the entire strength of a tank destroyer unit to be engaged against the enemy. For individual tank destroyers, offensive action consists of vigorous reconnaissance to locate hostile tanks and movement to advantageous positions from which to attack the enemy by fire. Tank destroyers avoid "slugging matches" with tanks, but compensate for their light armor and difficulty of concealment by exploiting their mobility and superior observation. . . .
>
> The characteristics of tank destroyer units are mobility and a high degree of armor-piercing firepower, combined with light armor protection; strong defensive capacity against attacks of combat aviation; and flexibility of action permitted by generous endowment of means of communication.[34]

FM 18-5 indicated that tank destroyer battalions would operate as mobile reserves and not as part of the front-line defense. The tactics prescribed presumed that large tank destroyer forces would swarm to the point of an attack and maneuver to strike at the enemy's flanks—from ambush if at all possible. Reconnaissance would be key both to finding the enemy and to identifying primary and alternate firing positions. Individual tank destroyers (TDs) would fire several rounds and then displace to another position before firing again. The manual suggested that this activity would take place semi-independently of other combat elements but suggested vaguely that units should call for help if confronted by enemy infantry.[35]

Put another way, a tank destroyer officer described the doctrine this way: "The idea is that if [boxing great] Joe Lewis is sitting in the corner with his back turned, you hit him behind the ear with brass knuckles. Then you get the hell out before all Harlem breaks loose."[36]

Bruce selected as the motto for the new force: "Seek, Strike, Destroy."[37]

*   *   *

With 20-20 hindsight, many observers have sharply criticized this doctrine. Indeed, combat would reveal major shortcomings. The doctrine utterly missed the realities of combined-arms warfare. It suggested no role for TDs during advances by friendly forces. And it presumed German use of tanks on a large scale that proved very much the exception rather than the rule. Several factors are worth keeping in mind, however, as one follows the story:

— The U.S. Army had never fought a mechanized war before. It was starting from scratch in almost every regard. One of the few "facts" available to the drafters was that on all fields of battle to date, neither tanks nor static antitank defenses had stopped the German war machine.

— Tank destroyer thinkers were not, for once, trying to refight the last war. The program would nevertheless become mired in a cycle of re-fighting the last campaign as critics weighed in.

— The psychological environment was one of fending off further German advances, for the Nazi high-water mark had yet to come.

Thinking naturally gravitated to the seemingly most pressing problem; failure to solve it might make worrying about tank busting under other circumstances an academic exercise.

Moreover, tank killers and their comrades in the units with which they would fight were a pragmatic lot, and the problems embedded in the official TD doctrine do not appear to have had much effect on the war effort. The doctrine would gradually shift to reflect battlefield lessons, but these twists were of little direct concern to the battalions in battle. In the words of the Army's post-war General Board report on tank destroyers: "Suffice it to say that the self-propelled tank destroyer proved to be a most versatile weapon on the battlefield, and although its use did not follow pre-combat doctrines, it did fill a need and became a very highly respected part of the successful infantry-armor-artillery team."[38]

Building an Organization

Bruce concluded that self-propelled (SP) battalions were the best way to implement the new doctrine. The Louisiana and Tennessee maneuvers had suggested that it would be impossible to save emplaced towed guns if the infantry was forced to retreat. American observers in Africa had reported that emplaced British antitank guns often survived only long enough to fire four to eight rounds.[39] The SP formation became standard on 5 June 1942.[40]

The standardized tank destroyer battalion initially comprised 35 officers and 807 enlisted men organized into:

A headquarters company with communications, transportation, and motor-maintenance platoons included.

A reconnaissance company consisting of three reconnaissance platoons and a pioneer (engineer) platoon.

Three tank destroyer companies, each consisting of two 75mm gun platoons and one 37mm platoon, a two-gun antiaircraft section, and a twelve-man security section.[41] The TD platoons inherited the four-gun configuration of their forebears, the field artillery batteries, rather than the five-vehicle formation standard in Western armored units.

Interestingly, McNair objected to the choice of SP guns, arguing that they would be too difficult to conceal on the battlefield. He pushed the use of towed antitank guns. Marshall, however, favored pursuing the SP option.[42] The Army would swing wildly back and forth on this question once it began to gather battle experience.

The Army wanted TDs that would be fast and light, and not only to permit them to maneuver rapidly from one firing position to another. The light vehicles also would be able to cross bridges, ford streams, and skim through swamps that tanks could not manage. There were some skeptics. George Patton Jr., for one, argued that the tank destroyer was destined to become nothing but another tank.[43]

The new battalions received the ad hoc equipment immediately available while Bruce set about convincing Ordnance to procure modern, fully tracked SP gun carriages for the new force. During the summers of 1940 and 1941, the Army had begun experimenting with improvised self-propelled antitank guns. In late 1941, fifty of the new halftracks were fitted with the venerable 75mm field gun (also mounted in the General Lee and Sherman medium tanks) and shipped to the Philippines in time for the Japanese invasion. With the 75mm mounted, the vehicle was at or above its load-carrying capacity. The gun bore was almost seven feet off the ground, and the gun could safely traverse at most 21 degrees to the side. Swinging the gun any further could lift a track off the ground, and firing under such conditions risked flipping the vehicle.[44] This was a far cry from McNair's vision of a "stable shore gun" with which to fight tanks.

Standardized as the M3 gun motor carriage, this vehicle was issued to the tank destroyer battalions to equip their heavy platoons. The halftrack had just enough armor—one-quarter inch of face-hardened plate—to ward off small arms fire. A gun shield for the 75mm cannon was five-eighths inches thick and rated enough to stop .30-caliber rounds at two hundred fifty yards. The M3 was completely open on top. TD crews found that it was hard to turn, which could prove a major problem in battle.[45] The vehicle could move at 45 miles per hour on level terrain—much faster than even a light tank—but it had less than one foot of ground clearance. There were five men in the crew.[46]

The M3s were the good news. The light platoons were first issued Ford "swamp buggies" mounting a 37mm gun. These were replaced in early 1942 by the M6, a 3/4-ton four-wheel-drive Dodge weapons carrier with a 37mm gun mounted on a 360-degree swivel in the bed.[47] In practice, the gun was viewed as facing to the rear, because firing it forward would shatter the windshield and injure the driver and front crewman.[48] Other than a quarter-inch splash shield on the gun, the four-man crew was completely exposed to enemy fire. The Army said that the vehicle would allow crews to move quickly to points of vantage—the M6 could travel at 55 miles per hour—and pack enough firepower to destroy a light tank.[49] In truth, it was well aware that the 37mm gun had proved to be a poor antitank weapon in British hands long before American forces drove the M6 into combat.[50]

AGF in May 1942 ordered production of yet another expedient, the M10 motor gun carriage. The M10 was constructed on the proven M4 Sherman tank chassis and had a crew of five. The first model was powered by twin diesel engines, while the M10A1 used a Ford gasoline engine. The vehicle had between one-half inch and two inches of frontal armor and between three-quarters and one inch on the sides, as compared with two inches and one and a half to two inches, respectively, on the early model Sherman tank. Oddly, since doctrine drove the selection of thin armor to retain speed, the vehicle was pre-equipped with bosses for mounting auxiliary armor on the hull. A 3-inch (76mm) converted antiaircraft gun was mounted in an open-topped turret, which also had a .50-caliber antiaircraft machine gun mounted toward the rear.[51] A large number of 3-inch guns were available because they were being replaced on submarines with 5-inch models and in antiaircraft units with 90mm guns.[52] The turret had a manual traverse mechanism instead of the powered system used on the M4 Sherman.[53] The Army designed the M10 to be able to outmaneuver and outshoot the then-standard Sherman and German Mark IV tanks.[54] Unlike American tanks, the stock TD lacked coaxial and hull-mounted machine guns.

Just as Patton had predicted, the M10 looked much like a tank. The somewhat arbitrary distinction between the two armored vehicles would be reflected in frequent references in tank destroyer battalion records to the vehicles as "tanks," once the M3 had been replaced. Actual tankers in the 1st Armored Division referred to the TD crews as artillery men, but artillery men in the same division called them tankers.[55] Tankers in the 743d Tank Battalion conceptualized the difference by referring in radio chatter to tanks as "cans" and to TDs as "can openers."

Bruce opposed the decision to produce the M10 because he wanted to speed development of a custom-designed M18 Hellcat TD. Battalions that used the M10 nonetheless thought highly of it. Unfortunately, the M10 did not become available until September 1942, so the first tank destroyer battalions entered combat in North Africa using the M3.

Training the Men

The Tank Destroyer Force gained full control over its own training, a situation that differed considerably from the haphazard arrangements that characterized the Army's separate tank battalions. A Unit Training Center became the heart of Camp Hood and was subsequently augmented by an Individual Training Center and a Replacement Training Center.[56] Battalion records during the war suggest that while units did not always get as many replacements as they needed, the ones they did get were generally properly trained to fight in TDs. Separate tank battalions, in contrast, often had to hastily train replacements who had never seen a tank before.

Tank killers were trained not only to fight with their guns but also to conduct "dismounted tank hunting." Crews of disabled TDs were expected to ambush enemy tanks and raid his tank parks using small arms, grenades, mines, and improvised weapons. Bruce sent Maj Gordon Kimbrell to visit the British Commando School and patterned tank-hunting training on the Commando model. The course employed live grazing fire and exploding practice grenades for the first time in the Army during simulated battlefield conditions.[57] The men underwent a grueling schedule that included conducting night reconnaissance, crossing deep streams, climbing slippery barbed-wire-covered banks, scaling steep walls, detecting booby traps, street fighting, and mastering demolitions.[58] The training in urban warfare would prove particularly important in Europe, where crews in separate tank battalions would face a steep learning curve because they had received no such instruction.

After surviving this unusually rigorous training regimen, the TD men tended to think of themselves as an elite force.

* * *

There were teething problems, of course. Before the training centers were established, units trained where and as they could. The 667th, 803d, and 899th Tank Destroyer battalions initially pooled their resources and in March 1942 established a joint training center at Fort Lewis, Washington.[59] The 628th may have set a record for training on simulated guns—eleven months!—before having an opportunity to fire some borrowed 75mm guns in November 1942.[60]

Some of the first battalions received sparse instruction before they had to embark for operations in North Africa. The 701st Tank Destroyer Battalion, for example, was able to conduct its first real range firing with its 75mm SP gear at Fort Dix, New Jersey, on 15 May 1942. The battalion shipped out for the United Kingdom only fifteen days later to prepare for Operation Torch.[61] Other battalions received only seven to eight weeks of training before boarding the transports.[62]

Thomas Sherman was one of more than two hundred mostly Nebraska men who reported to Camp Bowie, Texas, in February 1942 to join the 636th Tank Destroyer Battalion. They arrived without having received any basic training. The new soldiers received a compressed course from battalion noncommissioned officers (NCOs) but quickly shifted to training on 37mm guns, small arms, and vehicles. Sherman recalled that he never got very good at close-order drill and was always out of step. He would nonetheless become a recon sergeant within a few short months.[63]

Even at the new training center, the force at first suffered from a severe shortage of ammunition for the main guns. Crews had to practice with sub-caliber firing using .22-cal rifles bolted to the big guns. The round had a similar trajectory to that of the big guns, but differences in the muzzle velocities caused crews some confusion as they tried to learn how to lead a moving target.[64]

Another problem revolved around TD battalion opportunities to train with other units. AGF took steps to organize joint training involving divisions and units that would be attached to divisions in late 1943 and early 1944, but the practice did not become well established until many tank destroyer outfits had already shipped out.[65]

Chapter 2

North Africa: Seeing the Elephant

The lessons learned from combat by American troops in North Africa
have been manifold, and it has been repeatedly shown that
maneuver mistakes in the past have become the
Battlefield mistakes of the present.

— U.S. Army observer's report, January 1943

On 2 and 3 October 1942, Companies B and C, the 2d
Reconnaissance Platoon, and part of the medical detachment pulled out
of the scattered encampments of the 701st Tank Destroyer Battalion in
Northern Ireland.[1] They had been in the United Kingdom since early
June, training with the American 1st Armored Division and, for several
days, the British 61st Infantry Division. One battalion gunner—Corporal
Stema, who had no idea that he would soon be killed in action—had even
fired an impressive demonstration for the King and Queen.

The departing men knew they were headed somewhere via
Macclesfield, England, but no more than that. Captain Gilbert Ellmann
led a party of sixty-five enlisted men onto a train. Lieutenant Robert
Whitsit and other platoon leaders commanded columns of halftracks and
wheeled vehicles, which wound through the countryside following
British motorcycle guides who were unfamiliar with the route. "Thus,"

recorded the Company B diary, "did [we] move from the Emerald Isle to new adventures."

The 701st elements were attached to Combat Command B (CCB), 1st Armored Division. The command incorporated the 13th Armored Regiment (less 3d Battalion's medium tanks); 1st Battalion (light), 1st Armored Regiment; 1st and 2d battalions, 6th Armored Infantry Regiment; 2d Battalion, 503d Parachute Infantry Regiment; 27th Armored Field Artillery Regiment; and an assortment of engineer, antiaircraft, signal, and maintenance units. The diversity reflected the sound theoretical grasp that the all but untried U.S. Army had of the requirements of combined-arms warfare. How that would work in practice remained to be seen.

During a brief stay at an English country estate, the men of the 701st waterproofed their vehicles and learned of the complexities of loading men and equipment onto ships. Only two halftracks from the 2d Reconnaissance Platoon had gone missing during the transfer, never to be seen again. It was clear to the tank destroyer men that the Americans and British had never before worked together on a project such as this, and many confusing and conflicting orders ensued. On the other hand, the men viewed the landscape and the women—in fact, just about everything but the British rations—as distinct improvements over Northern Ireland.

On 9 October, a last-minute payday was imposed on the 701st, with—as the unit diary records—"the inevitable aftermath." The next day, the first elements—minus several men AWOL—traveled to Weymess Bay, Scotland, and Liverpool to board transport ships. A day later, the remainder embarked, including the missing men, who had been rounded up. The only major foul-up resulted in the assignment of all of the drivers from 2d Platoon, Company B, to the wrong transport; they would not rejoin the platoon until after it had already been committed to battle.

The troops were destined to spend twenty-five days aboard the HMS *Misoa*, HMS *Derbyshire*, and SS *Batery* with several thousand other American and British soldiers. The vessels formed part of a convoy that loitered off the Scottish coast for the first two weeks. Evacuation and landing drills filled the long days, the latter involving clambering down the ship's side on ladders to the waterline in full gear, and back up again. Company C participated in landing exercises, but Company B did not.

The men in "Baker," however, somehow obtained from shore a violin, a guitar, and a ukulele, with which they were able to provide entertainment to themselves and those around them. Finally, on 26 October, the convoy of about sixty ships departed.

On the nearby SS *Latita*, Capt Michael Paulick commanded Reconnaissance Company of the 601st Tank Destroyer Battalion. His company had separated from the battalion at Tidworth Barracks, an old British cavalry facility that also hosted elements of the 1st Infantry Division, to join the assault force as an asset of II Corps.[2] The remainder of the outfit was scheduled to follow in several weeks.

On 2 November, the men learned their fate: Operation Torch, the invasion of North Africa. Commanders received their first battle orders and sheaves of maps and aerial photographs. Morale was high.

The convoy passed the blacked-out mass of Gibraltar at about 2100 hours on 6 November.[3] Unbeknownst to the men, LtGen Dwight Eisenhower, overall commander of the Allied invasion force, was inside a tunnel beneath the Rock. Further on, towns glimmered on the shores of Spain to port and Spanish Morocco to starboard—the first lighted towns the men had seen since leaving the United States five months earlier. Before dawn on 8 November, the darkness was broken by the flashes of naval gunfire off Oran, Algeria. The transports dropped anchor off St. Leu.

"At that time," recorded the 701st's Company B diary, "we were ready for combat."

* * *

Perhaps.

Captain G. V. Nicholls, a British tank officer and combat veteran who visited the 2d Armored Division before Torch, noted a supreme overconfidence among American troops of all ranks—an observation that he probably could have offered regarding the men of the 601st and 701st Tank Destroyer battalions, as well. The Americans, he recorded, believed that continuous maneuvers had made them ready for active service and that their individual training was up to British and German standards. "In this opinion they were entirely wrong," he concluded.[4]

Indeed, American confidence was high. The old warhorse Lesley McNair was one of the few to sound a cautious note. Responding after the Carolina maneuvers to the oft-asked question from reporters as to the battle readiness of the troops, McNair said, "It is my judgment that, given complete equipment, they certainly could fight effectively. But it is to be added with emphasis that the losses would be unduly heavy, and the results of action against an adversary such as the Germans might not be all that could be desired."[5]

Fortunately, the first foe was not German.

* * *

Combat Command B, 1st Armored Division, formed part of Center Task Force, which had as its objective the capture of Oran and important nearby airfields. Second Corps, under the command of MajGen Lloyd Fredendall, controlled the ground element of the task force, which also included the 1st Infantry Division and parts of the 34th Infantry Division. This force was all that could be brought to bear from bases in the United Kingdom because of shipping constraints. Further east, an American-British task force landed at Algiers, while to the west, MajGen George Patton Jr. commanded American troops coming ashore in Morocco.[6] The Allied objective was to push 350 miles and more eastward after the landings to seize Tunisia, thereby threatening Generalfeldmarshall Erwin Rommel's rear and providing air bases from which to establish air superiority over the central Mediterranean. Some elements would remain behind in Morocco to encourage Spain to remain neutral, which was crucial to protecting Allied supply lines.

The Vichy French colonial forces defending Algeria and Morocco had some 125,000 men—including fourteen poorly equipped but trained and professionally led divisions—and five hundred combat aircraft at their disposal. French mechanized cavalry units in Algeria fielded 110 obsolete tanks and 60 armored cars.[7] Eisenhower believed that these forces were sufficient to thwart the invasion if they offered more than token resistance, and he oversaw a clandestine diplomatic effort to ensure that this did not transpire. The outcome of that bid remained uncertain as of D-day, however, and seven weeks before the invasion Eisenhower informed Washington that "the chances of effecting initial landings are better than even"—hardly an assertion of confidence![8]

Few of the American troops probably had any idea that they were embarking on an operation that senior American commanders had opposed. Chief of Staff George Marshall had objected that an invasion of North Africa would delay the planned landings in France. The British, however, were keen on the idea, in part to ease pressure on their forces in Libya and Egypt, which were suffering a drubbing at the hands of the Desert Fox, Erwin Rommel, and his Afrika Korps. President Roosevelt came down on the side of the British to ensure that American ground forces would engage Germany before the end of 1942 and meet his commitment to Josef Stalin to open a second front. In the event, British LtGen Bernard Montgomery launched his famous offensive at El Alamein on 23 October, two weeks before the Allied landings.

Operation Torch was a hurriedly organized affair. American and British political and military leaders did not reach agreement to pursue the project until late July 1942, and substantial differences between the Allies over where the landings should occur continued through August. Eisenhower was named overall commander on 26 July, leaving him a mere three months to pull together the until-then largest amphibious operation in American history.[9] Torch required a complete reorientation for staffs that had been working on the plans for landings in France. Improvisation was the imperative as they scrambled to train troops and supply the necessary sea-lift capacity amidst heavy shipping losses to German U-boats.[10] The tools of later amphibious operations, such as Landing Ships, Tanks (LSTs), were not yet at hand. Amphibious training for the naval and ground forces was inadequate, a fact recognized by commanders but deemed an acceptable risk.

* * *

Oran is situated in the middle of three bays that form a large bight between Cape Falcon on the west and Pointe de l'Aiguille to the east. Arzew, a secondary port, lies 20 miles farther east on the shore of a hilly and wide promontory. Hill masses behind the shoreline offered defenders advantageous terrain and channeled movement. The French defenses boasted forty-five fortified coastal guns at Oran and another six at Arzew. The Oran Division had nearly 17,000 men to defend the approaches to the city.[11]

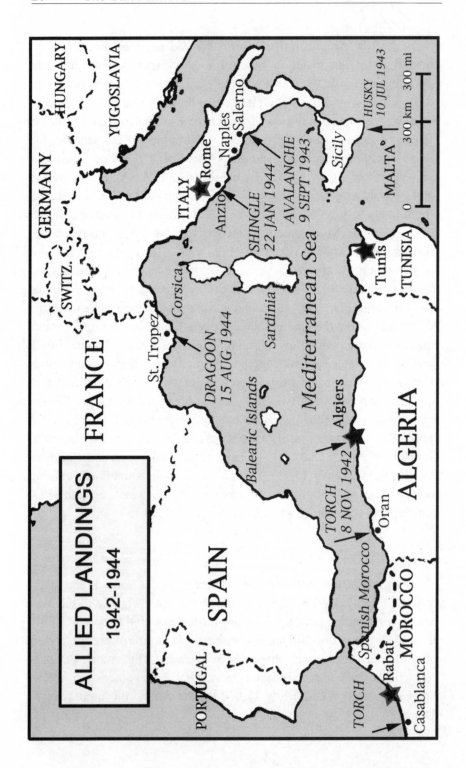

ALLIED LANDINGS
1942-1944

The invasion plan called for simultaneous landings at three major beaches—labeled Beaches X, Y, and Z—and one minor beach. One armored task force, designated Green and including the men of Company C, 701st Tank Destroyer Battalion, would land at Mersa bou Zedjar. A second, designated Red and including Company B, 701st Tank Destroyer Battalion, would land near Arzew, where the reconnaissance troops of the 601st Tank Destroyer Battalion would also come ashore. "Flying columns" from the assault force were to push inland in a double-envelopment maneuver and initially seize airfields and approaches to Oran while other units captured shore batteries. Airborne troops flying all the way from England were to drop at two crucial airstrips, La Sénia and Tafaraoui, and link up with armored columns advancing from the beaches. The French Army airfield at La Sénia lay about six miles south-southeast of Oran, while the Navy airfield at Tafaraoui was located twelve miles southeast of the city.[12]

*   *   *

The landings around Oran began as scheduled between 0100 and 0130 hours on 8 November and achieved complete surprise.[13] The 1st Infantry Division cleared the way for Combat Command B to begin landing its men and tanks from Maracaibo transport ships (converted tankers).[14] The Maracaibos required seven feet of draft, so pontoon bridges were constructed—a task requiring three hours—over which vehicles drove to shore. This was hardly a viable solution for any future assault landing under fire.[15]

Lieutenant Robert Whitsit and his 3d Platoon, Company B, 701st Tank Destroyer Battalion, and Lt John Eggleton's 2d Platoon from Company C disembarked at about 0600 hours in their respective landing areas. The remainder of both companies would unload at a frustratingly slow pace—one vehicle at a time ferried in landing craft—over the next two days. As corps assets began landing, Capt Michael Paulick and his recon men from the 601st clambered down rope nets from the deck of the SS *Latita* to small assault boats waiting below. Inexperienced and confronted with the slap-dash arrangement, many of them became entangled in the nets.[16] Nevertheless, they were soon ashore.

The tankers of the 1st Armored Division de-waterproofed their vehicles. West of Oran, Task Force Green—built around one armored and one armored-infantry battalion from Combat Command B—deployed a small task force dubbed a flying column to spearhead the advance. The column set off from Merza bou Zedjar for Misshergin about 0900 hours.[17] Lieutenant Eggleton's tank destroyers took the point, an order completely at odds with tank destroyer doctrine. Racing down the highway between Oran and Sidi bel Abbes, the Americans came under fire from emplaced French 75mm guns. Sergeant Mitchell's M3 crewmen replied with their own—a copy of the very guns firing on them—and destroyed two of the French weapons. The tank destroyer force's first engagement had been a success but had nothing to do with fighting tanks. Doctrine was taking a beating, and it was not even noon yet.

On the other side of Oran, Task Force Red—built around two CCB armored and one armored-infantry battalions—advanced to Tafaraoui Airfield. Lieutenant Colonel John Waters, a son-in-law of Patton, commanded a second flying column that consisted of the platoon from the 701st Tank Destroyer Battalion, two light tank companies, and one company of armored infantry. As in Task Force Green, Lieutenant Whitsit's M3 tank destroyers were put at the point.

About 1100 hours, the flying column reached the airfield. The arriving troops found no sign of the paratroopers from the 503d Parachute Infantry Regiment who were supposed to have landed there. The American forces quickly overcame light resistance and took three hundred prisoners.[18]

The missing airborne unit, it transpired, had been thoroughly dispersed during the long flight from England, and several of the aircraft had set down in a dry lake bed near Oran. American tanks found the paratroopers, and Waters requested by radio that they relieve his command so that he could pursue the enemy. Lieutenant Colonel Edson Raff, commanding the airborne expedition, agreed. At 1400 hours the paratroopers and American-piloted Spitfire fighter aircraft that were to operate out of Tafaraoui were ordered to the airfield. As the C-47s carrying the paratroopers approached some fifteen miles from the landing strip, French fighters and bombers struck the American aircraft and the flying column. A 500-pound bomb demolished one of Lieutenant Whitsit's M3s, wounding three enlisted men. The C-47s were forced down, and the airborne had to walk the rest of the way to Tafaraoui.[19]

Shortly before sundown, Whitsit's platoon engaged with long-range fire a mixed French battery of seven guns that had been shooting into the area of the airfield from the northeast. The French guns fell silent.

* * *

French aircraft and artillery again struck Tafaraoui the morning of 9 November. After Spitfires had driven off the enemy aircraft, Lt Whitsit's platoon accompanied a company of light tanks southward to deal with a French tank concentration reportedly in the vicinity of St. Barbe du Tlelat. The American force engaged the French at a range in excess of two thousand yards. As the TDs laid down a base of fire, the American light tanks advanced in two V's abreast, followed by a third V five hundred yards behind. The Americans destroyed fourteen Renault AMC35 light tanks armed with 47mm gun. Two were officially credited to the guns of the 701st Tank Destroyer Battalion; Lieutenant Colonel Waters later attributed all of the kills to the TDs, while one of the now bona fide tank killers suggested that an honest guess would be six. Waters commented, "It was a shame to shoot at these French tanks as we could almost see the shells go right through their thin armor. It gave our men lots of confidence."[20]

Task Force Green overran the La Sénia airfield the morning of 9 November and captured five hundred prisoners and ninety aircraft. At the beachhead, meanwhile, a new column under the command of Lieutenant Colonel Bruck was formed consisting of two medium tanks, five light tanks, and the M3s of Lt Arthur Edson's 2d Platoon, Company B, 701st Tank Destroyer Battalion. Once again, the tank destroyers were put in the lead. After several changes in orders, the column—now less two M3s detached to provide security in La Mecta—was directed toward La Sénia.[21]

As the day ended for the men in North Africa, thousands of miles to the rear the U.S. Army ordered the replacement of the light platoons in TD companies with heavy platoons. The decision did not affect the battalions already in action. Instead, they would fight with a now officially obsolete configuration.[22]

Both B/701st platoons participated in Task Force Red's capture of the town of La Sénia early on 10 November. Advancing from the south, they came under heavy sniping and artillery fire. One M3 in Lt Whitsit's

3d Platoon was struck by a shell and demolished, and the battalion suffered its first five deaths in action.

Waters ordered his flying column to bypass La Sénia and charge into Oran, and 3d Platoon TDs maneuvered around the town. Bruck, however, ordered his command to continue into La Sénia. When resistance continued, he called his column back to follow Waters around the outskirts.

Lieutenant "Ace" Edson in the 2d Platoon command M3 did not receive the transmission because of the notoriously unreliable radio. Edson, a former civil engineer who had joined the army as a private and risen to sergeant before accepting a commission, was following a tank, which was hit at a roadblock and began to burn. Edson's halftrack provided covering fire for the escaping crew but became stuck in the roadblock debris until the next vehicle in line pushed it free. Edson proceeded through the town under small-arms fire and out the other side. The brakes had been damaged by the roadblock, and the vehicle was smoking as it raced ahead. Edson suspected that the defenders thought he was already on fire.

Three miles down the road, Edson encountered a column of French trucks where drivers were standing in vineyards to the side of the road. As the halftrack barreled by the Frenchmen, someone in the vehicle yelled out, "Hey, Lieutenant, there's nobody behind us!" Sure enough.

Edson ordered the driver to turn around and head back. As the halftrack raced by the French trucks again, it broke down near the end of the column. Edson decided he had better shoot at the enemy, which he did. The French drivers decided to surrender. Edson arranged for four French trucks to tow his halftrack and carry his fifty prisoners back to La Sénia, where he negotiated the surrender of another three hundred combatants. The French officers did not want to capitulate to a mere lieutenant, but Edson told them, "Well, we have contact with a general." That sufficed to convince the officers to approach him one-by-one, salute, and surrender their pistols while the men stacked arms.[23]

*   *   *

Both Task Forces Red and Green entered Oran on 10 November, seized the city center, and linked up with elements of the 1st Infantry Division as it pushed in from the other direction. After suffering constant

French small arms fire on the way into the city, the tank killers were surprised to be met in the streets by clapping civilians.[24] Recon Company, 601st Tank Destroyer Battalion, followed the Big Red One into the city but saw no real fighting.[25] The men would later suggest off the record that they had probably accidentally expended most of their ammunition shooting at each other as they nervously ducked into and out of hallways hunting for French snipers.[26]

The French commander of the Oran area surrendered to BrigGen Lunsford Oliver, commanding general of Combat Command B.[27]

That night, Captain Paulick's reconnaissance troops from the 601st slept on the sidewalks of Oran. The city was dilapidated and down-at-the-heels in November 1942: "Trolley tracks, the odor of automobiles burning alcohol, wine doped with a sort of hashish, chic French women and slovenly dressed men, dirty Arabs and dirty streets," recalled a history of the 1st Infantry Division.[28] Even after six weeks of occupation the Center Task Force special service officer would note, "The only forms of amusement for men in Oran on pass are movies in French at the civilian theaters and the cheap French bars."[29] Paulick's men were awakened by the whack of oranges the natives were dropping out of windows by way of welcome. "Hi-Ho, Silver!" was the first password, and within a day, it seemed that every Arab street urchin was shouting, "Hi-Ho, Silver! Away! Bon-bon! Cigarette! Choo-gum!" "Chief" Gomez, Recon's first sergeant, thought the password undignified and was almost shot when he refused to respond "Away!" when challenged by a sentry.[30]

With the fall of Oran, the campaign in Algeria ended. The tank killers had "seen the elephant," as the British called the first experience of combat. Lieutenant Colonel Waters obtained a captaincy for Whitsit in recognition of his performance, although with most of the battalion still in England, Bob Whitsit remained a platoon commander. Waters cautioned his men, however, "We did very well against the scrub team. Next week we hit the Germans. Do not slack off in anything. When we make a showing against them, you may congratulate yourselves."[31] He was not alone in his view. Patton told observers from Washington that had the landings been opposed by Germans, "we never would have gotten ashore."[32]

On 11 November, the 701st Tank Destroyer Battalion and elements of Combat Command B were detached and ordered to proceed to Tunisia to join the British First Army. The tank killers of Company C were among the first to move. They arrived in the vicinity of Medjez el Bab by 24 November, at which time the command was attached to the Blade Force, British 78th Infantry Division.[33]

* * *

Several days later, the rest of the 601st Tank Destroyer Battalion (except for Company B, which was delivered to Algiers by mistake) joined Recon Company at Oran under the watchful eye of LtCol Hershel Baker. The two-hundred pound, roly-poly CO had a cherubic face, but he spoke with a foghorn voice and was a ball of fire. The World War I veteran had scheduled a beer party for the entire battalion the day he took command in December 1941. He had a taste for booze and gambling, and he was both a showman and something of a martinet with his officers. But Baker was "proud as hell" of his outfit.[34]

The battalion bivouacked at St. Lucien, where the men had their first taste of the exotic: "prowling, *vino*-peddling, cigarette-buying natives and howling native dogs," according to the outfit's unofficial history. The local *gendarmerie* also demonstrated its quaint custom of encouraging people to move along with a touch of a whip. Baker threw a big party for his old friends, MajGen Terry de la Mesa Allen and BrigGen Theodore Roosevelt Jr., commanding general of the 1st Infantry Division and his deputy, respectively.[35]

Tunisia: The War Begins in Earnest

Major General Orlando Ward, 1st Armored Division's commanding general, described Tunisia in a letter to Armored Force chief LtGen Jacob Devers. "First, the country is bigger than anyone can imagine—great wide expanses of plains and jagged, rugged mountains, and in many cases up-turned rocks standing up in the middle of the plains. Many of the hills and plains are tank-proof, although some are rolling and smooth, over which tanks can pass without difficulty. Dry wadies cut the plains, which are dotted with Arab huts and adobe houses. There are a good many trees on the mountains but few elsewhere."[36]

German combat aircraft and a handful of troops began landing at an airfield near Tunis on 9 November, the first of fifteen thousand reinforcements—including one hundred tanks—that arrived by the end of the month. Nine thousand Italian troops also moved in, most having shifted west from Tripoli. British forces, meanwhile, advanced from Algiers by land and short seaborne and airborne hops. Thanks in part to the Axis incursion, the Allies persuaded the French in North Africa to join their cause as combatants on 13 November. On 17 November, a German parachute battalion encountered French holding forces and the British spearhead at Medjez el Bab. The bold German commander bluffed the Allied forces into pulling back.[37]

Medjez el Bab lay only ten minutes flying time from the hard-surfaced German airfields around Tunis. Allied reinforcements, supplies, and air support had to make a three hundred fifty-mile journey to the new front. Allied fighters could loiter only ten minutes over the battlefield and operated off dirt airstrips, which any rain quickly turned to muck.[38] And starting in late November, there were downpours aplenty in Algeria and Tunisia as unseasonable wet weather preceded the expected rainy season by two months.

*   *   *

For Combat Command B and the elements of the 701st Tank Destroyer Battalion, the trek was even farther to Medjez el Bab: seven hundred miles from Oran. Departing on 16 November, Companies B and C of the 701st arrived the following day in Algiers where, much to their surprise, the company COs were greeted by Eisenhower. The Allied commander explained to Capt Frank Redding and Capt Gilbert Ellmann—commanding Companies B and C, respectively—that he had wanted to meet the first American troops sent to the Tunisian sector. The next morning, the company commanders met with British LtGen Kenneth Anderson, commander of the British forces pushing toward Tunis. Anderson told them that transportation bottlenecks were dramatically slowing the deployment of tank units to the front, while the tank destroyers were light enough to make the journey on their own. The pressing need for additional forces was why such high-level officers were so personally interested in the activities of two humble companies.[39]

Companies B and C of the 701st traveled together over curved mountain roads as far as Souk Aras, where Company B turned aside for Tebessa on 21 November.

The Main Effort: Fighting Around Medjez el Bab

Company C continued to Souk el Arba and arrived mid-afternoon on 22 November. The men received a warm welcome from the Luftwaffe: Twelve Me-109 fighter-bombers and six Ju-87 Stuka dive-bombers bombed and strafed the company assembly area, as well as the headquarters of the British 78th Infantry Division and a nearby airfield. Six Me-109s attacked again forty-five minutes later as the company drove to its bivouac at Bulla Regia. The company lost one halftrack.[40]

Indeed, the famous bent-winged Stuka, the screaming terror of the blitzkrieg in Poland and France, was very much in evidence from the front all the way back to Algiers, as were Ju-88 bombers. The Stuka had yet to become the sitting duck for Allied fighters that it would when the Luftwaffe lost air supremacy. For now, Germany's Me-109 and FW-190 fighters enjoyed the edge. Moreover, invasion planners had given low priority to antiaircraft formations, often removing them from convoys to make room for other units, a philosophy that resulted in a general shortage of antiaircraft artillery (AAA) into 1943. The AAA units that landed were often unfamiliar with just-issued equipment, poorly trained, and had not exercised with other arms.[41] Official observers reported an "almost complete lack of air-ground cooperation" on the American side.[42]

On 23 November, Capt Frank Redding reported to Brigadier Cass, commander of the British 11th Infantry Brigade. The brigade group made up the southernmost of a three-prong British advance toward Tunis. The 36th Infantry Brigade was pushing eastward on a road roughly ten miles inland from the coast, while Blade Force advanced along the center axis. All three British commands were to receive help from elements of CCB. Cass informed Redding that his forces had made contact with unidentified German units of unknown strength somewhere east of Beja in the broad Oued Medjerda Valley. The command was preparing to advance, and Cass expected the American tank destroyers to participate in an attack the next day. During the conversation, three enemy fighters attacked the brigade CP.[43]

Arriving in Beja by mid-day on 23 November, Company C received orders to secure the high ground west of Medjez el Bab with the help of two British bren carrier-mounted infantry platoons from the Surrey Battalion. The Americans determined that they would not be able to communicate by radio with the British because of incompatible gear. No reconnaissance of the area had been conducted by the British, which meant that the small mixed command would function as brigade reconnaissance. Lacking effective protection against air attack, Redding decided to space his thirty-five vehicles out over the length of some five miles.[44]

The command moved out at 1300 hours. On either side, rolling hills gave way to steep heights cut by wadis. The bren carriers led. The M6 light TDs followed by some two hundred yards and conducted reconnaissance by fire to the flanks with machine guns and 37mm cannons. Just past the crest of the last rise before the town of Medjez el Bab, the advancing force encountered a roadblock, which at first appeared to be undefended. Heavy and accurate 81mm mortar fire quickly disabused the men of their mistaken impression. Four of the thin-skinned bren carriers were disabled in the initial barrage, and the rest scuttled to cover.

Nobody could determine the source of the enemy fire. Redding deployed his three platoons to shoot at likely points. German fire soon zeroed in on the TDs and forced them to begin shifting about after firing. As the command group gathered to discuss next steps, the German fire adjusted to their location and forced the men to scatter. The incident, at least, demonstrated that the German observation post was located on a low mountain that provided line-of-sight to the location of the command group. Redding reasoned that the German mortars would be located on the reverse slope, which he had no means to engage. An attempt to maneuver the M6s into position to fire from the flank while the infantry advanced came to naught.

Help arrived in the form of a British artillery observer in a radio-equipped vehicle. His battery had not yet come into range, however, and the task force settled in to wait.

German aircraft again dive-bombed and strafed the tank destroyers repeatedly while mortar rounds pounded the position. German pilots were enjoying brilliant flying weather over their Tunisian bases, while bad weather was playing hob at Allied air bases.[45] Miraculously, only one man was killed.

Shortly before dark, the battery was ready to execute fire missions. The observer had only a 1:200,000-scale French road map and did not know his own or the artillery's position with any accuracy. The battery loosed a single round, and Redding and the observer rose to their feet to spot the impact. They quickly hit the dirt as the 5-inch shell landed only thirty feet in front of them. By the time the fire was corrected to the suspected German position, it was too dark to see or to support a planned night attack by the Surries.

The British tried valiantly anyway, but the Germans caught them on the slope with flares and badly shot up the attacking troops, who fell back. The next day, as the task force endured renewed strafing and dive-bombing attacks, the still unseen German force withdrew from the mountain.[46]

*   *   *

British troops set out to take Medjez el Bab under a bright moon the night of 24–25 November. The plan called for two battalions to simultaneously enter the town from the north and south, but the German paratroopers—now buttressed by two 88mm guns, seventeen tanks, and an Italian antitank company—threw the British back with heavy losses. At 1730 hours, Captain Redding received orders to take his TDs into Medjez el Bab to eliminate the antitank guns. Considering what had happened to the British force, the orders appear bizarre in retrospect. Even more bizarre, perhaps, is that the tank destroyers were able to enter the outskirts of town. Darkness was falling already, however, and the TDs navigated the final distance by heading toward the sound of gunfire. Redding and his men could see little more than a few fires in town and the flash of tracer rounds, and they were unable to distinguish enemy from friend. It was the Americans' first real experience with the fog of war. Redding later noted, "Abysmal ignorance became our prime noteworthy characteristic."

That night, while British artillery pounded the town, the Germans slipped out and withdrew to Djedeida, only ten miles from Tunis.[47]

When the Allies advanced again Thanksgiving Day to seize Medjez el Bab, the TDs were attached to the 2/13th Armored Regiment. The tanks passed Company C's bivouac in the first gray light of dawn, and the TDs swung into their place in the column. Redding noted the flash of light reflecting off aircraft wings to the right front as one German and one Italian plane began a strafing run against the exposed Americans. His spirits lifted when he spotted eleven twin-boom P-38 Lightning aircraft racing toward the column—the first friendly air cover he had seen since near Beja. The Axis aircraft fled but left behind three wounded men from a Company C gun crew.

As the column pressed forward, Redding nervously eyed a large flight of Ju-88s that had appeared to the east. Suddenly, the vicious roar of aircraft cannon and machine gun fire came from the rear. Aircraft were diving at the column, pulling up, and circling to strike again. Redding and his men saw twin booms and American stars on the fuselages as the planes tore fifty feet overhead, engines snarling.

The P-38 squadron from the 14th Pursuit Group of the U.S. Twelfth Air Force raked the column five times, spitting explosive shells and bullets at men running for cover. The Lightning, its nose packed with a 20mm cannon and four .50-caliber machine guns, was if anything more terrifying than the Stuka to men on the ground in its sights. The P-38s finally pulled away, their mission apparently accomplished. Seven of the "enemy" soldiers lay dead and twelve wounded. Every vehicle in the company except for one M3 and one M6 had been knocked out, and nine of the vehicles were in flames.

The Twelfth Air Force would later admit to an official observer mission that its pilots were not well trained in ground-troop identification. The air arm noted that to a pilot in a speeding aircraft, American and German halftracks, trucks, tanks, and helmets—especially dirty ones—looked pretty much alike. The risk was high in that policy was for pilots over the front to attack any ground targets "not clearly identified" as friendly.[48]

The men of Company C were shocked and demoralized, and it would take Redding four days to restore his command to even minimal mission readiness. As there were no replacement vehicles, Redding set his men to exhausting work to build as many functioning tank destroyers as possible out of the wrecks. When they were finished, all but one of the M6s and one of the M3s would move under their own power (although one more M3 eventually gave up the ghost).[49]

*   *   *

While the tank destroyers were refitting, the Anglo-American advance ground to a halt following several sharp engagements. On 28 November, Captain Redding was ordered to rejoin British forces. As the company drove down the Beja–Medjez el Bab highway, enemy planes appeared in the sky. The now airwise soldiers quickly dispersed, a tactic, they had learned, that usually convinced a pilot that a strafing run was not worth the risk of being shot down.[50]

On 1 December, Company C was ordered to join CCB's 6th Armored Infantry Regiment at Tebourba. The Allies were preparing another attempt to break through to Tunis, with local operations scheduled to begin at noon the next day. The TDs played virtually no direct role in the ensuing action, during which the tanks and armored doughs were badly mauled by the Germans. Inexperienced American tankers charged German antitank gun defenses and paid a steep price.

During two days of fighting, Redding's 75mm TDs performed several indirect fire missions as artillery, the first such use of tank destroyers in combat. (The 705th Tank Destroyer Battalion had used most of its guns as artillery during an exercise in August 1942, so the idea had been in circulation for some time even though it was not part of TD doctrine.[51]) Redding noted, "Although little good was accomplished because of unsuitable sighting equipment, we added in a highly satisfactory fashion to the general din of battle."[52]

The Allies gave ground, and by 10 December they had established a defensive line back at Medjez el Bab.

*   *   *

Company C was alerted the morning of 10 December while it was protecting the tank harbor of the 1/13th Armored Regiment in an olive grove near the Medjez–Tunis road. The company had been conducting daily reconnaissance missions in cooperation with the armored unit. Teams normally consisted of a two-gun TD section, a tank platoon of five M3 light tanks, a self-propelled mortar section with one halftrack-mounted 81mm mortar, and a detachment from the armored battalion reconnaissance section, probably equipped with jeeps and halftracks. The Germans patrolled the same area with similar equipment, and sharp clashes were frequent.

By now, the men had learned to meticulously camouflage their vehicles and to erase any tracks left by their passage. All movement into or out of positions took place after dark. These were the only ways available to defend effectively against the Luftwaffe.[53]

Reports indicated that a German armored column of fifty-five mixed vehicles was approaching. Indeed, the Germans had about thirty medium tanks and two of the massive new Mark VI Tigers in the column. A French battery brought the Germans to a halt only two miles short of Medjez el Bab. Rain had been pouring down for three days, and the panzers became temporarily bogged when they tried to maneuver around the guns. The 701st tank destroyers and Company A of the 13th Armored Regiment deployed to strike at the German flank. The light tanks of Company A also became mired, however, leaving the TDs on their own.[54]

Tanks to Destroy, and Guns to Do It

The German Wehrmacht fielded two medium tanks in large numbers in North Africa, the Panzerkampfwagen III and IV. American troops invariably referred to them as the Mark III and Mark IV. The Mark III carried a 37mm or 50mm main gun and was protected by 30mm (a bit more than one inch) of steel armor. The Mark IV was fitted with a range of guns from the 50mm to the long-barreled 75mm. The latter type was initially known in Allied ranks as the "Mark IV special." Early models of the panzer carried 50mm (two inches) of armor on the front and 30mm to 40mm on the sides and rear. Beginning in June 1942, the Wehrmacht began to add armor to vehicles in the field that increased the frontal armor to 80mm (three inches). In March 1943, the model H entered production with the frontal armor thickened to 85mm.[55] The blocky Marks III and IV resembled one another closely, which accounts for the uncertain enemy vehicle identification in many American after-action reports from this period.

The Mark VI heavy tank had 100mm (four inches) of frontal armor and 80mm on the sides and rear.[56] In practice, no American antitank gun fielded in North Africa could achieve a penetration of the Tiger's armor from the front. The main gun was the fearsome 88mm high-velocity cannon.

The main medium tank used by Italian forces encountered in Tunisia was the M13/40. The vehicle mounted a 47mm high-velocity gun and was protected by armor ranging between 30mm and 9mm in thickness.[57]

In theory, the American 37mm gun on the M6 could penetrate up to 2.4 inches of armor (depending on the type of round fired) out to five hundred yards, and the 75mm gun on the M3 tank destroyer could penetrate three inches of face-hardened plate at one thousand yards. The U.S. Army claimed that the 3-inch gun on the M10 tank destroyer could penetrate four inches of face-hardened armor plate at one thousand yards.[58] But it was not until the introduction of tungsten-core rounds late in the war that the weapon could achieve kills against that much armor from even three hundred yards.

*   *   *

As they had been taught, Capt Frank Redding's crews displayed a boldly aggressive spirit and engaged the far more numerous German tanks. Redding sent his six available M3s toward the German armor and arrayed his M6s to cover his rear. The TDs remained on the road surface to avoid sinking in the muck, so to avoid bunching up, Redding sent three TDs down a side route toward Ksar Tyr.

The three crews still on the main highway soon had their hands full. A concealed 47mm gun opened fire from a patch of trees to the south of the road but missed. Staff Sergeant Matthew Dixon maneuvered his M3 into position, and his 75mm barked back. Immediately, the enemy gun and its ammunition caught fire.

Through the smoke, five or six Mark III and Mark IV tanks emerged at point-blank range. The thin armor on an M3 had no chance whatsoever of stopping a shell from the main gun on either panzer model. Staff Sergeant Louis Romani turned his halftrack toward the threat. His gunner, Pfc Herman Lenzini, fired, but the round went high. Lenzini hurriedly adjusted as German shells whistled by, and he began firing as fast as his cannoneer could load. Lenzini's next four shots killed four Mark III tanks. The third M3 advanced to engage the remaining German tank or tanks, which had withdrawn under the murderous fire. A hidden armored car stitched the M3 with machine-gun fire, which killed the commander and two crewmen.[59]

A new threat emerged as a column of Mark IV tanks appeared at a bend in the road about a thousand yards distant. One of the remaining two guns drove the Germans back with hits on two of the lead tanks, while the crew of the second TD rounded up thirteen German prisoners. One gun of the second platoon on the nearby path was able to get into position to fire on the German column from the flank. It disabled three Mark III or IV tanks. Meanwhile, the light gun platoon drove off a probe to the company's rear by two armored cars and one light tank.

During the entire action, Redding had to run from TD to TD to issue orders, the radios having been rendered useless by days of rain and little maintenance and Redding's jeep having been sent to the rear on a supply mission.

German tanks had by now spotted the mired American light tanks and methodically shot them to pieces. The fire from the tank destroyers allowed many of the crews to dash to safety.

At 1630 hours, Redding received orders to disengage. All guns laid down heavy fire and backed down the highway.

The German column withdrew as well. The tank killers' first encounter with German tanks had been a resounding tactical success.

Fate, however, would snatch defeat from the jaws of victory. As CCB—accompanied by the tank destroyers—attempted its own withdrawal under cover of darkness, the column was shelled at the bridge across the Madjerda River. The column was ordered to reverse course and proceed across country more or less in the direction from whence it had come. One by one, the vehicles became stuck in the mud and were abandoned. Later in the campaign, the 701st would encounter one of the Company C guns lost here in German service. Eventually, the entire column was immobilized, and the Americans retreated to Medjez el Bab on foot. CCB was crippled. Redding's men, having lost all of their equipment, were assigned military police duties, where they remained until ordered back to the 701st in late January 1943.[60] The armored battalion officers responsible for the fiasco were relieved of command.[61]

The Southern Flank: The Tunisian Task Force

Company B of the 701st had parted ways with Company C on 21 November and proceeded southeast toward Tebessa, Algeria, a frontier town of twelve hundred inhabitants at the foot of the forested Atlas Mountains.[62] Waiting for their arrival was the Tunisian Task Force, a small venture consisting of the 2d Battalion of the 509th Parachute Infantry Regiment and French troops from the 3d Regiment of the

Chasseur D'Afrique, all under the command of LtCol Edson Raff. The American paratroopers had dropped at Youks-les-Bains airfield on 15 November in order to deny its use to the Germans and to protect the flank of British-led operations to the north. The French troops on the scene had proved friendly, much to the relief of the paratroopers, who thought they might be Germans.[63]

Raff obtained permission from headquarters in Algiers to occupy a smaller airfield at Gafsa, a lush oasis town of ten thousand people eighty miles to the south and roughly half the distance to the coastal road that was Rommel's only link to the German forces in Tunisia. Raff sent forty men there on 17 November. The French, who were receiving intelligence reports from coastal towns by phone, reported that a combined German-Italian force, including tanks, was advancing toward the area from the east. The defenses at Gafsa as of 20 November—a scant one hundred fifty men—had no artillery or antitank guns. Raff called for help.[64]

On 21 November, Raff ordered the destruction of fuel at the Gafsa airfield and pulled the elements there back to the vicinity of Youks-les-Bains, where he at least now had the support of a squadron of P-38s that had recently flown in. That morning, Company I and the antitank platoon from the 26th Infantry Regiment, 1st Infantry Division, arrived by air from Algiers. And just before midnight, the TDs of Company B pulled in, having completed a thousand-mile road march in seven days.[65]

Second Lieutenant Arthur Edson and the other tank destroyer men were tired, and their vehicles needed attention, but they were ordered to press on to Feriana, a village about halfway to Gafsa and just south of a place called Kasserine. Arriving in Feriana, the men were given one hour to sleep. At 0300 hours, Edson and the other company officers roused the men, and the company resumed its march toward Gafsa. Raff had ordered an attack at dawn on 22 November to evict a German parachute unit that had taken up residence.

At 0700 hours, P-38s strafed Gafsa and the Tunisian Task Force advanced. The tank destroyers were deployed as assault guns, and the infantry followed the halftracks—which were banging away with their 75s—into town. Lady Luck smiled, and the 'tracks missed all of the mines that the Germans had laid at a roadblock north of town. After a bit of sniping, the German defenders slipped away.[66]

Raff now faced a dilemma. The French reported that enemy forces were advancing toward Feriana to his rear, and shortly thereafter a motorcycle rider roared into town to report that a French armored car was in contact with an enemy tank force at El Guettar, a dozen miles further to the southeast. Raff pulled together a tank destroyer-infantry force and rushed to El Guettar.[67]

Company B arrived at El Guettar about 1700 hours. The trees of the oasis were visible to the right, and the Americans reasoned that the enemy had probably placed guns there. Company CO Capt Gilbert Ellmann sent two TD platoons to cover the trees. The men of the reconnaissance platoon continued down the road, manning the .30-caliber machine guns mounted on pedestals in their jeeps, and Edson and 2d Platoon followed. Generally, reconnaissance men depended on their wits to avoid ever having to use their machine guns because practically everything else on the battlefield was better protected than they were.[68]

Recon found ten Italian M13/40 tanks rather suddenly after cresting a small hill.[69] The lead jeep was lost as fire struck the American column, but the crew dashed to safety. Several Italian tanks advanced on the American column. The first M3 in Edson's platoon smashed the lead tank as it clanked over a rise, but then its gun jammed. The second TD pulled by just in time to destroy the next enemy tank.

The Italians decided to withdraw. Edson's crews spotted another tank in the distance and opened fire, but they could not hit the vehicle. Just before the tank disappeared from view, Edson climbed aboard one of the gun halftracks, straddled the 75mm, and dead-reckoned a last shot. The shell pierced the engine compartment at a distance later measured at 3,500 yards. Nightfall ended the battle, but the enemy column had been routed.[70]

After giving his men a few hours rest, Raff dashed back north to deal with the reported threat beyond Feriana. The task force arrived in Kasserine on 23 November and, having encountered no enemy troops, advanced east toward Sbeitla. Recon once again took the point, followed by Edson's platoon. Edson by now had figured out that because he was the most junior officer in the company, his platoon would almost always be in the lead. Once again, recon's jeeps ran into the enemy—a mixed group of German and Italian units—just short of Sbeitla. This time, the jeep drivers slammed into reverse and backed out as fast as they could, almost colliding, while the men on the machine guns fired at the enemy.[71]

A sharp fight ensued. Edson was riding in one of the gun halftracks instead of his command vehicle. When the firing started, he simply reacted rather than call the company CO on the radio. Edson led his platoon to the left, while Capt Robert Whitsit's platoon, directly behind, deployed to the right. Edson's M3 was struck by a 47mm round and disabled. The vehicle coasted to a stop in a dip with an excellent field of fire on the Italian and German tanks below. The lieutenant took over as gunner and opened fire, accounting for three light tanks. The remainder of the company destroyed five more light tanks—most from a range of only nine hundred yards—and captured seventy Italian soldiers and considerable equipment. Few Germans were taken because they withdrew when it became clear that the battle would go against the Axis forces. The tank killers suffered only one casualty, a man hit by mortar fragments.[72]

After clearing Sbeitla, the task force withdrew to Kasserine and then Feriana. Having raced one thousand miles and fought two decisive engagements that stopped the Axis push westward in southern Tunisia, the tank destroyer men were able to rest and enjoyed pancakes prepared by the kitchen crew. Raff received the French Legion of Honor for Company B's destruction of enemy armor at Sbeitla and a promotion to full colonel (the tank killers claimed that he had not even been present at the Sbeitla fire fight). Captain Gilbert Ellmann and the company received the Croix de Guerre with palm, and Arthur Edson a promotion to first lieutenant. The tank killers recorded in their operations report, "Although we had been attached to Colonel Raff and a few of his paratroops, we had done all the fighting in the recent engagements and had won the victories. Ours was a proud company."

On 1 December, during fitful action in the sector, Company B was strafed by American P-38s. Three men were killed and two wounded, a tragedy that demoralized the outfit.

Shadow Boxing

By early December, the Allied advance had come to a halt. An angry Eisenhower wrote Chief of Staff General George Marshall that American and British operations had thus far managed to violate every accepted tactical principle of warfare and would be condemned in the military school system for decades to come.[73] Be that as it may, the buildup of Axis forces assured near parity on the ground at the front by mid-December, a factor that had much to do with the Allies' difficulties. So, too, did the weather. Anderson launched a new offensive toward Tunis on 24 December, but Eisenhower realized the futility of the effort after examining the crippling mud at the front. He took the bitter decision to postpone the attack indefinitely.[74]

*   *   *

The men of the 701st Tank Destroyer Battalion considered the next month to have been perhaps the most miserable of their lives. Incessant cold rains turned the theater into a sea of mud. When the weather was clear, the air raids returned. Bivouacked near Sidi bou Zid, the men of Company B suffered German air attacks every day for a week beginning 3 December. The men spent Christmas Eve sitting around fires, singing songs and thinking of home until driven to bed by cold. It would be another week before they would see the first letters from home since the landings.

The 601st Tank Destroyer Battalion arrived in Tunisia on 21 December. In its first few hours at Souk el Khemis, in the heart of what by then had been dubbed "Stuka Alley," the men experienced their first German air attack. The strafing left soldier Michael Syrko dead on the sand. Ten minutes later, the enraged outfit shot down its first Spitfire.

*   *   *

During the last week of 1942 and the first six of 1943, the Allies and Axis sparred to gain any advantage in central Tunisia.[75] As ground was lost and gained and then lost again, some of the veteran tank killers wondered whether the generals in charge knew what they were doing.

In early January, the TDs of Company B of the 701st acted as artillery for French troops fighting to capture Hill 354 near Sidi bou Zid. Lieutenant Arthur Edson was awarded the Croix de Guerre with star for the effectiveness of his platoon's fire.

As had happened to the 701st, the companies of the 601st were widely dispersed. Company A was assigned to train and support troops belonging to the French XIX Corps near Ousseltia and engaged in its first fighting on Christmas Day. Company B deployed to support Colonel Raff's paratroopers around Feriana, and Company C was shuttled to the British and thence to the French at Fondouk Pass.[76]

The Germans struck at the juncture of the French and British sectors on 18 January, and the hard-pressed French appealed to Eisenhower for help. Eisenhower instructed the II Corps commanding general MajGen Lloyd Fredendall to send a suitable force, and the latter—bypassing the chain of command—told BrigGen Paul Robinett by phone that his Combat Command B, 1st Armored Division, had the job.[77] On 20 January, CCB—with the 601st Tank Destroyer Battalion (less two companies) attached—was assigned to the French XIX Corps in the Ousseltia Valley. Company A's TDs took up positions overlooking a valley dotted with small buildings and haystacks. Just as the sun was setting, the huts and haystacks transformed into camouflaged German tanks that assaulted the Americans. The tank killers pulled back gradually and then battled the panzers at a crossroads until it was too dark to fight. Only five TDs remained in action. The next day, CCB and the rest of the 601st arrived and drove the Germans off.[78]

Allied troops over the next week pushed the Germans back into high ground and captured a pass leading to Kairouan. For several days during the action, Company A of the 601st was reduced to a single officer because a captain had been killed and another captain and two lieutenants had become temporarily trapped behind enemy lines.[79] On 28 January, Combat Command B moved to rejoin the rest of the 1st Armored Division.[80]

The rest of the 1st Armored Division, meanwhile, was dealing with a German attack toward Sidi bou Zid, launched against French defenses in Faid Pass on 30 January. Combat commands C and D of the 1st Armored Division that day moved to intercept the German thrust. The 701st Tank Destroyer Battalion (less two companies) was attached to Combat Command D. The next day, the combat command launched an attack on Station de Sened and captured the town, which was lightly held by Italian troops. Assaults by Combat commands A and C on Faid and Maizila Passes ran into determined resistance, however, and both attacks were abandoned. American troops withdrew to Sidi bou Zid.[81]

On 2 February, Combat Command B was detached yet again and sent north to join the First British Army. It would soon be missed.[82]

An official observer who visited Capt Gilbert Ellmann's men of B/701st on 31 January near Pichon noted that the unit had received no break since the landings in November. The company had earned a high reputation, but it had already lost twenty-five men killed in action, and the strain of continual fighting and repeated air attacks by both German and Allied aircraft was beginning to tell.[83]

Some new blood, if not relief for the tank destroyer units already in action, was arriving. The 1st Tank Destroyer Group landed in Algeria on 17 January and took up the task of overseeing TD battalions when they were not directly attached to divisions. The 805th Tank Destroyer Battalion disembarked at Algiers and the 813th at Oran on 17 January, and the 894th shipped in about the same time. The 805th and 894th were transported to the II Corps area of the front by mid-February, but the 813th would not arrive until March. The 899th, meanwhile, arrived at Casablanca but did not rush to the line. Instead, the battalion was delighted to be issued the newest weapon in the TD arsenal, the M10. The men would have to learn to maintain and operate the new hardware before the unit would be ready for combat. The battalion CO, LtCol Maxwell Tichnor, had shown the foresight while still in the States of sending drivers for several weeks of training with a medium tank battalion, which made the conversion far easier than it might have been.[84]

* * *

By January 1943, a few tentative conclusions regarding the tank destroyers suggested themselves.

On the plus side, the idea of light, fast, hard-hitting tank destroyers worked, at least under certain circumstances. The Tunisian Task Force would have had no mobile antitank capability when it first encountered Axis armor had it not been for the ability of the TDs to cover long distances at high speeds beyond the capabilities of tanks. Moreover, as of January, the cheap and easily produced tank destroyers were well ahead of the enemy tanks in terms of their kill/loss ratio in combat. Later critics would seemingly forget this stage of the campaign. The tank destroyer had also demonstrated its potential utility as highly mobile field artillery.

On the negative side, the tank destroyer battalions had never been able to operate according to key prescriptions in the force's doctrine. The companies were dispersed and generally at the front line, not held back ready to deal with armored penetrations. The TDs' obvious tactical utility despite this fact suggested that the doctrine was, at least, incomplete. Fortunately, TD, infantry, and armor officers in the field were working out practical solutions as they went. Of course, some were better than others.

The Germans, moreover, did not usually behave as the doctrine assumed they would. U.S. Army observers noted that typically, small groups of German tanks preceded attacking infantry. Well-concealed high-velocity 88mm guns were placed to provide a defensive base of fire if necessary in practically every tank movement. Indeed, German tanks often towed the 88s into position. The German gunners often waited to fire until American tanks passed them in pursuit of the German tanks, catching the Americans from the rear. German air-ground cooperation was excellent, and artillery fire was adjusted accurately.[85] When the Germans had not acted thusly—as during the armored probe at Medjez el Bab on 10 December 1942—the tank destroyers had proved lethal in a scenario that at least approximated some aspects of doctrine.

Finally, combat experience had demonstrated that the M6 was not effective as a tank destroyer. Troops complained that its rounds bounced off German tanks.[86] In addition, the silhouette was too high, and there was insufficient space in the vehicle for the crew to properly serve the weapon.[87] The ineffectiveness of the 37mm gun, which was the infantry's standard-issue antitank weapon, presaged continual pressure from line units to parcel out TD battalions in order to provide the GI at the front with adequate protection against tank attack.

Chapter 3

From Gloom to Glory

"Probably the worst performance of U.S. Army
Troops in their whole proud history."

— Omar Bradley, *A General's Life*

Ike knew his front was not all it should be. After canceling offensive operations on 24 December 1942, he ordered II Corps Headquarters under MajGen Lloyd Fredendall to move from Oran to Tebessa and assume responsibility from the small Tunisian Task Force for guarding the flank of the main forces to the north. Second Corps' initial component was the 1st Armored Division, which had been extricated from its support to British formations. The 1st Infantry Division, elements of which were scattered along the front, received orders to concentrate in the II Corps sector. The 34th and 9th Infantry divisions were to gradually move forward into the area, the former turning over security responsibilities along the lines of communication to the French. By early February, the 26th Infantry Regiment, 1st Infantry Division, and the 168th Infantry Regiment, 34th Infantry Division, were established in Fredendall's sector.

Eisenhower's deputy and forward representative, MajGen Lucian Truscott Jr., later offered this description of Fredendall: "Small in stature, loud and rough in speech, he was outspoken in his opinions and critical of superiors and subordinates alike. He was inclined to jump at conclusions that were not always well founded. He rarely left his command post for personal reconnaissance and visits, yet he was impatient with the recommendations of subordinates more familiar with the terrain and other conditions than he was."[1]

Eisenhower visited Fredendall's CP on 13 February and was appalled to find that he had hundreds of engineers digging tunnels into the walls of a ravine for him and his staff. Ike noted that it was the only time during the war that he saw a commander at that level so concerned over his own safety that he dug underground shelters.[2] Omar Bradley, then a major general just arriving in North Africa, judged that Fredendall lacked personal courage.[3]

German successes against the poorly equipped French troops in the center during January had necessitated the deployment into the area of British units as well as elements of the 1st Armored Division. By Eisenhower's own admission, his front by late that month was "a long tenuous line stretching from Bizerte to Gafsa, with units badly mixed and no local reserves." On 26 January, Eisenhower gave British LtGen Kenneth Anderson command of the entire battle line in order to bring order to the chaos.[4]

*   *   *

Hundreds of miles to the east, Generalfeldmarschall Erwin Rommel was nearing the end of his skillfully executed sixteen hundred-mile withdrawal through Libya, cautiously pursued by Monty and his Eighth Army. Hitler had lost faith in Rommel's winning magic. On the same day that Anderson took command of the Allied battle line in Tunisia, Rommel was ordered to consolidate his forces in the modest French-built fortifications of the Mareth Line along the Tunisian frontier, turn his command over to an Italian general, and return to Germany "for health reasons." The successes achieved by the German commander in Tunisia—Generaloberst Jürgen von Arnim—against the French during

January, however, inspired Rommel to press again an idea he had formulated as he foresaw the merging of the two North African fronts.

The Mareth Line, Rommel reasoned, would be in grave peril with American troops only some one hundred thirty miles to the rear at Gafsa. Rommel proposed leaving a holding force at the Mareth Line, shifting his remaining strike force westward, and in cooperation with von Arnim, launching a surprise attack deep into the Allies' rear area in Tunisia. Generalfeldmarschall Albert Kesselring, who was responsible for coordinating the two German forces in Tunisia, and the Axis Comando Supremo approved the idea. On 9 February, the three German commanders met at Gabes to discuss the offensive. Von Arnim would attack at Sidi bou Zid with the 10th and 21st Panzer divisions, and Rommel would strike at Gafsa with elements of his Panzerarmee, the remnants of the Italian Centauro Division, and any forces that could be spared from the 21st Panzer Division after its initial operations. Fortunately for the Allies, command arrangements were left rather vague.[5]

*   *   *

Two clusters of passes pierced the mountain chain—called the Eastern Dorsale—running north to south inland from the coast in eastern Tunisia. In the north, passes at Fondouk and Pichon debouched into the French sector. Roughly fifty miles south, the Faid and Maizila passes sent roads down to the American-held oasis of Sidi bou Zid. Von Arnim's attacks in January had secured Pichon, Faid, and Maizila passes for the Germans.

The British Ultra code-breaking operation detected the German preparations for an offensive and alerted Allied headquarters in Algiers. Intelligence officers deduced from the traffic that the blow would fall at Fondouk, in the north.[6] Lieutenant General Anderson, acting on the best information available to him, decided to keep the 1st Armored Division's CCB behind Fondouk to deal with the threat.

To the south, II Corps' own intelligence collectors—ignorant of the Ultra data—had pulled together a growing body of evidence that the Germans were preparing an attack at Faid Pass. Fredendall heeded the warning. He instructed 1st Armored Division CG MajGen Orlando Ward in excruciating and insulting detail on how he was to dispose of his forces in preparation.[7]

On 11 February, Eisenhower received his fourth star. Nonetheless, a worried rather than cheerful Eisenhower inspected the II Corps area on 13 and 14 February. Despite Fredendall's awareness of a threat, Ike later recalled that he detected a certain complacency among the line units, illustrated by an unconscionable delay in preparing defensive positions. Eisenhower concluded that lack of training and experience among commanders was the chief cause of the problem. He also recognized that the 1st Armored Division had been too thinly spread to fight effectively.[8]

Two hill masses flank the road that runs from Faid Pass by Sidi bou Zid and thence to Sbeitla. To the north lies Djebel Lessouda and to the south Djebel Ksaira. In accordance with Fredendall's orders, a battalion of the 168th Infantry Regiment, 34th Infantry Division, defended each hill. Local commanders had objected that this disposition risked having the battalions cut off and cut up because they could not support one another, but Fredendall and his staff had declined to take a personal look at the terrain. Lieutenant Colonel John Waters had been given control over the troops on Djebel Lessouda on 12 February. In addition to the 2/168th, Waters had at his disposal a company of light tanks, a battery of 105mm howitzers, and the 2d Platoon, A/701st Tank Destroyer Battalion.[9]

Waters's job was to stop any attacking force long enough for LtCol Louis Hightower to launch a counterattack from Sidi bou Zid with his mobile reserve of some forty tanks from the 3d Battalion, 1st Armored Regiment. The rest of A/701st and two artillery battalions supported Hightower's force.[10] Company A was the only line company in the TD battalion that had virtually no combat experience.

*   *   *

At 0400 hours on 14 February, Waters rose and went to the lookout position atop Djebel Lessouda. Before turning in the night before, he had called the commander of the 2d Battalion and told him to inform his company commanders to expect an attack. Peering toward Faid Pass, he could neither see nor hear anything. A windstorm was blowing through the pass, carrying an obscuring cloud of sand with it. Waters returned to his tent just as a call came in from Col Peter Hains, the deputy commander of CCA, who wanted to know what the shooting was all about. Waters was mystified but said he would check. He returned to the top of the hill. Now he heard the rumble of artillery through the wind.[11]

Two battle groups of the 10th Panzer Division, covered by artillery fire and led by the Tigers of the Schwere Panzer Abteilung 501, were erupting from the pass. Dismounted panzergrenadiers from the 21st Panzer Division supported the attack. To the south, mobile elements from the 21st Panzer Division were preparing to sweep through the thin American defenses in Maizila Pass.

A small covering force of American infantry and the tank destroyers of 2d Platoon barred the exit from Faid Pass. Lieutenant Armbruster ordered his green tank destroyer crews to open fire. Their 75s would cause no more harm to the advancing Tigers than would throwing rocks, though the men later said they had managed to knock out three or more panzers of some type. The German force quickly overran the American positions. Men broke in panic and pelted back toward Sidi bou Zid. "Tigers! The Tigers are coming!" men shouted as they reached Waters' position. Two M3s and a few jeeps from A/701st joined the rout. These vehicles may have later fetched up with a combat group built around the 3d Battalion, 168th Infantry Regiment, which was deployed at Djebel Ksaira and at 1400 hours reported that it had been joined by some retreating tank destroyers.[12]

At 0650, Waters reported that he was under attack by infantry and armor. Waters ordered his light tank company forward. Armed with 37mm popguns, the light tanks stood even less chance than had the TDs and were quickly destroyed. At 0730, Hightower received orders to launch his planned attack to stabilize the situation. Climbing into his command Sherman, he instructed the forty-odd Shermans of Companies H and I, 3d Battalion, 1st Armored Regiment, and the eight tank destroyers of A/701st under the command of Captain Wray to advance.

About this time, Waters was able to count roughly sixty German tanks around his position, and there were more that he could not see. When Hightower saw the number of tanks that he faced, he radioed that the best he could do was to delay the enemy. He was not only outnumbered but outgunned.[13]

The tank destroyers deployed to the right flank of Company I. They drove to high ground east of the Lessouda-Sadguia road, advancing through a cactus patch over the rise. The crews were shocked to see about thirty Mark IV tanks heading west from the pass a mere two hundred yards distant. The Americans opened fire, including small arms in the heat of the moment. But a slugging match against so many panzers at short range was utterly hopeless. Three M3s and two M6s rocked and burst into flames as cannon shells struck home.

The outnumbered American tanks, meanwhile, were taking a pounding, especially from 88s, including those on a few Tiger tanks. Dust made identification of friend and foe extremely difficult.[14]Four more tank destroyers were knocked out as the confused melee continued. Fortunately, elements of the 168th Infantry surrounded on Djebel Lessouda spotted a flanking movement by six Tigers and were able to reach the tankers and warn them, which prevented a potentially devastating surprise.[15]

Hightower knew it was time to go. He later told LtGen Omar Bradley that the TD men of Company A stuck it out to the bitter end and were utterly fearless.[16] They had also earned the distinction of being the first Americans to knock out a Tiger tank by direct fire.[17] As the attacking force withdrew, the remnants of the TD company turned and raced toward Sidi bou Zid. They linked up with the roughly twenty surviving tanks under Hightower, who ordered a withdrawal in the direction of Sbeitla. Just west of town, German fighters—which completely controlled the air during the initial onslaught—bombed and strafed the Americans, who were fleeing in no particular order across the plain. The air strike knocked out Company A's last M3 and the maintenance trucks.

The Company A party decided to cut southwest across a wadi. The men soon spotted six German tanks moving slowly toward the main clump of retreating Americans. Bereft of firepower, the men dispersed and hid in the grass. The panzers passed, and the TD men could soon hear their cannons firing.

A radio message informed Hightower of the attack. He tried to reach some of his tanks up ahead but had no luck. The colonel ordered his driver to stop, and he traversed the turret and engaged the enemy himself. Although the Sherman was struck several times, he and his crew continued to slug it out. Finally, when he had only three rounds left, a German shell penetrated the Sherman and set it on fire. Hightower escaped with his crew and made it back to American lines. He had seven tanks left. According to the men from Company A, Hightower knocked out several of the panzers and saved the column.[18]

The remnants of Company A also made it back to American lines. They left behind two officers killed, one officer who was both wounded and missing, five enlisted men killed, six known captured, and forty-two missing in action.

*   *   *

On 14 February, the 1st Armored Division operations report recorded, "Enemy tank attack started on wide front. Djebel Lessouda surrounded by more than forty tanks. Our positions held even though Djebel Ksaira surrounded by more tanks and infantry. The whole operation was supported by continuous and heavy air bombardment." By the end of the day, American commanders realized that the Germans had broken out of Faid Pass, and that strong enemy thrusts were directed at Sidi bou Zid and out of Maizila Pass.

Combat Command A estimated that it had been hit by a tank force twice its own size. Division intelligence identified elements of the 10th, 15th, and 21st Panzer divisions and Panzer Abteilung 601 (Tigers) in the attacking force. The 15th Panzer Division was not there, and the Schwere Panzer Abteilung was actually the 501st, but the division correctly deduced that it faced a substantial portion of all German armor in North Africa.[19]

This was the very scenario imagined by the brain trust back in the Tank Destroyer Command. Now was the time for the tank destroyer battalions to sweep to the penetration and annihilate the panzers. There was only one problem. The companies and even platoons of the only battalions in the vicinity—the 701st, 601st, and newly arrived 805th—were scattered like thrown pebbles across the front.

Responding to battle reports during the morning hours, II Corps shifted a single company—A/805th Tank Destroyer Battalion—and an attached reconnaissance platoon from Feriana to Sbeitla.[20]

*   *   *

At 1930 hours, 1st Armored Division artillery reported that one of its officers had established contact with the 805th Tank Destroyer Battalion. They were discussing a plan for offensive operations by the outfit to back up the shaky line.[21]

The remnants of CCA rallied at dusk near Djebel Hamra and reorganized for the defense of Sbeitla. Allied commanders underestimated the size of the German offensive and decided to keep CCB near Fondouk. Nevertheless, in accordance with previous assessments that Gafsa could not be held against a major assault, they ordered an orderly evacuation of the town for the night of 14–15 February. The tank destroyers of B/805th had only just arrived in the vicinity on 9 February, their first deployment at the front. The TDs had taken up positions at Zannuch Station about twenty miles east of Gafsa. Almost daily, a few enemy tanks appeared at a distance and retired after exchanging a few rounds with the M3s. The company screened the evacuation of Gafsa and was the last unit to leave the town.[22]

Just after noon on 15 February, CCC/1st Armored Division, reinforced by the 2d Battalion of 1st Armored Regiment and led by Reconnaissance Company of the 701st Tank Destroyer Battalion, counterattacked from assembly areas northeast of Djebel Hamra in the direction of Sidi bou Zid thirteen miles away.[23]

Lieutenant Arthur Edson and the men of B/701st mounted their vehicles. "Glasscock, follow Milo!" Edson bellowed. The TDs would move so frequently over the next ten days—and Edson yell that order as many times—that the phrase would become a company slogan.

Combat Command C advanced through clear, dry afternoon air, raising clouds of dust behind it. Tanks took the lead. The tank destroyers of 3d Platoon, under Capt Robert Whitsit, took up position on the right flank, while Lieutenant Edson's vehicles swung behind the center with orders to move to the left flank if needed. 1st Platoon protected the rear.

Repeated German air strikes slowed the advance. The official U.S. Army history records that one of the TD platoons was destroyed in a Stuka attack on the village of Sadaguia. If men died there, they were not from the tank destroyer force.

The tanks became engaged in a wild battle against emplaced 88s and panzers. The Germans executed a well-conceived multi-pronged envelopment, striking around the flanks toward the American rear. Whitsit's platoon engaged German tanks that appeared on the south flank. A few moments later, a panzer column led by Tigers maneuvered to cut off escape from the north. German practice was to put a Tiger at the center of an attacking formation with lighter tanks on the wings; one flank of the formation would be stronger than the other.[24] Edson ordered his M3s into action. They could see the panzers, but the only passage across an intervening wadi was blocked by a crippled American tank. The tank killers took up position under some trees and opened fire at long range. Whitsit's TDs returned to help deal with this more serious threat.

A third German tank column appeared, and the command found itself under fire from four different directions. Fortunately, the radios worked this time, and Company B received orders to extricate itself.

All elements that were not too far forward beat a hasty retreat westward. During what the TD men would later characterize as a rout, one M6 and one jeep were abandoned. Remarkably, only one man in Company B had been hurt, a gun commander in Edson's platoon who fell victim to a shell that burst over the hood of his M3. When the day was over, only four American tanks had returned from the inferno. The 1st Armored Division had lost an entire tank battalion.

Late on 15 February, Lieutenant General Anderson instructed II Corps to withdraw to the Western Dorsale mountain range and insure the security of Sbeitla, Kasserine, and Feriana.[25] Accordingly, the 1st Armored Division gave ground, under orders from II Corps to use tank destroyers from the 701st and infantry as the rear guard. That night, LtCol John Waters was captured as his command tried to exfiltrate from Djebel Lessouda.

Delaying Actions: Sbeitla and Feriana

By 16 February, the 1st Armored Division had pulled back to Sbeitla, where it prepared to make a stand. It had already lost nearly one hundred tanks, almost two hundred men killed or wounded, and nearly one thousand men missing or captured.[26]

Combat Command B—with the 601st Tank Destroyer Battalion (less Company C and Reconnaissance Company) in tow—rejoined the division and rushed to shore up the other battered elements gathered at Sbeitla. Combat commands A and C manned the northern half of the division's defensive arc before Sbeitla, and CCB moved into positions to the south. Fredendall verbally ordered Ward to hold the line there at all costs until 1100 hours, 17 February, an order subsequently amended to an indefinite period. The Allies needed time to move British forces and the American 34th Infantry Division to Sbiba and Thala, northwest of the breakthrough; bring the American 9th Infantry Division's artillery forward to support them; and concentrate the 16th Regimental Combat Team (RCT) of the 1st Infantry Division at a new line to the rear.

As panzers probed the defenses late on 16 February, Lieutenant Colonel Hightower commanded a screening force in front of the CCA and CCC units just moving into position. Two platoons of Company B, 701st Tank Destroyer Battalion, participated in an effort to extricate the 6th Armored Infantry, which had been unable to disengage from the enemy. The maneuver succeeded, but the TDs became embroiled in a rear-guard action against three German tank columns, during which the tank destroyers were cut off.

The rest of Company B had spent the day searching out firing positions until ordered to deploy in a cactus patch with no field of fire whatsoever. Hidden by the plants, Lieutenant Edson and the rest of men were unaware that German armored columns passed to the north and south in the evening gloom.

Lacking orders to withdraw and unable to contact combat command headquarters where the battalion CO had gone in search of instructions, the battalion executive officer, Major Walter Tardy, ordered battalion elements to escape if they could. He could not reach Company B by radio, so he told Company A to find a Company B patrol to pass the instructions. About midnight, the tank destroyers dispersed and filtered back to American lines under heavy machine-gun fire. Following a route scouted by the pioneer platoon, the men drove through or around various obstacles and wadis that they never would have attempted in daylight. Machine-gun tracers paralleled one column on both sides. Most of the TDs crept into Sbeitla by dawn. The town presented a picture of crowded confusion as the TDs worked their way through the streets amidst exploding German shells.[27]

Captain Redding led Company C into Sbeitla somewhat later and found the town deserted. He contacted division headquarters to offer the services of his six remaining guns but was told to get off the net. He next radioed the combat command, which instructed him to take up positions at a spot that by now was behind German lines. Redding wisely joined the rest of the battalion west of Sbeitla.[28]

*   *   *

At 0314 hours on 17 February, 1st Armored Division transmitted to all subordinate units, "We are going to hold. Use every available trick you know. We are going to stick here. We will lick those bastards yet."[29]

German troops attacked in force at 0900 hours.[30] CCB had deployed the men of the 601st Tank Destroyer Battalion in an outpost line a few miles east of the main line of resistance.[31] The tank killers were strafed there by Allied aircraft and shelled by American artillery during the morning.[32] About 1145, the 601st reported that its command post was under attack by fifty tanks from one direction and a combined tank-infantry force from another. Lieutenant Colonel Herschel Baker requested reinforcements but was told to fall back on American lines, fighting a delaying action as he came.[33] Some of the TDs fired smoke and were able to shift about and maintain fire for about half an hour, but the battalion gave way under overwhelming pressure.[34] The informal battalion history recorded what happened next: "Confusion was king that day. There was no communication between units, no traffic control, no organization, and no order. It was every man for himself, and Heinie take the hindmost. Halftracks went sailing by jeeps as if the jeeps were standing still, and M4s tore down the road, three abreast, in chariot race style! It was a sad day for the new, inexperienced American Army."[35]

Several hours later, men from the 601st were spotted passing the CCB CP. Upon questioning, they said that the battalion had been dispersed, and that they had been ordered to regroup at Kasserine. Staff officers regrouped all the TD men they could find on the spot and turned them over to Baker when he reappeared.[36]

The Americans held their ground at Sbeitla until 1500 hours. II Corps now ordered the 1st Armored Division to withdraw through Kasserine Pass—except for CCA, which departed northward via Sbiba. Combat Command B screened the main retreat. The remnants of the 601st Tank Destroyer Battalion, supported by a company of infantry, was ordered to act as rearguard. They were nearly overrun. As German fighters strafed the retreating Americans, the 601st's CP radio halftrack stalled. Sergeant Jagels dismounted, calmly extracted the air filter, held it up to the sunlight, and observed, "Look at the dirt in that goddamn thing!" The last American troops cleared the pass at about 0300 hours on 18 February. By its own admission, the 1st Armored Division had suffered defeat in detail.[37]

The 701st screened the withdrawal of CCA, with its remaining guns falling back in leap-frog fashion. When darkness fell, the command disengaged and slipped away. It lost one M3, but no men, during the action.

*   *   *

Rommel's attack on Gafsa, meanwhile, had found the town abandoned, so Rommel advanced with his detachment from the Afrika Korps and some twenty-five tanks from the Italian Centauro Division toward Feriana. As of 16 February, Stark Force (built around the 26th RCT, 1st Infantry Division, commanded by Col Alexander Stark) was dug in around Feriana protecting the withdrawal of units into positions on the heights north of Thelepte.

The green 805th Tank Destroyer Battalion had moved into Feriana on 10 February,[38] and its recon men quickly became the eyes and ears of Stark Force; they conducted daily patrols of likely approaches to the town. Company A had left the battalion for Sbeitla on 14 February, but Company B returned following the evacuation of Gafsa.

The battalion's reconnaissance jeeps the morning of 16 February rolled down the road toward Gafsa, and the men noted that the usual Allied military traffic had disappeared. At 1130 hours, the patrol reported that it had sighted the enemy. Shortly thereafter, the first shells fell on a Stark Force outpost at Djebel Sidi Aich. TDs from Company B deployed beside the road to Gafsa to cover the recon team as it barreled back into Feriana.

Captain William Zierdt of Company C had deployed one TD platoon supported by a recon platoon to guard the pass leading to Feriana. A German fighter flew low over Zierdt's position. When its pilot waved, Zierdt waved back. Weeks later, after experiencing combat and learning to fear aircraft, Zierdt would accidentally shoot down a Spitfire.[39]

In the early afternoon, Stark ordered Zierdt to destroy the guns that were thought to be firing on the American outpost. The company sent two platoons through the pass, but the crews could spot no guns. Stark now ordered the two platoons to take up positions along the Feriana-Gafsa highway. Unable to reach the company by radio, the battalion operations officer had to deliver the order in person.

The Company C TDs came under fire from the north, and the men became a bit excited as it was their first time in combat. The M3s engaged what the crews thought to be 75mm guns. Months of training and demonstrations for congressmen and senators while back at Fort Belvoir, Virginia, paid off, and the crews performed extremely well.[40]

Perhaps because they had revealed their position, the tank destroyers soon were taking fire from the rear, as well. The TDs withdrew closer to Feriana. Company B, meanwhile, spotted approaching tanks and opened fire. After a brisk fight during which two TDs were knocked out, the company pulled back somewhat on orders from Stark.

Late in the day, Colonel Stark issued orders for a counterattack the following morning. The tank destroyers were instructed to execute a flank attack from the east in support of the main effort. Inasmuchas Company C still could not be reached by radio, the instructions were passed to the battalion operations officer over a field telephone located at an outpost near the tank destroyers. Colonel Anderson Moore, meanwhile, was instructed to take elements of his 19th Engineer Combat Regiment and a battalion of the 26th Infantry Regiment to Kasserine Pass and organize a defense.[41]

Company C mounted up at dawn on 17 February and moved out for the flank attack. The reconnaissance platoon at about 0830 reported that there were approximately fifty Italian tanks supported by 88s advancing along the highway from Gafsa. As the TDs pulled into sight of the highway, platoon commander SSgt John Spence saw German and Italian tanks and other vehicles driving bumper-to-bumper toward Feriana. There was no main American attack from the north in sight. Spence realized something had gone awry almost immediately. A few crews opened fire, but the order came almost at once in the face of such overwhelming odds: Pull back![42]

Zierdt still had no radio contact with higher command. The battalion operations officer, who was still with the company, raced to the Stark Force outpost to use the field telephone. The outpost—and its phone—were gone.

Stark had changed his mind and ordered that Feriana be abandoned. The outpost pulled out per orders, but nobody thought to tell the men of Company C. Battalion headquarters, which had had received its movement orders at 0300 hours, was unable to raise Company C by radio, so it sent a recon platoon to inform Zierdt. By the time the platoon tracked the company down, the tank killers appeared to have been surrounded.

Shortly after noon, Zierdt realized that he was almost completely encircled, so he ordered a withdrawal toward Kasserine. Gas and oil supplies were low, so he instructed vehicle commanders to destroy all faulty machines. As the halftracks, M6s, and jeeps pulled out, the enemy spotted the movement and machine-gun fire lashed the column. Recon took the lead, followed by Staff Sergeant Spence's M3s. Soon, tank fire howled in from the west.

The recon men and Spence's platoon returned fire to cover the rest of the column. One TD was knocked out, and several crewmembers were wounded. Almost immediately, heavy gunfire came crashing in from the east, and the other two platoons were committed. Company C had circled the wagons. The tanks to the west pulled back, evidently intending a flanking maneuver to the north.

Just as things looked hopeless, a flight of sixteen friendly aircraft strafed the enemy lines. The Germans were caught by surprise, and the fire slackened. The planes flew over the company, and each airplane waggled its wings as the flight swooped away to the north. "Look!" someone shouted, "They're trying to show us the way!" Indeed, along the line indicated by the fighters' flight Spence saw a cow path over a mountain that blocked the way. (The official operations report says that the planes did not attack the enemy, but Spence remembers that the air strike saved the company.)[43]

The Germans had recovered, so the two platoons facing east had to disengage separately under cannon fire. They were last seen heading northeast. The remainder of Company C traversed the rough high ground into the next valley. On the way across, the lead jeep tipped over and blocked the escape route; men grabbed the vehicle and righted it.

After coming under fire again near Thelepte airfield, the column turned toward Kasserine Pass. About 1515 hours, Zierdt finally reestablished radio contact with battalion headquarters, which ordered the company into positions at the foot of the pass. Company C had to borrow 75mm ammo from Sherman tank crews for its last two M3s.[44] Patrols were sent out to find the missing platoons, but to no avail.

By the end of the day, Company C had lost one officer killed, seventy-four men captured or missing, and most of its vehicles.

*　　*　　*

The Allies enjoyed a bit of a respite on 18 February as German commanders argued over how to exploit their initial successes. Rommel wanted to continue his thrust deep into the Allied rear, an idea von Arnim strongly opposed. Comando Supremo late in the day split the difference and authorized a less sweeping envelopment—a maneuver that would unknowingly send the Germans into the strong Allied defenses building up in the Thala area. The immediate consequences were in many ways the same for American troops at Kasserine Pass: Rommel ordered the Afrika Korps strike force to break through and then swing north toward Le Kef.[45]

Clobbered at Kasserine

The headquarters group of the 1st Infantry Division's 26th RCT arrived in Kasserine Pass about 0730 hours on 19 February to take charge of defenses that were already under attack. Fredendall had called Colonel Stark late on 18 February and told him to move to Kasserine Pass immediately and "pull a Stonewall Jackson." Stark took command from Colonel Moore and found four companies of the 19th Engineer Combat Regiment deployed on the right side of the line while his own 1st Battalion held the left. About 1705 hours, the 3d Battalion, 39th Infantry Regiment, 9th Infantry Division, along with an antitank company, began to move into the left sector in a more-or-less piecemeal fashion. Stark deployed a few tanks from Company I, 13th Armored Regiment, and what was left of the 805th Tank Destroyer Battalion after the Feriana engagement near the entrance to the pass on the right (Company A had rejoined the battalion minus four TDs lost near Sbeitla).[46]

Kampfgruppe Deutsches Afrika Korps launched a strong frontal attack during the day; casualties were heavy on both sides. Under heavy artillery fire and attacked by an estimated tank battalion, the 805th Tank Destroyer Battalion wildly reported that it had destroyed between twenty-five and thirty armored vehicles while losing eight of its own TDs. The official U.S. Army history's account suggests that the battalion destroyed no tanks, but *Stars and Stripes* credited the tank killers with sixteen panzers in the action.[47] The tank destroyers had to pull back at about 1600 hours because German infantry had infiltrated its positions. During the night, the battalion's last ten guns shifted to the left flank.

The following day, at about 0400 hours, a small British task force of eleven tanks, a company of motorized infantry, one battery of artillery, and some antitank guns arrived courtesy of the British 26th Armoured Brigade at Thala. During the afternoon, the 894th Tank Destroyer Battalion pulled into the pass. Stark deployed two companies to strengthen the right flank and one company to help the men of the 805th on the left.[48]

Rommel, however, was pressing his attack with reinforcements of his own—the 10th and 21st Panzer divisions—and his usual determination. By noon, German tanks had penetrated the line held by the engineers. As the afternoon progressed, the American line crumbled. Men fled, abandoning prodigious quantities of equipment. Lieutenant Colonel A. C. Gore, who commanded the British detachment, fought on valiantly until his last tank was destroyed. He then withdrew, accompanied by the five remaining TDs of the 805th.[49]

On 20 February, BrigGen Paul Robinett, commanding general of Combat Command B, was ordered to take charge of all troops defending Kasserine Pass. He, in turn, would report to the commander of the British 26th Armored Brigade, which was operating just to the north. The command spent that night rounding up and feeding stragglers from retreating units, including the 805th and 894th Tank Destroyer battalions. Both were initially incorporated into the command, but the 805th was in such a poor state—it had over the course of seven days lost eleven men killed, fifty-five wounded, and one hundred and sixty-eight missing or captured—that it could not be made combat-ready for at least a day and was sent north to Thala.[50]

At 0335 hours on 21 February, II Corps reported that the Germans had taken the heights on both sides of Kasserine Pass. Tanks were beginning to probe the plain on which sat Tebessa, II Corps headquarters, many of the largest American supply dumps, and the critical airfield at Youks-les-Bains.[51] Combat Command B advanced during the wee hours of 21 February to Djebel el Hamra in the Bahiret Foussana Valley to block the projected German advance. The Germans attacked the new line at about 1400 with forty tanks backed by motorized infantry and artillery. The tanks of CCB would not be budged and stayed in hull-defilade positions rather than charge into waiting antitank fire. Artillery fire poured into the German ranks. The 894th Tank Destroyer Battalion maneuvered its halftracks to the enemy's south flank and pounded the advancing Germans. The Americans held. Combat Command B's Brigadier General Robinett reported that he believed the Germans had begun to retreat back into Kasserine Pass.[52]

Major General Orlando Ward, CG of 1st Armored Division, on 22 February assumed command of all operations in Kasserine, Thala, and Haidra. That day, the Germans were reported to be burning some of their vehicles, but Rommel nevertheless threw one more jab at CCB; more tough fighting was required to restore the line.

The next day, 1st Armored Division elements advanced against little resistance. Rommel, worried about Monty's Eighth Army at his back, had decided to end his offensive.[53] By 25 February, German forces had withdrawn to the line Faid–Djebel Sidi Aich–Gafsa, and the following day the battered 1st Armored Division went into corps reserve.[54] Eisenhower deemed the Kasserine line stabilized as of 26 February.[55]

The first major American battle with German forces had cost the U.S. Army more than six thousand casualties, including three hundred dead, and two-thirds of the tank strength of the 1st Armored Division.[56] Some of the tank destroyer men realized for the first time why the British, saddled with inferior equipment, might feel proud of a successful evacuation.[57]

Ward concluded in a letter to Armored Force chief LtGen Jacob Devers written a few days later, "I now have a veteran division. Its losses have been great, but I hope before long to have it better than ever, based on past experiences."[58] His words doubtless applied to the tank destroyer units fighting as part of his command.

*   *   *

The troops were quickly losing faith in their equipment. Tank killers nicknamed their M3 the "Purple Heart Box."[59] The vehicle had no more punch than a Sherman and offered much less protection. After the fighting at Feriana and Kasserine, SSgt John Spence, of the 805th, realized that one had to move quickly in the M3, because if the halftrack were hit by a German tank round, "it was like lighting a match."[60] Indeed, the halftrack in general was getting a very bad name. One soldier, when asked by an officer if German aircraft bullets would go through the halftrack, replied, "No, sir. They only come through one wall and then they rattle around."[61]

Word had gotten all the way back to TD men training at Camp Hood. When the 899th Tank Destroyer Battalion shipped out for North Africa in January 1943, the men all hoped that they would not have to fight in the M3. They were elated when they were issued the first M10s in North Africa upon their arrival at Casablanca.[62]

By March 1943, official U.S. Army observers concluded that the 37mm gun was ineffective against German Mark III and Mark IV tanks. Only a side or rear shot had much chance of achieving a kill, and effective German coordination of tanks and infantry made this difficult to do in battle.[63] There were now enough M3s in North Africa to replace all of the M6s.[64] Company B of the 701st Tank Destroyer Battalion gleefully got rid of its M6s, which it judged "utterly worthless." Reconnaissance Company got stuck with some of them, however.

On to Victory

Eisenhower reacted to the debacle at Kasserine Pass by reorganizing his command. British General Sir Harold Alexander took control of all ground forces. The British—who viewed the American performance as incompetent—would play the lead role in the next phase of operations. Major General George Patton Jr. assumed command of II Corps and started to beat it into shape. Two fresh British divisions arrived, and the Americans and French rearmed. And the Allies finally deployed enough fighters to contest control of the air. With that, the Allies took the offensive.[65]

On 13 March, the 776th Tank Destroyer Battalion was attached to the 1st Armored Division, paving the way for the detachment three days later of the 701st.[66] A partnership that had seen the toughest times of the North Africa campaign came to an end until renewed in Italy. The newly arrived battalion, equipped with M10s, deployed near Maknassy, where the men almost immediately experienced their first German dive-bombing.

The first mission for the 776th was to act as lead element for the 1st Armored Division in II Corps' mid-March advance through Gafsa. Doctrine remained firmly tucked away in the field manual. The battalion CO concluded, however, that TD battalions were actually a logical choice for such work. They had organic antiaircraft protection, scouts, de facto infantry in their security sections, and the ability to destroy any German tank on the battlefield. The only real downside, he judged, was that his men had never fired a shot in anger.[67]

American forces recaptured Gafsa on 17 March, five days later passed through Maknassy, and advanced into the hills beyond.

The Perfect Test: Action at El Guettar

On 23 March, the Germans threw one last major armored punch at the Americans. Von Arnim counterattacked II Corps' 1st Infantry Division with the 10th Panzer Division just east of El Guettar. At about 0500 hours, the Germans advanced slowly in a hollow-square formation of tanks and self-propelled guns interspersed with infantry carriers. Additional infantry followed in trucks.

Sergeant Bill Harper, an M3 commander in Company C of the 601st Tank Destroyer Battalion, watched the advancing force with concern from the crest of the ridge above the pass to El Guettar. Harper counted seventy-five German tanks, and one platoon leader thought he spotted at least one hundred. These guesses were not bad, as the 10th Panzer Division had fifty-seven tanks and about the same number of armored cars and halftracks. The outnumbered TD battalion—on that day fielding thirty-one M3s and five M6s—was filling a two-and-a-half mile gap in the American lines.

The tank killers had expected trouble. Recon, which had established a picket line across the valley early that morning, spotted the advancing steel storm. After a brief exchange of fire, the recon jeeps, accompanied by a few TDs, raced back ahead of the foe. The lieutenant in charge of one group kept repeating over his radio, "Let the first three [vehicles] through, and then give 'em hell!"

The battalion's TDs were arrayed on the reverse slopes of the ridgeline and nearby hills. Companies B and C held positions in front of the 1st Infantry Division artillery, while Company A guarded the pass to El Guettar. The German formation split into three prongs and overran some American positions. Lieutenant Fred Miner in Company A reminded his men that the Americans had fled from the panzers in

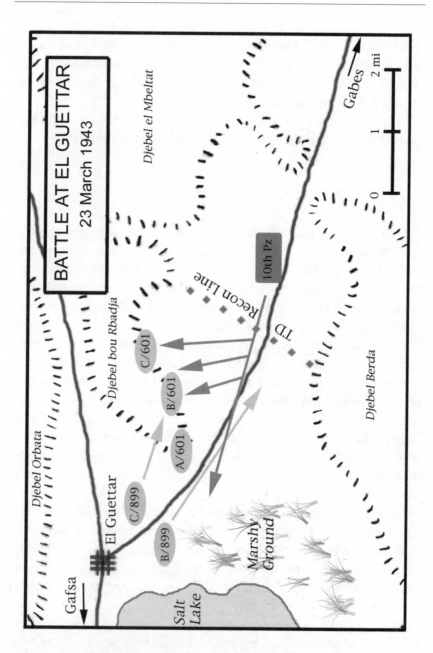

BATTLE AT EL GUETTAR
23 March 1943

Ousseltia Valley and at Sbeitla; he told them that this time they would
stand and shoot it out no matter what the odds.

In the weak light of early morning, the TD crews engaged the
Germans as they came into range. Sergeant Raymond, of Company B,
spotted a giant Tiger moving past and maneuvered to put six shots

(probably from the flank) into the panzer, four of which ricocheted but two of which did the job. Raymond next set a Mark IV alight. German rounds found Raymond's M3, and three hits set the halftrack on fire.

Guided by forward observers, most of the TDs raced over the crests of the ridges and hills, fired, and backed out of sight, only to pop up and do the same again at another location. The German gunners never knew where a TD would appear next. Except, it seemed, for one crew, which found itself the object of heavy fire every time their M3 crested the rise. They finally realized that their radio antenna was standing proudly tall and revealed their approach every time. They lowered the aerial.

After Company A's TDs had knocked out eight tanks, the German assault force withdrew and circled to reinforce the attack on the rest of the battalion's line. The panzers penetrated to within one hundred yards of the Companies B and C TDs. Some of the M3s were no longer moving, and a few were burning. The Germans were so close that Sgt Bill Harper at one point thought the outfit was surrounded. Even as ammunition ran low, the battalion doggedly held its ground. At the height of the assault, some TDs were forced to abandon the duck-and-strike tactics; they stood and fired as fast as the guns could be loaded. The crews also had to beat back German infantry using small arms, machine guns, and 75mm HE shells.

The German tide receded about noon, leaving a litter of burning tanks on the slopes and approaches. The tanks withdrew into defilade positions among wadis and small hills on the northeast side of the valley.

The untested 899th Tank Destroyer Battalion was in mobile reserve near Gafsa when, at 0845, it received orders to move to El Guettar. German tanks had overrun a field artillery battalion, and the 601st had already lost most of its 75mm guns. Company B entered the valley to engage the Germans while Company C provided overwatch from the ridgeline to the west.

Second Lieutenant Gerald Coady's platoon led the Company B charge through the gap into the valley. As the M10s rolled by to their first test against an enemy, LtCol Herschel Baker stood among his remaining Purple Heart boxes and shouted an unprintable but heartfelt welcome.

The Germans had skillfully selected their firing positions and—combined with an American minefield—they left Coady little room for maneuver. Coady tried to rush his force into covered positions to the north three times, and three times he fell back with losses. After two of his own TDs had been disabled, Coady saw that the platoon leader in the next platoon had been killed. He dismounted under heavy tank, antitank, artillery, and small-arms fire and organized the remnants of the two platoons to continue the battle.

Corporal Thomas Wilson commanded one of the Company B M10s. His destroyer received two direct hits and had two fires aboard. Wilson helped extinguish the fires while his gunner, T/5 Stephen Kurowski—who was wounded in both legs—continued firing his 3-inch gun at the Germans. Kurowski knocked out two emplacements, an artillery piece, and several machine guns before the M10 absorbed a third hit in the fuel tank, which started another fire. Wilson decided that he could not allow the Germans to capture their first M10 and directed his driver to a place where American forces would be able to recover the crippled vehicle.

At 1645 hours, the Germans struck again, supported by Stuka and fighter attacks. Infantry advanced first, overwatched by tanks and antitank guns. On the ridgeline, as the crews of C/899th watched the advance as if from an opera balcony seat, the gunners itched for something to come into range. The TDs of the 601st and 899th blazed away, and American artillery pounded the German troops. Thirty-eight panzers pressed the attack until almost 1900 hours but gave up after suffering further heavy losses.

The TDs and the artillery together had wreaked havoc during the day. Twenty-seven of the 601st's thirty-six guns were knocked out and fourteen men had died, but its sharp-eyed gunners had destroyed thirty-seven German tanks and damaged an unknown number of others. The crews of the M10s claimed fifteen Mark IVs for a loss of five TDs and a halftrack.[68]

The battle at El Guettar had played out General Bruce's dream scenario and doctrine to a tee. And, despite substantial American losses—concentrated among the antiquated M3s—the concept had worked. It would be nearly a year before the Tank Destroyer Force would have another opportunity to meet a large armored attack with a full TD battalion.

*   *   *

Almost as if to show for the record just once that he had read the official doctrine, 1st Armored Division CG Orlando Ward on 30 March issued an order to the commander of the 805th Tank Destroyer Battalion that said, "You will place your battalion in a position of readiness in the vicinity of the high ground four miles northeast of Station de Sened. . . . You will reconnoiter positions and routes . . . and be prepared to move to these positions to block an enemy threat from the north and northeast. . . . Perform vigorous and continuous reconnaissance. . . . You will act aggressively against any enemy threat."[69]

Nonetheless, as the Allies pressed relentlessly through tough opposition toward Tunis, experimentation produced another effective role for the tank destroyers. TDs were deployed before a tank attack to search out and destroy German antitank guns from long range. The results were little short of amazing. The tankers advanced without loss, and they later said that had they known how many guns had been there, they would have been scared stiff. The 1st Armored Division found the experience so compelling that it began to construct advances around the initial phase of TD suppressive fires. The TDs and tanks would then leapfrog from ridge to ridge, allowing the destroyers to work over the ground before the tanks advanced, and then to conduct overwatch in case they had missed any targets. The technique worked despite the fact that the two types of armor had incompatible radio equipment.[70]

During the night of 29 March, Patton organized a task force under the command of Col Clarence Benson, CO of the 13th Armored Regiment, to cut through German lines in the hills east of El Guettar and link up with Monty's Eighth Army north of Gabes. The 899th Tank Destroyer Battalion formed part of the task force, which spent six days trying unsuccessfully to overcome stiff German and Italian resistance. Reconnaissance Company had been issued several light tanks for the assault, a field modification of the TO&E that gave the men—always at the bleeding edge—considerably more punch. Finally, at 0930 on 7 April, the entire battalion was ordered forward after a renewed tank attack showed signs of progress. The Americans broke through and, now freed, raced into the flat desert beyond. At 1600 hours, elements of the 899th established contact with the Eighth Army near Sobkret Sidi Mansour.[71] There was now only one front in North Africa.

Lieutenant General Omar Bradley replaced Patton at the head of II Corps on 15 April so that the latter could return to overseeing the planning for the invasion of Sicily. Pinched out of the line by the steady shrinkage of the Axis perimeter, II Corps shifted behind the British lines and took on responsibility for the left flank along the coast. The new objective was Bizerte.

The tank-destroying days were basically over for the TD battalions in North Africa. The terrain was broken and poorly suited to the use of armor. Instead, the TD battalions usually occupied antitank defense positions to fend off hypothetical attacks. At times, they performed the roles of assault guns and artillery.[72]

American forces captured Bizerte on 7 May—Recon Company of the 894th claims to have entered the city first—and pushed onward as British units pounded toward Tunis. Resistance collapsed on 9 May and ended completely three days later. The Allies bagged 270,000 prisoners of war, veterans who would not be waiting for them when they invaded the shores of Europe.

The First Accounting

Some senior American officers judged that the North Africa campaign had tested the tank destroyer and found it wanting. Patton was among the critics; he concluded that the tank destroyer had proved unsuccessful *in the conditions of the theater*. Lieutenant General Jacob Devers went farther; he argued that "the separate tank destroyer arm is not a practical concept on the battlefield."[73]

The tank killers had tripped over at least three obstacles. The first was the field commanders' lack of training in and experience with the use of the weapon in combat. They tended to order tank destroyers to expose themselves recklessly to enemy fire and assigned to them missions for which they were not suited. After surveying commanders at the close of the campaign, moreover, Allied Forces Headquarters concluded that the tank destroyer battalions had at times been too widely dispersed to be effective. The headquarters issued training notes urging that the battalions be kept intact—at least within one division's sector—to enable the TDs to repel large armored thrusts.[74]

A second issue was a certain degree of confusion among the tank killers themselves over how to implement the offense-minded doctrine they had been taught. The Army responded to these challenges by ordering the Tank Destroyer Center to rewrite FM 18-5 to clarify for infantry and armor commanders and tank killers alike the necessity for the force to fight using concealment and surprise.[75] As one experienced battalion commander told Camp Hood, the proper way to attack enemy armor was with massed firepower. Charging German tanks was a recipe for disaster.[76]

The third obstacle was the frequent mismatch between the flat, cover-less terrain and the tall vehicles issued to the battalions. Concealment in the desert was often impossible for a self-propelled tank destroyer, whereas a towed gun could be dug in with little more than its barrel exposed. Bradley, among others, indicated that he would prefer towed tank destroyer battalions. Tankers had told Bradley that dug-in German antitank guns were virtually impossible to spot, and that four hidden 88s could hold off a company of American tanks.[77] This was doubtless music to LtGen Lesley McNair's ears, and as early as January 1943, Army Ground Forces ordered the Tank Destroyer Center to organize an experimental battalion armed with towed 3-inch guns. A failure among senior American officers to ponder the conditions likely in the *next* campaign led to a decision in November 1943 that would dog the tank destroyer force until 1945: Half of all battalions were converted to towed guns.[78]

The view of the tank destroyer's utility was more enthusiastic at the fighting level up to the very end of the campaign. A 1st Armored Division report on the action at Mateur between 4 and 9 May, for example, indicated that the use of tank destroyers on the flanks as close support had yielded excellent results. The report credited the men of the 776th Tank Destroyer Battalion with putting the enemy to flight on several occasions merely through reconnaissance by fire. (The report lamented, however, that the recently arrived tank killers had been too interested in looting and had thereby given the enemy time to destroy his equipment!)[79]

Moreover, teething problems in the tank destroyer force to some degree resembled kinks elsewhere in the U.S. Army. Air-ground coordination had been a mess. Ground commanders accused the high command—almost as inexperienced as they were—of criminal negligence in ordering attacks at dawn, when the sun was invariably in the eyes of American gunners.[80] And the evolution in combat of task force-style groupings of armor, infantry, tank destroyers, and artillery revealed other holes in doctrine and training. Task force commanders, for example, were typically armor officers who viewed the infantry through the prism of the doctrine for employing specialized armored infantry, a situation that led to misunderstandings between commanders and infantry officers.[81]

A fair assessment of the tank destroyer battalions' performance would acknowledge Omar Bradley's overall observation on the North African campaign: "On reflection, I came to the conclusion that it was fortunate that the British view [in favor of Torch] prevailed, that the U.S. Army first met the enemy on the periphery, in Africa rather than on the beaches of France. In Africa we learned to crawl, to walk—then run. Had that learning process been launched in France, it would surely have. . . resulted in an unthinkable disaster."[82]

The tank destroyer program had, in any event, reached its high-water mark. In April 1943, McNair recommended that no more than one hundred six battalions be established, rather than the planned two hundred twenty. This was about the number of units that already existed or were in the activation process. In October, the War Department indicated it wanted to inactivate forty-two existing battalions, leaving only sixty-four. AGF thought this excessive but agreed to disband twenty-five tank destroyer battalions in light of the need to provide replacements for divisions suffering high casualties in Italy. Further inactivations would reduce the force to seventy-eight battalions by 1944.[83] Fifty-six would serve in the European or Mediterranean theaters and six in the Pacific Theater. Eleven would be converted to armored field artillery, amphibious tractor, chemical mortar, or tank battalions.[84]

*   *   *

The use of tank destroyers in the artillery support role during the North Africa campaign spurred Allied Forces Headquarters to inform the War Department that field commanders wanted tank destroyer battalions to improve their capability for indirect fire. A TD battalion had the same number of pieces as three battalions of light field artillery, and by the end of the campaign, TD battalions had fired more rounds in artillery missions than in any other role.[85] (Army Ground Forces suggested that tanks could make a similar contribution.)

In the spring of 1943, indirect-fire tests had been conducted at the Tank Destroyer Training Center. Thereafter, a demonstration of indirect fire was included in the curriculum of the Tank Destroyer School, and battalions were permitted to practice artillery missions after completing all other requirements.[86] In North Africa, the 776th Tank Destroyer Battalion, by June 1943, had begun training with field artillery units to coordinate their fire on specific targets.[87] The 701st also conducted artillery training upon receiving its new M10 TDs beginning in August.[88]

In early September, a board that included Major General Bruce from the Tank Destroyer Center recommended extensive use of the tank destroyers—but not tanks—as artillery. The fall maneuvers demonstrated that tank destroyers were fully capable of operating as reinforcing artillery. In November, the War Department ordered that both tank and tank destroyer battalions receive one month of artillery training.[89] This change would have a major impact on the activities of the tank destroyers in their next campaign.

*   *   *

The battalions received the equipment they needed for the artillery mission and their main job: Killing tanks. The M10 and the towed 3-inch gun replaced the vulnerable M3 halftrack as units prepared to leap the Mediterranean to their next objective.

Allied forces invaded Sicily on 10 July 1943. Tank destroyer battalions did not participate in the Sicily campaign as such. The 776th sent eighteen enlisted men who worked as radio operators and military policemen,[90] the 813th sent six officers and four hundred men to handle POWs,[91] and a detail from the 636th guarded Italian and German prisoners being transported back to the States.[92]

Instead, designated units prepared for the invasion of Italy proper. Men of the untested 645th Tank Destroyer Battalion entered the Fifth Army Invasion Training Center near Ain el Turck, Algeria, on 15 June 1943. There they fired thousands of rounds on ranges and trained in street fighting and air defense. In late July, the battalion moved to a staging area near Bizerte. In the first days of September, the men waterproofed their vehicles. On 5 September, they loaded their equipment onto the new-fangled Landing Ships, Tank (LSTs) and departed, destination unknown.[93] The equally inexperienced men of the 636th Tank Destroyer

Battalion boarded transports at Oran on 1 September and sailed to Bizerte to join the invasion convoy. On 6 September, a forty-five-minute air attack wounded three battalion men.[94] The war was about to get very real again.

Chapter 4

The Tough Underbelly

"The close country and rugged mountainous terrain greatly
restricted the employment of armor."

— *Lessons from the Italian Campaign, Training Memorandum Number 2*, Headquarters,
Mediterranean Theater of Operations, 15 March 1944

At one minute after midnight on 9 September 1943, riflemen of the
141st and 142d Infantry regiments, 36th Infantry Division, began
descending from troop transports into waiting landing craft off the Italian
coast in Salerno Bay. There was no naval bombardment under way—an
attempt to achieve surprise.

Monty's Eighth Army had already crossed the Straits of Messina
from Sicily to the toe of Italy on 3 September in Operation Baytown,
which was designed but failed to draw German forces away from the
Salerno area. That same day, Italy had secretly surrendered after quiet
negotiations in neutral Portugal. Eisenhower had announced the
capitulation only hours before the Salerno landings, but the Germans had
expected as much; they rapidly disarmed the Italians and deployed their
own troops in key positions.

Stubby landing craft prows turned toward shore, and at 0330 hours the initial wave hit the beach. Miraculously, all was quiet. The rumble and flashes of gun and rocket fire to the north, where two divisions of the British 10 Corps were conducting an assault closer to Naples, told a different story.

The first squads pushed inland toward their objectives. Suddenly, German flares began to pop in the night sky. A furious rain of mortar and machine gun rounds struck the men now crossing the beach.[1]

The main invasion of Italy—Fifth Army's Operation Avalanche—had begun. The Allied spear struck what British Prime Minister Winston Churchill had described as the "soft underbelly" of Hitler's Fortress Europa.

Waiting in a series of strongpoints along the shoreline and in the heights further to the rear was the entire 16th Panzer Division: 17,000 men, more than one hundred tanks, and thirty-six assault guns.

No tank destroyers were assigned to the initial waves, despite the waiting German armor. For the first several hours, infantrymen beat off small panzer probes with bazookas and hand grenades. By 0730, disorganized artillery elements joined the riflemen and established ad hoc batteries. At 0930, several 105mm howitzers of the 151st Field Artillery Battalion engaged German tanks and helped repel a counterattack. The first Sherman tank landed at 0830 hours, but the German fusillade prevented landing craft from delivering armor from the 191st and 751st Tank battalions except in dribs and drabs for most of the day.[2]

The infantry battled inland against poorly coordinated efforts by the 16th Panzer Division to stop them. Battered by bazookas, tanks, artillery, naval gunfire, and air strikes, the German division lost two-thirds of its tanks by the end of the day.[3]

That is when the TDs finally arrived.

* * *

The 601st Tank Destroyer Battalion landed one complete company of twelve guns, one partial company of eight guns, and one depleted company of four guns, plus command vehicles, on Red Beach near Paestum at 1630 hours. The veteran outfit's mission was to support the untried 36th Infantry Division. Upon landing, the battalion CO, Maj

Walter Tardy, reported to the CP of the 151st Field Artillery Battalion, where he received orders to support the artillery providing covering fire on the right flank of the beachhead and to cover the road from Ogliastro against possible tank attack.[4]

At 1900 hours, the men of the 645th Tank Destroyer Battalion landed on Red Beach. The battalion was also attached to the 36th Infantry Division and ordered to protect the division's left flank and help cover the seven-mile gap between the American VI Corps and British 10 Corps. The two Allied corps intended to anchor their abutting flanks on the Sele

River, but neither reached the objective on 9 September. The next day, the battalion was shifted to support the advance of the 45th Infantry Division—VI Corps' floating reserve—which was just coming ashore.[5]

Generalfeldmarschall Albert Kesselring, now in command of German forces in southern (and after November all of) Italy, ordered the 26th Panzer and 29th Panzergrenadier divisions to leave only delaying forces in front of the Eighth Army and to move the bulk of their organizations to the Salerno beachhead. He also set the 15th Panzergrenadier and Hermann Göring divisions—both rebuilding after taking a battering in the Sicily fighting—in motion from Rome. The Allies in Fifth Army could only wait for Monty to arrive, and he was, as usual, advancing with all due deliberation.[6]

*   *   *

Unaware that new German divisions were converging on the field, the men of the 36th Infantry Division were pleasantly surprised that they could find hardly any Germans at all on 10 September. The division easily seized its objectives on Fifth Army's right flank. Two regiments of the 45th Infantry Division, meanwhile, moved into position on the American left near the Sele River.

Amidst the seeming calm, twelve M10s from the 601st reembarked as part of a task force rapidly organized to help the British, who faced stiff resistance to the north. Built around an infantry battalion, the task force sailed on 11 September to support Darby's Rangers—who had been fighting beside the British Commandos since D-day—at Amalfi Peninsula. Various problems, including the offloading of the first M10 into deep water by the Royal Navy, delayed the TDs' commitment to battle. The next day, the entire task force was attached to the British 46th Infantry Division.[7]

*   *   *

On 11 September, the U.S. 45th Infantry Division was ordered to cross the Sele River into what had been the 10 Corps zone in order to link up with the British right flank, which had been unable to push south. Company C/645th Tank Destroyer Battalion and a platoon of Sherman tanks from the 191st Tank Battalion supported the advance of the 179th

Infantry Regiment. The infantry bypassed the town of Persano in the hills overlooking the beachhead, but German defenders amidst the buildings opened up with machine guns and cut communications between the doughs and the armor.[8] The doughs of 2/179th Infantry Regiment, meanwhile, were struck by an armor counterattack and thrown back across the Sele River.[9]

The tanks and TDs tried to force their way into Persano to clear the Germans out. The advancing armor encountered roadblocks and blown bridges and could not maneuver off the road because of swampy ground. German guns opened fire on the column and knocked out seven of the M10s. Company A was called forward, only to find itself isolated when the infantry and tanks pulled back. When the company tried to extricate itself, two M10s got stuck in ditches and one was destroyed by artillery fire. The company claimed to have knocked out two Mark IV tanks, one Mark VI, and an 88mm gun, but the battalion's first real contact with the enemy had not gone well.

The next morning, the newly arrived 29th Panzergrenadier Division tore into the 45th Infantry Division and the left end of the 36th Infantry Division line at Altavilla. The panzergrenadiers pushed the 36th off the strategic high ground at Altavilla and tried to drive to the sea. Over the next four days, a total of three panzer and three panzergrenadier divisions struck all along the perimeter of the tenuous Allied beachhead.[10]

Even as the men of the 36th Infantry Division fought desperately to hold their line, the crews of the 191st Tank and 645th Tank Destroyer battalions launched a second effort to reach the hard-pressed 45th Infantry Division doughs through Persano and this time succeeded. By 1500 hours, the infantry reported that the town was cleared.[11] The Shermans and M10s then supported a hard-fought attack by the 157th Infantry Regiment that pushed the Germans out of a "tobacco warehouse" (actually five stone storage sheds) on the high ground above Persano, where the defenders a day earlier had knocked out seven Shermans.[12] The men of the 645th had helped stop what a worried Fifth Army CG, LtGen Mark Clark, viewed as a spear pointing at the heart of the beachhead.[13] But the Germans controlled more firmly than ever the corridor between the American and British toeholds.

The first elements of the 36th Infantry Division's daughter unit, the 636th Tank Destroyer Battalion, began landing on 12 September. The transports bearing the green battalion had approached the Bay of Salerno under constant German air attack.[14] As Sgt Thomas Sherman waded through armpit-deep water from the landing craft, he was glad for the bath after being cooped up on a jam-packed transport for ten days. His joy ended abruptly when the recon men formed up on the beach. The roar of a plane and chatter of machine guns announced a German air raid, and Sherman dove for a depression in the sand as bullets kicked up sand around him.[15]

Among the first ashore with Sherman were some thirty men—all multilingual soldiers who had excelled at tank hunting and commando tactics during training—who were grouped together in what the outfit called the "Ranger Platoon." Second Lieutenant William Walter, who spoke fluent German and several other languages, led the platoon off the beach and into the hills. Doubtless guided by the hand of Providence, they soon found themselves in an Italian wine cellar. Their joy dissipated when they heard German voices around the building and realized they were surrounded and well behind German lines. The men would spend the night hiding, killing the occasional German soldier who wandered in to snoop around, and capturing an oberleutnant.[16]

A see-saw battle raged along the 45th and 36th Infantry division fronts on 13 September. The TDs of the 645th in midafternoon rushed forward to support the doughs when a dozen German tanks struck the left flank of the 157th Infantry Regiment and another fifteen struck the right. But the attackers drove to within one hundred fifty yards of the 1st Battalion headquarters, and the line began to give way. The panzers and panzergrenadiers threw the Americans back out of Persano and the tobacco warehouse.[17]

The hungry men of the 636th's Ranger Platoon, meanwhile, were trying to make it back to American lines. The men, who were wearing the uniforms of the German soldiers they had dispatched, spotted a German SP gun and infantry in a field. Lieutenant Walter decided to use their one bazooka round to knock out the vehicle when the time was right. About this time, doughs from the 142d Infantry Regiment attacked the Germans, who returned fire. To their consternation, the Germans came under fire themselves from three MG42 machine guns and from machine pistols at their flank and rear. The single antitank round hit the self-propelled howitzer—earning Walter the nickname "Bazooka Red"—and incapacitated the gun and crew. The bewildered Germans surrendered. Fortunately for the German-uniformed Ranger Platoon, the GIs had witnessed the action and did not cut them to pieces.[18]

Panzers penetrated the line in several places—at one point coming within half a mile of the beach.[19] A provisional 636th company consisting of six M10s from Company B and six from Company C—joined by Recon and the Ranger Platoon—rushed to reinforce men of the 158th and 189th Field Artillery battalions. The artillery crews had been just about all that stood in the path of an advancing German tank company and panzergrenadier battalion. One battery of 105mm howitzers had knocked out five panzers with six rounds at ranges of only two hundred to three hundred yards, according to a VI Corps observer.[20] Clark's Fifth Army headquarters was located just behind the thin line, and cooks, clerks, and drivers hastily established a firing line when it appeared the Germans might break through.[21]

The attack was narrowly stopped, but the official U.S. Army history concluded that Fifth Army at this point "found itself at the edge of defeat."[22] Clark mulled withdrawing VI Corps from the beachhead. He decided instead to add the 82d Airborne Division to the hard-pressed VI Corps sector, and the paratroopers made an administrative drop into the beachhead that evening.

* * *

The German counteroffensive reached its crescendo on 14 September.

The 636th Tank Destroyer Battalion was defending a fifteen hundred-yard wide sector in the critical area barely off the beach. Battalion CO LtCol Van Pyland and his staff worked through the night to prepare for a renewed German attack at dawn. The twelve available M10s were dug into firing positions south of the junction of the Calore River and F. La Cosa Creek. Reconnaissance Company dug in on the left flank, while the Ranger Platoon strengthened positions on a rocky mass dominating the right flank. An artillery barrage struck about noon, and the first German infantry came into view shortly thereafter. About the same time, eight Sherman tanks from Company C, 751st Tank Battalion, arrived and deployed to support the Ranger Platoon.[23]

Walter's Ranger Platoon and some infantry volunteers opened up first on the advancing enemy with machine guns, Browning Automatic

Rifles (BARs), rifles, and bazookas while artillery rounds exploded about them. Germans fell, and the Shermans accounted for four advancing panzers. But several Mark IVs overran part of the Ranger Platoon's position, killing one man and wounding several others. The Shermans reported that they were receiving fire from 88mm guns and pulled back.

Pyland ordered five M10s out of their positions and moved to the right to save his collapsing flank.[24] The 2d Platoon of Company C maneuvered through the artillery fire to engage the panzers. Sergeant Edwin A. Yosts's M10 "Jinx" reached the crest of a ridge and opened fire. The first round was short, but the second disabled a Mark IV, and the third exploded an ammunition truck. Jinx backed away to escape artillery fire, only to reemerge in a nearby hull defilade position. Yosts's gunner, T/5 Alvin Johnson, knocked out four panzers with his next four shots. Other M10 crews in the company, meanwhile, accounted for two more Mark IVs.[25] Company B's tank killers were just as busy; they KO'd seven tanks by the end of the day. The battalion lost only two men killed in action.[26]

Further inland, elements of the 16th Panzer and 29th Panzergrenadier divisions at 0800 hours advanced again near the tobacco warehouse at Persano. The American forces had adjusted their lines during the night, and the Germans unknowingly advanced across the 179th Infantry Regiment front. M10s from the 645th Tank Destroyer Battalion joined in raking the Germans with flanking fire that knocked out all of the panzers and forced the infantry to retreat.[27] The crews of B/645th got their revenge for their losses at Persano when a German tank attack struck their defenses late in the afternoon. These tank killers destroyed eight confirmed panzers for the temporary loss of only one M10.[28]

All Allied strategic and tactical air assets in the Mediterranean Theater were redirected against German troop concentrations and lines of communication. Allied aircraft flew more than nineteen hundred sorties during the day. Naval gunfire, meanwhile, pounded German positions close to the beach.[29]

By the evening of 14 September, Allied commanders concluded that the crisis was past. The beachhead would hold.

* * *

Within days of landing, the tank destroyer battalions in Fifth Army found themselves scattered across the map despite the brass's professed intentions not to repeat their mistakes in handling TDs in North Africa. Reconnaissance Company of the 601st, for example, had been sent to the 180th RCT, and both the 45th Infantry Division artillery CP and 141st RCT tried to issue orders to the battalion. The 601st operations report noted, "At this stage, no one seemed to know to whom the battalion was attached. . . . Officers and men of the 601st Tank Destroyer Battalion were rather perturbed by the attachments and detachments of companies and platoons to various organizations for support, not even in one division, but in several divisions, including British. . . . During most of the operations, the battalion commander and battalion staff were used as messenger boys between higher headquarters and the various gun companies and platoons detached from the battalion. In some cases, the battalion commander was left completely out of the picture. At various times, even company commanders were overlooked."

Extreme fragmentation and rapid reattachments of elements down to the platoon or even gun-section level became the norm in Italy to a degree seen in no other theater of combat. On 16 September, for example, a mere two guns from the 813th Tank Destroyer Battalion (two platoons of which had been sent to Italy to join an aborted 82d Airborne Division operation to grab Rome's airport upon Italy's surrender) were attached to Company B of the 601st. Company B was in turn attached to the 133d Field Artillery Battalion.[30] Moreover, assignments to Allied units occurred frequently.

In addition to the confusion that resulted, there were practical problems. As one TD officer later noted, "While attached to the 1st Armored Division, despite some differences about where and when TDs could be most effective, we were truly attached. I.e., Division took care of all our logistical needs. When attached to infantry divisions, as soon as they found out we needed diesel fuel and 3-inch ammo, they wanted no part of that supply problem, and we were usually sent to corps supply dumps for all our needs."[31]

*   *   *

The 776th Tank Destroyer Battalion arrived in the Salerno Gulf on 16 September 1943 amidst the crash of naval gunfire in support of the troops ashore. The convoy endured three days of German air attacks while the tank killers waited their turn to land.[32] After working with the 1st Armored Division in North Africa, the battalion had equipped its TDs with 500-series radios in place of their old 600s so that they could talk directly to armor on the battlefield.[33] Unfortunately, this practice had not been adopted force-wide, and the battalion was destined instead to work closely with the infantry, who used yet a different communications setup.

Beyond the Beachhead

Kesselring by late in the day on 16 September concluded that he would not be able to destroy the Allied beachhead. Not only had four days of German counterattacks failed to cause fatal harm, but Monty's Eighth Army was only hours away from linking up with Fifth Army. Kesselring authorized a fighting withdrawal to the Volturno River twenty miles north of Naples, where he ordered the line be held until mid-October.[34]

For the Allies, climbing the Italian peninsula would be like climbing a ladder of nettles. Ultra intercepts indicated that Hitler had decided to defend Italy south of Rome. Kesselring began to build a series of defensive lines north of the Volturno River, where the Barbara Line ran along a ridge to the Garigliano River and thence across the southern Apennines to the Trigno River. Next came the Reinhard (also referred to as Bernhard) Line, which stretched from coast to coast. Kesselring planned to hold this line until 1 November. German engineers received orders to put all command posts along this intermediate line underground, construct the main battle line on the reverse slopes of hills to escape Allied artillery fire, construct OPs on the crests and forward slopes, and clear all fields of fire. Twelve miles further north and anchored on the Garigliano and Rapido rivers, the Todt organization was constructing fortifications for the Gustav Line, where Kesselring planned to hold the Allies until spring of 1944.[35]

On 18 September, VI Corps troops found nothing to their immediate front. The Germans had begun their fighting retreat. As the 157th Infantry Regiment recorded, the Germans' withdrawal "was as lethal as their attack, and there was no hurtling forward."[36]

Over the next two weeks, VI Corps averaged a daily advance of only three miles in the face of delaying actions and demolished roads and bridges as it fought to move abreast of British 10 Corps, which on 1 October took Naples.[37] Indeed, one VI Corps observer would describe the campaign over the coming months as an "engineer war:" "The Germans are expert at demolition, and in the mountainous country through which the Fifth Army is operating all advance must cease until bridges are built and roads repaired."[38] From Naples, the U.S. Fifth Army would advance up the western side of the Apennines, while the British Eighth Army advanced in a loosely coordinated fashion on the eastern side.

This was not the country envisioned in tank destroyer doctrine. Indeed, some ideas stressed in training—such as the danger of canalizing tank destroyers in narrow valleys—were completely at odds with the reality of warfare in Italy.[39]

The problem, however, cut both ways. German Generalmajor Martin Schmidt explained the sitution from the perspective of the panzer crews, "The German panzer units, in regard to organization, equipment, and training, were intended primarily for action on terrain like that of western, central, and eastern Europe. . . . It was of decisive significance that the panzer organizations were fighting on the defensive during the whole campaign [in Italy], whereas they were intended for offensive action. Almost all the panzer and panzergrenadier divisions that came to Italy in 1943 had gained their combat experience during campaigns in France and Russia. . . . In Italy, these divisions had to change their tactics considerably and sometimes paid dearly for their lessons."[40]

The battle became one of infantry maneuver as soon as the GIs left the coastal plain. Advancing infantry regiments encountered countless small German strongpoints, usually defending a demolished bridge or some other roadblock. One battalion would try to pin the Germans down, while the other two scrambled across the mountainous terrain to flank the position. In a typical experience for the TD outfits during this period, the 601st Tank Destroyer Battalion (attached to the 3d Infantry Division after 19 September) found that, because of the terrible terrain and deep mud caused by continuous rain, it could do little but follow the doughs up main roads.[41] The official U.S. Army history concluded that the heavy and road-bound tank destroyers were often a liability in this kind of fighting rather than an asset.[42] The doughs, tank killers, armor, and artillery would have to figure out ways to profitably employ the tremendous firepower the TDs represented.

*   *   *

The reconnaissance companies from the tank destroyer battalions, however, were a perfect fit for the new style of warfare and were among the busiest elements during the first weeks of the push northward. Infantry division commanders seized on their presence to reconnoiter for advancing units and to maintain contact with neighboring Allied forces.

Reconnaissance companies operated, as they had in Algeria and Tunisia, with three platoons of six machine-gun and FM radio-equipped jeeps and a command halftrack (the company headquarters had additional trucks and halftracks, and four motorcycles).[43] Some battalions, however, had received M5 light tanks to replace the company headquarters' 37mm-armed halftracks, as the 899th had during the last weeks of fighting in North Africa.[44] Despite frequent orders to conduct reconnaissance on behalf of units to which they were attached, the tank destroyer recon platoons still lacked radio gear compatible with that used by infantry recon troops.[45]

About 21 September, Reconnaissance Company of the 776th was attached to the famous Japanese-American 100th Infantry Battalion, 34th Infantry Division. The company formed the spearhead of the 100th's operation to outflank German defenses around Naples by capturing Benevento. The mission proved to be a pain-staking assignment of sweeping mines (by the pioneer platoon) and scouting out hostile gun positions and enemy troop concentrations. Company commander Lt Shelden Thompson, one other officer, and four enlisted men were wounded on 29 September when their halftracks hit Teller mines while on a scouting mission. The 776th battalion CO, LtCol James Barney Jr., and two enlisted men became the first Americans to enter Benevento when they were conducting a reconnaissance around the city.[46]

Even maintaining contact with other Allied units was less easy than it sounds as various columns pushed up roads through mountainous terrain that blocked a clear picture of what "neighboring" units were doing. On 6 October, Lieutenant Rogers of the 601st Tank Destroyer Battalion led his 3d Reconnaissance Platoon to Linatola to contact a friendly unit, but they encountered German infantry supported by machine guns and mortars instead. Rogers returned minus his jeep—and his brand new bedroll. Other members of Reconnaissance Company/601st had better luck and were among the first few to reach the Volturno River that same day.[47]

*   *   *

The weather deteriorated rapidly in early October, adding immeasurably to the misery of the fighting men and often immobilizing even the tracked tank destroyers. Nonetheless, on 4 October, Eisenhower and General Sir Harold Alexander—now commanding general of 15th Army Group, incorporating the U.S. Fifth and British Eighth armies—concurred that Allied forces would march into Rome within the month.[48]

The first large units of Fifth Army closed on the rain-swollen Volturno River on 7 October. The high water and mud forced two postponements of a planned assault crossing. On the far bank, three German divisions waited.[49]

Finally, the night of 12–13 October, the Allies launched their first major river assault crossing of the war. VI Corps planned to send the 3d Infantry Division on the left and the 34th Infantry Division on the right across the river during the night. The 45th Infantry Division was pushing the Germans out of the upper Volturno River Valley to anchor the corps' right flank. The Americans engaged in deception operations, such as limiting the volume of artillery fire before the day of the assault, to assure surprise.[50]

Beginning at midnight, GIs waded across or paddled assault boats to the far shore. Recon Company men from the 601st Tank Destroyer Battalion, carrying radios with which to call in supporting fire, forded the river with the doughs of the 3d Infantry Division. An hour later, artillery opened up all along the front. As the sky brightened, M10s from A/601st commenced direct-fire support from the south bank and destroyed two tanks, an SP gun, and other German targets. Beginning about 1100 hours, waterproofed Shermans from the 751st Tank Battalion splashed across the Volturno, followed an hour later by the first M10s—also waterproofed—from C/601st.[51]

The 776th Tank Destroyer Battalion provided indirect-fire support to the doughs of the 34th Infantry Division, who crossed the Volturno in a section deemed impassable to armor. The infantry came to a stop in front of unbending German resistance in the brush-covered hills beyond the river. Early on 14 October, four M10s forded the stream and drove the defenders from their key strongpoint with direct fire.[52] The M10, as it turned out, could go places heavier Sherman tanks could not.

Sixth Corps gained a foothold above Capua, but German troops could rain observed fire onto all suitable bridging sites and thus greatly slowed the American buildup north of the river. A British crossing below Capua, meanwhile, was checked. A smaller crossing by two British divisions closer to the coast north of Naples provoked vigorous German counterattacks. Indeed, the Germans were able to hold largely in place until 16 October, when they withdrew to the next line of defenses fifteen miles to the north—exactly in accordance with Kesselring's schedule.[53]

As visions of a rapid advance on Rome faded for good, Eisenhower proposed to the Combined Chiefs of Staff that his forces mount a small amphibious and airborne operation to turn the German line. The chiefs turned down the idea because requirements for Operation Overlord, the invasion of France, precluded devoting additional resources to the Mediterranean Theater. Eisenhower realized that his men were condemned to a grueling series of costly frontal assaults.[54]

* * *

The Allies called the ground north of the Volturno and south of the Rapido River and Gustav Line the "Winter Position." The West Point history of the Second World War offers a superb description of what the tank destroyer crews found there: "On Kesselring's map there were two delay lines in the area, the Barbara and Reinhard. His subordinate corps commanders had added intermediate delay lines of their own. Naturally, German commanders at lower echelons had added outposts and reserve blocking positions, so that to the GI and Tommy, attacking through the area seemed like attacking one big defensive zone. All hill masses were occupied. Positions had been sighted to provide each other covering small arms fire. Engineers had constructed some of the major bunkers of concrete. They had cut others from solid rock with pneumatic drills. Infantrymen had improved less critical positions by rolling large rocks around their foxholes. Because of the treeless mountains, artillery forward observers had overlapping, unobstructed views of the approaches to other mountains in the area. The towns that dotted the valley floors, such as San Pietro, San Vittore, and Cassino, were converted into strongpoints. . . . The ultimate difficulty was, of course, the German infantryman, whose morale was high and who was glad to be ending his Army's 2,000-mile retreat from El Alamein, through Tunis and Sicily, to the Gustav Line."[55]

For the tank killers of most battalions, the slow march up the Italian mainland became a series of small-scale fire-support missions for the infantry. The 3-inch gun on the M10 was effective in the direct-fire role out to six thousand yards.[56] The TD crews encountered mainly well dug-in machine-gun and antitank positions supported by roving self-propelled artillery pieces.[57] The Tank Destroyer Command had advocated the use of TDs against fortifications in 1942 but backed off after being accused of over-selling tank destroyers.[58]

Enemy tanks to kill were rare. In both the attack and the defense, the Germans usually exposed no more than two to four panzers at a time.[59] The Germans were using tactics that could have come from the TD field manual: The panzers were deployed in depth where they could move to previously reconnoitered firing positions to engage Allied armor whenever the Allies attacked or achieved a penetration.[60]

Most personnel and vehicle losses in the TD battalions were the result of landmines, followed by German artillery fire.

Experimentation led to the formation of ad hoc teams that were better able to handle the mix of German defenses. The infantry was vulnerable to strongpoints and tanks, so separate tank battalions were attached to provide close support with their machine guns and 75mm cannon. The M4 Sherman tank cannon, however, lacked sufficient penetrating power to defeat the front armor of the Mark VI Tiger tank or the new Mark V Panthers that would soon be appearing. So tank destroyer units were added to deal with tough armored threats. The usual mix was one TD platoon per tank company, or one TD company per tank battalion.

As early as Operation Avalanche, elements of the 601st Tank Destroyer Battalion had been incorporated into an ad hoc team, with B/751st Tank Battalion actually attached to the TD command.[61] By October, the tank killers from the 601st worked routinely with the tankers from the 751st; the reconnaissance company at times provided the infantry element to the team. Infantry commanders were usually new at combined-arms fighting and unfamiliar with the capabilities of the 3-inch gun, however, and typically told the TDs not only at what to shoot but also from where to do so. They tended to think in terms of direct fire, which placed TDs in exposed positions that invited rapid counter-battery fire from the Germans. The TD crews much preferred to shoot indirectly from defiladed positions.[62]

Indeed, TD battalions that were primarily engaged in close-support roles fired numerous indirect artillery missions, as well. Company A of the 645th, for example, conducted a fire mission on 19 October against a German battery at 13,300 yards under the control of an artillery observer. During November, the battalion fired 8,899 rounds of HE in its artillery role and only 360 rounds of AP. On one occasion, the new CO of the 645th Tank Destroyer Battalion, Maj Edward Austin (a field artillery officer himself), complained that the infantry was using TDs for fire missions that could have been conducted by organic artillery with less risk of counter-battery fire.[63] But the big artillery was plenty busy. Up to forty battalions at once were used to saturate German-occupied hills while the doughs moved in to storm the positions with rifles and grenades.[64]

The TDs worked well with field artillery units, but they were stepchildren. Supported units at times failed to inform all concerned when a TD battalion moved into position and began firing missions. The 701st Tank Destroyer Battalion recorded that its M10s drew friendly counter-battery fire several times.[65]

The 776th Tank Destroyer Battalion made a specialty of artillery support. On 10 October, the 776th's firing companies were attached to the field artillery to conduct joint fire missions with the 125th, 151st, and 175th Field Artillery battalions. The men found that the months of summer training in Algeria adapting and perfecting coordination with the artillery paid off handsomely. The battalion adopted a provisional internal organization that divided each company into two six-gun batteries, and each company was normally attached to a light artillery battalion. (Other battalions also used this system at times when conducting indirect fire missions.[66]) Some reconnaissance and security personnel were cross-trained to help man company-level fire direction centers.[67]

The 3-inch gun proved to be particularly effective in certain artillery roles. It was best at long-range missions because of the gun's great range and the round's flat trajectory, which would endanger friendly troops if fired at targets too close to the front lines. The 3-inch gun was better than the 105mm howitzer for shelling roads over which American troops planned to advance because the former left almost no crater but had a similar burst radius to the bigger round. The M10s could also turn to new missions by merely rotating their turrets rather than having to reposition guns.[68] One drawback was that crews lacked a good white phosphorous round similar to the ones used by artillery to register their guns.[69]

Company A of the 636th Tank Destroyer Battalion, which had been firing artillery missions, was hunkered down under an enemy barrage one rainy morning in late November. A shell struck one of the M10s and damaged the gun. The crew was ordered not to fire until Ordnance had checked the weapon. In due course, a lieutenant from Ordnance appeared and examined the vehicle, but he offered no opinion as to the extent of the damage. When the next fire order reached the platoon, the crew opened up, too. A radio repairman from Battalion was working in the turret when the order came. When the gun fired, the concussion blew the barrel off and knocked everyone in the M10 to the deck. The repairman got to his feet and sadly observed, "I don't know how you guys can do this all day long."[70]

*　　*　　*

Recon companies, meanwhile, continued to perform a dizzying array of jobs, as needed. German demolitions frequently prevented the M10s from advancing until division or corps engineers could repair blown bridges. The terrain off the roads made jeep reconnaissance impossible, so the recon companies often turned to foot scouting to spot well-concealed German strongpoints.[71] Mine clearing also became common labor. Most recon troops had received little training on mines but a lot on explosives, which evidently was viewed as close enough.[72] TD recon OPs provided fire control for battalion indirect fire missions—and occasionally for artillery units up to corps level.[73]

*　　*　　*

The 805th Tank Destroyer Battalion debarked at Naples on 2 November. The outfit had reorganized as a towed gun battalion in October after the North Africa fighting ended, at which time it received thirty-six new 3-inch guns. On 15 November, the men received a foretaste of what awaited them as the only towed TD battalion in Italy. The crews were ordered to conduct service practice against a mountainside. The weather was by now not only rainy but, in the words of VI Corps CG MajGen John Lucas, "cold as hell," particularly at higher elevations.[74] The 3-inch gun M5 weighed 4,875 pounds with its carriage and thus confronted the crew with a wrestling match even under optimal conditions.[75] Company C had to winch its guns into position, lost all rounds fired in clouds or crevices, and then had to winch the guns back out.

The battalion advanced to a bivouac in what its operations report described as "alluvial mud" on the west bank of the Volturno river by 19 November. The 805th's operations officer was initially informed that there was not even room for additional guns firing indirect fire missions, but on 26 November the outfit was attached to the 18th Field Artillery Brigade, whose artillery battalions would provide telephone wire, survey, fire direction, and observation. Three days later, the men attempted to move their guns into firing positions. Most were winched through the muck, but bulldozers and tractors had to be brought in to move others. Usually, the vehicle sank in the mud. Because of the lack of experience with the 3-inch guns in both the battalion and the artillery, and because of the lack of space, the firing positions selected were poor. Company C's guns were lined up hub-to-hub.

Second Corps—which, with the 3d and 36th Infantry divisions under command, was just moving into the line between VI Corps and British 10 Corps—informed the 805th that it would have no antitank mission and would fire solely as artillery. On 1 December, the guns finally did so, firing some twelve hundred rounds in support of a planned attack by British 10 Corps. The attack was scrubbed.

By the next day, the crews had learned that trail shifts—or manually swinging the entire piece to point in a new direction—were necessary between practically all fire missions. Unless the guns could be positioned on the reverse slope of a hill, moreover, the crews had to dig trenches under the trails in order to obtain sufficient elevation for the guns. Sometimes, the prime movers (2-1/2-ton trucks at this time) had to be winched into position from which to winch the guns. It was going to be a tiring business.

* * *

On 13 December, the 805th received orders to replace the 776th in support of the 2d Moroccan Infantry Division at Celli.[76] The division, which had arrived in late November, was one of two selected from the ten French divisions training in North Africa to join the Allied effort in Italy. The U.S. 1st Armored Division had also arrived, accompanied by the 701st Tank Destroyer Battalion, and was in Fifth Army reserve pending an opportunity to employ large numbers of tanks.[77] The 701st got into the action immediately, however, by conducting indirect fire missions.[78]

Lieutenant Arthur Edson from the 701st now commanded Company A's tank destroyers. A TD company commander could expect to lead a fairly exposed life. He was issued nothing but a jeep and, armed with a pistol or carbine, often entered a new area ahead of his armor to scout out the best firing positions. Reports of captains and lieutenants from the firing companies being killed or captured while on reconnaissance appear with surprising frequency in the records of the TD battalions. It would be hepatitis, however, that would send Edson to the hospital in late 1943.

*   *   *

By December, tank destroyer battalions were firing an average of fifteen thousand rounds a month in indirect fire missions. Crews of the 701st were firing as many rounds in a thirty-hour period as they had during the entire Tunisian campaign.[79] One result was a temporary shortage of 3-inch HE rounds, which curtailed the TDs' use as artillery. At one point, the TDs of the 645th were allocated only seven rounds per tube per day, and the 701st was reduced to a single round per gun.[80]

The combination of terrible weather and difficult terrain forced the U.S. Army to bring back the mule train to supply its forward units, including the tank destroyers. The 645th Tank Destroyer Battalion, for example, in December 1943 had an average of fifty men per day assigned to division pack trains as "muleskinners."[81] Even the 805th, which was acting as artillery well behind the infantry's foxholes, had to use mules to support its OPs.[82] The muleskinners had to lead their charges over narrow, icy trails above deep precipices, almost always at night. It was nerve-wracking business.[83]

John Voss was a muleskinner for the 636th Tank Destroyer Battalion. He returned one December day with a swollen hand and explained what happened. "I carried that mule and the rations both up the mountain, then he fell down. I helped him up, and he kicked me. Then I hit him and broke my fist."[84]

The high mountains also played hob with radio communications. The 701st Tank Destroyer Battalion at one point later in the campaign issued carrier pigeons to its scattered companies so they could forward required daily reports.[85]

The divisions of battered VI Corps began to withdraw from the line in mid-December; they would soon have business elsewhere in Italy.[86] On Christmas Day, 1943, the 776th Tank Destroyer Battalion was withdrawn for rest after ninety-two consecutive days of action. The next day, orders came down for yet another reorganization of the tank destroyer battalions, which reduced manpower by one hundred thirty-six men.[87] Other battalions implemented the reorganization in December and January, as well.

*   *   *

On 15 January, the Allies finally approached the Rapido River and the Gustav Line. They had taken the Winter Position after three months of heavy losses to enemy fire and to the elements. The turnover of lieutenants in VI Corps, for example, had been 115 percent.[88] Fifth Army's battle losses were forty thousand men—far higher than German casualties—while the weather conditions had claimed another fifty thousand sick in the preceding two months alone.[89]

Fortunately for the tank destroyer units, the action set a pattern that would continue with few exceptions for the rest of the war: Casualties were substantially lower proportionately in TD outfits than in the infantry and separate tank battalions—although each man would be sorely missed, to be sure. The 636th, for example—which supported a bloody eighteen-day ranger and infantry attack on San Pietro beginning on 30 November—lost only three men killed and twenty-nine wounded during the entire month of December. The 776th would lose only seventeen men killed and one hundred four wounded during its one-year stay on the Italian front.

Chapter 5

Anzio and Two Roads to Rome

"Those were four of the most trying, most terrible, and most
exasperating months in the history of modern warfare."

— *An Informal History of the 601st Tank Destroyer Battalion*

On 22 January 1944, VI Corps executed Operation Shingle—an
amphibious flanking movement around the German Gustav Line—and
landed at Anzio, a mere thirty-five miles southwest of Rome. Landing
craft bearing the assault wave headed toward the shoreline at 0200 hours.
The invading forces achieved almost complete surprise, and only a few
coastal artillery and antiaircraft guns offered a brief and futile resistance.[1]
Harassment raids by the Luftwaffe began about 0815.[2]

A few men from the 701st Tank Destroyer Battalion, including
platoon commander Lt John Hudson, who was there almost by accident
after checking himself out of a hospital to stay with his outfit, splashed
ashore with a naval forward observer team. As the naval officer and two
sailors established radio communications with warships offshore and
directed supporting fire,[3] the 601st landed in force to support the doughs
of the 3d Infantry Division and therewith participated in its third D-day

assault. The tank destroyers rolled four miles inland against no opposition by the evening of the first day.

Recon Company elements from the 601st drove unmolested to within seventeen miles of Rome before turning back.[4] Tank destroyer reconnaissance companies had received new vehicles before the Anzio landings; the M8 Greyhound armored cars had replaced the M5 light tanks.[5] The six-wheeled M8 had a crew of four, sported armor as thick as 5/8 inches on its hull front, and carried a 37mm gun and coaxial .30-caliber machine gun in a fully rotating, open-topped turret.[6] The vehicle was capable of speeds up to 55 miles per hour. A utility armored car on the same chassis—the M20—also joined the TD battalions in place of some halftracks.

The British 1st Infantry Division landed to the left and also made easy progress inland; engineers and the Navy had the port of Anzio open by mid-afternoon. By midnight, VI Corps had thirty-six thousand men and thirty-two hundred vehicles ashore. It had lost only thirteen men killed and ninety-seven wounded.[7]

*   *   *

Discussion of a possible end run had ebbed and flowed from the time Eisenhower had first raised the possibility as German resistance solidified after the Salerno landings. Several strategic considerations were in play. The first was pressure from the Joint Chiefs on Eisenhower to release landing craft on schedule for the invasion of France. The second was an Allied assessment that even in the best case, available transport would support only a small expeditionary force. Alexander identified Anzio as the landing site as early as 8 November, but commanders viewed the entire enterprise as contingent upon making sufficient progress up the peninsula to guarantee a rapid link-up with the landing force. The virtual stalemate in the Winter Position persuaded Clark to recommend scrubbing the operation on 18 December.[8]

By December, Eisenhower had received the nod to take command of the invasion of northwestern Europe, and General Sir Henry Maitland Wilson had been named to take command of a combined Mediterranean and Middle Eastern Theater. The British were now unquestionably the senior partners in Italy, and Churchill wanted to pursue the Anzio option. On Christmas day, Churchill obtained Eisenhower's backing.[9]

The U.S. VI Corps would make the assault. The corps commander, MajGen John Lucas, would have the American 3d and British 1st Infantry divisions, the American Ranger Force of three battalions, a British special service brigade with two commando battalions, and an American parachute infantry regiment and an additional parachute battalion. A week before the landings, Clark promised Lucas elements of the 45th Infantry and 1st Armored divisions, with more to come if needed.[10]

Lucas wanted more time, but the deadline for surrendering landing craft for Operation Overlord permitted no delay. Preparations were rushed. Sixth Corps did not fully extricate itself from the line until 3 January 1944, and then the final landing rehearsal, on 19 January, was a fiasco. Lucas recorded that he feared he was in for another Battle of Little Big Horn and noted on another occasion, "[T]he whole affair has a strong odor of Gallipoli."[11]

*   *   *

Beginning on 12 January, Fifth Army had launched a furious attack against German positions along the Rapido and Garigliano rivers in the hope of drawing enemy units in striking distance from Anzio away to the south. On 17 January, British 10 Corps crossed the mouth of the Garigliano, but a subsequent assault crossing by the British 46th and American 36th Infantry divisions were repulsed.

Despite some progress, the offensive failed to crack the defenses. Nevertheless, the battle drew the 29th and 90th Panzergrenadier divisions away from Rome. The Eternal City lay defenseless.

Major General Lucas viewed his job as establishing and defending a beachhead at Anzio, not kicking open the door to Rome. He judged his initial assault force to be too weak to risk penetrating the Alban Hills that dominated the landing site from a dozen miles inland, although by doing so he could have cut the main highway—and supply route—from Rome to the Gustav Line.[12] Lucas's decision decided the terms under which the battle at Anzio would be fought.

*   *   *

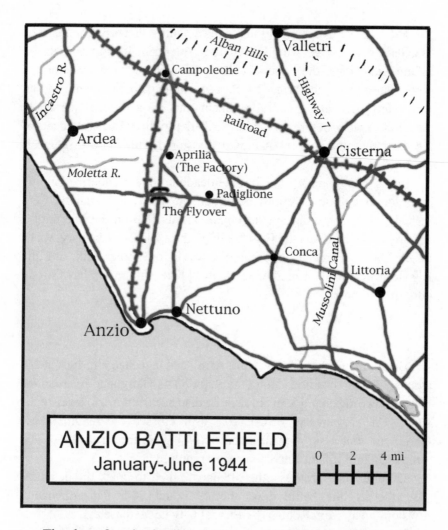

ANZIO BATTLEFIELD
January–June 1944

0   2   4 mi

The day after the landing, M10s from 2d Platoon, B/601st Tank Destroyer Battalion, engaged and destroyed a German tank as well as a machine-gun crew that had set up in one of the sturdy stone houses.[13] Their appearance suggested the enemy was beginning to react to the landings. Indeed, Generalfeldmarschall Kesselring and the German High Command in Berlin had quickly ordered the lead elements of twelve divisions and a corps headquarters into motion to contain the beachhead.

Sixth Corps spent the next several days slightly expanding and consolidating its holdings. By the third day, the Allies controlled a flat strip along the coast seven miles deep and sixteen miles wide. The left flank was anchored on the Moletta River and the right on the Mussolini Canal. A pine forest covered the center of the lodgement.

On 25 January, the British advanced up the Albano road toward Rome and captured the fascist model town of Aprilia, which the Allies dubbed "the Factory." The American 3d Infantry Division, however, encountered serious resistance as the doughs tried to advance toward Cisterna, a town in the Alban Hills. The lead elements of the 45th Infantry and 1st Armored divisions began landing that day. The arriving GIs soon shared Lucas's earlier misgivings regarding Operation Shingle. Informed that the Anzio operation would cut off the German forces defending Cassino, the men quipped, "Yeah, we've got 'em surrounded now." The history of the 157th Infantry Regiment recorded, "Anzio breathed disaster, and each man felt it."[14]

Rain, hail, and sleet began falling the next day while the 894th Tank Destroyer Battalion landed and deployed to support the British—who fielded only towed AT guns—the Rangers, and the 1st Armored Division.[15]

Lucas kept VI Corps sitting virtually still as he awaited the arrival of more troops. The Germans, however, were furiously active and threw units into the defensive line as they arrived.[16] Indeed, on 27 January, the tank killers of the 601st were ordered to provide close support to the doughs of the embattled 3d Infantry Division. They encountered a tough defensive line that exploited stone houses, ruins, and the natural cover offered by canals, stream beds, and draws as positions for strongpoints. Gunners dueled with German antitank guns at ranges of one thousand to seventeen hundred yards and knocked out three. The M10s of 3d Platoon, Company B, engaged a tank at only three hundred yards and destroyed it by firing 3-inch shells through two walls of the house behind which it was lurking.[17]

Lucas decided on 29 January that he was ready to break out, and he ordered an attack for the next day. The British 1st and American 3d Infantry divisions (the latter supported by the Rangers and the 504th Parachute Infantry Regiment) were to continue along their axes of advance. The 1st Armored Division's CCA (CCB was still in southern Italy) would swing around the British left and hit the Germans from the west. The ground units would receive support from naval guns, artillery, and air strikes. By then, however, Kesselring had stopped worrying that he could not contain the landing.[18]

The 1st Armored Division attacked on 30 January. Here was Lucas's strongest punch. The worst mud since the disaster at Medjez el Bab kept the armor road-bound, and the tankers fought much of the day just to reach their planned line of departure. The next day, the combat command—weakened by a requirement to loan a medium tank battalion to the British—tried again. It gained only a thousand yards. The division retired to the pine woods and dug in. The tanks would spend much of the next few months with nothing but their turrets exposed, firing artillery missions.[19]

The British 1st Infantry Division made better progress and in three days punched through the German main line of resistance and captured Campoleone. Early on 30 January, Sergeant Dixon of Company C, 894th Tank Destroyer Battalion, set of with a patrol of fifteen British riflemen to scout for gun positions that the TDs could use during the day's planned advance. German troops spotted the patrol, opened fire, and killed every man except for Dixon and a British sergeant. The two men crawled forward and shot the crew of a German machine gun. When another MG opened up and killed the British sergeant, Dixon fell to the ground and pretended to be dead. A German soldier approached and fired his pistol into the ground beside Dixon. Satisfied, he took the American sergeant's helmet, carbine, and pipe. Dixon lay still for forty-five minutes while German soldiers stood nearby talking. Finally, he saw his chance and crawled back to his M10.

The advance kicked off at 0630, when TDs carrying Tommies from the Irish Guards moved out. The M10s provided close support and engaged infantry and panzers that were carefully camouflaged and hard to spot beyond nearly point-blank range. One M10 KO'd a Volkswagen by driving over it. About 1530 hours, a hidden AT gun put four rounds through both sides of Sergeant Dixon's M10, killing him and wounding two crewmen. Sergeant Clark, who witnessed the action from five hundred yards distance, put four rounds of HE into the offending gun. Two other Company C TDs were damaged during the fighting.[20]

The 3d Infantry Division, meanwhile, launched an assault toward Cisterna that in three bloody days would gain no more than three miles before burning out in exhaustion. Tank destroyers from the 601st again provided close support and engaged German guns, machine-gun nests, and armored vehicles from ranges as close as fifty yards. The tank killers claimed four panzers during the last two days of January, one a Tiger

KO'd with three rounds of AP in the turret at one thousand yards. Recon troops were as usual far forward; 3d Platoon of Recon Company on 31 January beat off a counterattack with the help of their M8s, which at one point were firing pointblank with their 37mm guns.

The battalion CO, LtCol Walter Tardy, quickly concluded that his M10s were poorly suited to the close-support role. Commanders were highly vulnerable to small-arms fire, and he argued that the vehicles needed a sponson-mounted .30- or .50-caliber machine gun. Both the M10 and the M8 proved unable to move cross-country on the soupy ground. Other battalions quickly reached the same conclusions.[21]

The German Tide Rises

On 2 February, Alexander and Clark ordered Lucas to go over to the defensive. They told him to build a strong defensive line and to keep a powerful force in reserve to handle the German counterattack they expected at any time. The command also sent Lucas the First Special Service Force—a mixed American-Canadian outfit—and the British 56th Infantry Division, which would arrive in stages over the next two weeks.

As anticipated, the Germans struck the British sector of the line late on 3 February. A battalion of the Irish Guards and elements of the 894th Tank Destroyer Battalion were cut off during fierce night fighting. Platoon Sgt John Shoun led three Company C destroyers through the ring of German tanks and circled through the enemy rear. The M10s raced across an open field—the commanders madly firing the .50-cals—and roared back toward Allied lines over the heads of German infantrymen huddled in their foxholes. They made it out, but at least seven TD men were captured in the initial German assault.[22]

The next morning, Sgt Leo Dobson—whose crew, along with those of three other TDs, had also escaped encirclement the night before—found the battle situation extremely unclear. The Irish Guards sector had devolved into dozens of separate small-unit engagements, and heavy clouds, mist, and rain kept the air support away. Dobson spotted a Tiger tank backing out of one of the concrete houses. The huge tank had driven through the back wall and had been firing out through a window. The Mark VI was headed directly toward Dobson's M10 when it turned aside about six hundred yards away. The M10 gunner, Cpl Tom Perry, missed with his first shot, but the second caught the panzer broadside, and it caught fire so quickly that no crewmen escaped.

Some time later, an SP gun that had been trying unsuccessfully to hit Dobson's M10 pulled from a grove of trees, presumably to get a better angle. Perry fired rapidly, and the shells caved in the armor plate.[23]

Over the next week, repeated assaults drove the badly depleted British 1st Infantry Division back from Campoleone and the Factory at Aprilia. The TD crews from the 894th were constantly in the thick of the fighting and made heavy use of their .50-caliber AA machine guns against attacking infantry. M10s covered the final withdrawal from the Factory, and grateful Scots Guards dubbed the crews the "fighting tankbusters." Once again, a platoon of Company B became completely surrounded and had to dash three miles back to friendly lines. The crews waged a running battle using tommyguns, carbines, and grenades against the German infantry who barred the way.[24]

Lucas had to decrease the British frontage, and on 10 April he committed his two reserve regiments from the 45th Infantry Division to part of the British sector. The Americans tried to retake the Factory, but failed.

An uneasy lull settled over the Anzio beachhead.[25]

*   *   *

Companies A and C of the 701st disembarked at Anzio on 10 February and joined the 1st Armored Division; the rest of the battalion would trickle in over the next two weeks. The TD men were strafed as soon as they arrived at their assembly area, and air attacks were an almost daily occurrence for some time. Indeed, on 14 February, German planes attacked company gun positions five times during the day. The TDs joined division artillery in executing indirect fire missions.[26]

*   *   *

During the night of 15 February, 2/157th Infantry, 45th Infantry Division, moved into positions three thousand yards in front of a huge incomplete concrete highway overpass (sometimes called the "flyover") that would become the center of much of the fighting in the coming days.

The men moved into the holes dug by British troops and the 504th Parachute Battalion. The ground in front of the doughs was flat and open, and the Factory was to their right.[27] The Albano–Anzio highway at the overpass now formed the border between the American and British sectors.

At dawn on 16 February, the men of the 45th Infantry Division underwent the heaviest artillery barrage they had yet experienced. The shelling ceased, and German tanks supported by infantry advanced through a concealing fog down the Albano-Anzio road toward the American line. Although attacks also struck the positions of the American 3d and British 56th Infantry divisions to the right and left, respectively, this was the main assault.

The Germans put the tanks with the thickest front armor— Mark VI Tigers and newly arrived Mark V Panthers—at the point of each column.[28] The Panther was arguably the best tank fielded by any army during the war. The 45-ton panzer had 80mm (more than three inches) of well-sloped frontal armor and 40mm on the sides and rear. It was capable of reaching 30 miles per hour on roads—as fast as the much lighter Sherman tank. The Mark V carried a powerful high-velocity 75mm cannon that was the envy of American tankers, as well as a coaxial and hull-mounted machine guns.[29] It was prone to mechanical problems, however.

In the area held by the 157th Infantry, Company E was supported by a single M10 from the 645th Tank Destroyer Battalion—probably that commanded by Sgt John Kirk from Company C's 2d platoon. Panzers overran the left flank, but this exposed them to fire from the TD, which quickly destroyed two of the German tanks. Kirk identified the first of the two panzers he KO'd that day as a heavily armored Ferdinand SP gun (which carried an 88mm cannon protected by 200mm—eight inches!—of frontal armor on a rejected model of Tiger chassis). The remaining tanks withdrew, leaving the German infantry—who had broken into the center of the company area—to fight alone. The TD opened fire on the Germans with the .50-caliber AA machine gun and mowed down the attackers by the score. The doughs credited the TD crew with breaking up the assault, but the M10 had expended all of its ammo and had to withdraw. Company E was almost wiped out over the next twenty-four hours.[30]

The German attack pushed into the seam between the 157th and 179th Infantry regiments. Tanks, SP guns, and artillery pounded the line, but the men grimly held on. American artillery struck furiously in return. The TDs of the 645th engaged in a wild shootout with the advancing panzers. Second Lieutenant Jack Lindenberg's 2d Platoon, Company A, battled three Tigers and two Mark IVs in thick smoke at only three to four hundred yards. The American gunners caught two of the Tigers from the flank and forced the Germans to pull back. But Jerry destroyed one M10 in return and sent another limping to the rear with one of its two diesel engines shot out. Similarly, 1st Platoon killed one Mark IV for the loss of one TD, while 3d Platoon KO'd a Mark III and a Mark IV but left one burning M10 on the battlefield. Company C, meanwhile, claimed five panzers for the loss of three TDs.[31]

By day's end, the defenders had grudgingly backpedaled about one mile, but the Germans had failed to break through.[32]

Germany's Tank Destroyers

The fighting at Anzio took place at roughly the same time that the German armed forces began to field a class of armored vehicles specifically designed as tank killers. These were turretless, well-armored, self-propelled guns carrying cannon capable of dealing with the heaviest Allied (including Soviet) armor. Indeed, unlike the American designs, they were developed with the all too common slugging match in mind—not the rarely seen speedy response to an armored thrust.

The German Panzerjäger, or tank hunters, were an evolutionary product of assault guns designed to provide the infantry with close-in fire support that had seen service as early as the invasion of France. Indeed, when the Sturmgeschütz (StuG) III—the most widely produced assault gun—was given a powerful 75mm cannon and thicker armor in early 1942, the vehicle was initially used solely in an antitank roll on the Eastern Front. Official German sources credited the StuG III with twenty thousand Allied tank kills on all fronts.[33]

The Germans had built some jerry-rigged tank destroyers mounting AT guns in lightly armored superstructures on obsolete or foreign-made tank chassis. But in January 1944, the first Jagdpanzer IV vehicles entered service with combat units. This vehicle carried a long-barreled

75mm gun in an armored superstructure on the Mark IV chassis and had 80mm (three-plus inches) of well-sloped frontal armor. In February, series production of the Jagdpanzer V (Jagdpanther or Hunting Panther) began. The Jagdpanther carried the 88mm gun on a Panther chassis with sloped front armor 80mm thick.[34]

Other tank killers were produced, from the rare, giant Ferdinand to the widespread, diminutive, and deadly Hetzer. Unfortunately, American AARs often lumped the panzerjägers, assault guns, and SP artillery together under the "SP" heading. TD battalion kill statistics also broke out SP guns from the tanks, although the latter could be even more dangerous than actual tanks.

The German tank-killer units in practice operated more or less the same as their American counterparts, with platoons or companies parceled out in support of infantry or armored line units. A StuG III crew, for example, would typically take part in the pre-assault artillery barrage, join the main body in the attack, fire on strongpoints such as bunkers, and switch to the tank-destroyer role if enemy tanks appeared.[35] As in the U.S. Army, the tank hunters were not organized as part of the armored force (the assault gun crews were artillerymen), although they increasingly took on the role of tanks. After 31 March 1943, however, panzerjäger battalions not attached to the infantry were considered part of the Panzertruppe.[36]

*   *   *

The forward defenses buckled further on 17 February under the pressure exerted by three tank-supported infantry divisions. American troops gave ground almost to the line that Lucas had declared to be his final position. Further retreat, he said, would mean the destruction of the beachhead.

Realizing his peril, Lucas threw fresh armor into the fray. A battalion of the 6th Armored Infantry Regiment, vanguard of the 1st Armored Division, moved into the line to buttress the doughs of the 45th Infantry Division, and tanks advanced to help the slowly withdrawing 2/157th Infantry.[37]

The artillery barrage supporting the German attacks against the 45th Infantry Division during the day also hit the positions of Company A,

701st Tank Destroyer Battalion. One man was killed and another was wounded.

Company I of the 157th Infantry Regiment dug a semi-circular arc of foxholes in front of the overpass and at dusk repulsed the first of the infantry attacks that would crash into the position over the next several days. At approximately 1730 hours, the 1st Armored Division ordered the TDs of A/701st to take up firing positions at the overpass to support the doughs. The M10s arrived by 2300 hours, and the crews dug their vehicles in.

Lieutenant John Hudson deployed his 2d Platoon on the left in what was technically the British zone but contained many empty foxholes. The former infantry officer recalled from his training at Ft. Benning that a commander should never use a natural line—in this case the Albano–Anzio road—as the boundary between tactical units because neither outfit will view the feature as its problem. He sited his four M10s so that they could use the earthen ramp of the overpass as an ersatz revetment.

* * *

On 18 February, renewed attacks by fresh formations—the 29th Panzergrenadier and 26th Panzer divisions—broke through the 179th Infantry Regiment's line.[38] Two hull-down M10s from 2d Platoon, B/645th Tank Destroyer Battalion, engaged a dozen panzers pushing down the highway toward the overpass. Boggy ground made off-road maneuver impossible for the TDs, but it also forced the German tanks to stick to the roads. Sergeant Tousignant reported: "Three Mark VIs [were advancing], interval between them of approximately one hundred yards. We opened fire on first tank, knocked [it] out while broadside in road. Opened fire on second tank, which pulled in behind house out of view. Third tank came down road. Fired on him, knocking him out broadside in road, blocking road. In the meantime, second tank behind house turned around, started back north toward their lines, got out in the open, and we knocked [it] out."[39]

Return fire disabled the second M10, however.

As the Germans sought to exploit the hole in the American line, the massed fire of two hundred Allied guns fell on advancing panzers and infantry. The attack disintegrated, and artillery wrecked four more German thrusts over the next hour.[40]

By day's end, the 645th had lost a total of eleven tank destroyers battling the German offensive (plus six more abandoned in deep mud), but it had killed twenty-five panzers with direct fire, plus twelve through artillery concentrations directed by battalion personnel.[41] Company A, 894th Tank Destroyer Battalion, was attached to the 645th during the day to compensate for the 645th's losses. But February proved a costly month for the 894th, too: The outfit lost seven men killed, fifty-two wounded, and fourteen missing.[42]

*   *   *

Lieutenant John Hudson's men at the overpass itself were bombed and strafed frequently on 18 February, but the guns were well protected, and the outfit suffered no casualties. That night, Hudson crawled infantry-style down a drainage ditch that ran beside a rail line parallel to the road to do some scouting. As he neared a culvert, he could hear the voices of a German patrol from inside the pipe.

At 0400 hours the next morning, a strong German infantry assault supported by panzers tried to push down the Albano–Anzio road through the defenses at the overpass. Hudson's 2d Platoon stood right in the way of the advancing panzers.

Hudson spotted the panzer column as it clanked into view. A Tiger was the first vehicle in line. Hudson ordered his guns to fire at five hundred yards. Staff Sergeant Merle Downs, a small, quiet, but immensely competent noncom, opened up first. Hudson watched in dismay as fifteen 3-inch tracer rounds deflected off the Tiger's thick hide. He began to wonder how the encounter was going to turn out. Fortunately, the ground was still too soft for the panzers to deploy off the road and engage the outnumbered TDs.

Two more rounds had bounced off the Tiger when its turret began to rotate toward the flank as the panzer commander sought out his tormenters. The tank killers saw their opening and put three quick shots through the less-armored side of the Mark VI's turret. A hulking derelict now completely blocked the road, and the M10s engaged the panzers strung out in the column behind the Tiger.

When the Germans withdrew from the hopeless fight, they left behind two Tigers and five Mark IVs, all credited to the guns of 2d Platoon.[43]

In the neighboring British sector, the M10s of the 894th maintained such a high rate of fire that crews worried rounds would begin to "cook off" when shoved in the breech because of the heat. Corporal Arthur Wiest of Company C recalled the Southerners in the battalion whooping rebel yells as they fired machine guns at charging German infantry.[44]

*   *   *

On the night of 19–20 February, C/701st moved into positions along the Albano–Anzio road to relieve Company A. The last German attack struck the men at the overpass at dawn on 20 February. Seventy-two British 25-pounders—the major commanding had earlier set up a telephone link to Hudson's positions—delivered a barrage that broke up the attack.[45] (Indeed, seventy-five percent of all German casualties during the failed offensive were caused by Allied artillery.)[46] Two platoons from Company C joined tanks from the 1st Armored Division in conducting a reconnaissance-in-force against German positions. The TDs engaging German armor in the vicinity of Terre di Padiglione destroyed one Mark IV and one Tiger in exchange for two damaged but salvageable M10s.[47] The probe also destroyed two battered German infantry battalions.[48]

The German offensive was over. On 22 February, Lucas was replaced by MajGen Lucian Truscott Jr.

*   *   *

Anzio became a siege, a violent stalemate differentiated only by occasional offensive jabs by one side or the other. These were at times vigorous: The crews of the 601st Tank Destroyer Battalion KO'd twenty-five panzers and SP guns during one local thrust in late February.[49]

The Germans could survey and shell the entire beachhead, so the Allies hid by day and moved by night. (LtCol Harrison King, commanding the 701st Tank Destroyer Battalion, was critically wounded on 25 March when a shell fired not by the Germans but by the 894th Tank

Destroyer Battalion struck a branch over the heads of his party, killing or wounding several men.)[50] Yet the Allies steadily added to their assets ashore. Over the longer run, the Germans had no hope of matching this build-up.

Tank destroyers by and large reverted to the artillery role. The British now dubbed the men from the 894th who were providing them with indirect-fire support the "house-busters."[51] But a few platoons from each battalion were always at the front to provide antitank defense and close support for tactical operations. One day, Sgt Bill Harper's platoon from the 601st Tank Destroyer Battalion was dug in near some buildings at Isola Bella, while the Germans were dug in a few short yards away on the far side. Ordnance radioed forward and requested the serial number of Harper's gun. Harper's radio operator asked whether Ordnance wanted the number on the breech block or the one on the gun barrel, and was told the latter. The radioman replied that the fellow from Ordnance could come forward and get that number himself because it was in enemy territory.[52]

Reconnaissance Company from the 601st held part of the line at the edge of no-man's land. The men learned quickly to discern the difference between the *voom-voom-voom* sound of German tank engines and the steady *rrrrrr* of American engines. Platoons rotated forward for a week and then were relieved by another. "Relief" was relative: The men huddled in the basements of stone houses during the dangerous hours of daylight. One recon man, sent to the rear after sustaining an injury at Beja Letina, soon begged for a transfer back to Recon because of all the "incoming mail." "I can't stand it back here in the hospital," he complained. "It's too rough!"[53]

The TD commanders experimented with new ways of doing business in the confined and flat bridgehead. The 701st Tank Destroyer Battalion, for example, deployed two gun companies on the line and kept the third in reserve to fire indirect missions. The forward TDs were thus able to call for and receive effective and almost immediate artillery support. The tank killers also learned to position their M10s behind sturdy buildings. Although they had no immediate field of fire (a violation of doctrine!), the destroyers needed to move only a few feet to acquire enemy targets. The Germans adapted, however, and began to zero in their AT guns on the corners of buildings that they suspected of harboring tank destroyers.

This, in turn, allowed the Americans to spot and destroy some of the AT guns.[54]

The tank killers found new ways to use their well liked M10s more effectively. The crews began to add a covering of thick timbers and sandbags to the open turrets of their M10s when they were in positions in or beside a building, which gave them both protection and camouflage. (Later in Western Europe, when engagements with German tanks were more frequent, crews learned to cover the turrets only when in defensive positions. The open turret allowed the men to bail out quickly when the vehicle was hit—a great worry among crewmen in Sherman tank turrets who had to escape through a single hatch.) Some even built custom metal turret tops with hinged doors; the 804th Tank Destroyer Battalion, for example, fashioned covers out of wrecked halftracks and simply discarded them when the TDs had to move.[55] The crews learned to run their engines only at night so as not to expose their positions. The men had to start the engines for thirty minutes per day to recharge the battery, which suffered a constant drain from the radio because the M10 lacked the small "Little Joe" generator motor found in tanks. The crews also found that sandbags reduced the radiator's vulnerability to shrapnel and added to the protection afforded by the frontal armor.[56]

Some outfits took advantage of the relative inaction to establish schools for various specialties. The 894th put every man in the battalion through a course on laying, detecting, and removing antipersonnel and antitank mines. Some learned to drive M10s, while others took courses on diesel mechanics, mortars, wire communications, and repair of the 3-inch gun.[57]

Checked at Cassino

The landings at Anzio accomplished, Major General Clark on 23 January visited his three corps commanders and urged them to step up efforts to crack the Gustav Line and link up with the beachhead.[58] The Americans needed to drive up the Liri Valley to accomplish this mission. The keys to the German defenses were the Cassino massif, the town of Cassino, and the Benedictine Abbey that brooded over the valley from the mountainside.

The 34th Infantry Division launched the first attack toward the objective the night of 24 January. The rest of II Corps, the French Expeditionary Corps, and British 10 Corps entered the fray over the next several days, but progress was minimal. On 31 January, Company C of the 776th Tank Destroyer Battalion entered battle in support of the tankers of the 756th Tank Battalion, who in turn fought beside the doughs of the 34th Infantry Division still struggling to consolidate the crossing of the Rapido River southeast of Cassino.

The first American troops reached the outskirts of Cassino on 3 February. The Germans fought back skillfully from the thick-walled buildings, and the Americans withdrew. The 34th Infantry Division launched another major attempt to take the town on 7 February. This time, the TDs from the 776th crawled into town to support the tanks and doughs.[59] Street fighting was a rare and unwelcome experience for the TD crews in Italy, mainly because the streets in Italian towns were usually so narrow that armor could not operate. The 3-inch gun, as it turned out, was particularly effective against German pillboxes and fortified houses.[60]

In the northwest corner of Cassino, the infantry asked a TD platoon commander to knock out a 50mm gun the Germans had placed in the third floor of a building. The only catch was that American doughs were already on the first floor. The tank destroyer commander crossed his fingers, put four rounds into the structure, knocked out the gun, and never scratched a doughboy.[61]

During the day, a Company C M10 destroyed the battalion's first enemy tank of the Italian campaign. This was four-and-a-half months after battalion had entered the fray—a vignette that underscored the fact that the TD crews were fighting a war that bore little resemblance to the one envisioned in their doctrine.

But the Germans held on. The 34th Infantry Division had been bled white, so a newly created provisional corps consisting of the 2d New Zealand Division and the 4th Indian Division moved into the line to take another crack at Cassino.

On 15 February, American bombers struck the Benedictine abbey on Monte Cassino after a soul-searching discussion within the Allied chain of command had concluded that the action was necessary to support the New Zealand Corps offensive. Second Corps artillery added to the destructive bombardment,[62] and the M10s of B/636th contributed several concentrations of 3-inch fire into the rubble late in the afternoon.[63] The ruins, in the event, provided superb defensive positions to the Germans.

* * *

The fighting around Cassino once again demonstrated that tank destroying was a relatively safe occupation as compared with those of the rifleman and tanker. Infantry divisions were ground down to the size of regiments. During February, the 636th Tank Destroyer battalion lost only two men killed and seven wounded, all to German artillery fire. The casualties, however, included much of the command group who were in the battalion CP when it took a direct hit on 12 February.[64]

On 16 March, a flight of B-25 bombers dropped their load on the positions of C/636th (now attached to CCB/1st Armored Division), which were located behind the front line near Cassino. Thanks to the crews' now habitual construction of elaborate foxholes and dugouts near their vehicles, only one man was so badly wounded that he required evacuation. At least the American attack provided a break from the frequent German air strikes along the front.[65]

* * *

More than a month after the destruction of the abbey, the Allies were still trying to capture Cassino—the town itself having now been treated to a massive air bombardment, as well. On 15 March, the New Zealanders launched another effort to clear the town. By 21 March, both they and the Indian troops trying to clear the mountainside were exhausted, and Allied commanders were debating whether to abandon the assault.[66]

That day, Brigadier Burrows, commanding the 5th New Zealand Armored Brigade, asked 636th Tank Destroyer Battalion CO LtCol Van Pyland whether it would be possible to lay fire safely within two hundred yards of friendly troops. The conventional wisdom was that the 3-inch gun had too flat a trajectory to fire close to friendly positions. Pyland, however, said it could be done because his guns were registered on a building very near the spot Burrows wanted to hit. The 636th ran a telephone line to the Kiwi CP and made plans.

The next day, from 1100 to 1245, Pyland personally directed fire into the Continental Hotel in Cassino. An American officer in a tank near the Continental Hotel helped adjust the fire.[67]

Pyland now discovered the hazards of supporting Allied troops who had even less knowledge of TD doctrine than American commanders. On 23 March, he received orders via CCB to send four M10s into Cassino to "knock down some buildings and drive enemy tanks out." Pyland objected that this idea ran against every principle of tank destroyer tactics. CCB passed the buck and told Pyland to take the matter up with General Parkinson, CG of the New Zealand Division. Parkinson reiterated his orders, so Pyland and his operations officer (S-3) drove to the Kiwi headquarters, where Pyland met with Brigadier Burrows to coordinate the operation—and in all likelihood repeated his opinions on the matter. Some time later, CCB notified the 636th that the plan had been scrubbed.[68]

Once again, the Allies failed to capture Cassino. And the rains fell.

An End to Stalemate

In the early hours of 11 May, Capt Richard Danzi, 636th Tank Destroyer Battalion S-3, met with the commanders of the line companies and passed them fire mission orders. Men made ready. Night fell, warm and misty. It was so still that Sgt Tom Sherman could hear dogs barking on the far side of the Liri Valley.[69]

At 2300 hours, the M10s of the 636th and 804th Tank Destroyer battalions joined the cacophony of 155mm Long Toms, 105mm howitzers, and 75mm tank guns throwing HE rounds at the German defenses of the Gustav Line.

The crews in the 804th had only entered the line in the Cassino sector along the Garigliano River in March and engaged in artillery duels with the enemy. Now, doughs of the 88th Infantry Division advanced with the tank destroyers in close support. The M10s blasted machine gun nests and other strongpoints. Recon men roamed ahead, spotting German positions and clearing mines. The battalion nonetheless had two TDs damaged by mines.[70]

By 15 May, the Gustav Line had collapsed.

* * *

That same day, the 636th Tank Destroyer Battalion was pulled from the II Corps line for transfer to the Anzio beachhead, where it arrived on 19 May. Feverish preparations were underway there, and the battalion was immediately broken up. Company B was attached to the 1st Armored Division and further subordinated to the 701st Tank Destroyer Battalion. Company A was assigned to the 601st Tank Destroyer Battalion in support of the 3d Infantry Division. Each TD company received an extra M10 to use as a command vehicle. On 23 May, Company A of the 894th Tank Destroyer Battalion was attached to the depleted 636th.[71]

* * *

At 0545 hours on 23 May, a tremendous artillery preparation rained down on German lines. At 0630 hours, the breakout from Anzio—Operation Buffalo—kicked off.[72] The 3d Infantry and 1st Armored divisions made up the main assault force, supported by a limited advance by the 45th Infantry Division and diversionary attacks by the British.

Cracking the prepared German defenses was costly for the 3d Infantry Division, which suffered 1,626 battle casualties on the first day, the highest one-day toll paid by any American division in Europe during the war. But by late on 24 May, the offensive had advanced a dozen miles, and the doughs of the 3d Division had taken their first main objective, Cisterna.[73] The first phase was an infantry struggle, although the crews of the 601st Tank Destroyer Battalion—working closely with the infantry-support tanks—helped when they could by engaging strongpoints, guns, and tanks.[74]

Vast minefields resulting from months of siege warfare proved to be the greatest danger to the tank destroyers during the breakout. The 601st lost four M10s destroyed and ten damaged to mines (plus two TDs damaged by shellfire)—half the battalion's strength. Casualties, particularly among drivers, were unusually heavy as a consequence.[75]

To the left of the 3d Infantry Division, the 1st Armored Division's CCA blew holes through the German minefields with snakes—long, explosive-filled tubes—and crashed through the enemy line. A platoon of A/701st Tank Destroyer Battalion TDs and one of engineers accompanied each tank company to provide close support. As the armored force approached its objective—high ground beyond a railroad line—Cpl John Conlin spotted two Tigers rolling along a slope. He got a "lightning draw" on them, and his gunner put a 3-inch round neatly alongside the barrel of each 88mm gun. Both turrets locked because of the damage, and Conlin pounded the panzers with HE rounds until they caught fire. Informed over the radio that a counterattack by twenty-five Tigers was expected, Conlin's company commander, Capt John Wright, called back, "Make that twenty-three. I've just knocked out two." The company lost five men wounded, two M10s knocked out by mines, and one M10 destroyed by antitank fire.[76]

Lieutenant Arthur Edson, just transferred to take command of C/701st Tank Destroyer Battalion, had worse luck. CCB/1st Armored Division relied on riflemen instead of snakes to clear the mines. During the long siege, American troops had laid mines on top of mines, and the minesweepers did not discover the lower layers. When the heavy armored vehicles gradually compressed the earth, they detonated the lower layers and suffered the loss of twenty-three tanks and eight M10s from Company C. The command nevertheless reached its objective by nightfall. By then, Company A had KO'd eight panzers, and Company C scored two.[77]

On 24 May, a German Tiger tank battalion counterattacked the 157th Infantry Regiment, 45th Infantry Division, and all but wiped out one platoon of Company B. An unidentified TD element (possibly M10s from B/894th Tank Destroyer Battalion, which was attached to the 645th in support of the 45th Infantry Division) engaged the Mark VIs; 3-inch fire penetrated two of them and exploded their ammo. Artillery fire drove off the rest. The official U.S. Army history makes no mention of the role played by the TDs in beating off this attack, but the doughs said the TDs had saved the day.[78]

Lieutenant John Hudson, just appointed "Ace" Edson's exec, was riding in one of his M10s in place of an injured crewman when he spotted a Tiger as it poked its nose out of a barn. As the Mark VI pulled into full view, shaking off loose hay, the Americans could see that bales of hay were wired to the hull to provide very effective camouflage. Hudson told the gunner to fire his newly replaced 3-inch gun—so new that the red Ordnance tag was still on it. But the gun would not fire.

A hasty inspection revealed that there was no firing pin! Hudson ordered the crew to install the replacement pin from the on-board kit and aimed machine-gun fire at the panzer. The tracers set the hay ablaze, and the Mark VI backed slowly through the barn trailing flames and a one-hundred-foot column of smoke. Later in the day, the crew encountered a smoke-charred Tiger with hay around its exploded gas tank, but they could not tell for certain that it was the same vehicle.[79]

On 25 May, the southern front linked up with the beachhead. The men of the 701st by 26 May had been credited with destroying twenty-one German tanks, three self-propelled guns, and assorted antitank and artillery pieces during the breakout so far.[80]

*   *   *

The 36th Infantry Division came into the line from reserve positions and by 28 May was knocking at the door of the strategic town of Velletri. Recon men of the 805th Tank Destroyer Battalion—the towed-gun outfit's companies had been parceled out to reinforce self-propelled TD battalions—were working with the division. During the morning, Lt Arpod Sabo and his 1st Platoon spotted two Tiger tanks that refused to be drawn into the line of fire of nearby TDs. Arpod grabbed three soldiers and a bazooka and went after them. He sidled close to the first huge tank and fired three rockets into the thick frontal armor, but none penetrated. The frustrated lieutenant clambered to the turret top and blazed away with his carbine through a hatch. He killed every man but the driver, who backed the tank to safety—minus Arpod, who jumped free.[81]

*   *   *

It was 29 May, and one battalion of the 168th Infantry Regiment, 34th Infantry Division, had launched two assaults on German trenches near Villa Crocetta, only to be driven back each time. The infantry battalion S-3, Capt William Galt, volunteered to lead one more attack against the objective. When the sole surviving tank destroyer from a platoon of Company C, 894th Tank Destroyer Battalion, allegedly refused to go forward, Captain Galt jumped on the M10 and ordered it to precede the attack. As the tank destroyer advanced, followed by a company of riflemen, Galt manned the machine gun on the turret, located and directed fire on an enemy 77mm antitank gun, and destroyed it. Nearing the enemy positions, Galt stood fully exposed in the turret, firing his machine gun and tossing hand grenades into the zigzag trenches despite the hail of sniper and machine-gun bullets ricocheting off the tank destroyer. As the tank destroyer moved, Galt so maneuvered it that forty of the enemy were trapped in one trench. When they refused to surrender, the captain pressed the trigger of the machine gun and dispatched every one of them. A few minutes later an 88mm shell struck the tank destroyer and Galt fell mortally wounded across his machine gun. He had personally killed forty Germans and wounded many more.

Captain Galt was awarded the Medal of Honor. Every man in the M10—themselves credited with killing forty German soldiers—died, and they did not even receive mention in their own battalion's history.[82]

*   *   *

The informal history of the 601st probably spoke for many other TD outfits at this point: "The 601 that broke out of the Anzio beachhead was a tough, experienced, battle-hardened, confident battalion. The men had "got" forty-three Kraut tanks on the beachhead for the loss of three, and they weren't afraid of anything the Kraut had, or made, or manned. They'd knocked out his IVs and VIs and his Panthers and his Ferdinands, and they were going to get to Rome if they had to put wings on the M10s and fly 'em there!"[83]

Rome!

While all roads may lead to Rome, American troops in Italy cared about only two.

M10s from Company B, 636th Tank Destroyer Battalion, on 4 June were at the point of the 13th Armored Regiment's column, pressing toward Rome up Highway 6. The column plowed through several German delaying positions and entered Rome at 0715 hours. Company B's Charles Kessler recalled, "My tank destroyer rolled past a large 'Roma' sign marking the city limits and on into the capital. Ahead of me were five Sherman tanks and two TDs. Behind were the entire Fifth and Eighth armies. We had not gone two hundred yards into the city when a monster 170mm German self-propelled gun opened fire. The lead M4 burst into flame, and the rest of us deployed off the road. The enemy gun was well hidden, and it was several hours before we flanked and destroyed the SP gun."[84]

Company C/636th, meanwhile, was carrying doughs of the 141st Infantry Regiment, 36th Infantry Division, and spearheaded the advance up Highway 7. The column received orders to cross the Tiber River and establish defensive positions on roads departing Rome for the north. As the M10s rolled into the city, they encountered three Tigers deployed to place overlapping fire on a key intersection. One platoon was sent toward the right to swing around the panzers. While weaving through the maze of streets, the tank killers ran into three Panthers. Guns blazed in both directions. One Mark V took a direct hit, and the other two withdrew.[85]

Ellis Force, consisting of A/636th; elements of the 91st Reconnaissance Squadron, 143rd Infantry Regiment; and the 751st and 753d Tank battalions, advanced up a secondary road between Highways 6 and 7. Recon Sgt Tom Sherman was ordered to lead a platoon of M10s forward to deal with an SP gun menacing Highway 7 at the entrance to Rome. Sherman was amazed to find the road blocked by a gaggle of rear-echelon types who had raced ahead to grab choice housing for their units. The major in charge did not want to let the TDs get by. He remained obstinate even when M10 crewmen called out suggesting that he and his men take care of the SP gun themselves. Sherman finally suggested he would report this to "Colonel"—normally known as Lieutenant—James Graham, Company A's acting commander. The major relented, and the task force entered Rome in the early afternoon and linked up with the column headed by Company C.[86]

Other units rolled into Rome. The men of the 3d Infantry Division and 601st Tank Destroyer Battalion arrived, the latter pleased to observe that Rome was "clean, beautiful, full of lovely girls, and it had hardly been touched by the war."[87] The 1st Armored Division and 701st Tank Destroyer Battalion pulled in by 1500 hours.[88] Also late in the day, the M10s of the 804th Tank Destroyer Battalion entered Rome from the south. The difference between the Anzio and main forces had been completely erased, and the 804th joined Ellis Force the next day.[89]

Groping Toward Better Combined-Arms Solutions

With movement restored to the war, tank destroyer units found themselves at the point of advancing columns as they had been in North Africa. Nevertheless, tank destroyer outfits asserted that reconnaissance elements—not TDs—should lead any advance seeking to reestablish contact with the enemy in order to permit the destroyers to deploy and exploit their fire power when contact occurred. Recon men, it must be said, frowned on situations in which they were ordered to precede armored columns—ranging ahead of the far less vulnerable tanks in their little jeeps by up to fifteen hundred yards.[90]

After eight months of operations in Italy, basic communications issues between the tank destroyers and infantry units they supported remained unresolved. Major Charles Wilber, by June commanding the 636th Tank Destroyer Battalion, noted in his monthly report: "Tank destroyer companies attached to infantry regimental teams are usually broken down to one platoon with each infantry battalion. Although radios within the tank destroyer battalion are plentiful and no serious communications difficulty exists, there does exist a need for positive communication between the tank destroyer platoon supporting the leading infantry battalion and that battalion's commander. Personal liaison between the two has been tried with results that are not entirely satisfactory due to the time element and the distances involved. A possible solution is that the tank destroyer platoon leader be equipped with a 300 series radio on the same frequency as that of the battalion commander. . . ."[91]

Wilber's view that coordination with the infantry needed improvement was widely held in the TD battalions, and a Fifth Army review of operations during early and mid-1944 pinned the blame mainly on infantry commanders who did not understand the powers and limitations of tank destroyers. Fifth Army also pointed a finger at the frequent reattachment of TD outfits to new divisions, a practice that prevented the two arms from developing ties of mutual understanding and trust through experience operating together. (Similar problems dogged the cooperation between the doughs and the separate tank battalions in Italy.)

The Fifth Army report also noted that the commanders of the 636th and 894th Tank Destroyer battalions complained that, during the breakthrough to Rome, their M10s had been ordered to advance ahead of the infantry to overrun points of resistance—a tank mission for which they were not suited.[92] The tank killers' view was clear: It was imperative that the thinly armored, open-topped TDs have a screen of infantry to prevent enemy infantry from closing for a quick kill. The M10 was not capable of performing the role of a tank within small-arms range of the enemy, they argued.[93]

One "offending" unit—the 34th Infantry Division—was unapologetic. The attached 191st Tank Battalion had suffered casualties so severe during the breakthrough that it had become combat ineffective, the division asserted, and the infantry had no choice but to use the armor that was available, the 894th's tank destroyers.[94]

The Fifth Army review concluded that problems in TD cooperation with tank units evident early in the period had generally been overcome by summer. Surprisingly, the early troubles were attributed to a lack of aggressiveness on the part of TD commanders.

Perhaps this impression resulted from a key lesson learned by the TD crews. The 3-inch gun was able to destroy enemy armor and installations at a greater range than other mounted direct-fire weapons, and the tank killers concluded that M10s should remain to the rear of advancing tanks, from which they could provide effective supporting fire. Tank destroyers, they observed, should operate about four hundred yards behind friendly tanks in typical Italian terrain. Any closer and the TDs would be subject to the same fire hitting the unit supported; any farther and effective support would be impossible.

There were also two sides to the tanker complaints of lagging TDs. The 701st noted in a lessons-learned memo, "Tanks will sometimes storm ahead and seemingly forget about their supporting TDs. However, this need not occasion any worry among the TDs; the tanks will always be glad to send back a guide as soon as the TDs are needed."[95]

Poor-to-nonexistent radio communications between the two types of armor continued to plague operations. Several battalion commanders from tank and TD battalions had proposed a new approach to mixed operations: Rather than attach a tank destroyer element to the tank unit, the TD commander should be ordered to support the tanks and be held responsible for executing the mission effectively. They would then have the flexibility to provide close support even when communications broke down.[96]

The M18 Arrives

The first two Hellcats—still sporting their T70 test designation—arrived in Italy in April and were issued for battle trials to the 601st Tank Destroyer Battalion at the Anzio beachhead.[97] In June, the 805th—a towed battalion—became the first to re-equip with the M18.

Buick had designed the M18 with much input from the Tank Destroyer Force. The vehicle embodied the doctrine: fast, light, and lethal. At 40,000 pounds, the M18 was little more than half as heavy as the M10, and it could reach the remarkable speed of 50 miles per hour. The tradeoff was that armor was thin—a mere half-inch on the hull front (less than on the M8 armored car). The Hellcat carried a 76mm gun (a lighter version of the 3-inch gun) in a full-traverse open-topped turret, and, like the M10, had no machine guns other than an antiaircraft .50-caliber mounted at the turret rear.[98] The turret traverse speed was so high that gunners had to make final aiming corrections manually.[99]

Lieutenant Colonel Peter K. Kopcsak, CO of the 602d Tank Destroyer Battalion, opined that the Hellcat "was the best vehicle to come out of Detroit during the war."[100]

Buick, however, claimed it had designed the Hellcat as the answer to the Tiger which—since its gun could not penetrate the Mark VI front armor—it was not.[101] Some, moreover, disliked the Hellcat's thin armor and thus preferred the M10. One battalion—the 813th—in early 1945 fought conversion from the M10 to the M18 so vigorously that it was moved to the M36 instead. The battalion judged that "the M10 is a superior TD to the M18 in every particular."[102]

Much to the dismay of the crews, many American infantrymen thought the M18 resembled a German tank because of its barrel length and suspension. At least some crews responded by painting the white identification stars bigger and brighter.[103]

Coiling for the Next Strike

Several tank destroyer battalions slipped out of sight during the hot days of mid-summer 1944.

The 636th was typical. It moved to the Salerno area in early July. There, maintenance crews gave the M10s thorough overhauls and replaced worn guns and tracks. Vehicles were painted, camouflaged, and waterproofed. In view of the problems in combined arms operations experienced to date, all companies conducted training problems with the 753d Tank Battalion and the infantry battalions and regiments of the 36th Infantry Division. Recon taught its men to use 81mm mortars. The 636th took the unusual (but not unique) decision to get rid of all of its M20 armored cars and replace them with old M3 halftracks, which the battalion concluded had proved more suitable.[104]

Veterans of Salerno and Anzio thought, "Here we go again." The men did not know the destination, but they had learned that amphibious operations could be hazardous to one's health.[105]

The U.S. Army allowed that some of the first soldiers had made their contributions at the front and were needed more now at home. Lieutenant Arthur Edson, who had landed at Oran, rotated home in July 1944. The European war was over for him. He took up duties at the Tank Destroyer School at Camp Hood, Texas.

*   *   *

The battalions that remained behind in Italy—the 701st, 804th, 805th, and 894th—would continue to support the infantry and armored divisions as they pushed the Germans back to their last defensive stronghold before the Alps. The Gothic Line ran through the Apennine Mountains from north of Pisa to Rimini. American troops again began the grueling job of attacking pillboxes, concrete emplacements, and other strongpoints supported by tank destroyer fire. Progress would again be measured in yards, and casualties would again spike. This time, however, the Allies would decide to hunker down during the horrible winter weather and attack again in the spring. All they had to do in Italy was tie down German forces while events in northwestern Europe decided the outcome of the war.

Chapter 6

Storming Fortress Europe

"You are about to embark upon the Great Crusade, toward which we have striven these many months. The eyes of the world are upon you. . . . Your enemy is well trained, well equipped, and battle-hardened. He will fight savagely. . . . I have full confidence in your courage, devotion to duty, and skill in battle. We will accept nothing less than full Victory!"

— General Dwight Eisenhower's message to Allied soldiers,
sailors, and airmen, 6 June 1944

Just after midnight on 6 June 1944, men of the 704th Tank Destroyer Battalion, stationed at Tilshead, England, were disturbed by the deep, soul-shaking roar of hundreds of planes passing overhead on their way to France. The men knew that this was it.[1]

Soon, the parachutes of the British 6th Airborne Division caught the air in the dark sky northeast of Caen, while the men of the American 101st and 82d Airborne divisions leapt into the unknown near Ste. Mere-Eglise and Carentan. Their mission was to secure road junctions and exit routes from the invasion beaches on the coast of Normandy. When the sky brightened, gliders bearing more paratroopers landed in hedgerow-bounded fields, and Allied bombers and fighter-bombers began the first of the eleven thousand sorties they would fly that day against German emplacements, troop concentrations, and transportation nodes.[2]

At 0530 hours, those warships with fire missions among the seven hundred in the vast Allied armada off the choppy Norman coast turned their guns toward land and bombarded the beaches assigned to Commonwealth forces. Twenty minutes later, shells began to crash into the German defenses along the American beaches, codenamed Omaha and Utah.

At 0630, doughs of the 4th Infantry Division and amphibious Duplex Drive (DD) Sherman tanks from the 70th Tank Battalion hit the beach at Utah, the VII Corps landing area. Within three hours, they had overwhelmed the defenses and were moving inland to link up with the airborne, all at a cost of only one hundred ninety-seven ground-force casualties.

The V Corps landing at Omaha, conducted by elements of the 1st and 29th Infantry divisions and the 741st and 743d Tank battalions, encountered heavy seas and an extraordinarily difficult job. Most of the 741st's DD tanks sank and, as General Eisenhower had predicted in his message to the invasion force, the Germans along the beach fought savagely. Nevertheless, by the afternoon the doughs and tanks clawed their way off the sand. They left twenty-five hundred casualties in their wake.[3]

The North Africa veterans of the 899th Tank Destroyer Battalion, less Reconnaissance and B companies and the administrative elements, rolled off their landing craft at Utah Beach as part of the twenty-fifth wave on 6 June. About 2015 hours, the TDs—attached to 4th Infantry Division artillery—moved into positions just south of Audoville La Hubert to provide antitank defense to division and artillery headquarters. One platoon encountered sporadic light machine-gun and some small-arms fire.[4]

The Tank Destroyer Force had entered Hitler's Fortress Europa.

*   *   *

The U.S. Army had allocated forty-eight tank destroyer battalions for the fight in Western Europe, plus four that were scheduled to transfer from Italy when Operation Anvil (later called Dragoon)—the invasion of southern France—commenced in August. In accordance with the wishes of higher headquarters, half of these battalions were towed. As of 4 June,

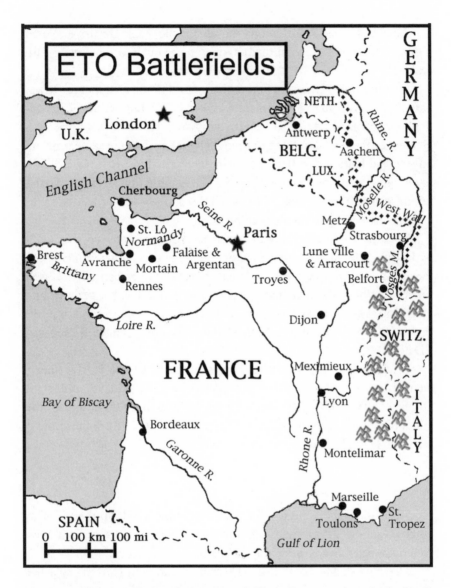

nineteen self-propelled and eleven towed battalions were ready for battle in England.[5]

The important role played by TDs in Italy as supporting artillery had made an impression on Army planners. All TD battalions in England were issued fire direction sets, switchboards, telephones, wire, aiming circles, and the other accoutrements necessary to accomplish basic surveys and fire direction. The battalions all conducted indirect-fire training as time allowed.[6]

June 1944 was a portentous month for the Tank Destroyer Force, although there is little sign that anyone on the chain of command fully realized it.

Amphibious maneuvers before the invasion indicated that the towed battalions were extremely vulnerable when offloading on the beach and deploying for battle. As a result, the Army reduced the towed-gun element of the invasion force to a single battalion.[7] At the same time, the only towed battalion in Italy was being converted to M18s. Clearly, the towed-gun concept was in trouble. The situation was somewhat reminiscent of the dispatch of the first TD battalions to North Africa with an obsolete organization and equipment.

The first M4 Shermans with 76mm main guns had arrived in England by D-Day. Although the new version did not enter combat immediately, the fire-power gap between tank and tank destroyer had been erased. Indeed, the new Sherman had thicker armor than a TD, boasted machine guns, and was about as fast as the M10. If a tank was as good or better than a TD in almost every respect, what was the point of having a separate TD arm?

On 16 May, Army Ground Forces had asked the ETO whether it wanted any of the new M36 tank destroyers under development by Ordnance. The M36 was essentially an M10 with a 90mm antiaircraft gun mounted in a redesigned, open-topped turret to perform the antitank mission. The ETO expressed no interest.[8]

*   *   *

The GIs and Tommies fell short of almost all of their D-Day objectives. Four days of hard fighting passed before the troops in the two American beachheads were able to link up.

The men of the 635th Tank Destroyer Battalion (towed) splashed ashore across Omaha Beach from LSTs and Rhino barges on D+2 and were initially attached to 1st Infantry Division artillery. By nightfall, the gun companies were parceled out to the infantry regiments and the gun platoons to the infantry battalions in what became standard operating procedure for the employment of towed TD battalions. As the outfit's AAR noted, "[the gun platoons] were not under 635th Battalion control but were part of each [infantry] battalion and were used by the battalion commanders as antitank guns."

This use reflected a recognition that the doughboys' standard-issue 57mm antitank gun could not handle the threat posed by German tanks. Indeed, the Army command planned before the invasion to attach a towed TD battalion to each infantry division and to hold the SP battalions in corps and army reserves. By D-Day, it had already amended this decision by attaching one SP TD battalion to each armored division.[9]

*   *   *

The 702d Tank Destroyer Battalion landed at Omaha Beach on 11 June. The men expected to surge ashore in six feet of water with guns blazing so were pleasantly surprised to roll ashore almost dry and find military police directing traffic. The battalion moved that night to La Mine, where the stench convinced the men that they were surrounded by German corpses. Dawn revealed a dead bull in the center of the CP.[10]

After consolidating the beachheads, Allied forces built up with amazing speed. In less than four weeks, nearly one million men and 177,000 vehicles landed, along with more than 500,000 tons of supplies to keep them fighting.[11] In the American sector, two more corps—VIII and XIX—became active during that time.

The Tank Destroyer Force kept pace. The 1st Tank Destroyer Group came ashore at Utah Beach on 12 June 1944, the M10s of the 803d Tank Destroyer Battalion rolled across Omaha Beach that same day, and more outfits followed. By the end of the month, the 801st, 612th, 607th, 823d, 821st, 813th, and 634th had arrived in a parade of clanking M10 and prime mover tracks.

*   *   *

The first major American objective inland was the port of Cherbourg, and by 18 June, MajGen J. Lawton Collins's VII Corps had wheeled from Utah Beach and cut across the Cotentin Peninsula on which the city is located. The 1st Platoon of A/899th Tank Destroyer Battalion joined the task force that accomplished the mission the night of 17–18 June. Company A was strafed four times by American P-51 fighters on 22 June, and one TD was set on fire but saved.[12]

The remnants of five German divisions defended Cherbourg, and they had orders from Hitler to fight to the last.[13] The M10s from the 899th pushed toward the port with the doughs of the 9th Infantry Division, and TDs engaged pillboxes and AT guns as the Americans approached the outskirts. On 22 June, one M10 crew from 2d Platoon of Company C—which was supporting the 47th Infantry Regiment—confronted a 77mm AT gun that commanded the road at Le Motel. Smoke was placed on the gun, and the M10 rolled onto the street and destroyed the German weapon from only three hundred yards distance. The next day, a second destroyer from the platoon boldly drove around a blind corner and from a distance of one hundred fifty yards engaged a concealed 88 that was pounding the infantry. The TD lost a track, but the 88 lost its crew.[14]

While the towed guns of the 801st Tank Destroyer Battalion placed direct fire on three of Cherbourg's fortifications, the doughs, M10s from the 899th, and tanks entered the city on 25 June. 2d Platoon of Company C helped knock out five 20mm and one 47mm guns during heavy street fighting. Twice, the only tactic available to the crews was to dash around a corner while under fire—shooting while moving—and to engage the target.[15]

Cherbourg fell, but the Germans sabotaged the port facilities so thoroughly that the engineers needed three weeks to repair them sufficiently to handle minimal shipping.[16]

With the capture of Cherbourg, LtGen Omar Bradley on 3 July turned First Army south to drive inland through the heart of the bocage, as Normandy's hedgerow country is known in French. The troops encountered stiff resistance at every turn. Casualties mounted alarmingly for little gain in territory. Indeed, the next three weeks would cause senior Allied commanders to worry that they were falling into a stalemate similar to that of trench warfare during World War I.[17]

Throwing Away the Manual

Allied planners had selected the invasion area in part because it offered superb natural inland defenses for the beachhead. The hedgerow-covered terrain in most of the zone was unsuitable for German armored counterattacks.[18]

The terrain also was not particularly suitable for Allied combined-arms attacks, either. The U.S. Army described the conditions in its lessons learned report on the fighting in Normandy:

The terrain in the area selected for the initial penetration of French soil was generally level or gently sloping. However, it was broken up into a "crazy quilt" pattern of small fields separated by hedgerows. These consisted of an earthen mound or wall eight to ten feet in width and four to six feet in height, covered with a scrub undergrowth.

Along the top of this wall grew rows of trees. Forming an important part of the obstacle thus created was the ditch that ran along one or both sides of the mound. The roads, narrow and winding, ran between these hedgerows, and offered the defenders many advantageous positions for ambuscades or surprise attacks on advancing foot-troops and armor. Observation was normally limited [to] from one hedgerow to the next. . . .[19]

The Germans exploited the conditions to establish an extraordinarily effective defense in depth. The bocage became a seemingly infinite series of strongpoints, each concealing infantry with "bazookas" (TD crews applied this catch-all phrase to one-man panzerfausts and larger crew-served antitank rockets), machine guns, AT guns, sometimes armor, and nearly always mortar and artillery support.

Incredibly, American forces had conducted virtually no training to operate in the hedgerows, and units on the line were left to work out the best approach through trial and error. The U.S. Army's Center of Military History attributes this lack of preparation to an assumption among invasion planners that the Germans would withdraw to the Seine River. Whatever the cause, the riflemen paid with a river of blood. A U.S. Army survey of casualties in portions of the 1st, 4th, 9th, and 25th Infantry divisions between 6 June and 31 July 1944 found that infantry companies lost nearly 60 percent of their enlisted men and more than 68 percent of their officers.[20] These casualties, naturally, were concentrated in the combat elements.

The key to the solution lay in creating effective tactics for the infantry, their supporting separate tank battalions, and, less problematic, the artillery. The fate of the tank destroyers revolved around this dynamic because—with a single exception—they were not called upon to fight large German armor attacks during the fighting in the Normandy beachhead.[21] The Germans faced the same difficulties as the Americans in the bocage and found that they could rarely employ more than a platoon or company of tanks at once.[22] On the VIII Corps front in June and July, for example, German tanks were rare, but the enemy had many

SP and assault guns that he employed in close support of the infantry. On the XIX Corps front, the TDs encountered some Mark IVs and Mark V Panthers, which were typically employed during frequent counterattacks in groups of between two and seven in support of the infantry.[23]

The Sherman tank could crawl across about half of the hedgerows, but in doing so it risked getting stuck, or exposing its thin belly to enemy fire, and having knocked loose everything inside the vehicle that was not tied down. The tankers first resolved the problem by using tank-dozers to knock holes in the hedges. Within two weeks of D-Day, the infantry-tank team began to develop through trial and error the technique that—with local variations—would see the men through Normandy. Engineers blew one or more holes through a hedgerow with explosives, and the armor raced through to support the riflemen on the far side. (Interestingly, the German Panzer Lehr Division also settled on using a mix of tank, infantry, and engineer companies amidst the hedgerows.[24]) The Germans naturally figured this out and quickly aimed their AT weapons at any gap that suddenly appeared in the far hedgerow.

This was as dangerous as it sounds. But there was nothing else to do.

The M10 Plays Tank

The U.S. Army concluded after the war that two factors determined the role self-propelled TDs wound up playing in the bocage.[25]

The first was the power of the terrain to force tactical decisions. Tank destroyers deployed even a few hundred yards behind the front line were unable to provide support and could not respond to the shallow, harassing German tank-infantry actions that characterized counterattacks. TDs, therefore, had to deploy more or less even with the infantry, no matter what doctrine said.

The second was the high attrition rate suffered by the separate tank battalions. Of those that landed on D-Day, for example, the 741st Tank Battalion lost most of its Shermans during the landing. From D-Day to 10 July, half the tanks in the 746th fell victim to enemy fire.[26] By 31 July, the 70th Tank Battalion was down forty Shermans and six M5s.[27] The 743rd Tank Battalion in June and July lost at least twenty-five officers and men killed in action and another one hundred sixteen wounded, or nearly one man in five.[28] The infantry divisions had little choice but to turn to the tank destroyers to augment the tanks in offensive operations.

803d Tank Destroyer Battalion CO LtCol Charles Goodwin described a typical SP outfit's experience during the hedgerow fighting in June and early July (in the course of which his men supported the doughs of the 2d, 29th, and 30th Infantry divisions and the 82d Airborne Division's paratroopers):

> This battalion has been utilized almost continuously as close support antitank defense immediately behind the front-line infantry and as actual tanks. . . . No previous theories or training directives contemplated the terrain or type of combat encountered in this zone. The hedgerows and heavily covered areas preclude observation and afford extremely limited fields of fire. Front-line infantry, with the exception of the 82d Airborne infantry, could not or would not point out targets of opportunity such as machine gun nests, pillboxes, etc. When such targets were located, however, excellent results were obtained from the 3-inch fire. OPs such as church steeples, tall trees, hilltops, etc., can be effectively eliminated.
>
> In the earliest combat, there was a tendency on the part of the infantry commanders to order the destroyers out in front of the infantry. It cannot be emphasized enough that this is fatal. The destroyer cannot substitute for the tank inasmuch as it is lightly armored and has no machine gun to keep hostile infantry down. The .50-caliber antiaircraft mount is useless for ground work. [We] suffered eight tank destroyer casualties during this early period, seven of which were caused by the German rocket launcher or rifle AT grenade. It is believed that these weapons possess a range not in excess of seventy-five yards. These weapons can penetrate any part of the tank destroyer, including the front and final drive. Had the destroyers remained behind the advancing infantry, these losses could have been avoided. This is evidenced by the fact that no tank destroyer casualties have been sustained from infantry weapons since infantry commanders have been prevented from using destroyers in front of infantry. It will be noted that Sherman tanks have suffered the same fate when operating in front of infantry. . . .
>
> While the assignment of the 803d Tank Destroyer Battalion in actual tank roles is contrary to basic policy, no member of this organization felt he could do otherwise. The infantry required every assistance they could obtain to perform their mission, and the morale factor plus the actual firepower of the tank destroyers did greatly benefit them. Casualties are no greater three hundred yards from the enemy than they were three thousand yards behind the front.[29]

As had his counterparts in Italy, Goodwin recommended in July that TD units be given a support mission—to be executed according to the best judgment of the TD commander—rather than being attached to an infantry unit. He also took the more practical step of welding the .50-caliber turret mounts on his M10s onto the front above the gun tube and providing crewmen with periscopes welded to the turret side so that they could fire the MG without exposing themselves. (Many other battalions adopted variants of this solution as the campaign progressed.) In July, Goodwin's men destroyed two tanks, two SP guns (plus one probable), at least a dozen machine gun positions, and two antitank guns. It lost eight men killed and thirty-eight wounded—but no more M10s.[30]

*   *   *

At 0300 hours on 11 July, Maj Hoyt Lawrence, commanding the 899th Tank Destroyer Battalion, was alerted to help doughs of the 9th Infantry Division repel what appeared to be a substantial German tank-infantry thrust in the vicinity of Le Desert. The infantry had reported the sound of tracked vehicles beginning around midnight, and fighting broke out a couple of hours later. Intelligence had detected the movement of the Panzer Lehr Division into the sector the day before. The armored division incorporated panzer tactics instructors from the training schools in Germany, but the unit had lost nearly one-third of its 15,000 men during fighting in the British sector. In the early hours of 11 July, division commander, Generalleutnant Fritz Bayerlein, counted only thirty-one tanks ready for battle. He also had two panzergrenadier regiments and three battalions of 105mm howitzers.[31]

Panzer Lehr deployed three columns in its attack, dividing the available tanks among two of them. The three axes were to converge at St. Jean de Daye. Unknown to the Germans, the spearheads struck the Americans where a gap had developed between the 39th and 47th Infantry regiments. The attackers overran a battalion CP and pushed as far as two thousand yards behind American lines.

The M10 crews engaged the attackers in the darkness, firing at dimly seen shapes despite the knowledge that the flash from the 3-inch guns betrayed their position to German panzers, infantry, and artillery. Sergeant Nicholas Peters and the other men in 1st Platoon, Company A, were holding defensive positions with the 39th Infantry Regiment, along with the rest of the company. The Panzer Lehr attack carried by their position about three hundred yards east of Le Desert. The TDs pivoted and raced down a parallel route until they could engage the head of the German column.

The TDs opened fire on the lead panzer, which burst into flames. The bonfire exposed three more Panthers, and Peters ordered his gunner to engage. The TDs set two more Mark Vs alight before the German column withdrew. But the Jerries accounted for one M10 before they left.[32]

The battle was the 899th's first encounter with the Mark V, and by dawn the crews realized that their guns could not penetrate the Panther's frontal armor.

The men knew what to do. They bravely maneuvered into flanking positions, often at nearly point-blank ranges. And the panzers burned.[33]

To the west of Le Desert, Pvt Pat Rufo sat in an M10 in 3d Platoon of Company A. The platoon had already destroyed a Mark IV—one of ten panzers advancing along an unimproved road—by firing at gun flashes in the darkness. One M10 had been KO'd during the fire fight, and the company commander requested infantry support.

Three Panthers were spotted on a nearby dirt road, and Rufo's M10 was ordered into an adjacent field to engage them. The M10 had the drop on the panzers, and a dozen rounds destroyed the Panthers and a halftrack.[34]

Later that day, SSgt Herschel Briles, from the 3d Platoon of Company C, dismounted to lead his M10 down the road in search of the enemy. Shortly after daybreak, he and his crew had destroyed a heavily camouflaged Panther. Now Briles carefully reconnoitered past the wreck. A second Panther appeared on the road just in front of the sergeant. Briles yelled for his gunner to fire as he dropped flat. The 3-inch gun barked, but the Panther's turret rotated toward the M10. The gunner corrected his aim, and the gun spoke again in awful harmony with the long-barreled 75mm on the Panther. Both shots killed. (One post-war account describes a more extended fire fight, but contemporary records portray the action as indicated here.)

Briles counted the men bailing out of his M10, and the total was one short. The sergeant raced back and leapt to the deck. Ammo was beginning to explode inside the turret, but Briles grabbed a fire extinguisher and managed to put out the flames. The last crewman, alas, was dead.[35]

Panzer Lehr conceded failure before dusk and coiled back. It had lost one Mark IV and twelve Panthers to the guns of the 899th, and more to fighter-bombers that joined the fray during the day.[36] The forward deployment of the tank destroyers with the infantry had worked, and the team had smashed the only major armored attack against the Americans during the beachhead fighting.

*   *   *

The attachment of tank destroyer companies and platoons directly to infantry regiments and battalions raised two major challenges for TD officers. The first was that TD outfits were neither trained nor organized to establish close and continuing liaison with the infantry units beside which they now fought in close quarters. Nor did the two arms share radio gear that could communicate with one another. In some units, the company administrative officer became the liaison contact with the infantry regiment, and a recon platoon was attached with the commander to take on the administrative duties. In other units, the battalion staff sent additional personnel down to the line companies to take on the regimental liaison duties. The TD platoon commander often set up shop at the infantry battalion CP and controlled his vehicles by radio. This left the burden of tactical command on the scene to the platoon sergeant.[37]

The second problem was that the attachment of TD companies and platoons to infantry regiments on a continuing basis effectively ended the TD battalion headquarters' control over them. The battalion staff soon exercised no more than a supply function, and in some cases it was unable to do even that. Once battle commenced, even company commanders lost most of their influence over the employment of their line platoons.[38]

*   *   *

Lieutenant Wilfred Ford commanded 2d Platoon of B/899th Tank Destroyer Battalion, which from 14 to 18 July supported the doughs of the 2/60th Infantry Regiment in the 9th Infantry Division's drive from Les Champs de Losque to cut the St. Lô–Periers road. The German infantry in this sector had armor support, too, and the panzers were extremely well camouflaged amidst the hedgerows and orchards. Company B, meanwhile, had only eight M10s still serviceable.

Early on 14 July German infantry penetrated Company B positions and attacked with grenades and small arms. Crews resorted to .50-calibers, carbines, and grenades to beat the raid off. After the shooting stopped, seventeen German bodies lay around 1st Platoon's positions alone.

When the doughs started forward in the morning light, one of Ford's M10s was hit and burned. In the bocage, it was practically impossible to tell where the fire originated.

Ford tackled the problem by personally accompanying the infantry forward on reconnaissance to spot not only the German positions but also concealed routes of approach and firing points for his M10s. He also hit upon the idea of asking the infantry to cover the sound of his vehicles' forward movement with noisy firing demonstrations.

Second Platoon got its first kill—a tank believed to have been a Mark V—at 1345 on 15 July with three rounds fired at only one hundred yards. The Panther burned. A short while later, the platoon had a second M10 damaged when a shell burst perforated the radiator of one motor.

The next day, Ford's TDs again moved out to provide direct-fire support to the doughs. Two panzers had been spotted, and the M10s crept forward and opened fire. One Mark IV began to smoke, and the other withdrew.

For all the reconnaissance and planning by the young lieutenant, the needs of the infantry commander took over once the shooting started. Several hours after the first engagement, Sergeant Ward pulled his M10 into a field. To his left, he could see three Sherman tanks working with the doughs. The infantry battalion commander ordered Ward to pull even with his forward line. As the M10 crossed the open area to the next hedgerow, a 75mm round penetrated the thin armor and set the vehicle on fire. Crewmen sprinted to safety in a ditch.

The infantry commander ordered another one of Ford's TDs to fire on some houses. Sergeant Shicks pulled up but first shot five or six rounds into the next hedgerow to flush out the suspected antitank gun. Shicks's gun jammed. About this time, another lieutenant arrived to relieve Ford, who was ordered to move over and take charge of 1st Platoon. The other lieutenant mounted Sergeant Lum's M10, which swung past Shicks and advanced. Ten minutes later, the M10 was hit by a round that severely wounded the lieutenant and Sergeant Lums, and killed or wounded most of the crew. Ford's transfer was off, and thanks to the arrival of a replacement M10, the platoon still had something with which to fight.

The 2d Platoon's gunners destroyed two tanks, two SP guns, and one halftrack-mounted 75mm gun between 14 and 18 July, despite the trying conditions.

One German Panzer Lehr tanker captured by nearby Company C told interrogators that the he and his comrades were not all that worried by bombing, but they did not like the TDs (even though four 3-inch rounds had bounced off his Panther before it was KO'd!).[39]

The Problem with Towed Guns

Despite having their guns deployed with the front-line infantry, the towed battalions did almost no tank killing and expended most of their ammunition in indirect fire. While working with the 1st Infantry Division, for example, the 3-inch gun crews from the 635th during all of June saw precisely one German tank—which had evidently suffered mechanical failure—and they encountered none in July. The battalion could only claim to have killed at least six enemy soldiers during exchanges of machine-gun fire.[40] The 801st, which landed on 13 June and supported the 4th Infantry Division, knocked out a single panzer (using a bazooka) in mid-July.[41] Despite many false alarms, the 802d did not see any panzers during its first month of fighting in July.[42]

The difficulty in actually bringing the towed guns into play is also reflected in the extremely low casualties suffered by the battalions. The 635th in June lost six men killed and ten wounded, and another three and ten, respectively, in July.[43] The 801st lost only one man seriously wounded in June and a handful more to mortar fire in July.[44] Other battalions suffered somewhat higher levels of casualties, but none approached the losses in the self-propelled—much less the tank—battalions.

The towed commands learned quickly that they had to dig in—and sandbag their positions, if possible—because of German artillery and mortar fire. This tended to make gun positions quasi-permanent. Because the barrels were so close to the ground, the crews usually had to cut their own roads to firing positions and then cut down one or more hedgerows in front of them to create a field of fire. All this left the guns more vulnerable to observation and made extraction for quick redeployment against armored threats from a new direction exceedingly difficult.

The towed units also discovered that they could not fight effectively on the move. Driving was painfully slow for the M3 halftrack prime movers and guns down the narrow dirt roads of the bocage. Experiments carried out by the 821st Tank Destroyer Battalion suggested that towed guns moving into even reconnoitered but unprepared positions would not have enough time to get off the road to a place with a proper field of fire quickly enough to combat a tank attack. This meant guns would have to deploy in the road itself—a recipe for disaster.[45]

The invasion had hardly begun when infantry division commanders realized the drawbacks to towed TD units and demanded SP battalions. To the extent that a surplus of SP battalions was available beyond the needs of the armored divisions, they were assigned to the infantry. The Army also raised the priority for SP battalions in the shipping schedules.[46]

The towed battalions had a somewhat easier time establishing radio links with the infantry because mobility was not an issue. Each gun company in the 802d Tank Destroyer Battalion, for example, was ordered on 12 July to send one SCR-608 radio to their supported infantry regiment's CP, while Battalion supplied one to 83d Infantry Division headquarters.[47]

A Sudden Feeling of Impotence

Early encounters with Panther tanks in the bocage demonstrated the alarming fact that the 3-inch/76mm gun could not penetrate the panzer's frontal armor except at near point-blank ranges or the occasional lucky shot. (Later clashes with Tigers would produce the same results.) Ike lamented, "You mean our 76 won't knock these Panthers out? I thought it was going to be the wonder gun of the war. Why is it I'm always the last to hear about this stuff? Ordnance told me this 76 would take care of anything the Germans had. Now I find you can't knock out a damn thing with it."[48]

On 6 July, the American European command cabled Army Ground Forces and requested that all M10 battalions be converted to the M36 and that no more M10 battalions be shipped to the ETO.[49] By mid-July, TD officers were discussing whether they could integrate 90mm antiaircraft guns into their operations.[50]

The tank destroyer crews had faced Tigers and Panthers in Italy and come away supremely confident in their ability to defeat the enemy. Now there was a widespread feeling of inadequacy regarding the very same equipment. What had changed?

The irony was that important aspects of the tank destroyer doctrine had worked in North Africa and Italy—imperfectly, as most plans will in the real world, but they had worked! The only times that American troops had encountered panzers in large numbers, the Germans had been attacking. Yes, reality had thrown a curve ball by confronting the tank killers with combined-arms attacks, but in every case in which a tank destroyer battalion had been able to respond more or less as a whole, the tank killers had beaten the Panzertruppe. El Guettar, Salerno, Anzio, and even Le Desert in Normandy had worked out more or less as General Bruce and his brain trust had foreseen. The massed fire of many TDs from various angles had been so effective that even when the crews had watched rounds bounce of the thick armor on the front of the Marks V and VI, other shots had struck home. Indeed, the TDs had usually dished out lopsided losses to the enemy. Only at Kasserine Pass, where TD units were committed piecemeal, had the tank destroyers failed.

Tank destroyers working together could beat the heavy German armor when playing defense, with all the advantages that accrue to the defender.

The problem, again, was that the doctrine was incomplete. While offensive in spirit, it was defensive in nature and offered no real plan for TD crews participating in attacks against small panzer elements spread out among dug-in infantry. The fighting in North Africa and Italy had hinted at this problem, but the best German armor had been scarce in the former, and mountainous conditions in the latter had usually precluded the use of large numbers of TDs at any one time.

Now, the Germans would enjoy the advantages of the defender against American armor in most situations. The question was, would they come out and attack en masse again and allow the Tank Destroyer Force to return to its game plan?

Chapter 7

Armored Thunder

"As of August 14, the Third Army had advanced farther
and faster than any army in history."

— George Patton Jr. *War As I Knew It*

On 25 July 1944, as LtGen Courtney Hodges's First Army launched
Operation Cobra, LtGen George Patton's Third Army waited impatiently
to the rear to become operational and exploit the hoped-for breakthrough.
The beachhead fighting had mostly involved the TD outfits attached to
the infantry divisions. Now armored divisions made ready to roll, and it
was time to test the TDs in blitzkrieg, American-style.

Lieutenant General Omar Bradley had conceived Cobra as a way to
end the bloody hedgerow war with a major breakthrough on a narrow
front west of St. Lô. He planned a massive air attack by strategic bombers
and fighter-bombers to crack the German line. As eventually formulated
by VII Corps, three infantry divisions—the 30th, 9th, and 4th—were to
punch a hole in the defenses. The 2d and 3d Armored divisions and 1st
Infantry Division (Motorized) were to provide the initial exploitation
forces. Eighth Corps—which would attack under First Army control and

go to Patton when Third Army stood up—had the 4th and 6th Armored divisions ready, as well as the 8th and 79th Infantry divisions. Behind them, three more Third Army corps were building up.[1]

The portents had not been favorable. Bad weather forced cancellation of the planned kickoff on 24 July, but the word did not reach most of the Eighth Air Force strategic bombers in time. Most were unable to identify their targets and did not bomb, but one flight dropped its bombs on positions of the 30th Infantry Division when the lead bombardier—who was struggling with a sticky release—inadvertently loosed his load and caused fifteen other B-17s to follow suit. Twenty-five American soldiers died, and one hundred thirty-one were wounded. A Ninth Air Force B-24 accidentally bombed an American airfield at Chippelle, France, and destroyed two medium bombers and the crews. And one P-47 Thunderbolt struck an ammo dump that, regrettably, belonged to the Allies.[2]

The omens did not dramatically improve in the early hours of 25 July. More than five hundred fifty fighter-bombers from the IX Tactical Air Command (TAC) dropped more than two hundred tons of bombs and a large amount of napalm. Fifteen hundred B-17 and B-24 heavy bombers from the U.S. Eighth Air Force dropped more than thirty-three hundred tons of bombs, while some three hundred eighty B-26 medium bombers unloaded more than six hundred fifty tons of high explosive and fragmentation bombs. Some seventy-five of the bombers dropped their loads within American lines, and short bombs killed one hundred eleven American soldiers. Among them was LtGen Leslie McNair, godfather to the Tank Destroyer Force, who had come to observe the breakout.

But the unfortunate Panzer Lehr Division, which had replaced some of its armor lost to the guns of the 899th Tank Destroyer Battalion two weeks earlier, absorbed most of the carpet bombing. The war of attrition in the bocage had been hell on the American GI, but it had hurt the Germans badly, too. In all of Normandy (including the British sector), the Germans between 6 June and 9 July lost two thousand officers and eighty-five thousand men and received only five thousand replacements. They had also lost one hundred fifty Mark IVs, eighty-five Panthers, fifteen Tigers, one hundred sixty-seven 75mm assault guns and antitank guns, and almost thirty 88mm guns.[3] They were running out of men, and the collapsing Eastern Front demanded every available replacement.[4] A mere five thousand men held the line in front of the six divisions of VII

Corps, and they were backed by no more than twenty-five thousand others in the area, counting reserve, supply, and headquarters personnel.[5]

Panzer Lehr was virtually annihilated by the air strikes. Generalleutnant Fritz Bayerlein estimated that 70 percent of his men were killed, wounded, or stunned.[6]

Where German troops survived the destruction, however, they fought on bravely, and VII Corps' initial advance was slow. The VII Corps commanding general, MajGen J. Lawton Collins, decided on 26 July to commit his armor and the 1st Infantry Division in the expectation that the extra weight would crack the German defenses.

Combat Command A/2d Armored Division crossed its line of departure at 0945 hours. By 1035, the tankers were through the German defenses. Accompanied by the M10s of the 702d Tank Destroyer Battalion (less Company B), CCA was off to wreak havoc in the German rear.[7] The TDs were held in reserve in the columns and had no initial contact with the enemy.[8]

By 27 July, the breakthrough had become unstoppable. The 3d Armored Division and attached 703d Tank Destroyer Battalion attacked at 0530 hours.[9] Combat Command B/2d Armored Division—supported by Company B, 702d Tank Destroyer Battalion—attacked that same day and, because of delays elsewhere, became the corps spearhead. On the fly, the combat command received orders to hook to the coast and cut off the retreat of German forces still holding out to the north. By the next afternoon, the command had established a long, thinly held line of roadblocks that barred the path to the trapped Germans.[10]

The Germans tried to break free, and a series of violent and isolated battles flamed along CCB's cordon. About 0900 on 29 July, fifteen panzers and several hundred paratroopers attacked the 78th Field Artillery Battalion—supported by four destroyers from Company B of the 702d—at a crossroads near La Penetiere. The assault collapsed a company-sized infantry screen. The M10s, two artillery batteries, and the antiaircraft section unleashed a fusillade of direct fire, while the third battery provided indirect fire support. Until reinforcements arrived thirty minutes later, these guns were all that prevented a German penetration. The attackers withdrew, leaving nine panzers and one hundred twenty-six men behind.[11]

*   *   *

The M10s of several TD battalions—including the 644th, 818th, and 893d—sported newly installed "Culin hedgerow devices."[12] Designed by Sergeant Curtis G. Culin of the 102d Cavalry Reconnaissance Squadron, the contraption (the 3d Armored Group referred to them as "Rube Goldbergs") was made from steel girders from German beach defenses. It amounted to a set of steel teeth protruding from the nose of the tank and could be mounted on tanks or TDs. The teeth allowed the vehicle to grip and plow through a hedgerow with hardly any loss of speed. A similar device that looked more like a blade was referred to as the "green dozer." Vehicles outfitted with the Culin device were called "Rhinos." Tank and TD battalions hurriedly installed the devices during the second half of July in preparation for Operation Cobra, and by the time Cobra began, 60 percent of the tanks involved had been fitted with Culin devices.[13] The invention gave American armor a decisive edge in mobility over German panzers during the final phase of the Normandy campaign. In fact, the use of the Rhino in combat was barred until the launch of Cobra in order to maintain tactical surprise.[14]

*   *   *

On 28 July, Patton took control of VIII Corps (he acted as the deputy 12th Army Group commander under Bradley for three days until Third Army officially became operational). Patton characteristically led with his tanks. The 4th and 6th Armored divisions lunged toward Avranche, the gateway to Brittany and central France, twenty-five miles distant.[15] Among the first targets fired on by the 4th Armored Division were men of the 2d Armored Division who had helped open the door. Pointed radio communications quickly resolved the matter.[16]

The 704th Tank Destroyer Battalion had been formed out of the 4th Armored Division, spent three-quarters of its Stateside training time with the division, and remained attached to the 4th Armored for most of the European campaign.[17] M18 crewman Roy Roberson recalled:

> The 4th Armored Division, with the 704th attached, plunged out through a dazed enemy. But the knockout was far from complete. Very soon, a German tank opened fire and knocked out five of our halftracks.
>   Lieutenant Addision took his 2d Platoon with Sgt [Joe] Schedevy's tank leading and roared forward to engage the enemy.

Sergeant Schedevy spotted the Jerry tank first. M18 driver Technician Fifth Grade Beck whipped the tank around into a firing position and gunner Corporal Treet laid the crosshairs on the center of the [German cross] and fired the first direct-fire round for the 704th. It was a good shot and did the job. Before the TD stopped rocking, Treet spotted another Jerry behind a hedgerow. The Jerry fired at our TD and missed. A second round from Treet left the Kraut going up in smoke. Two more enemy tanks, panic-stricken, tried to escape and exposed their positions. Second Platoon tanks fired four more shots and neutralized the enemy. . . .[18]

Eighth Corps charged through Avranches late on 31 July and crossed the Selune River. "Now that's my kind of fighting," Patton said. "Those troops know their business. We'll keep right on going, full speed ahead."

Patton ordered a two-pronged assault into Brittany: The 4th Armored and 8th Infantry divisions were to advance on Rennes, and the 6th Armored and 79th Infantry divisions were to seize Brest at the tip of the peninsula. Task Force A was created to clear the north coast.[19]

Task Force A was controlled by the 1st Tank Destroyer Brigade, an oddball formation in its only combat appearance. Only two TD brigades were ever organized, and the second disbanded before leaving the States. The brigade was envisioned as the controlling headquarters for a number of TD groups, each consisting of several battalions. Even the Army appeared unclear as to its purpose, but notionally that appeared to be to serve as the kernel for an add-hoc command to deal with massive enemy armored offensives. The task force included the 2d Cavalry Group, the 15th Cavalry Group, the 6th Tank Destroyer Group, the 705th Tank Destroyer Battalion, the 159th Engineer Combat Battalion, and the 509th Engineer Light Company. The command would advance to St. Malo, side-slip, and meet the 6th Armored Division at Brest.[20]

This task force is noteworthy because it established a pattern for Third Army's frequent use of M18-equipped battalions in concert with cavalry units. The speedy Hellcats were able to keep up with the fastest cavalry thrusts and provided firepower that the light units lacked.[21]

The task force also displayed the American ingenuity in combat. The 705th Tank Destroyer Battalion on 4 August ran into a heavily defended roadblock near Chateauneuf. Headquarters Company deployed as infantry, but the Germans held firm despite point-blank fire from supporting M10s. The battalion finally cleared the block with indirect fire from an 81mm mortar mounted on the outfit's wrecker.[22]

The TD battalions fought attached to widely dispersed units. As a consequence, reconnaissance companies sometimes performed their role for divisions rather than their battalions. The recon men of the 603d Tank Destroyer Battalion, for example, led the 6th Armored Division's advance to Brest—where it took five hundred prisoners—and subsequently to Lorient.[23] Other battalions, such as the 628th, split the recon company up and assigned one platoon to each of the scattered gun companies.[24]

* * *

A TD battalion operating with an armored division was blessed with a robust and effective integration with the big unit that tank killers with infantry divisions could only envy. A company commander, for example, could communicate by radio with his own platoon leaders and individual vehicles, the armored combat command, the artillery, and close air support. The company was far closer to being an organic component of the combat command than part of the distant and rarely encountered TD battalion to which it belonged.[25] Indeed, battalion CPs quickly lost even radio contact with their far-flung companies because of the large distances involved.[26] And armored divisions tended to view their attached TD battalions as an organic component—in part because the attachments tended to be lasting. The 3d Armored Divisions history, for example, notes, "Although originally wearing the [panther] patch of TD service, the fiercely independent 703d finally adopted the 'Spearhead' patch and was as much a part of the division as any of its own tank battalions."[27]

Captain Thomas Evans, CO of C/704th Tank Destroyer Battalion, described operations with the 4th Armored Division during the breakout:

> We traveled mainly on highways and on paved roads as much as possible. The forward elements of the combat command, usually reconnaissance, would travel ahead and on both the right and left of the columns. . . . A company of tanks would usually lead the column, and interspersed back, they'd tell [us our] position in the column, depending on what they were going to do that day. . . .

If [reconnaissance] hit any resistance, they moved off the road and the tanks set up to attack whatever it was if need be. Of course, the [armored] infantry pulled off, too. They immediately moved up on foot behind the tanks and decided whether they were going to attack that particular position. The same time they were getting ready, the mechanized artillery would pull off and set up to fire. So we had almost instantaneous fire support. . . .

We traveled twenty, thirty, sometimes forty miles each day, all the way across France. The whole column was just moving at lightning speed. We'd hit some resistance, get off the road, and fight to break the resistance. We didn't even mop up lots of times. We left that to the troops behind us. . . .

We, the combat command mostly, would call for air strikes [by the XIX Tactical Air Command] if we ran into resistance that would take a head-on attack to overcome. The P-47s would come in and drop their 500-pound bombs and strafe the area. In my command vehicle, I had a crystal in my radio so that I could call for an air strike if it was necessary.[28]

In Brittany, the 4th Armored Division reached Rennes on 1 August. The TDs of Evans's company made a demonstration against the defenders while the rest of CCA executed a double envelopment and drove through a ferocious storm of German artillery fire into the city. The M18s then pulled back a thousand yards and picked off eight or ten panzers and many trucks and horse-drawn artillery pieces as the defenders tried to escape. Two TDs were lost in this fighting.[29] Sergeant Roger Turcan, commander of one of the destroyed M18s, was awarded a Silver Star for continuing to load and fire his gun after three other members of the crew had been killed.[30]

The 6th Armored Division reached Brest by 9 August. During the subsequent siege, A/603d Tank Destroyer Battalion was ordered to fire indirect missions with the goal of provoking counter-battery fire by the big guns in the fortifications in order to locate and destroy them. The battalion's records to not indicate how the men felt about this mission.[31]

The informal history of the 644th Tank Destroyer Battalion, an M10 outfit that supported the 8th Infantry Division during the capture of Brest, recorded: "The operation was nastier than anyone anticipated. We found that we were facing a combination of paratroopers, marines, sailors, and fortress troops, well armed, cocky, and beautifully dug in. Hill 88, Kergroas, Pontanezan Barracks, the fort on the river, and a dozen other tight spots will stand in the history of this war as some of the toughest in

Europe. Company A had to pick up rations in M10s, the pioneers dug Company C's destroyers in on the outpost line at night, and Company B led the infantry from one critical point to the next. We watched the P-47s drop gasoline bombs, we put out red panels and were bombed by our own P-38s, watched a [B-17] go down when it collided with a Thuderbolt, began to take prisoners. Also, the Krauts had a few coastal guns that shook us up at night."[32]

*   *   *

Meanwhile, on the eastern flank of the Avranches corridor, fighting had been fierce. Combat Command A/2d Armored Division became embroiled in a costly drive on Tessy sur Vire in support of XIX Corps, to which it was temporarily attached. During a thirteen-hour fight against a German counterattack on 28 July, the crews of the 702d Tank Destroyer battalion knocked out eleven panzers.[33] On 1 August, the tankers and TDs battled a tenacious 2d Panzer Division defense near Tessy sur Vire itself. The Germans had deployed along the reverse slope of a hill before Tessy and engaged the American armor as the tanks crested the ridge and exposed themselves on the skyline. Working along the highway, the tank killers from B/702d Tank Destroyer Battalion accounted for two Panthers and five Mark IVs. Other TDs of the 702d were assigned to support a flank attack that began about 1500, and the M10s ran into a swarm of panzers. Company A KO'd two Panthers and four Mark IVs.[34]

The 893d (SP) and 612th (towed) Tank Destroyer battalions operated with the 2d Infantry Division in the neighboring V Corps sector in its attack toward the Vire River. The M10s worked just to the rear of the assault battalions to defend them against armored penetrations. The towed outfit came next, and its 3-inch guns took over positions from the self-propelled TDs and provided flank protection as the attack progressed.[35]

Nineteenth and V corps had their hands full, but most everyone else was off and running.

The history of the 3d Armored Division recorded with regard to CCA, "So fast was the advance. . . that, at Brecey [on 30 July], the speeding combat command caught German troops lolling under shade trees, drinking wine. This was a pleasure that tommygun fire and grenades quickly terminated. Brecey, however, was the scene of more vicious fighting later. Company A of the 703d Tank Destroyer Battalion found the town had been reoccupied after the lead elements of CCA passed through. With their 3-inch guns, the TD men thoroughly wrecked the little town and again routed its garrison."[36]

On 2 August, Patton ordered XV Corps to begin the drive into central France while VIII Corps cleared Brittany. The 5th Armored and 83d and 90th Infantry divisions rolled south and east to secure the narrow corridor through Avranches on which every advancing unit depended for passage and supplies. The left end of XV Corps' initial line was anchored at St. Hilaire du Harcouêt, located about eight miles southwest of a town called Mortain.[37] The corps then pressed on toward Mayenne.

Elements of First Army were also shaking free and driving eastward.

M3 prime movers pulled the 3-inch guns of the 823d Tank Destroyer Battalion—which had landed on 24 June and was attached to the 30th Infantry Division—through rolling countryside with ever larger fields on both sides of the road. The unit history recorded that this was the first of the "victory marches" through Europe. "Civilians lined the roads ecstatically greeting 'les Americaines' and showering the troops with flowers, cider, and cognac. In return, the soldiers scattered cigarettes, chocolate, and chewing gum among the populace. Happy throngs waved jubilantly at the passing columns."

The men observed that the terrain was increasingly suitable for maneuver warfare. The column's destination was Mortain.[38]

On 4 August, British General Bernard Law Montgomery—who was still in command of Allied ground operations—ordered the first major change to the invasion plan. Patton was told to use minimum force to clear Brittany and to throw most of his troops eastward, with an initial objective of the Mayenne River. First Army would continue to attack in the Vire–Mortain area, making a tighter wheeling movement. Anglo-Canadian forces, meanwhile, would pivot toward Falaise and Argentan. The goal was to encircle German forces west of the Seine River or, barring that, to trap them against the river and destroy them. Mortain was the pivot point for all Allied movement.[39]

Counterblow at Mortain

On 1 August, Generalfeldmarschall Günther von Kluge, who had replaced Gerd von Rundstedt as commander of the Western Front in July, realized that the Americans had kicked in the door to France at Avranches. He immediately made preparations for a counteroffensive to close the American corridor, which he concluded was the only way to stem the tide. Consultations with Berlin indicated that Hitler supported the idea and envisioned a concerted effort by as many as nine panzer divisions. Trapped in the reality of a rapidly decaying situation, the best von Kluge could arrange was an attack by elements of four.[40]

Some two weeks earlier, Generalleutnant Heinz Guderian, newly appointed Chief of the General Staff, had observed to Hitler that von Kluge lacked a "lucky touch" in commanding large armored formations.[41]

The 1st SS, 2d SS, 2d, and 116th Panzer divisions received orders to concentrate east of Mortain. These units, however, were already weakened by attrition and had no more than two hundred fifty tanks among them—fewer than the authorized equipment of two full-strength panzer divisions.[42] The entire 2d SS Panzer Division had only thirty operational tanks remaining, and the 116th Panzer Division had only twenty-five. The 1st SS Panzer Division, meanwhile, was strung out on the roads from Normandy.[43] The attack nevertheless would begin at Mortain the night of 6–7 August.

Allied air reconnaissance and the Top Secret British Ultra code-breaking system detected the scope of the German build-up, and Bradley reacted. He deployed five infantry divisions along eighteen miles of front between Mortain and Vire, backed by two armored combat commands, and held three of Patton's divisions to anchor the right flank to the west of Mortain. He also increased pressure at Vire on the assembling German forces. Nevertheless, the German attack achieved tactical surprise.

The 30th Infantry Division was settling into positions recently vacated by the 1st Infantry Division astride the German axis of advance. Each regiment had attached a company of towed 3-inch tank destroyers from the 823d TD Battalion.

*   *   *

At 0130 hours on 7 August, firing broke out at the security outpost of the 3d Platoon, A/823d Tank Destroyer Battalion, as panzergrenadiers from the 2d SS Panzer Division attempted to infiltrate Mortain. Soldiers leapt to the .50-caliber machine guns on the halftracks and beat the attack off. But other German troops had more success and entered the town. Platoon commander Lt Elmer Miller decided to stick it out. But concentrated small-arms fire at close range made it impossible to serve the 3-inch towed guns, and his position was overrun. A few of Miller's men were able to join the 2d/120th Infantry Regiment, which would remain surrounded on the nearby heights for the next five days. Others escaped in small groups.[44]

In nearby Barthelmy, 3d Platoon of B/823d Tank Destroyer Battalion during the night of 6–7 August positioned two guns to the northwest and two to the southeast. About 0300 hours, the men could hear hostile tanks and troops, but they could see nothing through a thick fog that blanketed the area. Three hours later, a seventy-five-minute artillery barrage crashed down on the infantry and gun crews. Close on its heels came tanks and grenadiers from the 1st SS Panzer Division advancing from the north, east, and south.[45]

Reduced crews manned the 3-inch guns while the remainder grabbed their carbines and deployed as infantry to help the doughs. Sergeant Chester Christensen carefully sighted his gun on the lead Panther advancing from the south and destroyed it with a hit on the hull machine-gun ball mount. The subsequent explosion blew the turret off the vehicle. The hulk blocked the road, but within an hour the Germans had dragged it out of the way, and the panzers advanced again. Christensen again KO'd the lead tank, this time at a range of only thirty-five yards.[46]

A German assessment noted, "Well installed American antitank guns prevented at first every penetration of our tanks."[47] Indeed, the TDs claimed three more panzers—including one with a bazooka—but the Germans overwhelmed the defensive line with a second effort. Platoon commander Lt George Greene was last seen by the men who escaped backing into a doorway and firing a .30-caliber machine gun from the hip in Hollywood style.[48] He was captured after being stunned by the explosion of a Panther's 75mm round, and many of the TD crewmen joined him in captivity.[49]

First Platoon of Company B, under the command of Lt Leon Neel, deployed its guns west of Barthelmy. Neel brought his first gun into Barthelmy just as the battle for the village erupted. It was destroyed by artillery fire before it could even uncouple, and only two of the crewmen reappeared. After 3d Platoon had been overrun, Neel obtained permission by radio to bring two more guns into town. One made the dash, but the second withdrew under fire and deployed to cover the road.

The first gun crew engaged a Panther supported by grenadiers advancing up the street. An AP round stopped the Mark V, and HE dispersed the infantry. Private Robert Dunham killed the tank commander, who had been leading his vehicle on foot, with his carbine at three hundred yards. A high-velocity round soon struck the destroyer, which had now revealed its position.

Neel pulled out and found the gun along the road, which he deployed in a field beside a 57mm antitank gun. The lighter gun withdrew just as more tanks appeared. The TD crew fired on a Panther that appeared on the main road out of the thinning fog and dispatched it at a distance of only fifty yards. The crewmen could now see two other tanks that had stopped just out of range. One of them circled through the fields and took up a dominating spot that the Americans could not bring under fire because of the hasty positioning of their gun. The second tank patiently surveyed the area for forty-five minutes, evidently trying to spot the American weapon.

Finally, the second tank advanced. Knowing full well that firing would reveal their position, Neel and three volunteers destroyed the panzer. The overwatching German tank fired as well, and the blast ejected the men from their position. Neel led his men toward the rear, carrying their wounded with them. The day had cost the company forty-two enlisted men and one officer, most of them presumed captured.[50]

* * *

The 3-inchers of Lt Tom Springfield's 1st Platoon, A/823d Tank Destroyer Battalion, were meanwhile deployed at a roadblock on the Abbaye–Blanche road with a platoon of doughs from Company F, 120th Infantry Regiment; an AT platoon; and a section each of machine guns and mortars. At 0500 hours on 7 August, one of the 57mm AT guns

A prototype M3 (T12) fires during training in August 1941 at Ft. Meade, Maryland, the first home of the Tank Destroyer Force. *NA*

An early M3 tank destroyer at Camp Hood, Texas, in summer 1942. *NA*

The M3 gun crew (left to right): gunner, loader, commander. *NA*

The woefully inadequate M6 tank destroyer. *NA*

A sign at the entrance to the tank destroyer section of Camp Hood, Texas, displays the black panther crushing a tank in its jaws that served as the TD symbol. Camp Hood became the home of the Tank Destroyer Force in September 1942. *NA*

TD crews were commando-trained to seek out enemy tanks after the loss of their own vehicle and destroy them with Molotov cocktails and sticky bombs. In practice, they did not do so. *NA*

Tank destroyers fire at a November 1942 Army war show in Texas. Many miles away, the first TDs were going to war. *NA*

An M3 finds a hull-down position in the Tunisian desert. But the long flat vista behind the wadi illustrates why this was often difficult to do. *Patton Armor Museum*

A reconnaissance team from the 894th Tank Destroyer Battalion begins a mission at Kasserine Pass in February 1943. *NA*

A reconnaissance team from the 894th Tank Destroyer Battalion (right) passes a wrecked M3 "Purple Heart box" in Kasserine Pass in February 1943. Several destroyed tanks are visible in the middle distance.*NA*

Captain Michael Paulick (front left) from Reconnaissance Company, 601st Tank Destroyer Battalion, examines a map at El Guettar on 23 March 1943. The recon peep behind Paulick carries the pedestal-mounted .30-caliber machine gun. The M3 TD in the background is in one of the defilade positions from which the Americans pounded the 10th Panzer Division. *NA*

View from American lines of the 10th Panzer Division attacking the 1st Infantry Division at El Guettar. *NA*

One of the first M10s committed to battle. This one near Maknassy, Tunisia, in early April 1943 belongs to the 899th Tank Destroyer Battalion. *NA*

The towed 3-inch gun undergoing testing at Aberdeen Proving Grounds. The Signal Corps caption observes, "Army Ordnance Department tests have proved the 3-inch antitank gun as superior to the German 88mm antitank gun as an antitank weapon." Ordnance was wrong. *NA*

Staff Sergeant Raymond G. Murphy and the crew of the "Jinx," who were awarded silver stars for their 25-minute spree of destruction against the German counterattack at Salerno. L to R: Murphy, Sgt. Edwin Yost, T/5 Alvin Johnson, PFC Joseph O'Bryan, and Pvts. Clyde and Clasoe Tokes, twins from Oklahoma. *NA*

Number-3 gun (M10), 2d Platoon, Company A, 701st Tank Destroyer Battalion, shells the enemy in the Mignano sector, Italy, in December 1943. *NA*

An M10 from the 601st Tank Destroyer Battalion moves up at Anzio Beachhead, 29 February 1944. Note the extra ammunition stacked on the rear deck. *NA*

An M10 engages a German machine gun nest on the outskirts of Rome on 4 June 1944. *NA*

BM10s approach the historic Coliseum as the Americans liberate Rome. *NA*

German prisoners pass a camouflaged M10 in the Normandy bocage in July 1944. The terrain forced the self-propelled TDs to operate as tanks or artillery because they rarely had long fields of fire. *NA*

An M10 blasts retreating Germans at St. Lô on 20 July 1944. *NA*

A 3-inch gun crew uses building parts for camouflage during street fighting
in France, in August 1944. *NA*

One of the Panthers dispatched by the 645th Tank Destroyer Battalion during the battle in Meximieux, France, on 1 September 1944. The panzer ran into a building after being hit. *NA*

Back in Brittany, an M18 crew in the streets of Brest, September 1944. *NA*

Black crewmen from the 614th Tank Destroyer Battalion fire their 3-inch gun in England before heading to the Continent, September 1944. *NA*

The battle for the border begins. An M10 fires on enemy positions at Riesdorf, Germany, on 14 September 1944. *NA*

The TDs engage in fierce fighting inside Aachen on 15 October. The image graphically illustrates the vulnerability of crews in open turrets to fire from upper stories during urban warfare. The wartime censor's pen has obscured the unit designator on the M10. *NA*

An M36 from the 607th Tank Destroyer Battalion in the streets of Metz in November 1944. *NA*

The crewmen of an 801st Tank Destroyer Battalion 3-inch gun reposition their weapon in Hofen. The battalion lost seventeen guns in the first day of fighting. *NA*

A Royal Tiger knocked out in Stavelot, Belgium. It appears to be the one nailed by the men of the 825th Tank Destroyer Battalion—who had been assigned to security duties—in their only combat action of the war. *NA*

The crew of this camouflaged 776th Tank Destroyer Battalion M36 destroyed five panzers during a German counterattack at Oberwampach, Luxembourg, in January 1945. *NA*

First Army troops clear Cologne on the Rhine River, 6 March, 1945. *NA*

destroyed a reconnaissance halftrack with a 75mm gun that was heading toward the roadblock. A following halftrack loaded with ammo exploded.

Artillery fire soon rained down on the roadblock. Twice during the day, rare Luftwaffe air strikes hit the tiny command. Unfortunately, so did one flight of British Typhoons, which wounded two of the TD men.

The Germans tried to rush the roadblock with tanks. Firing calmly at a range of two thousand yards, the TDs picked off at least a dozen armored vehicles, including three tanks, four armored cars, and four halftracks. The crews and infantry believed more vehicles had been hit but retrieved by the Germans.[51]

*   *   *

Lieutenant Francis Conners's 2d Platoon of A/823d Tank Destroyer Battalion, was emplaced between two companies of the 120th Infantry Regiment on Hill 285 overlooking the Le Neufborg road. At 0500 hours, the TD crews spotted a German tank moving through the fog from behind a house in a nearby field. A bazooka team, accompanied by an infantry lieutenant, went after the panzer, but after five hundred yards the lieutenant decided they had gone far enough. Sergeant Ames Broussard asked permission to carry on alone and pushed on until he spotted the Mark IV. Broussard knocked the tank out, but German infantry had infiltrated past him, and he was cut off for fourteen hours.

The Germans attacked the line on Hill 285 at 0900. Number-two gun destroyed two Mark IVs at a range of only one hundred fifty yards. Number-one gun later hit another panzer from fifty yards; this panzer limped away smoking and was later found abandoned. Second Platoon added two SP guns and an armored car to its total by the end of the day.

The main threat to the crews came from the Allies. Typhoons struck the position and killed one TD man. Later, friendly artillery and infantry took the men under fire. "We didn't have a friend in the world that day," commented Lieutenant Conners.[52]

*   *   *

By the end of the day, von Kluge was convinced that the offensive had failed, but he pressed ahead at the insistence of the Führer.[53]

The 823d Tank Destroyer Battalion fought beside the doughs for the duration of the bitter struggle, but no subsequent day saw the wild engagements against panzers witnessed on the first. The men at the Abbaye–Blanche roadblock would fend off more German attacks until 12 August and be credited by Col Hammond Birks, CO of the 120th Infantry Regiment, with being one of the most important factors in his outfit's successful stand against the German offensive. Conners held his hill against repeated assaults with his crews, a recon section, and a few infantry stragglers until ordered off on 9 August. Fewer than nineteen men were killed, wounded, or missing.[54]

The men of the 823d had demonstrated the strength and weakness of General McNair's vision of the steady shore battery engaging enemy ships. The towed 3-inch guns had, indeed, proved a lethal weapon in their first real test against a large armor force. But the overrunning of two platoons and other losses demonstrated the vulnerability of guns that could not move after they had revealed their firing positions nor when confronted with the choice to withdraw or die.

*   *   *

The 2d Panzer Division accomplished a minor penetration but was stopped by air strikes—particularly by rocket-firing British Typhoons—and by reserve tanks from the 3d Armored Division. The panzer division lost 60 percent of its committed strength on 7 and 8 August.[55] The 2d SS Panzer Division, meanwhile, captured Mortain but could not push the 30th Infantry Division off high ground west and northwest of town. Allied fighters intercepted Luftwaffe ground-support missions before they could reach the battle zone, and few German planes arrived.[56]

The M10s of the 629th Tank Destroyer Battalion rolled in to support the hard-pressed 30th Infantry Division on 8 August. And several other TD battalions—including the 899th and 629th—arrived as other American divisions converged to snuff out the counteroffensive. LtCol W. Martz, CO of the 654th Tank Destroyer Battalion, was captured near Mortain on 8 August while operating with the 35th Infantry Division.[57]

Battered by Allied fighter-bombers and facing stiff resistance, the German armored columns ground to a halt, and the attack broke down within five days, having advanced to a depth of between three and seven miles.[58]

Pocketing the German Seventh Army

While the fighting flared at Mortain, Bradley on 8 August proposed to Montgomery that he send Patton's Third Army in a sweeping envelopment of the German Seventh Army. The objective would be to link up with Canadian troops pushing south toward Falaise. Monty agreed.

Fifteenth Corps advanced from its positions around Le Mans on 9 August. The U.S. 5th and French 2d Armored divisions spearheaded the attack. The Germans tried to stop them at the Sarthe River, but XV Corps smashed through at a cost of thirty-nine tanks. Starting their long partnership with the 5th Armored Division, the crews of the 628th Tank Destroyer Battalion began to kill panzers. Staff Sergeant Flynn claimed the battalion's first armored victim on 11 August when he destroyed a Mark IV at five hundred yards near Le Mesle. Two days later, Corporal Kee—the battalion's only gunner from Chinatown in New York City—knocked out two Mark IVs at twelve hundred yards.[59]

The tanks turned due north and headed for Argentan. The columns reached that city on 13 August, but Bradley stopped them because he feared they would collide with the Canadians. The Canadians, however, were behind schedule and did not reach Falaise until four days later, a delay that allowed many thousands of German troops to escape.[60]

Hitler on 16 August reluctantly approved von Kluge's recommendation that Seventh Army extricate itself from the almost complete encirclement. He also sacked von Kluge, who committed suicide.[61]

*   *   *

The 607th Tank Destroyer Battalion on 15 August deployed its towed 3-inch guns with the 90th Infantry Division to relieve the 5th Armored Division in the Le Bourg St. Leonard-Chambois area northeast of Argentan at the eastern end of the pocket. Companies B and C of the

607th settled in with the doughs of the 359th Infantry Regiment at the point where it was expected the Germans would try to break free.

German infantry attacked the line at 0800 on 16 August but was thrown back by noon. A second assault supported by panzers briefly drove the Americans out of their positions. During the fighting, 607th CO LtCol Harald Sundt personally manned a Company C 3-inch gun directly in the path of the attack. Sundt, Sgt Harold Scott, and Cpl Orlin Shirley were decorated for playing a crucial role in stopping the onslaught.

The next day, the M10s of the 773d Tank Destroyer Battalion arrived from the Argentan area, where the men had just seen their first action. Artillery fire struck around the vehicles of Company A as they maneuvered into position south of Le Bourg St. Leonard about 1400 hours, and one M10 struck a mine. At 1600 hours, two platoons of TDs pounded the buildings of the town, after which the doughs of Company E, 1st/359th Infantry Regiment, advanced into the streets supported by the TDs of 3d Platoon. Corporal Carlston and Corporal Holmes from 3d Platoon each destroyed two Mark IV tanks during the action, while Corporal Hamilton in 2d Platoon accounted for one more. Two men died and twelve were wounded.

Company C, meanwhile, advanced on Le Bourg St. Leonard at 1930 hours with the riflemen of Company A, 2d/359th Infantry Regiment. 3d Platoon got into a fire fight, during which it destroyed a Mark IV but lost one M10.

The doughs and TD crews cleared the town, and the SP outfit turned its positions over to towed guns from the 607th on the morning of 18 August. The crews of the 773d then pressed on toward Chambois in support of the 90th Infantry Division's bid to seal one of the last holes in the wall of the pocket. When the doughs and TDs linked up with Polish troops (under Canadian command) at Chambois at 1600 hours on 19 August, the Falaise Pocket was closed! The two days of combat netted the 773d another dozen panzer kills.

At 0800 hours on 20 August, two platoons from Company A moved into firing positions near Chambois. When Lt Delbert Reck's 1st Platoon spotted a mixed column of Germans, Reck ordered his destroyers to take up hasty firing positions along a hedgerow and waited while the enemy drove into his trap before opening fire. Reck and his platoon sergeant, SSgt Edward Land, moved from M10 to M10 to orchestrate the deadly barrage. When the smoke cleared, 3-inch gunfire had destroyed one

Panther, seven Mark IVs, nineteen halftracks, twenty-nine trucks, nineteen command cars and Volkswagens, and assorted other vehicles and guns. Reck's men also rounded up nine hundred prisoners. They had suffered only two men wounded.

The doughs of Company E, 359th Infantry Regiment, were being pressed hard by German tanks and grenadiers when two TDs from 2d Platoon clanked up. The first 3-inch salvos found no targets. Sergeant John Hawk was a machine gunner who had helped drive off one attack already and been wounded in the leg by shrapnel. He approached Lt John Snider to report that panzers were lurking in the woods. Snider traversed onto the general area but could not spot the tanks. Hawk told Snider to aim directly over his helmet and climbed a knoll under enemy fire to act as a human aiming stake. The first shot missed.

Realizing that his shouted fire directions could not be heard above the noise of battle, Hawk ran back to the destroyers through a concentration of bullets and shrapnel to correct the range. He returned to his exposed position, repeating this performance until two of the tanks were knocked out and a third driven off. Still at great risk, he continued to direct the destroyers' fire into the Germans' wooded position until the enemy came out and surrendered. (Hawk was awarded the Medal of Honor for his heroics that day.)[62]

Company C's 1st Platoon was in positions on Hill 129 north of Fougy with doughs from the 3d Battalion, 359th Infantry Regiment. During the night, the men engaged German vehicles trying to slip by in the darkness at ranges between two hundred and four hundred yards and stopped four tanks and a dozen other vehicles. At daybreak, the Americans discovered that the Germans had flanked them to the left, and a wild fire fight broke out, during which the platoon destroyed two Panthers, two Mark IVs, an 88mm SP gun, and assorted other vehicles. One M10 was lost in the exchange, and the remaining two guns—out of ammo—pulled back to the company CP. Before leaving, Private Conklin, although wounded, returned to his knocked-out M10 and fired its last four rounds of HE at advancing German infantry only one hundred yards away.

Company C's 2d Platoon was located at Chambois proper when the wave of fleeing Germans troops crashed against the American line. The crews had a field day; they picked off eleven Mark IV panzers, three Panthers, five Mark III command tanks, three assault guns, and many other vehicles. Sergeant Schimpf's number-four gun alone KO'd eight panzers and assault guns and twenty-six other vehicles, and his gunner fired three basic loads of ammunition during the action. The platoon reported approximately five hundred enemy dead and approximately one hundred prisoners.

The 3d platoon was deploying at Fougy about 1000 when it encountered the Germans eight hundred yards away. Over the next eight hours, the M10s destroyed eleven Mark IV panzers, three Panthers, two Mark III command tanks, and about thirty other vehicles.[63]

By 21 August, American troops were rounding up stragglers, most of whom wanted to surrender. The 776th had busted forty-six tanks and SP guns and another seventy-seven vehicles. As a unit citation concluded, "The battalion inflicted staggering losses upon the enemy, attacking them relentlessly wherever they were encountered, contemptuous of overwhelming odds." The almost overlooked 607th's guns had destroyed thirty-four tanks, twenty-three SP guns, nine halftracks, and sixty-four other vehicles during the fighting.[64]

*   *   *

First Army, meanwhile, was compressing the pocket as it plowed north toward the British and Canadians. The 3d Armored Division hooked through Mayenne and then east and north after the fighting at Mortain, and the 703d's M10s followed close on the heels of the lead Shermans. CCA ran into the remnants of the 1st and 9th SS Panzer divisions around Joue du Bois on 14 August. The fighting was so vicious that staff officers and cooks had to join the battle to beat off the German counterattacks. Company A of the 703d knocked out three tanks and drove off the accompanying grenadiers. On 15 August at Ranes-Fromentel, an SS combat patrol infiltrated Company A's positions and captured a lieutenant, two security men, and two engineers. All but one engineer who escaped were later found shot to death.

Later that day, Cpl Joseph Juno from 2d Platoon, Company B, engaged two Panthers at a mere twenty-five yards. The 3-inch gunfire cracked the frontal armor on both panzers. Juno was killed by exploding ammunition when he dismounted to help the enemy wounded.[65]

*   *   *

The collapse of the Falaise Pocket was a disaster for the German Army. It left behind fifty thousand prisoners, ten thousand dead, as many as five hundred tanks and assault guns destroyed or captured, and most of the transportation and artillery of those troops who got away.[66]

Even as the resistance crumbled, Eisenhower decided to pursue relentlessly rather than stop at the Seine River to build up supplies, and Bradley unleashed a tidal wave of American corps across northern France. First Army, on the left, would receive priority in supplies over Third Army to enable it to support Montgomery's drive along the coast. Generalleutnant Heinz Guderian, father of Germany's armored legions, lamented, "While our panzer units still existed, our leaders had chosen to fight a static battle in Normandy. Now that our motorized forces had been squandered and destroyed they were compelled to fight the mobile battle that they had hitherto refused to face."[67]

River Hopping

The 3d Armored Division (with the 703d Tank Destroyer Battalion attached) recorded, "There was a quality of madness about the whole debacle of Germany's forces in the West, something which was not easily explained. Isolated garrisons fought as viciously as before, but the central planning and coordination which must go into decisive action was missing. . . . [For the men,] days merged into one long stream of fatigue and weariness in the endless pursuit."[68]

Lieutenant Jack Dillender, a platoon leader in the 814th Tank Destroyer Battalion, supporting the 7th Armored Division's blitz across France, recalled, "The weather was hot and the fumes from vehicles and no rest began to take their toll on our faces. Our eyes were in bad condition and our faces cracked and blistered so badly we could hardly open our mouths."[69]

The semi-official history of the 610th Tank Destroyer Battalion noted the wonderful side of the "rat race": "The natives along the route cheered the columns all the way, and arms began to ache from returning the waves and salutations along the way. The briefest stop was the signal for much bartering for bread, cognac, and wine, and as the convoy moved the French enthusiastically tossed apples, tomatoes, etc., into the vehicles. A steel helmet was a necessity, for a hard apple thrown at a speeding vehicle can be a deadly missile."[70]

As they had in North Africa, the tank killers sometimes formed the division's spearhead. Lieutenant Jack Dillender encountered division CG MajGen Lindsay Silvester and XX Corps commander MajGen Walton Walker in a small village where the advance had stopped under German fire. Dillender recalled:

> General Walker said, "What the hell is holding up my corps?" He received an explanation. . . . Then he said, "Put a TD unit in the lead and put me on the banks of the Seine by 3:00 PM. Where is the TD officer?"
>
> I jumped down and reported to him. He said, "Lieutenant, can you read a map?"
>
> I said, "Yes, sir," and he said, "Show me where you are." He said, "Fine. Now, do you see this road taking off to the right at the crossroads? Do you see that it turns back to our attack direction? Lieutenant, I want you to take your platoon and lead us to the Seine at Melun. I want you to run your destroyers as fast as you can, and don't deploy this column unless you run into armor and lots of it. Do you understand?"
>
> I said, "Yes sir."
>
> He said, "Lieutenant, move out and good luck."
>
> I said, "Yes, sir," saluted, and ran back to my destroyer, and off we went. . . . We were about thirty miles from the Seine, and we were really pushing those diesels. Along the way I saw a small German convoy (no tanks) to my left front headed for the same intersection.   We were on a road lined with trees, and they had not seen us. I halted my platoon and brought all four guns broadside. . . . We fired the first round together and then it was at will after that. We finished off that convoy so that there wouldn't be any traffic congestion at the intersection and then moved on. We reached the Seine at 3:10 PM.[71]

Captain Fred Parkin, the intelligence officer of the 813th Tank Destroyer Battalion (attached to the 79th Infantry Division), drove ahead, left the edge of his last map, got lost, and with his jeep driver liberated Roubaix, a city of 175,000 souls.[72] During the 1st Infantry Division's advance on Juvigny on 13–15 August, the otherwise underemployed 635th Tank Destroyer Battalion (towed) ferried the doughs forward in its halftracks.[73]

* * *

French and American forces from First Army captured Paris on 25 August. Ike had hoped to bypass the city, but a Resistance uprising got into trouble, and—subject to strong pressure from Charles De Gaulle—Eisenhower had to order troops into Paris.

The 4th Armored Division assaulted Troyes on the River Seine the next day with the goal of forcing a crossing. The armor advanced in sweeping "desert formation"—with tank destroyers following in a secondary line—expecting the mere five hundred defenders reported by reconnaissance. Instead, they encountered two thousand determined SS soldiers.[74]

Artillery pounded the city while the tanks, armored infantry, and M18s of the 704th Tank Destroyer Battalion advanced. The SS waited until the attackers were almost upon them before they opened fire from basements and buildings. Heavy return artillery fire struck the Americans until Capt Thomas Evans maneuvered one of his M18s into position and knocked out the German OP in a church steeple.

One of Evans's M18s was hit as the SS mounted a counterattack. The captain leapt to the deck of the crippled vehicle and raked the oncoming storm troopers with the .50-caliber machine gun until the M18 was hammered by another devastating blow.[75] But the charge had been repulsed. The 4th Armored Division slugged its way through the city.

By early the next day, the division owned the ruins of Troyes. The last river crossings along the Seine were denied to the Germans on 29 August.

* * *

The M10s of the 702d Tank Destroyer Battalion soon left the Seine and Somme rivers behind, and the men adopted "One More River to Cross" as a favorite unit song.[76] There would be no other organized defensive line in northern France.

The enemy had lost all but about one hundred of the twenty-three hundred tanks and assault guns he had deployed in Normandy.[77] Perhaps half that number had been destroyed in the American sector by a combination of TDs, tanks, artillery, fighter-bombers, antitank guns, and bazookas. TDs had accounted for roughly one hundred fifty panzers in fairly sizable engagements, and probably that many again in numerous scattered encounters. The tank killers were carrying their share of the load.

Operation Dragoon

On 15 August, MajGen Lucian Truscott's VI Corps, Seventh Army, made an assault landing at St. Tropez in the French Riviera. As before the Anzio operation, the Americans and British had disagreed over the wisdom of the project. Churchill judged that it would fatally weaken the Italian campaign by drawing off too many divisions. The Americans were thinking in terms of logistics and wanted to capture the ports of Toulon and Marseilles. Indeed, once the northern and southern fronts linked up, these ports were to satisfy one-third of the logistical needs in northern France until Antwerp was opened in December.

The 3d, 45th, and 36th Infantry divisions stormed ashore (west-to-east, respectively) at 0800 hours supported by air strikes, naval bombardment, DD tanks, and parachute drops inland from the beaches. They encountered virtually no initial resistance because only two German infantry regiments from separate divisions stood in their way.[78] With a self-propelled TD battalion attached in addition to the usual separate tank battalion, the truck-rich American infantry divisions were equivalent to full-strength panzergrenadier divisions.[79]

The men of the 601st Tank Destroyer Battalion added one more D-day to their list and hit the beach with the 3d Infantry Division. As far as the 601st was concerned, the operation was less trouble than the practice landings at Naples had been. Recon sent platoons in several directions, and another rat race across France began.[80]

The line companies of 645th Tank Destroyer Battalion landed with the 45th Infantry Division. The M8s and M20s of Reconnaissance Company landed the next day and moved ahead of the advancing infantry, who in some cases rode on the battalion's M10s. Battalion destroyers linked up with the paratroopers and helped capture Le Muy on D+1.[81]

Three platoons of the 636th Tank Destroyer Battalion landed on Green Beach with the 36th Infantry Division at H+40 minutes. The 1st Platoon of Company B drove to Drammont to assist the doughs against strongpoints and pillboxes, while the 2d Platoon of Company C established a roadblock to protect the left flank of the 141st RCT. The 1st Platoon of Company B helped clear Yellow Beach and captured forty-five POWs.[82]

The Italian campaign veterans, already clued in to the importance of combined arms operations, comfortably formed up into task forces to drive inland. The 36th Infantry Division, for example, established three such commands. One of them, Task Force Butler, included elements of the 141st RCT, 753d Tank Battalion, 636th Tank Destroyer Battalion, a cavalry squadron, and a SP artillery battalion. Division ordered Reconnaissance Company to race ahead of the columns and establish contact with Allied paratroopers. By 19 August, TF Butler had reached the Digne-Sisteron area some sixty miles from the coast and encountered no organized resistance along the way.[83]

The 3d and 45th Infantry divisions raced west and then hooked north up the Rhone Valley east of the river—between Germany and most of the German troops in southern France. Behind them, four French divisions began to come ashore and turned initially to the task of taking Marseilles and Toulon. The Maquis emerged to assist the American advance and the French assaults on the major port cities.

Stripped almost bare to feed the attrition machine in Normandy, the German Nineteenth Army had only one mobile formation left in southern France, the 11th Panzer Division. One mountain and seven understrength infantry divisions would be nothing but stuffing for the POW cages if they could not escape what, in effect, was a massive encirclement.[84]

On 16 August, Berlin accepted the inevitable and ordered a general withdrawal from southern France, but Hitler ordered that garrisons be left behind in Marseilles, Toulon, and a few other ports to deny their use by the Allies.[85] The two main cities nevertheless fell to the French by 28 August.

Alarmed at the speed of the American advance, the Germans moved the 11th Panzer Division to Montelimar, where it tangled with the 36th Infantry Division for over a week. The clash built in scope and energy as the two divisions brought their full strengths to bear over the first several days, culminating in a series of indecisive battles on 25–26 August.

The crews of the 636th Tank Destroyer Battalion saw only limited action in the course of five German attacks on 25 August. That night, however, Generalmajor Wend von Wietersheim, commanding the 11th

Panzer Division, ordered his panzergrenadier regiment, reinforced by artillery and ten tanks, to attack American positions threatening his escape route north of Montelimar. About 0100 hours on 26 August, the German force struck a roadblock near La Concourde manned by two infantry companies and two platoons of B/636th. German infantry infiltrated the position and located the M10s, and a German panzer company commander then fired flares that illuminated the armor for his tanks standing off in the dark. Five M10s quickly burst into flames and a sixth was hit. Following a two-hour exchange of fire, the Americans retreated to the MLR fifteen hundred yards to the rear. The Germans had also lost heavily among the panzergrenadiers.

The 11th Panzer Division during the day received orders to join the withdrawal to Lyon. By evening, TF Butler had so many targets in its sights that it had to call for extra artillery observers to help dispatch the retreating German columns.[86]

*   *   *

Mostly, these were good times for the tank killers.

During their first two weeks in France, TDs from the 645th encountered scattered German armor, claiming two Tigers, one Panther, one Mark IV, one Mark III, and one SP gun for the loss of ten casualties (most from Reconnaissance Company), two M10s, two M8s, and two M20s.[87]

By 31 August, the 3d and 45th Infantry divisions had pulled nearly abreast of Lyon. The French 1st Armored Division, meanwhile, led a Gallic sweep northward along the west side of the Rhone River.[88]

On 1 September, the 11th Panzer Division launched a spoiling attack against the 45th Infantry Division. A strong tank-infantry force struck Meximieux, which was defended by two reserve companies of the 179th Infantry Regiment and the regimental headquarters—including clerks and kitchen personnel—supported by 2d Platoon, A/645th Tank Destroyer Battalion.

Lieutenant Joseph Dixon was just moving two of his M10s into the village when the Germans attacked. The two TDs took up positions near the center of town, with the first about one hundred yards ahead of the second. The TD commanders, Sgt Robert Fitts and Sgt Wayne Menear, positioned their vehicles so that they were partially concealed by buildings.

Ten minutes later, a platoon of Panthers raced up the wide main street into Meximieux, firing their machine guns in all directions and crushing everything in their path. Fitts's gunner, Cpl William McAuliffe, waited until the lead Mark V was only seventy-five yards away before he fired his 3-inch gun. The round penetrated the right front hull of the Panther, which burst into flames and coasted another twenty-five yards. McAuliffe nailed the next tank seconds later at one hundred yards. This tank also caught fire and drove into a building, setting the neighboring houses ablaze. The other three tanks flew by Fitts.

Menear's gunner, Pvt James Waldron, hit the third Panther at a range of only twenty-five yards. For some reason, he used a round of HE. The shell did not penetrate the armor, but it shattered the driver's periscope, and the Panther plowed into another building between the American TDs. American doughs killed or captured the crewmen as they bailed out.

One of the last two Panthers stopped about fifty yards beyond Menear's TD and turned around. Waldron immobilized the Mark V with a shot to the right track. The infantry opened up on the tank with 81mm mortars and took care of the crew when it, too, bailed out. The last Panther fled.

The Americans beat off 11th Panzer Division attacks until dark. By day's end, the defenders had killed or captured nearly one hundred thirty Germans and destroyed eight medium tanks, four light tanks, three assault guns, and seven other vehicles. Losses totaled about thirty men killed or wounded (and one hundred eighty five presumed captured) as well as two tank destroyers and about twenty-five other vehicles destroyed or damaged.[89]

* * *

Tank destroyer recon elements in jeeps and M8s ranged far ahead of the advancing columns with no contact other than radio communications. They fought innumerable tiny actions against small roadblocks and surprised German columns. Reconnaissance Company of the 636th Tank Destroyer Battalion entered Lyon at 1630 hours on 2 September and reported the city clear of the enemy but all the bridges blown. Recon later amended its report to say there was considerable sniper fire. A few days later, Battalion won approval to begin rotating the recon platoons so that men could get some rest and their vehicles receive critical maintenance.[90]

The advancing columns nipped at the heels of the retreating German forces. On 14 September, the M10s of A/636th were advancing with C/753d Tank Battalion and 36th Infantry Division doughs.[91] The 753d's AAR recorded, "First Section [of the 1st Platoon] . . . had run into numerous enemy withdrawing. In fact so close to the enemy and so many, [that] one tank moving down the road to St. Sauver from Allencourt was given a stop sign by an enemy MP to allow enemy vehicles to continue along the road perpendicular to the advance of the troops."[92]

Sergeant Tom Sherman from the 636th was near the column's point. He reported: "The destroyer driver who was just ahead of my jeep realized that the [German] bus driver didn't intend to stop, so he slammed on his brakes and brought the destroyer to an abrupt stop. As the bus roared by, we could see that it was loaded with German soldiers. The driver of the destroyer in front of my jeep started to pull forward, so his gunner could get a better shot at the fleeing bus when another bus loaded with German soldiers following closely behind the other bus collided with the barrel of the destroyer's gun [which stripped the mechanism]."[93]

The tanks and TDs shot up the enemy column.

* * *

The advance was so rapid that maintenance and supply problems posed the greatest challenge. Lack of fuel, supplies, and replacement parts gradually slowed the Seventh Army's pace. At one point in September, almost half of the M10s in the 645th Tank Destroyer Battalion were deadlined, most because of worn-out tracks.[94]

The history of the 157th Infantry Regiment summed up the advance this way: "The men drank champagne, cognac, white wine, red wine, and eau de vie (White Lightning), flirted with the French girls, and chased the Germans. Said they, 'This is the way to fight a war. . . . Chase them for six days, fight them for two. . . . We never had it so good.'"[95]

General Johannes Blaskowitz, CG of Germany's Army Group G, might have summed the situation up differently. He had lost more than half the 150,000 troops who had been manning southern France on 15 August.[96]

End of the Rat Race

Near the extreme left of First Army's advance, the 3d Armored Division reached the high ground west of Mons, Belgium, on 2 September. First Army CG LtGen Courtney Hodges, alerted by Ultra that the Germans were concentrating in that area, had sent VII Corps to spring a trap. The tanks and accompanying 703d Tank Destroyer Battalion TDs encountered an estimated thirty thousand German troops who were attempting to withdraw into the defenses of the West Wall. The Germans were now caught between VII Corps to the east, XIX Corps to the west, V Corps to the south, and the British to the north. The 3d Armored Division, joined by the 1st Infantry Division, proceeded to annihilate an entire corps. A platoon of TDs under the command of Capt Bill Smith destroyed twenty vehicles in six hours of fighting. Twenty-five thousand Germans surrendered to the American divisions.[97]

By 3 September, the British had liberated Brussels, and they took Antwerp the following day (although the Germans would block sea access through the Schelde Estuary for nearly two more months). Eisenhower told his senior commanders that resistance along the entire front showed signs of collapse.[98] In the face of these grim developments, Hitler on 5 September reinstated von Rundstedt as overall commander of the western front. Hodges told his staff on 6 September that with ten more days of good weather the war would be over.[99] On 11 September, patrols from Third and Seventh armies made first contact and the two fronts soon became one. But things were about to change.

For one thing, the supply situation was becoming terribly constricting across the entire front. Progress had far outstripped pre-invasion planning, and logisticians had to resort to ad hoc measures—including air deliveries and the famous Red Ball Express truck route—to get supplies from the beaches to the spearheads. Neither First nor Third armies by the end of August had meaningful ration or ammunition reserves, and fuel was used as quickly as it arrived. In Third Army, the 814th Tank Destroyer Battalion was rationing ammunition—nine rounds per day for each M10—and on 29 August

CCB/7th Armored Division literally ran out of gas in the middle of the World War I battlefield at Verdun. (The attached TDs, which burned diesel, still had some reserves).[100] The 610th Tank Destroyer Battalion kept moving only because the "gas noncom," Corporal Bruff, was able to supply the entire outfit with captured German fuel.[101]

Likewise, Seventh Army dangled at the end of a 500-mile supply line that ran back to Marseilles and the other southern French ports.

Moreover, the Allied advance was reaching the outer glacis of Germany itself. There lay the defenses of the Siegfried Line, or West Wall as the Germans called it, and considerable stretches of inhospitable terrain.

*   *   *

First Army's 3d Armored Division occupied Rötgen, Germany, on 12 September. Beginning under cover of darkness (and Hodges's authorization for "reconnaissance in force" until sufficient fuel and ammo arrived), the division launched one of the first attacks on the Siegfried Line the next morning. The unit's history recorded, "The plan was simple; the first waves of infantry, supported by direct tank-destroyer fire, were to secure high ground just beyond the dragon's teeth. Immediately following this part of the operation, men of the 23d Armored Engineer Battalion would move forward and breach the obstacle line with high explosive charges. The tanks, which were usually considered point of the 'Spearhead' [the division's codename], would then go on into Germany behind the 'Queen of Battles' and the engineers."

Combat Command A's Task Force Doan tackled a cluster of pillboxes behind dragon's teeth northwest of Schmidthof. Mortar fire disrupted the first wave, but the doughs rallied and pressed on. Even pillboxes that had taken direct hits from the 3-inch guns on the supporting M10s continued to spew death. The tanks were unable to advance until the discovery of a secondary road where German farmers had filled in the dragon's teeth with dirt so they could cross the line to their fields. The M4s pushed forward. Assault guns and German soldiers with panzerfausts engaged the Shermans, and at one point, Col Leander Doan could see seven of his M4s burning among the pillboxes. Progress was slow and demanded a high price in blood, but CCA bashed a path through the first band of defenses.[102] Third Platoon, B/703d Tank Destroyer Battalion, was probably the first TD unit to penetrate the Siegfried Line.[103]

By 15 September, the 3d Armored Division had punched all the way through both bands of the West Wall in its sector. The tankers and supporting TD crews were only the first to discover that the villages on the far side provided superb defensive positions, too. A half-dozen panzers ambushed Task Force Lovelady and destroyed seven tanks and one of the supporting TDs. The command pulled back to the fortifications, and the division's forward progress all but ended. The worn out 3d Armored Division had only 25 percent of its authorized tank strength fit for combat.

Nonetheless, the advance had enabled the 1st Infantry Division on the left to take high ground at Eilendorf and encircle Aachen on three sides. Almost defenseless, Aachen was ripe for the taking, but the overextended 1st Division lacked the resources to snatch it. On the right, the 9th Infantry Division on 16 September advanced through the West Wall to within seven miles of the Roer River. But German reinforcements were arriving in large numbers to plug the gap. Confronted by fresh German reserves, Collins on 17 September ordered his exhausted corps to consolidate its positions. Only the 9th Infantry Division would continue to press the attack on the right, plunging into the forbidding gloom of the Hürtgen Forest.[104]

*   *   *

Far to the south, Seventh Army's 636th Tank Destroyer Battalion recon men reached the Moselle River on 20 September and scouted crossings for the 36th Infantry Division. The 141st RCT crossed the river the next day, but the race stopped rather suddenly. Over the next several days, recon teams reported strong enemy positions in every direction. Resistance became fiercer, artillery barrages heavier, and minefields thicker. Recon had to turn to foot patrols.[105]

Likewise, the recon men from the 601st Tank Destroyer Battalion ran into determined resistance at Faucogney. "From there on," recorded the battalion's informal history, "it was slow, tough going."[106]

*   *   *

The armored spearheads could run no longer. The infantry—that Queen of Battles—and its supporting tanks and TDs again took center stage.

The officially recognized U.S. Army campaigns in northern and southern France, characterized by rapid movement and isolated pockets of German defense, ended on 14 September 1944; on 15 September, the Rhineland Campaign began, a slugfest that was to drag on by official count until 21 March of the next year. Yet there was one more clash of charging armor left to be fought in France.

The Tank Battles of Lorraine

Eisenhower conferred with Montgomery and Bradley from 9 to 11 September to discuss operations in light of the tight logistic situation. SHAEF continued to underscore that the primary Allied effort would be in the north, in the direction of the Ruhr, as urged by Monty. But on 13 September, Eisenhower gave Patton the inch the fiery general needed to take a mile. Patton gained leave to push only far enough to establish "adequate bridgeheads" beyond the Moselle River. A day later, Patton was across the river in strength. He ordered his corps commanders to press on to the Rhine.[107]

On Third Army's right, the French 2d Armored Division pierced the German defenses west of the Moselle River and penetrated the German Nineteenth Army's rear area. Further north, the American 4th Armored Division formed the edge of a wedge driving into a gap between the German Nineteenth and First armies. German commanders had wanted to strike a blow against the U.S. Seventh Army advancing from the south, but this new peril appeared even graver.

Hitler ordered a counterattack, and on 17 September the Fifth Panzer Army received instructions to seal the gap in the German front by attacking the southern flank of the Third Army columns advancing toward Metz. To the rear, German commanders struggled to find the resources to construct a forward defensive line before the Vosges Mountains, and success against the U.S. Third Army offered the only hope of gaining enough time. Fifth Panzer Army set taking control of the town of Luneville as its objective. It had available badly understrength elements of the 15th Panzergrenadier and 21st Panzer divisions and three panzer brigades either present or on the way. The 11th Panzer Division, having completed its rear-guard action against Seventh Army, was promised by 25 September.[108]

The panzer brigades—the 111th, 112th, and 113th—had recently been formed for service on the Eastern Front but were committed to the west instead. They consisted of two panzer battalions (forty-five each of Marks IV and V), two panzergrenadier battalions, and other assorted elements. They lacked artillery and salvage capabilities, and the men had never even met the officers who took command when the units began detraining in France. The 112th Panzer Brigade, moreover, had been mauled by air strikes and lost roughly sixty tanks while attacking the French 2d Armored Division on 13 September.[109]

The closely linked series of actions that followed constituted by some measures the largest tank battle to take place on the Western Front.

*   *   *

On 18 September, seventeen tanks and the panzergrenadiers of the 111th Panzer Brigade advanced northward toward Luneville. Men of the 42d Cavalry Squadron and CCR/4th Armored Division held most of the town but were still battling elements of the 15th Panzergrenadier Division in the streets. The panzers swept the cavalry aside and, attacking in concert with the panzergrenadiers already in Luneville, pushed the Americans back into the north part of the city.[110]

Company B/704th Tank Destroyer Battalion, was bivouacked on high ground northwest of the city. Third Platoon rolled into Luneville under heavy artillery fire to aid the defenders. During fighting that lasted until well after dark, the M10s claimed three Panther kills.[111]

Combat Command A/4th Armored Division rushed a task force to the scene to help out.[112] Second Lieutenant Richard Buss and 2d Platoon, C/704th Tank Destroyer Battalion, accompanied elements of the 37th Armored Regiment on the rescue mission. A sergeant led Buss's destroyers toward the south part of town, to a spot where the buildings thinned out and a railroad embankment was visible across a field. A large deserted factory loomed over the scene. Buss noticed that there were no civilians to be seen on the streets. Buss related later:

After a while, a Lieutenant Walle arrived back from the embankment and announced that he had spotted two Panthers hidden in some trees across the field on the other side. We both took off at a run and peered over the rails. There they were! Two beauties at about three hundred yards range! The enemy had been so considerate as to place one sideways to our position. The other was positioned facing us at a three-quarters angle. With hand signals, I called Sergeant Romek's tank up and had him dismount and join us on the embankment. I pointed out the targets. He ran back and mounted. His tank trundled up and laid its tube across the railroad tracks. Romek briefed the gunner, Corporal Mazolla, and the tube traversed onto the target.

I gave the signal to fire. The concussion was deafening. Mazolla rose up from the telescopic sight and signaled a hit, except that nothing happened. I was terribly disappointed. I called for another round, and Mazolla indicated another hit, but there was still no indication that we had put the target out of action.

Suddenly, I saw billowing flames. It was not the dramatic kind of explosion that one would have expected. The flames were a transparent orange, rising with startling swiftness. They rose through the branches of the trees to a height of nearly sixty feet. When I looked for the second target, it was gone.[113]

The platoon lost only one man to a sniper during the action. Third Platoon, meanwhile, knocked out one of three panzers advancing to the railroad line. The German attack was beaten off. But LtCol Bill Bailey, CO of the 704th, would die under mortar fire in the streets of Luneville the next day.[114]

The 603d Tank Destroyer Battalion's Company C—preceding the main body of CCB/6th Armored Division, which was hustling east from Brittany—also deployed at the southeastern edge of Luneville during the day.[115] That evening, the combat command began to relieve the defenders of Luneville.[116] On 21 September, the M10s of the 773d clanked into town and took up positions on the eastern edge.

On 22 September the Germans probed Luneville from the north and east but met with no greater success.[117]

*   *   *

The rest of CCA/4th Armored Division and Company C of the 704th were located a dozen miles to the north in the area of Arracourt. The 113th Panzer Brigade was on its way there, too.

About midnight 18–19 September, an American outpost near Lezey heard tracked vehicles to the front and called in an artillery barrage. The noises stopped. At about 0730 hours, Capt William Dwight was driving down a nearby road in a thick morning fog when he encountered the rear of a German tank column. He avoided detection and radioed his battalion CO, LtCol Creighten Abrams. A half-hour later, a section of Shermans south of Lezey found the head of the column when a Panther emerged from the fog seventy-five yards away. The Shermans destroyed three Panthers in short order, and the rest of the panzers disappeared in the murk.

Captain Dwight appeared at CCA's CP at Rechicourt and was ordered to lead a platoon of tank destroyers—the only unit available—to reinforce the defenses at Lezey. Company C's CO, Capt Thomas Evans—who had been shaving beside a TD when the first German shell struck near the CP—selected Lt Edwin Leiper's 3d Platoon for the mission. Northeast of Rechicourt, the small column spotted German tanks moving through the fog.

The M18s raced into hull-defilade positions in a depression and opened fire at one hundred fifty yards. The CCA executive officer, LtCol Hal Pattison, described the action: "It was so foggy that even at one hundred fifty yards the gunners could not see the enemy tanks through the telescopic sights. Consequently . . . when a German tank was spotted, the TD would come out of the depression just enough to fire on the enemy. Then one round of HE was fired to adjust on. Captain Dwight adjusted the fire. Having adjusted, AP would be utilized to destroy the enemy tank. When our TDs fired, the Germans would lay their guns on the muzzle flash. In this manner, they were successful in knocking out [three] of the TDs. One TD was lost rather unfortunately. It had pulled up out of the saucer-like depression to render fire upon the enemy. In that position, the motor stalled, leaving it exposed. Another of the TDs was taken up to try to withdraw it to cover. The Germans fired on them, and the TDs answered fire. Firing at the muzzle blast, the German tanks almost put a round down the tube of the recovery TD. . . . They then hit the stalled TD."[118]

Corporal Frederick Stewart, gunner in Sgt Emilo Stasi's TD, rapidly knocked out two Panthers before return fire crashed into the M18 and damaged the turret. Stasi and Stewart suffered leg wounds, another man was injured, and a fourth was killed. About one hour later, gunner Cpl John Eidenschink in Sgt Pat Ferraro's crew killed three panzers before the Hellcat was hit and put out of action. Sergeant Steve Krewsky's men destroyed four panzers before being knocked out, with several men injured. Sergeant Edwin McGurk's destroyer was the only one to escape damage, and his gunner, Cpl Dominick Sorrentino, accounted for two panzers.[119] (One post-war study claimed an even higher number of kills.[120] Combat Command A physically surveyed only eight German tanks positively destroyed, however, so there probably was some double counting at work.)

American and German tanks, meanwhile, battled in the fog, which protected the Germans from air attack but forced all action to take place at relatively close quarters, where the better German guns had less advantage. Captain Evans deployed his remaining two platoons on high ground south of Rechicourt. The M18s and C/24th Engineers were all that stood between the Germans and CCA's CP and artillery positions.

About 1200, the 113th Panzer Brigade made another stab toward Arracourt. As the fog lifted, Evans could see thirty to forty panzers advancing on his position. He later recalled, "We waited and waited until they were within fifteen hundred yards [CCA's after-action maps indicate that all kills took place at between five hundred and one thousand yards]. Then we fired. The two leading tanks were hit and stopped dead, aflame. The others, the crews apparently confused, turned sideways. I really don't know why. That's where they made their big mistake. It was a turkey shoot! From our position, with only our turrets showing, we hit eleven more as fast as we could load and shoot. . . ."[121]

The TDs were well concealed in defilade and repositioned after firing, so the Germans never had a good target and returned little fire. The 113th Panzer Brigade withdrew. Combat Command A officially credited Company C's TDs with eight Panther kills. Private Frank Amodio, in his first action as a gunner, accounted for five of them.[122]

That evening, Patton visited Evans's small CP on the hillside overlooking the burning armored hulks. Colonel Bruce Clarke, CO of CCA, indicated that Evans had been in charge of the shootout. Patton told

Evans, "This is the kind of thing that's going to end the war quicker than anybody had hoped." He then walked to his jeep and left.[123]

*   *   *

CCA formed up in two columns in heavy fog the next morning. The enemy appeared to have withdrawn, and the Americans moved out to the northeast about 0900. At 0930, the 113th Panzer Brigade renewed its attack and threatened to strike the rear of the American columns. Both were ordered to turn around, even though B/704th Tank Destroyer Battalion had combined with the artillery and tanks defending Arracourt to chalk up another six panzers while beating off the attack.[124]

Working with the 35th Infantry Division's 320th RCT and elements of the 691st and 602d Tank Destroyer battalions (the latter arrived about noon after some stiff fighting around Luneville), the combat command established a defensive perimeter at Arracourt. The 37th Armored Regiment battled the panzers all that day, losing seven Shermans in exchange for eighteen enemy tanks.

There was little contact the next day when the 4th Armored Division initiated sweeps of the area through thick fog. One German armored probe struck positions held by the 25th Cavalry Squadron near Juvelize and destroyed five light tanks. Lieutenant Marvin Evans's 2d Platoon, Company B, was nearby, where its M18s had been under sporadic friendly artillery fire for almost a day, despite heated comments by radio to the artillery observer by Evans. With the cavalry pulling back, Evans sent one TD back to cover the withdrawal of the rest. The overwatching crew spotted a column of German tanks and opened fire at six hundred yards, destroying three. The platoon then withdrew in leap-frog fashion.[125]

By the end of 22 September, CCA and the 704th Tank Destroyer Battalion claimed to have accounted for a total to date of seventy-nine panzers in exchange for fourteen Shermans, seven M5s, and one M18 damaged beyond repair.[126]

On 23 September, a tank-infantry assault by the 111th Panzer Brigade developed from the east. American tanks maneuvered onto high ground northeast of Juvelize and picked the panzers off as they came in. When German infantry moved into Marsal, fighter-bombers wreaked havoc on them.[127]

Sometime during this period, Captain Evans won the Silver Star. He recalled, "They attacked again toward Arracourt. Two of our M18s were hit. One was set afire, and next to it was one with a track shot off, but the gun was still good. I was more mad than anything else and maybe a little foolhardy, but I got up in the second M18 and was able to load and fire long enough to get two more Panthers. Then the Germans wised up. I got down on the ground and crawled away. Eventually, they hit and burned that M18, too."[128]

*   *   *

The 11th Panzer Division concentrated in the forest south of Dieuze on 24 September. It had left a battle group to the south but incorporated the thirty surviving Panthers of the 111th Panzer Brigade (only three of which were battle-ready). The division had twenty of its own Mark Vs and ten Mark IVs, was about 70 percent fit for combat, and had well trained men with good morale, but it lacked its antitank battalion, which was being outfitted with new Jagdpanzer IV tank destroyers. Workshops labored to rehabilitate as many of the panzer brigade's Panthers as possible and distributed them to division units as they were repaired. The division was ordered to advance toward Rechicourt on 25 September despite the poor terrain and repetition of the line of attack.[129]

The panzers and grenadiers struck into the teeth of the 4th Armored Division's defenses on the hills near Juvelize and drove the defenders off Hill 264. Renewed attacks the next day netted Hill 257 and Juvelize as the 4th Armored Division pulled back its forward units to straighten its line.[130]

The 602d Tank Destroyer Battalion covered the tactical withdrawal. In apparent reference to this action, battalion CO LtCol Pete Kopcsak later recollected: "Barthold (platoon leader, Company B) with his TDs held his ground until enemy infantry were passing him and the 4th Armored Division artillery was shelling him. I talked with [LtCol Creighton] Abrams of the 4th Armored who said he had to pull back as he was losing too many tanks. When I arrived at the battalion CP, Major Conlin said he thought I had been captured. I had waited to see that Barthold's unit had evacuated safely. Our fighter planes were strafing the Germans on both sides of my vehicle. I saw AA tracer bullets from the Germans firing at those planes. My driver sped down the road while

Smith, the radio operator, fired machine-gun bullets to both sides of the road and to our front."[131]

On 27 September, the panzergrenadiers occupied a line of concrete fortifications left from World War I—this was the area in which Corporal Hitler had served—and found themselves safe from even heavy artillery fire. The division renewed its attacks on 28 September. The spearheads came close to Rechicourt but bogged down, and one prong suffered heavy casualties.[132]

The 11th Panzer Division had achieved enough for the Germans to man a thin defensive line between the German First and Nineteenth armies. Fifth Panzer Army viewed its mission as accomplished.[133]

*   *   *

On 29 September, American air strikes shattered the 11th Panzer Division's forward elements. A/602d Tank Destroyer Battalion was attached to the 2d Cavalry Group in the vicinity of Arracourt and proceeded to the scene of the German rout. The company's gunners claimed eight "Tiger" tanks (no Tigers were present), three armored cars, and an unknown number of enemy personnel.[134]

To the south, the 813th Tank Destroyer Battalion was operating with the 106th Cavalry Group in support of the 79th Infantry Division near Luneville. The cavalry believed it had spotted a force of well-concealed German tanks near Bauzemont, and the cavalry commander suggested that the tank killers investigate. The 1st Platoon of Company C advanced at about 1100 hours and an M10 engaged and knocked out a Mark IV tank. The exchange may have provoked movement, because a second Mark IV and a halftrack pulled into view, both to be dispatched by the TDs. The 3d Platoon arrived, and the eight TDs continued to fire as more vehicles became visible, setting more alight. The Germans' problems were compounded when Allied fighter-bombers struck their positions.

Nearby, Company A's 3d Platoon also spotted the Germans and cut loose. Soon, three more Mark IVs, one halftrack, and a small vehicle had been disabled. The Germans tried to withdraw to the northeast at about 1500 hours, but Company A's 2d Platoon engaged the column and destroyed a Mark V, a Mark IV, a truck, and numerous infantry. The 1st Platoon, meanwhile, shelled and silenced a German artillery battery.

By the time the dust settled, the tank killers had destroyed thirteen Mark IVs, two Panthers, and three halftracks and trucks, and killed or wounded forty-five foot troops. They had lost not a single man or vehicle in exchange.[135]

By 29 September, the Fifth Panzer Army's offensive efforts had run out of steam. Hitler called off the operation and ordered most of his surviving armor northward. The Allies by now held a 20:1 advantage in tanks along the Western Front.[136]

Changes in the Force

Combat experience caused commanders to settle on a major realignment of the Tank Destroyer Force in the ETO. The U.S. 12th Army Group requested that the number of towed battalions be cut to twelve and that ten be reequipped with T5E1 90mm guns. On 29 September, HQS, European Theater, approved the conversion of all twelve towed battalions to 90mm guns. How close the tank killers came to fielding an even more unwieldy weapon! Fortunately, no 90mm towed guns were immediately available.

Of the remaining forty battalions, twenty were to receive the M36 TD and the remainder to retain M10s or M18s at the discretion of the army commanders and within the constraints of supply of the weapons.[137]

A Gun for Hunting Big Game

Standardized in June 1944, the M36 Jackson was an adaptation of the M10A1 (the gasoline-powered variant), and many were in fact returreted M10A1s. The vehicle mounted the 90mm M3 gun in an open-topped turret equipped with power traverse.

The gun was rated as capable of penetrating three inches of homogenous armor at forty-seven hundred yards. In practice, it could kill most big cats—the Tiger I and Panther—at typical combat ranges. A crew from the 610th Tank Destroyer Battalion made the *New York Daily News* when gunner Cpl Anthony Pinto (1st Platoon, Company A) destroyed a Panther with a remarkable shot from forty-two hundred yards.[138] Lieutenant Alfred Rose from the 814th Tank Destroyer Battalion on 1 December 1944 scored a panzer kill at forty-six hundred yards—the maximum range of the telescopic sight—with eight rounds.

Tests conducted by the 703d Tank Destroyer Battalion in early December using captured Mark Vs, however, indicated that the Panther's front armor could deflect some shots fired from as little as one hundred fifty yards. The battalion concluded that the M36 should still maneuver for side shots even against the Panther, that if that were not possible two TDs should engage the target, and that the 90mm gun would not penetrate the front armor of the Royal Tiger (Tiger II) at any range. The battalion called for better ammunition rather than a bigger gun.

Once again, the only machine gun was a rear-mounted .50-caliber for antiaircraft defense.

The hull was identical to that of the M10, except for minor modifications to provide stowage for the larger ammunition, and the vehicle was equipped with a small auxiliary generator, which had often been requested by M10 crews. The pressing requirement for 90mm antitank weapons at the front convinced the Army to put M36 turrets onto one hundred eighty-seven M4A3 Sherman chassis, which retained the thick armor and hull machine gun. This variant, dubbed the M36B1, further blurred the distinction between the tank and the tank destroyer.

Production of the M36B2 began in early 1945. This series used retired M10 hulls (diesel engines), provided folding flaps of steel to cover the turret top, and incorporated a muzzle brake on the main gun.[139]

*   *   *

The first M36 Jacksons arrived in the ETO in September. The First and Ninth armies channeled arriving M36s to TD battalions supporting armored divisions, while Third Army used them to convert towed battalions. The 610th Tank Destroyer Battalion (towed) was the first to reequip, beginning 25 September.[140] (The 776th Tank Destroyer Battalion—in Naples to prepare for transfer to France—was probably the first outfit in Europe to actually receive the M36 in September, but it did not arrive in the ETO until early October.) The 703d Tank Destroyer Battalion (M10s) began the transition on 30 September and first used the new TDs in combat in October. The 703d almost immediately cut the .50-caliber machine-gun mounts off the backs of the turrets and welded them to the left front corners. By year's end, only seven battalions had received the M36.[141]

The first trickle of Hyper-Velocity Armor Piercing (HVAP) ammunition for the 3-inch and 76mm guns began to arrive in September, as well. The tungsten-core round offered TDs and tankers the possibility of destroying the Panther and Tiger from the front, but combat reports indicate the American vehicle still had to close, in most cases, to within several hundred yards. The ammunition remained extremely scarce until the end of the war. Anecdotal reports on ammunition supplies in TD and separate tank battalions suggest there is some truth to the assertion that tank destroyer outfits received top priority in allocation of the "souped-up" ammo.

Chapter 8

The Battle for the Border

"It was the doughboy, the tanker, and the TD who cracked 'The Line'
and broke through the vaunted defense system."

— History of the 823d Tank Destroyer Battalion

The German High Command judged that the West Wall would hold
if the Americans failed to break through immediately. The generals
anticipated a concentrated American thrust through the line at Aachen in
mid-September. By 25 September, the High Command concluded the
immediate crisis had passed.[1] On 27 September, Ultra codebreakers
deciphered a message sent several days earlier directing that all SS
divisions—beginning with four panzer and one panzergrenadier
divisions and three Tiger battalions—be withdrawn for rest and
refitting.[2]

A war of attrition took hold in October 1944 that engulfed the front
along or near the German border from British and Canadian positions in
the Dutch tidal lowlands to American and French foxholes near
Switzerland. The tank destroyer crews were intimately involved,
although for months the fighting bore no resemblance to the conditions
postulated by doctrine.

Montgomery had tried to flank the German border defenses with Operation Market-Garden beginning 17 September. His uncharacteristically bold plan to leap the lower Rhine by using American and British airborne divisions to capture a series of strategic bridges for use by follow-on armor had fallen just short. Monty's offensive effectively ended on 23 September. In the aftermath, Eisenhower opted to continue his strategy of applying pressure along the entire front. The Wehrmacht, however, was no longer hopelessly fragmented and reeling. The Siegfried Line provided the bracing a defending army needed to plant its feet and fight back.

The West Wall, construction of which began in 1936, ran nearly 400 miles from north of Aachen along the German frontier to the Swiss border. The Germans had neglected the defenses after 1940, so Hitler worked furiously during the collapse in France to put together a scratch force of 135,000 men to partially rebuild and man the line. The rehabilitated defenses were, on average, three miles deep. The strongest portion faced Patton along the Saar River between the Moselle and the Rhine. The second most formidable section was a double band of defenses protecting the Aachen gap, with the city of Aachen lying between the two. Immediately behind the West Wall in this sector was the Roer River, which gave the Germans a backstop that they could flood by releasing water from dams farther south near Schmidt.[3]

Pillboxes in the West Wall typically had reinforced concrete walls and roofs three to eight feet thick and were generally twenty to thirty feet wide, forty to fifty feet deep, and twenty to twenty-five feet high, with at least half of the structure under the ground. In some areas, rows of "dragon's teeth"—reinforced concrete pyramids—acted as antitank obstacles. In other areas, the defenses relied on natural features—rivers, lakes, forests, defiles, and so on—to provide passive antitank protection.[4]

The 702d Tank Destroyer Battalion recorded one view of the Siegfried Line in the area near Übach, Germany, in October: "The average pillbox had only one, or at most, two apertures, from which the enemy was able to deliver small-arms, machine-gun, and AT fire. Much more dangerous than the pillboxes, which could usually be reduced without much difficulty, were numerous AT guns—dug in and skillfully camouflaged between the pillboxes, and protected by infantry in firing trenches and bomb-proof dugouts."[5]

The defenders also had artillery. Lt Leon Neel of the 823d Tank Destroyer Battalion said of the incoming shells, "There wasn't enough room in the sky for any more."[6]

* * *

The official U.S. Army history noted, "The fighting during September, October, November, and early December belonged to the small units and individual soldiers. . . . A company, battalion, or regiment fighting alone and often unaided was more the rule than the exception."[7] The period also marked the point at which the American combined-arms team began to gel in the ETO. Riflemen, tanks, and TDs supported by artillery worked together better than they had in the bocage. Shared experience had much to do with the improvement.

Panzers appeared rarely and then in small numbers, while pillboxes, fortifications, towns, cities, and trench lines posed the main challenges to infantry and armored divisions along the border. The result was that, as in the bocage, the self-propelled tank destroyers frequently filled in as assault guns, little different from the role played by the tanks.

A memo from the 803d Tank Destroyer Battalion described a typical action in which the TDs of Company B, one company of tanks, and doughs from the 30th Infantry Division's 119th Infantry attacked the Siegfried Line near Rimburg on 2 October: "Each platoon was equipped with a 300-series radio borrowed from the infantry battalion whom they were supporting. . . . All pillboxes were encountered in pairs, mutually supporting. The TD platoon was employed with two guns firing, one into each of the pillbox embrasures, and the other two guns overwatching. This pinned down the enemy personnel and allowed our infantry to infiltrate to the blind side. When in position to make the final assault, infantry would call by radio for fire to be lifted. In a few cases, fire from the M10 would drive the enemy out of his position. . . . Unless the M10 could get into position to fire into the embrasure, [it] was useless. No amount of fire from the 3-inch gun could penetrate the thickness of these defenses."[8]

Company C of the 803d, meanwhile, coordinated fire plans with the infantry and acted as the forward observer for artillery via a telephone link at one of the infantry battalion CPs. Company A provided fire control for a platoon of Sherman tanks from the 747th Tank Battalion.[9]

The widespread installation in infantry-support tanks starting in October of SCR-300 radios compatible with the walkie-talkie used by the doughs contributed tremendously to battlefield cooperation, and the case of Company B at Rimburg showed that the TDs were more effective when so equipped, too. Oddly, however, TD units were not issued the SCR-300, despite pleas from at least some battalion commanders for the radios.[10]

The Battle of Aachen

Of the four American armies along the front, only First Army was able to claim a major milestone in October. Ninth Army, having finished clearing Brest, entered the line between the First Army and the British beginning in early October and—short of men and supplies—dug in. Third Army began its first frustrating and bloody attacks aimed at capturing Metz—which became an obsession to Patton—while Seventh Army probed the German defenses along the Vosges Mountains.

First Army CG MajGen Courtney Hodges took aim at Aachen, which had been the seat of Germany's First Reich under Charlemagne. Hodges judged that he lacked the resources to both contain the city and drive through the German defenses before the Rhine River. Prominent military historian Stephen Ambrose concluded, however, "The Battle of Aachen benefited no one. The Americans never should have attacked. The Germans never should have defended. Neither side had a choice. This was war at its worst, wanton destruction for no purpose."[11]

Hodges ordered XIX Corps to punch through the West Wall north of Aachen and complete the encirclement of the city. After days of artillery preparation and a substantial but generally ineffective air strike, the 30th Infantry Division crossed the Würm River and began working through the West Wall on 2 October. The doughs suffered heavy casualties and were on their own the first day because tanks and TDs were unable to advance through the deep muck to provide fire support. The 29th Infantry Division aided the assault on the left with limited-objective attacks.

Combat Command B/2d Armored Division entered the fray through the 30th Infantry Division's sector in the fiercely contested town of Übach on 4 October. The M10s from the 702d Tank Destroyer Battalion provided overwatch while the Shermans pounded pillboxes from close range in support of the advancing riflemen. The attackers finally began to make noticeable progress the next day and soon cut the main highway to Aachen.[12]

On 5 October, the men and towed 3-inch guns of the 823d Tank Destroyer Battalion crossed the Würm River and passed through a gap in the Siegfried line opened by the 30th Infantry Division. The battalion CP set up shop in the basement of a schoolhouse in Übach. The gun platoons deployed into defensive positions with the line battalions of the 29th Infantry Division, and then with their usual partners in the 30th Infantry Division. The guns fired direct missions against pillboxes and indirect ones against more distant German targets.

Covered on the left by the 2d Armored Division, the 30th Infantry Division now pushed south to link up with the 1st Infantry Division east of Aachen. The doughs from the Big Red One, meanwhile, were clawing their way through heavy resistance southeast of the city. On 10 October, with encirclement seemingly ensured, the Americans delivered a surrender ultimatum to the Aachen garrison. Ordered by Hitler to fight to the last man, the commander refused.[13]

*　　*　　*

The Germans gathered reserves and, after a series of unsuccessful piecemeal counterattacks, struck back in growing strength with the 1st SS Panzer Corps beginning on 10 October. A tank-infantry force hit the lines of 120th Infantry Regiment, 30th Infantry Division, at 1300 hours. As Lt Leon Neel directed the action under heavy German fire, a single gun from his 1st Platoon, B/823d, destroyed three Mark IV tanks and two Panthers over six hours, while a second gun KO'd another Mark IV. The battalion's history claims that Cpl Jose Ulibarri personally accounted for four of the tanks with seven rounds in only sixty seconds. The engagement took place at between thirteen hundred and twenty-three hundred yards, and the 3-inchers required an average of three rounds per panzer destroyed. The platoon was also credited with assisting the 230th Field Artillery in disabling three more German tanks. The platoon suffered no casualties.

The Germans tried again the next day at about 1600 hours but pulled back after losing two more panzers. This time, however, they destroyed one 823d gun with direct fire and killed one man and wounded eight more. The guns of Company A shifted forward to strengthen the antitank defense.

Evidently having learned little about the futility of driving toward emplaced guns with long fields of fire, the panzers tried one last time on 12 October. The determined assault closed to within four hundred yards of the American positions, and 2d Platoon of Company B smashed two Panthers and a Tiger, while Company A's guns claimed one Mark V and two Mark VIs. Each TD company lost one 3-inch gun in the exchange, while Company B was left to find three new halftracks—including one to replace a vehicle buried beneath a collapsed building.[14]

Massed artillery fire—capped by a dramatic appearance by American fighter-bombers—smashed German tank-infantry attacks aimed at the 1st Infantry Division on 15 October. The American circle closed around Aachen the next day.[15]

The Big Red One, meanwhile, had launched its assault on the city itself on 10 October with a bombardment by three hundred fighter-bombers and twelve artillery battalions.

Lieutenant Colonel Derrill Daniel's 2/26th Infantry Regiment, backed by TDs from A/634th Tank Destroyer Battalion and tanks from the 745th Tank Battalion, was tasked with clearing the south and center of Aachen. While dug in at the outskirts prior to the assault, Daniel had used the tanks as "snipers" against MG nests and the TDs to blow up buildings suspected of harboring OPs.[16] But now he had to take the buildings—a lot of them.

Initially, Daniel assigned a mixed force of three or more Shermans and two TDs to support an infantry company. The armor's job was to blast ahead of the infantry, drive the enemy into cellars, and generally "scare the hell out of them." Tanks and TDs had prearranged infantry protection in return, but small arms fire forced the doughs to move cautiously, dashing from door to door and hole to hole. One 2d Platoon M10 was knocked out approaching Triererstrasse by a bazooka fried from a pile of logs only twenty-five yards away. It took the doughs from Company F some time to spot the offender and take him out with a BAR.

The 3/26th Infantry Regiment, meanwhile cleared a factory district on the east side of the city. M10s from 3d Platoon, 634th Tank Destroyer Battalion, and Shermans played backup. When the doughs came under fire, a tank or TD would return fire until the riflemen moved in and cleared the building with grenades.

The two battalions launched their attack on the city proper on 13 October. Companies F and G from 2d Battalion each had three Shermans and one M10 attached, while Company G had three tanks and two TDs. The armor had difficulty negotiating embankments along the main rail line; several successfully slid down a ten-foot bank, while others went under the tracks only fifteen yards from the main underpass in which German demolitions were visible.[17]

Lieutenant Colonel Daniel soon developed a more frugal tactical approach for the urban fighting: A tank or tank destroyer went into action beside each infantry platoon. The armor would keep each successive building under fire until the riflemen moved in to assault it. The crews usually fired HE rounds on fuse-delay through doors, windows, or thin walls to explode inside. Only once a building was cleared and the doughs became safe from muzzle blast would the tank or TD fire on its next target. Machine guns mounted to the front of the TD turrets added invaluable support during the street fighting. The process quickly produced tremendous teamwork. Light artillery, meanwhile, crept two or three blocks ahead of the advancing troops, while heavy artillery dropped beyond that.[18]

Colonel John Seitz, commanding the 26th Infantry Regiment, described the approach in a lessons-learned report: "We proceeded without undue hurry, realizing that street fighting requires great physical exertion and considerable time if buildings are to be thoroughly searched and cleared. Our policy of searching every room and closet in every building, blowing every sewer, and mopping up each sector paid dividends in later security. . . . We placed tanks, TDs, and SP guns in position just before daylight or at dusk. We would have the engineers and [TD] pioneer-platoon men blow holes in the near walls of buildings. Then we would run the vehicles into the buildings and provide apertures for the gun barrels by blowing smaller holes in the far walls."[19]

The tank destroyers expended tremendous amounts of ammunition—one platoon, for example, fired two hundred fourteen rounds of HE and thirty-six rounds of AP at strongpoints in one thirty-six-hour period. The TDs encountered German armor only once during the push to the center of Aachen, when two panzers thought to be Tigers supported by infantry attacked 3d Battalion's Company K near the Kurhaus on 15 October. One Tiger penetrated to some woods within two hundred yards of the battalion CP, where two 3d Platoon M10s engaged it by firing at its muzzle flash. Corporal Wenzlo Simmons, who was acting as gunner because his commander was absent with a toothache, was credited with making a kill. During the drive to Aachen's center, only two men were killed and five men wounded, and two TDs were lost.[20]

By 21 October, American troops had reached the German CP and were using 155mm guns to bash holes through the thick walls of medieval buildings that were impervious to TD and tank fire. The first time an SP 155mm was used, an M10 fired sixteen rounds at a wall to create a hole through which the gun could fire. The German commander surrendered, commenting, "When the Americans start using 155s as sniper weapons, it is time to give up."[21]

No Fire-and-Maneuver Here

The muck along the West Wall played havoc with towed 3-inch guns during the autumn (even SP guns were often road-bound). Some battalions called for replacing the M3 halftrack prime movers with fully tracked vehicles, such as modified M5 light tanks. There was also a call for wider tires for the 3-inch gun carriage. The 635th noted in its AAR for October, "Speed is not as essential as getting in and out of the positions tactics demand."[22] But commanders also realized that this meant that the towed guns had to be in place already to stop an armored attack, because they could not be repositioned speedily enough to deal with unexpected threats.[23]

The lack of natural cover and concealment in front of many West Wall defenses meant that towed guns had to move into well protected, previously prepared positions to survive intense artillery and mortar fire. The prime movers and other vehicles also needed to be dug in and sandbagged—a single piece of shrapnel in the gas tank of a halftrack would usually set it alight. The change of terrain had in no measure changed this lesson from the thick bocage.[24]

*   *   *

Far to the south, the U.S. Seventh Army was fighting through the rough, forested terrain before the Vosges Mountains. The thick woods cut down fields of fire so much that the TDs were often of little use beyond providing a boost for infantry morale. And even that was debatable: The Germans usually reacted with artillery fire to the sound of TD engines, thus putting the doughs at greater risk. German armor, when it was encountered, was usually pre-placed in woods and more vulnerable to bazooka attack by the infantry than to TD gunnery.

The 773d and 813th Tank Destroyer battalions became embroiled in fighting to clear the Foret de Parroy and Foret de Haguenau east of Luneville with the doughs of the 79th Infantry Division. The fighting in the forests offered a heavy dose of the danger TD crews faced in their open turrets from artillery shells exploding amongst the treetops. On 7 October, the 779th began to install steel covers on the tops of its M10 turrets to protect its crews from airbursts. For good measure, the outfit moved all .50-caliber machine gun mounts to the turret fronts.[25]

The 813th did not cover its turrets until early 1945. Corporal Harry Dunnagan of the 813th recalled one incident. "We had one man stranding up in the turret on guard. The rest of us were lying down in the tank sleeping. Shortly after dark, a loud explosion shook me awake. That was a [tree-burst] directly over the open turret, and it was on its mark. Fortunately, I was not hit. As I looked up, the man in the turret, Clancy A. Jordan, was sinking down, saying "Mother" and other words I couldn't understand. I reached for him and tried to see if I could give him some [morphine]. There was no time; by the time he reached the floor, he was dead. I put my hand on our sergeant, George M. Richey, to try to wake him; he was silent. He was dead. The lieutenant's legs were chopped up."[26]

Dunnagan was promoted to sergeant and took over the M10. The very next day, Dunnagan's destroyer advanced with the infantry. Both sides were using artillery, and the other gun in the section was hit, and its crew bailed out when the .50-caliber ammo caught fire. Dunnagan's replacement gunner blindly fired HE into the trees wherever the infantry said there were Germans. Before the day was out, the new gunner was wounded by shrapnel from a 20mm shell that struck a tree limb overhead.[27]

The weather deteriorated steadily as snow and ice alternated with rain and mud. That meant that the TDs could not advance until engineers cleared the roads of mines, and that as a consequence the infantry had usually reached its objective before the destroyers could move up.

The M10s frequently served as artillery pieces, although the steep slopes meant that often the flat-trajectory 3-inch guns could not hit desired targets. Recon established listening posts from which they directed artillery fire and provided antitank defense warning. And men learned to fire the bazooka.[28]

*   *   *

Even where TDs could fight, the heavy combat all along the front resulted in serious artillery ammunition shortages by October. Once again, TD battalions showed they could step into the breach. Between 16 and 26 October, for example, M18s from the 602d Tank Destroyer Battalion conducted one hundred thirty-eight indirect fire missions under the control of XII Corps Artillery in support of the 26th and 35th Infantry and 4th Armored divisions.[29]

*   *   *

With tank destroyers operating almost entirely like tanks when performing direct-fire missions, a simple improvement made to infantry-support tanks as early as the bocage fighting finally came to some TDs. On 1 November, the 9th Infantry Division informed the 899th Tank Destroyer Battalion that field telephones would be installed on its M10s once installation on the attached tanks was completed. The division thought there would be enough phones to cover the entire battalion. This simple expedient permitted a rifleman to talk to the commander in the turret while crouching—with at least some cover—at the rear of the vehicle. In view of the continued lack of radio links between the doughs and most TD outfits, this fix permitted some relatively safe communication while under fire.[30]

The 3d Infantry Division demonstrated that more could have been done on the communications front more broadly. By October, the division had introduced a common radio frequency for use by the doughs, the tank killers from the 601st Tank Destroyer Battalion, and the tankers of the 756th Tank Battalion—a fix that produced a high degree of cooperation among the arms.[31]

A Grim Struggle

November was like October for the TDers, only more so: more bloody attacks against well-dug-in defenders, and more bloody bad weather. Casualties had been so heavy in front-line infantry units in October they were suffering severe shortages of riflemen. The worsening weather was cutting dramatically into the number of close-support missions the Air Corps could fly to ease the job faced by the infantry and armored divisions—and their supporting tank destroyers. However, by the end of the first week of the month, the transportation system was finally delivering most of the supplies needed by the front-line troops.[32]

* * *

The under-publicized Seventh Army—dubbed "America's forgotten army" by military historian Charles Whiting—set the pace for the entire Western Front in November. Major General Alexander "Sandy" Patch on 29 September had gained control of XV Corps after his men had linked with Third Army, and the Normandy veterans settled in beside the Italian veterans of VI Corps. The divisions had burned themselves out trying to break through the German Vosges Mountain defenses in October, but November brought three fresh formations—the 100th and 103d Infantry and 14th Armored divisions—into the line.

Seventh Army and the First French Army to its right (together comprising the 6th Army Group) had one slight advantage over the troops farther north: The terrain was awful, the weather conditions terrible, and the defenders tenacious, but the men had not yet confronted the West Wall. Moreover, the German forces facing them—in the estimation of the German Nineteenth Army commanding general—were incapable of stopping another concerted offensive.[33]

A blanket of wet snow covered the XV Corps front the morning of 13 November after heavy rains had given way to blizzards in the preceding days. Streams and rivers were swollen and many bridges were under water. Nonetheless, the 44th and 79th Infantry divisions jumped off as scheduled toward Strasbourg, some fifty miles ahead on the Rhine. On 15 November, the German line in front of the 79th Infantry Division all but collapsed after doughs from the 315th Infantry Regiment—supported by tanks and by TDs from the 813th Tank Destroyer Battalion—hit the

German reserves just as they were assembling for a counterattack. Company A's M10s nailed six SP guns, while Shermans from the 749th Tank Battalion destroyed most of rest of the 708th Volksgrenadier Division's assault guns. By 18 November, the 553d Volksgrenadier Division's defenses were unraveling under the steady pressure from the 44th Infantry Division.[34]

The French 2d Armored Division—formerly a First Army command—began to ease into the line on 16 November and was ready to strike when a hole opened two days later. Armored task forces enveloped the Saverne Gap in the Vosges Mountains. After only five days of fast moving against little resistance, the French tanks rolled east across the Alsatian plains and entered Strasbourg at 1030 hours on 23 November.[35] Recon men from the 813th Tank Destroyer Battalion operated with the French division during the final dash. Company C, 776th Tank Destroyer Battalion, meanwhile, worked with the 106th Cavalry Group, which screened the French north flank.[36]

The 3d Infantry Division and the rest of VI Corps pushed through the High Vosges and joined XV Corps on the Rhine River. The M10s from the 601st acted as assault guns during the 3d Infantry Division's breakthrough and fired on strongpoints. No German armor was encountered. A platoon of Recon Company led the advance into Strasbourg to relieve the French on 27 November.[37]

*   *   *

The 636th Tank Destroyer Battalion also battled through the Vosges with the 36th Infantry Division. One night, Sgt Tom Sherman had to drive a new lieutenant forward to one of the gun platoons. Crawling up a winding mountain trail with no lights, Sherman just made out a hand waving him to a stop. The sergeant recognized one of the outfit's old campaigners, a veteran of every fight since Salerno. The soldier motioned Sherman and the lieutenant to silence. "See those lights over there?" he whispered in a voice tight with fear. "That's a German tank."

"Why don't you go get it?" queried the lieutenant quietly.

"I don't want it," replied the soldier.[38]

*   *   *

Not far to the north, Patton's dashing Third Army spent most of November deep in mud as it prosecuted the almost medieval reduction of the fortifications at and around Metz. The tank destroyers played the role of modern-day siege engines. Twentieth Corps had the mission to capture the city and three infantry (the 5th, 90th, and 95th) and one armored (the 10th) divisions—supported by seven tank destroyer battalions—with which to do so.[39]

The first assaults on the nearly impervious fortresses had begun as early as 27 September, when the 818th Tank Destroyer Battalion participated in a costly and ultimately unsuccessful 5th Infantry Division bid to take Fort Driant, one of the outer defenses around Metz. The TD fire proved completely ineffective against the works—but no great shame, because heavy artillery and air strikes failed as well.[40]

By November, XX Corps planners had decided to invest the fortifications the corps could not storm and to isolate and capture Metz itself. The entire Third Army launched an offensive on 8 November in weather so atrocious that the attack caught the Germans by surprise. The TDs provided direct fire support to the attacking doughs when they could, but between the rushing Moselle River and the mud, the vehicles often had trouble reaching the forward positions. Two platoons from B/773d Tank Destroyer Battalion helped beat off a vigorous German tank-infantry counterattack launched against the 90th Infantry Division's 358th Infantry Regiment at Distroff on 15 November. Two gun sections of Company B were overrun. When the TDers withdrew, one M10 overturned, and three crewmen were wounded by enemy fire. The German attack carried into Distroff, where the remaining M10s engaged several German SP guns, with both sides losing one vehicle. The street fighting was so close and the issue in such doubt that the American commander called artillery down on his own positions. The panzergrenadiers eventually pulled back.[41]

Patton's pincers clamped shut around Metz on 18 November. Two days later, elements of the 5th and 95th Infantry divisions (with the towed 774th and 607th Tank Destroyer battalions attached, respectively) had fought their way into the city. Resistance ceased two days after that.[42]

Elsewhere in the Third Army's sector, ground conditions were so poor that even when the 4th Armored Division and 704th Tank Destroyer Battalion clashed with the Panzer Lehr Division near Baerendorf in mid-November, both sides' road-bound armor could only act as artillery support for the armored infantry and panzergrenadiers.[43]

The Fifth Panzer Army mysteriously slipped away from the front by 20 November, but the German infantry holding the West Wall defenses remained to trouble the tank killers.[44] Where the doughs tried to clear the pillboxes, the tank destroyers provided fire support.

Much of the Siegfried Line around Saarlautern incorporated the local towns, which forced the TD crews to remember everything they had been taught about street fighting. The 607th Tank Destroyer Battalion—which had been re-equipped with M36s during the battle for Metz—supported the doughs of the 379th Infantry Regiment, 95th Infantry Division, in the capture of Saarlautern. The assault across the Saar River began the night of 2–3 December, and early the next morning, Lt Richard Reynolds led his TD platoon across a captured bridge still wired for demolition. (The 607th's informal history attributes the action at the bridge to Lt Calvin Stone, but the official U.S. Army history cites a DSC award in attributing command to Reynolds.) The Germans counterattacked with tanks and infantry supported by heavy artillery fire. Reynold's M36s helped repulse wave after wave of assaults—including a night-time attempt to run tanks loaded with explosives onto the bridge that the TD crews stopped only two hundred yards short—and destroyed four panzers for the loss of one destroyer.

Two M36s from Company C, meanwhile, supported the infantry attack on southern Saarlautern and Linsdorf. The TDs were advancing carefully up a street to eliminate a roadblock when a window shutter opened and a German bazooka crew fired at the lead vehicle. The round struck the turret, but a bedroll and a turret lifting ring detonated the warhead and saved the destroyer. The covering M36 pounded the adjacent houses, and thirty-five German soldiers emerged to surrender.

The grinding advance continued toward the suburb of Fraulautern, with the TDs engaging pillboxes and other strongpoints in support of the infantry. Each advance was met by heavy artillery and mortar fire. Eighteen hundred rounds struck the 607th's positions at Fraulautern in a single day. During the battle for the town, Pvt Eugene Esposito from Company C had to take charge of his M36 when his commander was killed by machine-gun fire. Esposito destroyed the MG and its crew. He then ordered his vehicle forward and spotted a bazooka crew hiding behind a stone wall, and he dispatched them as well. He next spotted a flamethrower team creeping toward him along the wall. This time, his 90mm fire dropped the wall on top of the Germans. And the fighting went on.[45]

*   *   *

To Patton's north, Hodges's First Army received the nod to undertake the main effort for the American 12th Army Group when Eisenhower, Monty, and Bradley conferred on 18 October. Hodges decided he had to try again to clear the Hürtgen Forest before he could push on to the Rhine River. General Omar Bradley years later conceded, "What followed . . . was some of the most brutal and difficult fighting of the war. The battle . . . was sheer butchery on both sides."[46]

The Hürtgen was a dense fir forest covering a broken land of gorges and sharp ridges. The Germans had embedded a seemingly endless series of camouflaged defensive positions through the forest. A few narrow trails and fire breaks offered TDs and tanks the only routes for maneuvering forward, and these were often mined and covered by AT guns. Indeed, armor could offer help to the doughs only occasionally.

On 2 November, V Corps' 28th Infantry Division, which had recently replaced the exhausted 9th Infantry Division, kicked off an attack aimed at seizing control of the Monchau-Schmidt area. The 112th Infantry Regiment advanced up the narrow Kall Trail and took Schmidt by the next day. American commanders had failed to reckon with the fact that the Germans would view the operation as being aimed at the nearby Roer River dams, and the men were therefore surprised when a vigorous tank-supported counterattack exploded out of the trees. The doughs were driven out of Schmidt and fell back to a village called Kommerscheidt.

Three Shermans from the 707th Tank Battalion executed a daring advance up the Kall Trail on 4 November to support the doughs in Kommerscheidt, but the M4s were hard-pressed by the German panzers. The next day, six more Shermans and nine TDs from C/893d Tank Destroyer Battalion traversed the treacherous trail to bolster the defenses, but to no avail.

TD platoon commander Lt Turney Leonard earned a Medal of Honor for his part in the action, which his citation described in these terms: "During the fierce three-day engagement, [Leonard] repeatedly braved overwhelming enemy fire in advance of his platoon to direct the fire of his tank destroyer from exposed, dismounted positions. He went on lone reconnaissance missions to discover what opposition his men faced, and on one occasion, when fired upon by a hostile machine gun, advanced alone and eliminated the enemy emplacement with a hand grenade. When a strong German attack threatened to overrun friendly positions, he moved through withering artillery, mortar, and small arms fire, reorganized confused infantry units whose leaders had become casualties, and exhorted them to hold firm. Although wounded early in battle, he continued to direct fire from his advanced position until he was disabled by a high-explosive shell which shattered his arm, forcing him to withdraw. He was last seen at a medical aid station which was subsequently captured by the enemy. By his superb courage, inspiring leadership, and indomitable fighting spirit, 1st Lt Leonard enabled our forces to hold off the enemy attack and was personally responsible for the direction of fire which destroyed six German tanks."

The defenses at Kommerscheidt collapsed on 7 November. The 28th Infantry Division's offensive ended in failure at the cost of six thousand casualties, thirty-one Sherman tanks, and sixteen M10 TDs. The division and its attached units moved to the quiet Ardennes sector to recover.[47]

* * *

Company C, 628th Tank Destroyer Battalion accompanied CCR/5th Armored Division into the gloomy forest in early December to support the doughs of the 4th Infantry Division, who had replaced the men of the 28th Infantry Division. The 628th recalled this as "by far the most intense period of combat experienced by any unit of this battalion." Artillery fire confined the men to their armored vehicles for long periods, but the open turrets on the M36 still left them vulnerable to air bursts and shrapnel. After a shell caught two crews in one turret—the second had taken refuge after the M36 hit one of the ubiquitous mines—the battalion resolved to build armored covers for all its TDs (accomplished by January). At one point, only a single Company C M36 was operational because of combat losses in vehicles and crewmen.[48]

On 13 December, the newly committed 83d Infantry Division finally emerged on the far side of the Hürtgen Forest. But the Germans still held Schmidt and the Roer River dams.[49]

* * *

The Ninth Army had drawn the assignment of driving to the Roer River from north of Aachen in conjunction with First Army's VII Corps. The terrain was generally flat, and villages across the plains provided strongpoints that the Germans typically reinforced with trench lines. The terrain offered the German tank killers long fields of fire that gave maximum advantage to their excellent optics and high-velocity antitank weapons. The frequent rains restricted armor on both sides to the roads, which gave even greater advantage to the defender.

The Ninth Army's offensive began at 1245 hours on 16 November. The Roer River lay at its farthest point twelve miles east of American lines.[50] Nineteenth Corps, supported on the left by gradual commitment of XIII Corps, made good initial progress, but German resistance built and forward progress slowed.[51]

The 702d Tank Destroyer Battalion was operating as usual with the 2d Armored Division—which was the northernmost element in XIX Corps—while the newly arrived the 771st Tank Destroyer Battalion had been attached to the neighboring 102d Infantry Division. The former battalion was just converting to the M36.

The 2d Armored Division captured the town of Puffendorf within hours of jump-off on 16 November. The Germans viewed this effort as the most pressing threat, and von Rundstedt authorized the use of the reserve 9th Panzer and 15th Panzergrenadier divisions to contain the menace. The former, accompanied by a Tiger tank battalion, struck back on 17 November.[52] The panzers included the new Mark VI Royal Tiger—a 70-ton monster with 150mm (six inches) of sloped frontal armor and an 88mm gun with an even higher muzzle velocity than that found on the regular Tiger.[53]

Combat Command B's Task Force 1 was just forming up for the day's attack when about twenty panzers, supported by infantry and artillery, burst through heavy morning mist into its positions. A tank battle ensued which the Americans lost decisively. 9th Panzer Division attacks struck other CCB task forces during the morning. The M36s (and a few remaining M10s) from the 702d Tank Destroyer Battalion engaged the attackers and KO'd six panzers during the day. The fighting cost the 2d Armored Division eighteen medium and seven light tanks destroyed and about the same number damaged.[54]

The Germans and Americans generally took a defensive posture the next day, but the 2d Armored and 29th Infantry divisions captured the town of Setterich, which provided enough room to commit CCA. On 20 November, the 9th Panzer Division retaliated with a force of between sixty and eighty Tigers and Panthers. LtCol John Beall, CO of the 702d Tank Destroyer Battalion, threw an old North Africa German trick back at the enemy. A few American tanks approached the Germans and then fled, which lured the Germans within range of his new 90mm guns.[55]

The Jerries had their own tricks, however. The 702d's AAR for 17–21 November recorded: "The enemy used the heavy armor of his Mark VI tanks to full advantage. In several instances, the enemy maneuvered his heavily armored tanks into position between three thousand and thirty-five hundred yards from our TDs and tanks and opened fire. At this distance, our TDs could not penetrate the front of the Mark VI and the enemy evidently knew this for he [kept] only his heavily armored front exposed. At this distance, our 90mm gun would ricochet off the Mark VI, and usually the high-velocity gun of the Mark VI would penetrate and knock out our vehicles."

The 9th Panzer Division attack also struck the positions of the 102d Infantry Division's 405th and 406th RCTs on 19 and 20 November, and the crews from the 771st Tank Destroyer Battalion experienced a major tank battle as their first real action. Shortly after dawn on the first day, the German thrust penetrated the American lines. Company C's Lt George Killmer ran from vehicle to vehicle in the confusion and brought his guns to bear against four Mark IVs and four Panthers. When wounded crewmen evacuated one M10, Sgt Walter Nedza recruited two riflemen to help him serve the gun. The three climbed into the turret under fire and dispatched a Mark V. The rest of the company eliminated the remaining seven panzers and lost only one M10 in the fire fight. A few hours later, the company's gunners KO'd three more Panthers.

The action on 20 November cost Company C more dearly. The TDs in the course of three engagements accounted for two Royal Tigers, but the massive panzers knocked out six M10s. Several times, the crews watched in frustration as their 3-inch rounds bounced off the Tigers' thick hides. Company A, meanwhile, fired on Royal Tigers about noon and stopped two of them. The battle against the panzers cost the battalion five men killed and twenty-two wounded.[56]

By 21 November, the 2d Armored Division was again making slow forward progress, although German tanks, often dug in, remained a major problem. The 702d Tank Destroyer Battalion gunners had destroyed a total of twenty-four panzers in the course of the 9th Panzer Division's attack. The battalion lost three M36s in exchange.[57]

Ninth Army did not clear the west bank of the Roer River until 9 December. Army headquarters in late November sought permission from 12 Army Group to convert two of its four towed battalions to M10s on an emergency basis because "self-propelled tank destroyers of all types are urgently needed in combat."[58] The tough fighting cost ten thousand American battle casualties.[59]

Cannons at Climbach

The M20 scout car advanced cautiously toward yet another picturesque but probably deadly French village on the margins of the Siegfried Line. It was 14 December 1944, and a task force under command of LtCol John Blackshear had as its objective the town of Climbach, France, and a German armored concentration reported to be there. The task force consisted of one company from the 411th Infantry Regiment, 103d Infantry Division; a heavy weapons platoon with machine guns and mortars; one platoon of tanks from the 14th Armored Division; and 3d Platoon, Company C, 614th Tank Destroyer Battalion (towed).[60]

Company C's Lt Charles Thomas, commanding the TD detachment, was riding in the lead scout car, followed by a section of his 3-inch guns. As the vehicles reached some high ground three hundred yards east of Climbach, a storm of fire erupted from German tanks and antitank guns about seven hundred yards away. Thomas's M20 was hit, and although severely wounded, the lieutenant motioned the column to halt and helped evacuate his crew from the wrecked vehicle. He suffered additional wounds to his chest, legs, and left arm. Thomas nevertheless directed the deployment of his two guns so that they could engage the Germans, and only then turned command over to platoon leader Lt George Mitchell. The guns unlimbered in an open field affording no protection. This was the only place from which they could fire on the German positions.

The bombardment by the 3-inch guns drove the panzers to pull back and seek defilade positions. But small-arms, mortar, and artillery fire began to strike the American gun positions. Men dropped, killed or wounded, and one gun was quickly knocked out. Mitchell ordered his other two guns forward, but he fell wounded. Despite the loss of their commanders, the crews of the two guns manhandled their weapons into position. The American tanks had become mired and could not advance to help them, and the infantry remained behind the gun positions.

The Germans now mounted an attack using a few tanks and some infantry. Skeleton crews manned the guns by now. Private First Class Whit Knight manned one gun alone. He sighted, loaded, and fired his weapon at the attacking Germans as explosions heated the air around him. Realizing that his gun would not stop the infantry, Knight leaped to a machine gun on a burning halftrack and opened fire. Nearby, other men grabbed small arms and machine guns to fend off the infantry assault. Private First Class Leon Tobin and Cpl Peter Simmons—the only survivors of their crew—continued to pour fire into the attackers until both were struck by bullets. As the Germans fell back, the few remaining tank killers returned to their last serviceable gun.

The American doughs finally pushed forward in a two-pronged assault on Climbach, and American artillery began to seek out the German tanks. The last TD supported the advance and knocked out at least one more machine gun nest for the riflemen.

The action illustrated the unsuitability of towed tank destroyers for mobile operations against a prepared enemy, no matter how determined the tank killers. The engagement had cost the TD company dearly: four enlisted men were killed or mortally wounded, and two officers and seventeen enlisted men were wounded. These heroic soldiers were members of one of the three TD battalions with black enlisted personnel and mostly white officers to see action in Europe with the then-segregated Army. (The other two were the 827th in the ETO and the 679th in Italy.) Lieutenant Thomas was awarded the Medal of Honor many years later, one of seven black recipients from World War II.

*   *   *

While German panzers had appeared to challenge America's tank killers now and again during the fighting along the border, they had rarely done so in any substantial numbers. Granted, the Anglo-American strategic air campaign was reducing panzer production, but Germany in November and December delivered 2,299 tanks and assault guns (new or repaired) to the Western Front. Indeed, during the same period, only 921 went to the Eastern Front.[61]

Where were all the panzers?

Chapter 9

The Battle of the Bulge

"The present situation is to be regarded as one of opportunity
for us and not of disaster."

— General Dwight Eisenhower to his American
army commanders, 19 December 1944

On 19 August, Hitler—who evidently understood that Germany's armies in the West would have to fall back to the West Wall—had told a group of intimates that he planned to launch a major counteroffensive in early November, when bad weather would hobble the Allied air forces. The Fhrer calculated that a devastating victory would break the Western Alliance and permit him to strike a separate peace, so he could deal with the Soviet Union. By mid-September, Hitler had already settled on the Ardennes for his bold strike, the seemingly impassable forested and broken plateau where Germany had successfully attacked in 1914 and 1940. He would dole out just enough men and equipment to keep the border defenses from crumbling while gathering his resources in utmost secrecy.[1]

Delays slowed the project, but by early December, Hitler had assembled twenty-eight divisions for his offensive—Operation Wacht Am Rhein (Watch on the Rhine)—and another six for a supporting offensive—Operation Nordwind (Northwind)—in Alsace. This was the largest reserve Germany had been able to accumulate in two years, albeit much weaker than the strike force available when German troops had slashed through the same area in 1940.[2] Moreover, troops below the level of officers and NCOs were often new to battle.

The U.S. 12th Army Group intelligence assessment for 12 December asserted: "It is now certain that attrition is steadily sapping the strength of German forces on the Western Front, and the crust of defense is thinner, more brittle, and more vulnerable than it appears on our G-2 maps or to the troops in the line." Three days later, the British 21st Army Group appreciation observed: "The enemy is at present fighting a defensive campaign on all fronts; his situation is such that he cannot stage major offensive operations. Furthermore, at all costs he has to prevent the war from entering a mobile phase; he has not the transport or the petrol that would be necessary for mobile operations, nor could his tanks compete with ours in the mobile battle."[3]

Bradley understood that a German attack in his thinly held Ardennes sector was a possibility, but believed the risk was acceptable. He had placed no major supply dumps in the area, and he judged he could hit any attack from the flanks and stop it before the Meuse River.[4] The consensus view in the Allied camp was that the Fifth and Sixth Panzer armies (the latter controlling the SS armored formations withdrawn from the fighting beginning in late September) formed a mobile reserve to counterattack any American drive to the Rhine across the Roer River.[5]

Those armies had far different orders than the Allies imagined. Hitler's plan, delivered to Generalfeldmarschall Gerd von Rundstedt complete to the last detail with "NOT TO BE ALTERED" scrawled across it in the Führer's own handwriting, called for a three-pronged offensive along a 75-mile front between Monschau and Echternach.[6] In the north, the Sixth Panzer Army was to strike to and across the Meuse River and then northwest for Antwerp. In the center, the Fifth Panzer Army was to attack through Namur and Dinant toward Brussels. The armored divisions in the first echelon had nearly a thousand tanks and assault guns, while the armored and mechanized reserve possessed another four hundred fifty.[7] The German Seventh Army was to reel out a line of infantry divisions to protect the southern flank of the operation. A "Trojan Horse" unit under special operations veteran SS Hauptsturm-führer (Lieutenant Colonel) Otto Skorzeny, using captured American vehicles and uniforms, was to ease the way to the Meuse once the initial breakthrough was achieved.

Allied forces in November and early December gathered a steady trickle of information suggesting that a German buildup was under way in the Eifel, just behind the Ardennes front. Both sides had deployed into this thus-far quiet sector inexperienced divisions for a low-pressure first taste of war or battered ones for rebuilding. The American divisions, north to south, were the 99th Infantry (green), 106th Infantry (green),

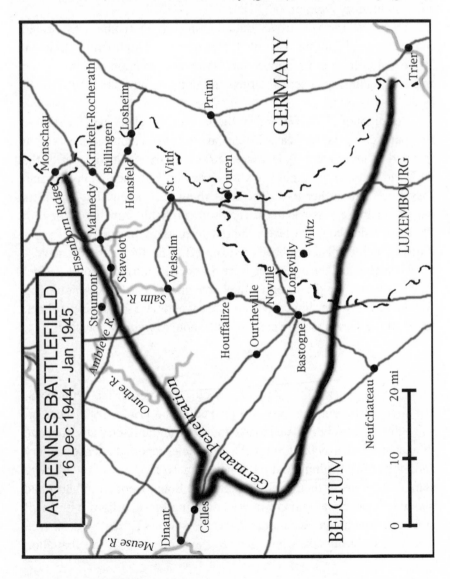

ARDENNES BATTLEFIELD
16 Dec 1944 - Jan 1945

28th Infantry (rebuilding), 9th Armored (green), and 4th Infantry (exhausted).

Towed Guns Tested

Most of the tank destroyer battalions along the front line when the German offensive began were towed outfits deployed, as usual, with forward infantry regiments.

The 801st Tank Destroyer Battalion in early December was located in the Honsfeld-Büllingen-Krinkelt area with the 99th Infantry Division. Its towed 3-inch guns almost daily fired interdiction and harassing missions against unobserved targets in the thick forests behind German lines.

The night of 15–16 December, Sgt James Gallagher heard the rumble of approaching tanks near Hoffen and led a reconnaissance section forward to investigate. A German patrol appeared suddenly out of the dark and ordered the Americans to surrender. The men complied, and they were led further east. The next thing they knew, huge panzers became visible amidst the trees. They were probably from the 1st or 12th SS Panzer division, the lead armored formations of the Sixth Panzer Army, which had been dubbed the main effort for the entire offensive.

Gallagher and the other men were questioned and then shunted aside. Dawn was not far off when Gallagher realized that he was not being watched closely. He slipped away into the woods and found his way back to report the Germans were coming. But soon, everyone knew that.[8]

* * *

Near the center of the Ardennes sector, the men of the 820th Tank Destroyer Battalion had only just arrived at the front on 9 December, when they were subordinated to the untested 106th Infantry Division and its attached 14th Cavalry Group. All companies reported intense artillery and mortar fire beginning at 0400 hours on 16 December, and all wire communications to them were quickly cut. Soon, German infantry had pressed so close that gun crews were fighting for their lives with small arms and hand grenades. Gunner Private First Class Rosenthal destroyed five tanks during the day, but by evening almost all battalion elements—some on foot—were in retreat along with the infantry and cavalry.[9] By early the next morning, the Germans surrounded the two forward infantry regiments.

Just to the south, the towed guns of the 630th Tank Destroyer Battalion were deployed with the regiments of the 28th Infantry Division when the German offensive hit. Most of the armor controlled by the German Seventh Army (which consisted largely of infantry divisions) attacked in the division's sector, as did much of the Fifth Panzer Army.[10] The 630th moved its 3-inchers into previously prepared positions when tank-infantry formations struck the forward lines. But German infantry pushed forward rapidly, and one gun section accompanied by a recon platoon stumbled into a fire fight before it could even reach its assigned spot. By dusk, the 28th Infantry Division was just managing to hold on to some strongpoints at road junctions while the German flood flowed around them. That night, two TD guns were overrun at Hupperdange.[11]

At the southern extreme of the assault zone, the 802d (towed) and 803d (M10) Tank Destroyer battalions were in southern Luxembourg with the 4th Infantry Division, which had been moved to the Ardennes to rest after suffering terrible casualties in the Hürtgen Forest. Although spared the brunt of the panzer assault, the doughs had to fight desperately to hold the line. The 803d deployed Reconnaissance Company, the security section, and cooks as infantry. Nonetheless, the 803d did not record a single confrontation with a German tank during the first two weeks of the battle, and the M10s were employed mostly in the indirect-fire role.[12] The 4th Infantry Division would bend but not break and, soon reinforced by the lead elements of the 10th Armored Division, would form the southern shoulder of the German penetration.

*   *   *

Eisenhower was meeting with Bradley when the first reports of the German offensive reached him. Ike thought it a major operation, but Bradley suspected it was only a spoiling attack. Nonetheless, they agreed to order the 7th Armored Division from Ninth Army and the 10th Armored Division from Third Army to redeploy to the Ardennes as a precaution. The next day, Eisenhower alerted his reserves, the 82d and 101st Airborne divisions, for movement.[13]

*   *   *

At 0500 hours on 17 December, the 3-inch gun crews of 3d Platoon, A/801st Tank Destroyer Battalion watched the main road southeast of Honsfeld. The second section of the recon platoon was deployed a short distance forward. Elsewhere around the town, another platoon from the 801st and several towed guns from the 612th Tank Destroyer Battalion supported the doughs of a provisional infantry unit culled from division rest camps.[14] The men had been under frequent artillery fire since early the day before. But the 99th Infantry Division had been putting up a defense so stiff that the Sixth Panzer Army had been forced to commit the SS armor to help the infantry assault wave.

The sound of tanks reached the men from the gloom ahead. Sergeant James Gallagher, the recon section leader, had been told to expect the arrival of an American cavalry unit; Gallagher set out to investigate, but not before telling his men to pull back if he did not return. The sergeant approached the lead vehicle and was relieved to make out the lines of an M5 light tank. Gallagher called out to the commander in the turret. Suddenly, a rifle butt struck the back of his head.

The rest of the column consisted of Mark IVs.

The column stopped at the road junction in front of 3d Platoon. Recon men creeping back reported that the vehicles were German, so the gun platoon leader ordered his crews to swing their 3-inchers to the right and fire. As the men struggled to shift their ungainly weapons, German infantry who had dismounted from the panzers heard the sounds and cut loose with machine pistols and machine guns. With nothing between them and the Germans but air, the crews hit the dirt and returned fire with their small arms. Turrets turned, and 75mm shells crashed among the 3-inch pieces, wrecking equipment and flesh. The platoon leader yelled for his men to pull back. The men—including Gallagher, who had crawled away and made his second miraculous escape—raced toward the cover of a railroad line as bullets whipped around them.[15]

Oberstleutnant Joachim Peiper's 1st SS Panzer Regiment spearhead joined the flow of retreating American vehicles and rolled into Hongen against virtually no further resistance.[16]

A short while later and not far away, a section of 1st Platoon was shifting its guns into position west of Hunningen to deal with an armored column that had been spotted headed toward Büllingen and Hongen in the thin gray dawn. The crews opened fire and efficiently destroyed four Mark IV tanks and a halftrack. The rest of the panzers withdrew. Counter-battery fire crashed into the 1st Platoon's positions, wounded the platoon commander, and disabled one gun. The men hitched up their weapons and withdrew to Mürringen with the infantry.

By the end of the day, the 801st had lost to enemy fire or deliberate destruction to prevent capture seventeen 3-inch guns, four M8 armored cars, and many of its other vehicles. Known casualties had thankfully been relatively light, but several tens of men were missing. By dark, most of the remaining crewmen were fighting as infantry. The battalion nevertheless KO'd another five panzers with landmines.[17]

*   *   *

The next day, the 801st was ordered to withdraw toward Camp Elsenborn. The consensus among platoon leaders was that the battalion's losses of guns and the failure to destroy more of the enemy was due to "the non-mobility of the towed gun and the lack of armor protection for the gun crew."[18]

In a similar experience, 630th Tank Destroyer Battalion had most of its towed guns overrun between 16 and 18 December, although the 3d Platoon of Company B claimed to have destroyed fourteen tanks, one 88mm SP gun, and several other vehicles. Nearly two hundred men quickly went missing in action.[19] Likewise, by the evening of 17 December, the 820th Tank Destroyer Battalion had lost twelve towed guns and nearly one hundred thirty men missing.[20]

*   *   *

The freedom to maneuver quickly to good firing positions could make a tremendous difference in the face of overwhelming odds.

The M18s of 1st Platoon, C/811th Tank Destroyer Battalion, and the 3d platoon of Reconnaissance Company, arrived near Ouren early on 17 December, among the first SP destroyers to respond to the German penetration. The CO of the 112th Infantry Regiment, 28th Infantry Division, ordered the guns into position east of town, where German tanks were reported to be concentrating. The TDers learned while under way that the Germans had already seized the hill they were to occupy.

Confirmation came in the form of small arms fire and retreating doughs, who said that panzers were advancing up the far side of the hill.

Lieutenant Dan Orr decided to try to stop the enemy. His gunners opened fire as eighteen German tanks, supported by infantry, silhouetted themselves atop the crest. Return fire killed seven men and wrecked the recon vehicles and two M10s, and the German infantry began to flank the position. But panzers were burning—ten in all—when Orr ordered a withdrawal. Sergeant Dominic Zacharilla took up a position from which he could cover the retreat by the rest of the platoon, while the recon men grabbed a bazooka and provided flank support. Zacharilla held his lonely position for twelve hours under constant fire, destroyed three more German tanks, and helped knock out a fourth. The small band held up the German advance long enough for the regimental headquarters and trains to evacuate.

The elements of the widely scattered TD company, including Orr's platoon, made their way toward Bastogne. Company CO Capt David Collins encountered disorganized elements of the 9th Armored Division parked along the road and ordered them to join his column. At Bastogne, Collins was instructed to proceed to Neufchateau, where he discovered that his column had grown to more than one hundred fifty vehicles. Other men from the 811th trickled in to Bastogne over the next few days, mostly on foot, and joined the town's defenders.[21]

The Hitler Youth Grab a Porcupine

On the northern edge of the battle zone, the 2d Infantry Division had orders to organize a defensive line along the Elsenborn Ridge. The twin villages of Rocherath and Krinkelt sat astride the Wirtzfeld road, which the division had to hold if it was to extract both its forward elements and those of the 99th Infantry Division. But by early on 17 December, tanks from the 1st SS Panzer Division had been spotted in the vicinity of nearby Büllingen, the division's supply point. Indeed, M10s from 1st Platoon, C/644th Tank Destroyer Battalion, arrived just in time to drive off a German armored probe toward Wirtzfeld by combining with an AT gun to destroy four panzers and a halftrack. One reconnaissance platoon entered Büllingen to establish and maintain contact with the panzers only to be surrounded and captured except for 2d Section, which broke free. A few towed guns from the 612th Tank Destroyer Battalion also knocked out several panzers near the town of Butgenbach.[22]

The 2d Infantry Division's 38th Infantry Regiment, supported by battalions of other regiments as conditions permitted and required, established a defensive line at the twin villages to screen the withdrawal. There was snow on the ground, and the fog was thick—as was the seeming confusion. The few available destroyers from the 644th (Company C and 2d Platoon of Company A) could provide only spot antitank defense, and the doughs mostly fought panzers with mines and bazookas when they first struck the defenses at Krinkelt the night of 17 December. (The 741st Tank Battalion was the spine of the antitank defense in Rocherath.)

Two surviving platoons of Reconnaissance Company joined the doughs and TDs in heavy street fighting that surged back and forth among the burning buildings of the village for hours. The Germans reached the recon company CP, but headquarters personnel grabbed their guns and helped drive the attackers away at midnight. Sergeant Melvin Mounts and his crew narrowly escaped a rude surprise when the building behind which their M10 was hiding collapsed, revealing two Panthers twenty yards away.[23]

About dawn on 18 December, a panzergrenadier regiment supported by a battalion each of tanks and assault guns—all from the 12th SS "Hitlerjugend" Panzer Division—concentrated near the twin villages to join the volksgrenadiers already engaged. The SS panzers were about evenly divided between Panthers and Mark IVs.[24]

The 644th Tank Destroyer Battalion, which had left a company behind with the 8th Infantry Division when it had joined the 2d Infantry Division in the Ardennes in early December, received control over the towed guns of Company C, 612th Tank Destroyer Battalion. Three guns from the 801st were also attached.[25]

The Germans again penetrated Krinkelt on 18 December. Lieutenant Robert Parker of Headquarters Company saw seven Panthers approaching his position. He secured a bazooka and made his way to a ruined barn, from which he scored a direct hit on one tank. Parker worked his way through the hail of fire in the streets until he was within forty yards of the panzers. The lieutenant fired again and soon had one Panther burning nicely and a second immobilized. Cannon shells and machine gun bullets now sought Parker out, but he was able to damage three more

Mark Vs before he was wounded. Out of rockets, Parker made his way back and organized two bazooka teams from recon that were able to finish the panzers off.[26]

Five more panzers carrying infantry reached the 38th Infantry Regiment's CP. A TD located fifty yards away (probably the M10 with Pvt Henry McVeigh acting as gunner) knocked out the first tank, and when the column stopped, it finished off the second and third. CP personnel in the upper floors of the building blazed away at the grenadiers, few of whom escaped, while a doughboy knocked out the fourth panzer with a bazooka. The surviving tank turned around and left, despite a shot from the TD that hit the turret. McVeigh was credited with destroying two Panthers, two Mark IVs, and a halftrack.[27]

The 2d Infantry Division pulled out of the twin villages on 19 December to man the defenses along Elsenborn Ridge, its mission successfully completed.[28] During the withdrawal, a column of twelve Panthers approached a heavy walled church near the northern edge of Krinkelt, firing into every house, until Private McVeigh knocked out the lead panzer with a HVAP round at seventy-five yards. The others pulled back.[29]

All told, the 644th Tank Destroyer Battalion accounted for seventeen panzers, two SP guns, and one halftrack during the fighting around Krinkelt.[30]

The defense at Krinkelt and Rocherath had accomplished far more than the men involved knew: It had thrown the Sixth Panzer Army hopelessly off schedule. Asked after the war why the 12th SS panzer Division had failed to break through, then-Sixth Panzer Army Chief of Staff Generalmajor (Waffen SS) Fritz Kraemer attributed the failure to "tank destroyers and heavy resistance."[31] By 20 December, Generaloberst (Waffen SS) Sepp Dietrich, commanding the Sixth Panzer Army, privately concluded that the Ardennes offensive had failed.[32]

Slowing the Surge at St. Vith

Generalfeldmarschall Walter Model, commanding Army Group B, believed that the Ardennes offensive would become a battle for road junctions because of the restrictive terrain.[33] With the Sixth Panzer Army tangled by the tenacious defense offered by the 99th and 2d Infantry divisions, and with the German Seventh Army making slow progress on the southern shoulder, the Fifth Panzer Army in the center badly needed one such road junction: St. Vith. It expected to capture the objective by 17 December.[34]

The town was still in the hands of what was left of the 106th Infantry Division when the lead combat elements of the 7th Armored Division arrived late on 17 December after a sixty-mile road march over clogged and slippery roads. The men in the attached 814th Tank Destroyer Battalion (who had been in Holland converting from the M10 to the M36) had seen the fear on the faces of the Belgian civilians they had passed en route, but they did not know the cause.[35]

The CG of the 106th Infantry Division passed command to BrigGen Bruce Clarke, commanding CCB. Clarke set about organizing a horseshoe-shaped defensive perimeter around the town, supported by CCB/9th Armored Division and the remnants of a regiment each from the 106th and 28th Infantry divisions. The TDs and recon teams of the 814th were parceled out to support division elements manning roadblocks along the defensive line.[36]

Clarke's goal was to delay the Germans as long as possible, not to hold St. Vith indefinitely. The Germans were preoccupied with reducing the two surrounded regiments of the 106th Infantry Division (both eventually surrendered) and first attacked the defenses at St. Vith in any strength on 20 December. That day, the Führer Begleit (Escort) Brigade—formed around the cadre of a battalion that had protected Hitler's Eastern Front headquarters—tried to push down the roads behind St. Vith to bridges across the Salm River. At dusk, a company of Mark IVs crested a hill in front of 1st Platoon, A/814th Tank Destroyer Battalion. The waiting M36s cut loose with their 90mm guns and destroyed five Mark IVs with seven rounds. The remainder retreated into the growing darkness.[37]

Late on 20 December, patrols from the 7th Armored and 82d Airborne divisions established contact. The paratroopers were establishing a defensive line on the far side of the Salm River, and the defenders of St. Vith were now subordinated to the XVIII Airborne Corps.[38]

The following morning passed in ominous silence.[39] As evening approached, the 18th and part of the 62d Volksgrenadier divisions launched an attempt to reach St. Vith in the wake of a terrific artillery barrage. Third Platoon of A/814th was supporting Company B of the 23d Armored Infantry Battalion at the far right of the 7th Armored Division's lines southeast of St. Vith, where a six-hundred-yard gap separated the men from CCB/9th Armored Division. The volksgrenadiers began infiltrating about 1630, and the doughs were soon in trouble as the Germans detected the gap and charged in. The platoon's three M10s and one M36 quickly ran out of HE shells, and the crewmen resorted to .50- and .30-caliber machine guns, side arms, and hand grenades.

The infantry began to backpedal under the pressure, and two M10 crews—bereft of infantry support—were alarmed to discover that their vehicles were sunk too deeply in mud to move. The German fire was too heavy for the other destroyers to pull them free, so the men bailed out and accompanied the rest of the platoon back to St. Vith to set up a roadblock.

Royal Tigers from the Schwere Panzer Abteilung 506 now joined the attack and wreaked havoc on a few Shermans that tried to cover the widening gap in the line. The remaining 3d Platoon gun section laid mines that knocked out three panzers. The volksgrenadiers pressed on fiercely and came close enough to disable the one M36 with a bazooka about 2330 hours. The crewmen in the last TD faced a column of eight approaching Panthers and knocked out the leader, which blocked the road. Return fire damaged a track, but the crew was able to repair it.[40] The stubborn little roadblock held the main route through St. Vith until nearly midnight.[41] This was just one example of the many small, desperate fights waged throughout the sector by isolated groups of American soldiers that created a domino effect and wrecked the German timetable.

Heavy snow was falling through the freezing night air as Tigers carrying volksgrenadiers crawled past burning buildings into St. Vith. Clarke ordered a retreat to a new defensive line west of the town, but in the chaos many small units never got the word.[42]

The Führer Begleit Brigade drove a wedge between Combat Commands A and B of the 7th Armored Division on 22 December, and Clarke withdrew to another line with his headquarters in Commanster, a town set deep in the forest. The remaining M36s of A/814th shifted one mile to the vicinity of Crombach and dug in with the doughs from 23d Armored Infantry Battalion. The exhausted men repulsed repeated infantry attacks with the help of artillery called in as close as twenty-five to one hundred yards in front of the foxholes. First Platoon M36s claimed three Tigers with direct fire and one by indirect fire, but one M36 sustained a hit that destroyed it.[43]

*   *   *

During the day, differences surfaced between MajGen Maxwell Ridgeway, commanding XVIII Airborne Corps, who wanted to hold on to the territory between the Salm and St. Vith, and 7th Armored Division general officers who believed the command was in danger of imminent destruction. Clarke's CCB had already been reduced by half. British Field Marshall Bernard Montgomery, who on 19 December had taken command of all Allied forces on the north side of the salient, decided the men at St. Vith had delayed the Germans long enough and ordered a withdrawal across the Salm.[44]

The extrication began the next morning when the temperature dropped far enough to freeze the mud and permit vehicles to move. Tanks and TDs bearing riflemen were just forming up at Hinderhausen when the Führer Begleit Brigade struck again. Cavalry deployed as a rearguard while two M36s engaged the lead panzers.[45] Lieutenant Jack Dillender related:

> A German tank attempted to round a curve into Hinderhausen. We were fighting our TDs over the rear end to help out maneuvering and our withdrawal. I was with my lead destroyer. James Cochran, the gunner, attempted to point the 90mm at the tank (a Panther). He could not get low enough because a camouflage net stopped the tube. We could see that German tank gun traversing our direction. My number-two TD was just across the road, and I [ran over and] called to Gilbert Dahms to get him quick. When he fired, we could hear the click—we had a misfire. Needless to say, our pucker strings were straining.
>
> Dahms and Cochran kept each other supplied with chewing tobacco and both were cool country boys. Dahms reached up to the top of that 90mm breechblock and quickly moved the cocking lever to recock the gun. He then checked his aim and fired, and we hit that tank with an APC [armor piercing, capped] round head-on. We quickly loaded an HE round and let him have it again. That started him to burn.
>
> A German opened the hatch and attempted to jump off. Cochran on the other side of the road aimed a rifle and shot the guy. He then spat a big wad of tobacco and said, "That's one you missed, Dahms."

Fortunately, it had turned cold, and we had had some snow the night before. If that hadn't happened, we would not have been able to make it. Anyway, we took a couple more tanks trying to enter Hinderhausen. [The battalion's AAR indicates three Tigers were destroyed.] I was on the deck of my number-two TD with [James] Foss, the commander. We had to back up for some shots, and in doing so we were no longer covered by a building on our right side. Shortly thereafter, we took a hit in the side. Foss was knocked off the deck. They repeated with another hit, which gave me a wound to my left leg and knocked me off the deck. I fell on top of Foss, who was not wounded, but I fell on him as he was getting up, which really clobbered him.

Our TD was starting to burn so we started helping to get everybody out and rolled in the snow to put the fire out. Everybody got out burnt and wounded, some worse than others, but all alive. . . . We could not put our wounded inside the other TDs because we still had to fight, so we strapped them on the outside of the TDs. It hurt us to do that, but it was the only way to get them out. Our mad run out of Hinderhausen was successful, and we got to a ridge near Commanster where we could make another stand.[46]

Indeed, the two remaining M36s engaged the pursuing panzers and destroyed one Tiger and two Panthers. One more TD fell victim to German fire, however. The remaining gun joined the withdrawal through Neuville.[47]

Lieutenant Colonel Robert Jones, CO of the 814th, commanded a task force that fought a rear-guard action to cover the retreat. Jones had two of his TD companies, his recon company, a company of light tanks, and the remnants of the 14th Cavalry Group.[48]

All but the last elements had crossed the bridges across the river when Lt Hugh Bertruch saw more panzers from the Führer Begleit Brigade approaching. His four TDs began a raging fire fight that cost the Germans seven tanks and the 814th all four M36s. The crewmen retreated through the moonlight, where they found engineers who were just finishing preparations to blow the bridge. The TDs had won the time needed to close this road.[49]

The 2d SS Panzer Division, however, had worked its way to the west side of the Salm from the south, and Task Force Jones had to fight for every mile toward the safety of the 82d Airborne Division lines. The command broke up into small groups, many of which made it back to American lines over the next several days.

Jones's battalion escaped the St. Vith battle with remarkably low casualties: Two men were killed, nineteen were wounded, and twenty were missing in action. Nevertheless, nearly half the 814ths M36s had been damaged or destroyed. But the 814th's gunners had KO'd eight Tigers, twelve Panthers, six Mark IVs, six other tanks of unknown type, and various other vehicles.[50]

The stubborn defense at St. Vith, combined with that at Rocherath-Krinkelt, had limited the Sixth Panzer Army to a twenty-mile-deep but only five-mile-wide salient carved out by Oberstleutnant Joachim Peiper's 1st SS Panzer Division spearhead. To the south, the Fifth Panzer Army sent the 2d Panzer and Panzer Lehr divisions racing for a second key road junction: Bastogne.[51] But Fifth Panzer Army's commanding general, General der Panzertruppe Hasso von Manteuffel, on Christmas Eve recommended to Hitler's adjutant that the attack be abandoned because of the time lost at St. Vith.[52]

Channeling the Flood

The American response to Wacht am Rhein followed the outlines foreseen by Bradley, although by 19 December he had largely lost his ability to control the northern wing of First Army.[53] Reinforcing divisions initially deployed mostly along the flanks of the German penetration to build two solid containing walls. On the north, the 1st and 30th Infantry divisions and 82d Airborne Division shifted into what would become an east–west line anchored on the shoulder formed by the 99th and 2d Infantry divisions at Elsenborn Ridge.

The battle-tested 30th Infantry Division on 17 December had been ordered south from the Roer sector, and the crews of the 823d Tank Destroyer Battalion—who had never fired their new M10s' guns in anger—accompanied the division on its march south through a bitter cold night along unfamiliar roads. Worse yet, Company B still had several towed 3-inch guns, while Company A remained entirely towed. By dawn on 18 December, the men arrived in the area of Malmedy, Belgium. Company B deployed its towed guns forward and held its M10s back as a mobile reserve. Company A received orders to move to Stoumont, while Company C was sent to Stavelot.

In Stavelot, where Peiper's 1st SS Panzer Regiment had pushed through a day earlier without leaving a holding force behind, columns from the two sides arrived almost simultaneously on 18 December. The M10s had hardly taken up firing positions when panzers struck from the east and west. Second Platoon claimed between nine destroyed and eleven tanks probably destroyed, while 1st Platoon accounted for a Panther and a halftrack.

A platoon of towed guns from the 825th Tank Destroyer Battalion—which had been engaged in rear-area security duties since arriving in France four months earlier—had also arrived in Stavelot about 0330 hours to establish two road blocks with the doughs. Two halftracks trying to move guns to high ground south of town had come under fire and been knocked out. One of the two surviving 3-inchers began pounding German-occupied buildings until the men spotted four Tigers approaching at about 1000 hours. Both crews turned on the panzers, and each gun knocked out a pair. A fifth panzer, however, could be heard nearby. It had entered via another route, and was now crawling through town conducting reconnaissance by fire.

One crew moved its gun into the center of the street, where it could engage the panzer. The men were doubtless appalled when they saw the house-size form of a Royal Tiger. The men fired fifteen rounds as quickly as they could, one of which struck the base of the panzer's main gun. The Germans decided to back away from the fight, but the driver miscalculated and steered into a building that collapsed and pinned the Tiger. Ordered to withdraw, the unnamed TD platoon leader and another noncomm continued to fire the gun until the rest of the crew had gotten away, at which time they destroyed the weapon and withdrew on foot.

*   *   *

The TD crews crouching behind their 3-inch guns in Stoumont heard Peiper's tanks maneuvering in the dark early on 19 December. Company A requested permission to fire flares so that the guns could engage the panzers, but the local infantry commander refused. About 0600, amidst fog so thick that the men could see no more than fifty yards, panzers were discovered already in the outskirts of town. The doughs began a fighting withdrawal, which exposed gun after gun to enemy assault. The Germans overran 1st and 3d platoons; nine crewmen had been wounded and sixteen were missing when the company pulled out to the north with the remaining 2d Platoon guns. The gun-less platoons drew four 3-inch and two captured 75mm guns held by battalion maintenance.

It was a cruel twist of fate that the men of the 823d had to experience again the vulnerability imposed by towed weapons one day after its conversion to self-propelled TDs was to have taken effect. The M10s of Company C back in Stavelot, meanwhile, claimed five Tiger tanks during fighting that day. One more twist of the knife awaited the 823d: The outfit was repeatedly bombed and strafed by American aircraft on 24 and 26 December and lost three men and several vehicles. The battalion history noted, "The men feared our own planes as much as they did the enemy."[54]

*   *   *

The 703d Tank Destroyer Battalion was detached from the 3d Armored Division and sent south with the 823d. When Company B was attached to the 82d Airborne Division on 20 December, the paratroopers were trying to contain the German along the Salm River between Trois Ponts and Salmchateaux as the battle progressed around St. Vith.

It was cold. So cold, in fact, that one 3d Platoon M36 turret froze solid and stayed that way for days, and some vehicles would not start again once shut off.

Lieutenant Roberts's 2d Platoon joined the 504th Parachute Infantry Regiment, which was attempting to retake the village of Cheneux near Stoumont. The TDs were ordered to advance with the infantry and make as much noise as possible to give the impression of great strength. They were also told to shoot at anything that moved in front of them. It was so dark that the crews could see no more than twenty-five yards as they entered town.

A 20mm flak gun opened up on the paratroopers, who hit the dirt. One M36 advanced to destroy the gun and almost ran into a German halftrack. The gunner tried to engage the vehicle, but as the turret traversed, the 90mm gun barrel struck the halftrack. This was enough for the panzergrenadiers, who bailed out and scooted. By now, the driver had the Jackson in reverse and backed up far enough for the gunner to destroy the halftrack. This accomplished, the men knocked out the troublesome

20mm gun. The paratroopers and TDs were able to clear the town the next day. But the German pressure had only begun.

First Platoon, commanded by Lieutenant Ball, joined the 505th Parachute Infantry Regiment. The infantry drove back a German attempt to cross the Salm River on the night of 22 December.

Early the next day, Ball—who was with his first section—spotted two well-camouflaged SP guns emerging out of the forest two thousand yards away on the far side of the river. Rather than fire on them, he waited to see whether any more interesting targets appeared. Shortly, three Panthers moved cautiously into view. Unfortunately, the SP guns were now almost out of sight close to a draw from which they could menace the paratroopers. Ball ordered his M36s to fire, and almost immediately both SP guns started to burn. The Panthers backed out of sight before the TDs could traverse and shoot.

Direct HE fire crashed into Ball's position. One round struck a tree only thirty yards from one destroyer, and a shell fragment killed a crewman.

The Germans shifted their efforts to another sector and successfully crossed the river at Vielsalm. During the night of 24 December the 82d Airborne began a withdrawal to new defensive positions near Basse Bodeaux.[55]

*   *   *

With every spare unit rushing to stem the German offensive, Ninth Army went over to the defensive along the Roer River north of the Bulge. Dug-in tank destroyers and tanks were positioned in depth along the line. Supplemental, alternate, and decoy positions were prepared. Skeleton crew manned captured German AT guns of all types. And, behind the TDs, 90mm antiaircraft guns moved into direct-fire positions.[56]

The Battered Bastards of Bastogne

The men of Company C, 609th Tank Destroyer Battalion, were fighting along the Sauer River when they were alerted on 18 December to deploy to a place called Bastogne, Belgium, with CCB/10th Armored Division. The M18s, less one platoon, followed the Shermans north. The lead elements arrived in Bastogne about dusk and formed a screening force consisting of three small task forces east of town. The men in the destroyers had no idea what was going.[57]

Also on 18 December, the 705th Tank Destroyer Battalion, located near Aachen, received orders to report to the CG of VIII Corps in Bastogne. The M10s rolled south, and the advance guard arrived in La Roche the next day. Battalion CO LtCol Clifford Templeton noted that "visual and oral evidence" suggested "a certain degree of confusion in the general situation." Templeton deployed his men in defensive positions until he was able to obtain orders that attached his command to the 101st Airborne Division, which had hiked into Bastogne the preceding night and was exchanging its first shots with the spearhead of Panzer Lehr Division. Templeton encountered a small German tank-infantry force while returning to his men but escaped harm.[58]

By evening, the battalion had entered Bastogne. The terrain was rolling; open fields interspersed with heavily wooded tracts were the only obstacles to cross-country tank movement. The command was deployed in defensive positions along the front lines within two hours of arrival. The battalion's sector of the perimeter would extend to 13,000 yards.[59]

*   *   *

Early the next morning, 3d Platoon, C/609th Tank Destroyer Battalion, commanded by Lt David Hagen, pulled into Noville (north-northeast of Bastogne) to join the fifteen Shermans and four hundred soldiers, mostly armored infantrymen, of Major William Desobry's team from the 10th Armored Division's CCB. Artillery rounds exploded around them, and even before a single German was seen, a sergeant was killed and another man wounded. Sergeant Richard Beaster's M18 raced through town and arrived on the northern edge in time to join a veritable cannonade from tanks, bazookas, and just about anything else that would fire that knocked out two Mark IVs that had appeared on the road to Houffalize.[60]

Lieutenant Hagen employed the gun section commanded by Sgt John Pilon in static positions on the east edge of town, where the M18s took advantage of buildings for cover. The other two destroyers of his platoon roved through the village and were ready to respond on call. The fog swirled about, sometimes so thick that the crewmen could see barely ten feet.

About 1000 hours, the fog lifted suddenly and revealed some thirty tanks from the 2d Panzer Division, the closest no more than 300 yards away. The M18s and Sherman tanks opened fire. The gunners knocked out nine of fourteen tanks on a ridgeline to the north. The destroyer commanded by Sergeant Beaster claimed five Panthers with six rounds, but the M18 was struck just as it loosed its last killing shot, and the gun crewmen were wounded and the driver killed. Sergeant Pilon later recalled being able to hear the Germans in two approaching halftracks shouting to one another; the vehicles pulled back when they realized their peril, but Pilon's gunner, Cpl Justin Double, got them both. Pilon then spotted a Panther approaching from his left. The M18's turret traversed, the 76mm gun spat fire, and the Mark V started to burn.[61]

Desobry sought and received permission to withdraw his own small force but decided to attack instead when he was reinforced by a platoon of M10s from C/705th Tank Destroyer Battalion and a battalion of paratroopers from the 506th Parachute Infantry Regiment.[62]

A meeting engagement ensued, in which the paratrooper battalion, supported by a few tanks and TDs, attempted to take high ground east of Noville while an estimated battalion of German grenadiers backed by panzers tried to push westward. For some reason, the German tanks generally held back, and when a few advanced, the TDs engaged them from the flank and destroyed five at fifteen hundred yards range. The clash resulted in a draw. Overnight, artillery pounded the American lines, and Major Desobry was badly wounded; panzer engines growled in the dark along the perimeter.[63]

The Germans attacked again out of thick fog at about 0400 on 20 December, when C/705th reported contact with German infantry near Foy and Noville. Between 0800 and 1000, heavy artillery concentrations crashed down on the defenders, followed by the appearance of panzers and grenadiers out of the murk. The fog did not lift until mid-day, and until then the action took place at distances of only a few yards. The eight remaining Shermans were out of AP ammo, and Company C's 1st Platoon M10s moved forward. When the fog lifted suddenly as it had the day before, the gunners could see a skirmish line of fifteen panzers. The TDs fairly quickly dispatched five Mark IV tanks and raked the escaping crews with .50-caliber machine gun fire while the remaining panzers retreated out of sight.[64]

The battered command was now surrounded, however, and late in the day fought its way back through fog and smoke to the main Bastogne defensive line. Lieutenant Hagen ordered Sergeant Pilon to join the rearguard, which consisted of a paratrooper company and four TDs. Looking back into the village, Pilon spotted German infantry accompanied by a panzer entering the ruins. He fired HE at the infantry and was pleased to hear cries for medics in German. Armor piercing rounds convinced the panzer to pull back. Pilon then ordered his driver to follow the rest of the column westward.[65]

Team Desobry had lost about half its men, eleven Shermans, and five tank destroyers, but it had held up the German advance on Bastogne for two critical days.[66]

*   *   *

While the 609th's 3d Platoon fought in Noville, 2d Platoon, commanded by Lt Edward Gladden, had joined Team Cherry in Longvilly due east of Bastogne. The destroyers mainly fought against infantry attacks, but the platoon claimed a single Mark V, with the credit going to an M10 destroyer that battalion records say was manned by a makeshift crew composed of personnel from company HQ. The M10 had been recovered under fire, manned, and successfully employed. This M10 may actually have been crewed by men from Company C, 811th Tank Destroyer Battalion, who made their way through German lines and attached themselves to the 609th on 20 December.[67]

After waging a more scattered and confused defensive action than that in Noville, the remnants of Team Cherry fell back to the MLR near Neffe, one mile outside Bastogne.

*   *   *

Company B/705th's 1st and 3d platoons were deployed near Neffe with the 327th Glider Infantry Regiment when the panzers and grenadiers attacked at 1930 hours on 20 December. 1st Platoon's M10s fired flares to illuminate the enemy and destroyed three panzers while raking the infantry with machine-gun fire. Third Platoon also reported destroying three panzers.[68]

Company A/705th was at Ortheuville helping defend a roadblock. The crews drove off the first German force to appear and KO'd a Mark III and several halftracks during the exchange. Artillery fire soon exploded around the M10s, and this time a large force of tank-supported infantry appeared. The outnumbered Americans fell back toward Bastogne.[69]

*   *   *

The Germans probed the main line at Bastogne on 21 December, by which time they had enveloped the town. The TDs shifted firing positions as needed by the paratroopers, although the 705th's AAR suggests that the coordination did not gel until late in the day. Still, that battalion's M10s knocked out four panzers and three halftracks during the fighting.[70]

On 22 December, the Germans launched a concerted effort to take Bastogne, this time from the west.[71] This would be the day on which BrigGen Anthony McAuliffe, acting CG of the 101st Airborne Division and all other troops in the pocket, issued his famous reply to a surrender ultimatum: "Nuts!" The 705th committed the men of Reconnaissance Company to the foxhole line to fight beside the paratroopers for the remainder of the siege. The recon platoon from the 609th also manned the front line, and the 101st Airborne Division placed 2d Platoon, A/705th, in mobile reserve. By 1000, the platoon had already had to deploy once to the outlying village of Monty, where it destroyed a panzer and helped convince the enemy to withdraw.[72]

The skies finally cleared on 23 December. Planes dropped supplies to the defenders of Bastogne and vast quantities of explosive ordnance on the enemy.[73] The defenders grimly held on and hoped that relief on the ground would follow soon.

By Christmas Eve, the 705th Tank Destroyer Battalion had worked out a standard procedure for supporting the paratroopers (who had little prior training or experience working with armor of any type). Guns worked by platoons. One section took up positions in or within a few yards of the MLR, while the second section stood back one to two hundred yards to provide supporting fire. The Germans, for their part, were by now typically attacking in small battle groups of four or five panzers supported by fifty to a hundred infantrymen following an artillery preparation.[74]

The defense, meanwhile, was reorganized into combined arms teams built around the four regiments of the 101st Airborne Division. Roadblocks were established on all routes into Bastogne, each supported by two M18s from C/609th Tank Destroyer Battalion. Four M10s and forty men from the 705th formed part of a small new central reserve force.[75]

At 0400 hours on Christmas morning, tanks and panzergrenadiers struck the defenses after a mortar preparation. The panzers preceded the infantry by about two hundred yards, and a few succeeded in making a potentially disastrous penetration. The 705th's AAR describes how the defenders exploited the situation: "The infantry of the 101st Airborne Division permitted the tanks to pass through them and then effectively stopped the following enemy infantry. In some instances, our guns permitted the tanks to pass them and were enabled to place effective fire on their flanks and rear. In places, the enemy armor was able to penetrate the MLR but denuded of their own infantry were excellent targets for the antitank defenses of all arms of the division as well as our own guns. In several instances, the tank destroyers were able to effectively assist friendly infantry by HE and .50-caliber machine-gun fire on the enemy infantry."[76]

1st Platoon, Company B, was able to KO seven of ten panzers that penetrated the MLR between Champs and Hemroulle at about 0300 hours. Other platoons claimed their prizes, too, and by day's end the crews had destroyed fifteen panzers, two AT guns, and an armored car.[77]

Everyone was learning. Colonel W. Roberts, CCB/10th Armored Division, wrote shortly after the battle: "The TDs taught me and my tanks a lesson that is being straightened out right now in this command. Properly employed in the defense, some tanks must be up with the infantry (I do not say what proportion) and some in reserve in the "socker" role. Those with the infantry must act in the TD role 98 percent of the time. The TDs know how to do it. Tankers are not as well trained, and they suffered. My eight TDs lost only three while getting twenty-two sure kills. My tanks did not approach that proportion."[78]

* * *

Far to the east, in Berlin, Generaloberst Heinz Guderian met with Hitler on Christmas Day and urged him to suspend the offensive because it had failed. Guderian was already thinking privately about whom he would prefer occupying Berlin and wanted to shift the armored reserves to the Eastern Front. Hitler refused.[79]

The German attack resumed on 26 December, but with less vigor. The TDs used the same successful tactics to handle the armor. The Germans escaped the day's encounter with the guns of the 705th short four panzers.[80]

During the period 19–26 December, the 705th accounted for thirty-nine German tanks, three halftracks, and assorted other vehicles and weapons. The battalion suffered casualties of twenty men killed, thirty-five wounded, and twelve missing. Five M10s were destroyed as well.[81]

The men of C/609th KO'd fifteen enemy Mark V tanks and one Mark VI tank as well as three SP guns. Losses amounted to thirteen men and eight vehicles, including two M-18s destroyed by AT fire. The other losses were principally the result of nightly enemy bombing.[82]

Armored Crush

Anticipating orders from SHAEF, Patton on 18 December began to turn the weight of his Third Army more than 90 degrees so as to rip into the southern flank of the Bulge. Third Corps, including the 4th Armored and 80th and 26th Infantry divisions—each with an SP tank destroyer battalion attached—attacked on 22 December to relieve Bastogne, while Devers's Sixth Army Group began to take over most of Third Army's area of responsibility. Patton's spearhead dashed one hundred twenty-five miles through a blizzard to accomplish this feat, and through 23 December, 133,178 motor vehicles traversed a total of 1,654,042 miles. German commanders who calculated that Patton would never be able to react so quickly were wrong.[83] On the other hand, German intelligence easily detected the Third Army shift, and by the time Third Army's spearhead arrived, the Germans had deployed strong blocking forces on all approaches.[84]

Captain Thomas Evans, now S-2 of the 704th Tank Destroyer Battalion, recalled, "We moved from around Sarreguemines, where we were engaged, and came back and got into Longwy, which was maybe twenty miles from Bastogne. It was about eighteen or twenty degrees below zero. There were maybe eight or ten inches of snow on the ground. And cold! It took us all night to move from Sarreguemines. They had MPs stopped every twenty miles. They had these big cans and logs burning so we could get out and warm our hands up. But we were only allowed to stay for two minutes."[85]

The 4th Armored Division was battle weary. It was short on trained men and material, and most of its tanks were worn out.[86] The 704th Tank Destroyer Battalion was just as tired after fighting along the Siegfried Line. Patton instructed the division—which would advance along and parallel to the road from Arlon—to attack with tanks, TDs, artillery, and armored engineers in the van, trailed by the armored infantry. The command was to use wide-envelopment tactics against any strongpoints.[87]

The division jumped of at 0600 hours on 22 December. It bridged the Sure River the next day after meeting light initial resistance, and commanders were optimistic that they would reach Bastogne in short order. Early in the afternoon on 24 December, a message from Patton relayed by VIII Corps arrived in Bastogne: "Xmas Eve present coming up. Hold on." But the 4th Armored Division had run into a stiff German defense supported by antitank and assault guns around Chaumont, Warnach, and Bigonville.[88]

There would be no armored dash into Bastogne. Instead, the armor and infantry began the painful process of ejecting the Germans—mostly elite troopers from the 5th Parachute Division—from their path. Captain Thomas Evans spent Christmas day with his old Company C comrades, in the bitter cold, pinned down by German artillery fire.[89]

The official U.S. Army history declares the siege of Bastogne ended as of 1645 hours on 26 December, when the 326th Airborne Engineer Battalion reportedly spotted three light tanks, thought to be friendly.[90] They were actually Shermans from CCR's 37th Tank Battalion. Eleven M18s from B/704th Tank Destroyer Battalion soon followed the tankers into Bastogne. Their first kill was a captured Sherman manned by German troops.[91]

*   *   *

North of the German salient, VII Corps readied itself to counterattack on orders from Field Marshall Montgomery, but it became embroiled in the defensive battle long before Monty was ready to move. The corps included the 2d and 3d Armored and two infantry divisions. Early on 21 December, "Hell on Wheels" began its march from the Roer front toward the German spearhead. The 2d Armored ran under radio silence, and its recon elements had orders to make sure that no one was captured.[92]

The 2d Panzer Division, low on fuel and badly strung out, had almost reached the Meuse River near Dinant. The 2d Armored Division's reconnaissance patrols established contact on 23 December. After going round and round with higher command in order to get permission to attack, MajGen Ernest Harmon sent his CCA to bore into the German positions at 0630 on Christmas Eve. A roadblock supported by a Panther with a very skilled gunner barred the path of CCA's Task Force A. One of the M36s recently acquired by the 702d Tank Destroyer Battalion crawled up the face of a defile and placed three rounds through the side of the Panther's turret.[93]

Thus began a three-day engagement during which the 2d Armored Division annihilated its opposite number, and bits of Panzer Lehr Division to boot. At 0930 hours on Christmas day, CCB descended on the 2d Panzer Division's main concentration at Celles. The Germans lacked enough fuel to maneuver, and the panzers often fought as strongpoints where they stood. The battle was a combined-arms extravaganza as American tanks, TDs, artillery, and fighter-bombers (including some British Typhoons) combined to destroy more than eighty German tanks and sixteen other armored vehicles. The crews of the 702d fought no large engagements, but its tank kills here and there added up to a tenth of the total.

On 26 December, Bradley—aware of the 2d Armored Division's smashing victory—told SHAEF that he believed Hitler's offensive had reached its high water mark.[94] Indeed, the tide was already on its way back out.

The Smaller Bulge

The veterans of the North Africa desert in the 601st Tank Destroyer Battalion were hunkered down near Strasbourg. The outfit's informal history recorded, "Christmas week 1944 was cold, miserable, and anything but joyous. The destroyers were all over the division area, firing at the Kraut, blocking roads, and catching plenty of hell. The news from the north was terrible. There was constant talk of a coming Kraut push. Recon was up in the hills with the French Ghoums [North Africans]. Morale was 'excellent' in the morning reports, but nowhere else!"[95]

American and French troops in the now thinly stretched Sixth Army Group sector along the upper Rhine were glumly ushering in the new year amidst cold and snow when Hitler's secondary offensive—Operation Nordwind—struck out of the midnight darkness. The German First Army executed the main attack, driving south through Bitche and the Wissembourg Gap. The Germans threw into the fight seven battle-worn divisions and one SS mountain division fresh from Finland. Their mission—straight from the Führer's mouth—was to destroy as many American formations as possible.[96]

Allied intelligence (including Ultra) provided forewarning of the attack, and Eisenhower ordered Sixth Army Group CG LtGen Jacob Devers to give ground in order to prevent a rip in his lines—but to fall back no further than the Vosges Mountains under any circumstances. Indeed, Ike was willing to abandon Strasbourg if need be, but threats of outright insubordination from the French persuaded him to abandon the idea. Seventh Army's CG, LtGen Alexander Patch, in turn opted to shorten his lines by withdrawing to a new MLR before the mountains, although not until several of his divisions had been badly bloodied in the first week of fighting. The American line eventually stabilized on the Moder River, which flowed from west to east into the Rhine. The French, meanwhile, fought fiercely to contain the German Nineteenth Army, which still held a substantial area west of the Rhine around the city of Colmar and which launched a drive to capture Strasbourg from the south.

The weather was dreadful. Blizzards and fog often blinded the combatants, and roads iced into slick sheets that could send tracked vehicles sliding into ditches and snow banks. Sergeant Tom Sherman in the 636th Tank Destroyer Battalion watched one M10 whip by down a hillside road at an impressive rate of speed. The captain standing beside him asked in surprise, "What's their hurry?" Evidently only Sherman had noticed that the M10 had been sliding backwards.[97]

Between the conditions and the limited armor available to the Germans, the battle became primarily an infantry struggle.

The 813th Tank Destroyer Battalion's experience was typical. The outfit was with the 79th Infantry Division on the left wing of VI Corps. The battalion lost nineteen of its M10s during the fighting and reluctantly re-equipped partially with M18s because no replacement M10s were available. Despite the fact that the once-proud 21st Panzer Division was active in the sector beginning 6 January, tanks appeared only sporadically and in small numbers, and targets were mainly infantry and halftracks. All but a few M10s were lost to German infantry assaults or because they became immobilized on the roads.

The 813th Tank Destroyer Battalion headquarters briefly filled the role once imagined for the tank destroyer brigades and coordinated antitank defenses in its sector. On 7 January, the M18s of the 827th Tank Destroyer Battalion (another nearly all-Black unit) arrived and was subordinated to the 813th's CO, Maj George McCutchen.[98]

Once Seventh Army had withdrawn to its Moder River line, the tank killers of the 636th had one of the few sizeable run-ins with panzers experienced by any TD outfit had during the fighting. Company C held positions near Hanhoffen on 21 January, as recounted by the 36th Infantry Division's newspaper:

> The warning net alerted Company C three hours before the German tanks ground into range. The 3d Platoon, commanded by 2dLt Lee Kiscadden, was emplaced along a heavy thicket with a clear field of fire in three directions. Two guns were there, about twenty yards behind the infantry. Six enemy tanks slid out of a tree line about two thousand yards to the east. The T-Patch [36th Infantry Division] TD men moved forward to the edge of the woods and sat there waiting.
>
> A driver, Cpl Lem J. Luke, marked the enemy's progress. "Yonder they go, yonder they go," he repeated. The enemy tanks kept coming. They crossed a small bridge and stopped.
>
> [Battalion CO LtCol Charles] Wilber was standing next to Lieutenant Kiscadden. "When are you going to shoot?" he asked impatiently. Lieutenant Kiscadden was standing next to the destroyer commanded by Sgt Rufus Brantley. He called to gunner Cpl Wiley Johnston, "When you're ready!"
>
> The enemy tanks were sitting ducks, halted just across the small bridge about twelve hundred yards away. It was Sergeant Brantley's first combat as a tank commander—the day before he had been a medico and private first class. He spotted what he later described as the "biggest damn tank on earth." Two rounds smashed into the tank, two columns of orange fire and black smoke

roared into the gray snowy sky. His monster was two Mark IVs sitting hull to hull. They both were destroyed.

Sergeant William Rutledge spotted two other tanks at the same time. Short a loader, he had to observe fire and handle the gun by himself. Two Tiger tanks had forced their way past the infantry defense line and were two thousand yards across the plain, going towards the rear. Rutledge poured three rounds into one, shifted his fire, and hit the second. The second tank withdrew; the first one was crippled. Another round disabled it.

The 3d Platoon had accounted for three tanks in less than two minutes. The left flank of the open field was secure.[99]

Second Platoon, meanwhile, spotted a dozen mixed medium and heavy tanks and accounted for another four panzers. The tanks were barely visible across the snow and against a grey sky. One Panther met its doom when it became silhouetted by an exploding smoke round. The carnage persuaded the crewmen in the surviving eight panzers to withdraw.

Digging the destroyers in along the Moder River line was a major undertaking. Explosives had to be used to break through the deep frozen layer on top. Bulldozers were then used to scoop out pits, but the subsoil was so mucky that they often became stuck and had to be dragged free by tank-recovery vehicles. Finally, log floors were installed to prevent the TDs from sinking. Frequent air strikes by German jet fighter-bombers added to the strain.[100]

The fighting was bitter and casualties were high on both sides, but Operation Nordwind blew itself out by the end of January.

*   *   *

Back in the Ardennes, First Army on 3 January 1945 began a full-scale attack on the northern flank of the Bulge through deep snow, cold, wind, and fog. In less than two weeks, First and Third armies fought through fierce resistance to link up at Houffalize, about halfway up the length of the salient. The next day—17 January—Bradley regained command of First Army. By the end of the month, Hitler had sent the Sixth Panzer Army to deal with a crisis on the Eastern Front, and American troops had completely eliminated the Bulge.[101]

Lessons Learned

The tank destroyers in First and Third armies were credited with knocking out more than five hundred panzers during the Battle of the Bulge.[102] That number stands as a summation of the efforts of thousands of TD men who fought with skill and courage under some of the most trying conditions of the war. They did what they were asked to do—kill tanks—and much else besides. Far beyond the statistics, the irreplaceable role played by those men in crucial battles at Krinkelt, St. Vith, and Bastogne—as well many secondary engagements that sealed what Churchill called America's greatest victory—bears witness to the Tank Destroyer Force's contribution to American arms.

The Ardennes fighting dealt the deathblow to the towed TD battalion concept because of the high losses suffered by towed units. The Army decided to convert all remaining towed battalions to SP formations, but supplies of the vehicles were not adequate for immediate implementation, and some outfits dragged their 3-inchers all the way to VE Day.[103]

Self-propelled outfits that had been directly in the path of the German offensive had suffered as well. The 811th Tank Destroyer Battalion, for example, lost nine men killed, thirty-five wounded, and eighty-two missing in action, as well as seventeen M18s and most of its armored cars.[104]

Despite the contributions made by the TD battalions during the Battle of the Bulge, Patton on 14 January 1945 recommended to the chief of Ordnance that production of tank destroyers be ended. He urged further that all TD battalions attached to infantry divisions be replaced by tank battalions.[105] The tank destroyer vision had clearly not answered all questions in some very influential minds.

*   *   *

The tank destroyer battalions learned from their experiences and continued to refine their methods. Army Ground Forces noted that the Battle of the Bulge had provided a laboratory to compare the effects of attaching tank destroyer units to armored and infantry formations versus issuing TD units no smaller than company-size general support orders with the freedom to implement them as seemed fit. In divisions using attachments, TDs were parceled out so widely that they were unable to concentrate against armored threats—one armored division, ordered to consolidate a single TD company as a reserve, reported that it could not comply. "Mission-type" orders where used maintained tactical integrity of the TD units, precluded misemployment of the destroyers, allowed for better rotation of the men and equipment in the line, and improved morale. Ultimately, however, it was up to the battalion CO or TD group staff to persuade division commanders to adopt "direct support" practices in lieu of attachment.[106]

Other refinements emerged as well. By January 1945, the 803d Tank Destroyer Battalion kept a TD air liaison officer at the closest airstrip at all times. At the first sign of a tank attack, he took to the air, from where he could communicate directly with individual vehicles and was able to position single guns to best respond to the enemy.[107] He could also call in artillery strikes. Major General A. D. Bruce had tested such employment of light planes to help TDs in late 1942, but the practice had not been adopted in combat.[108]

Chapter 10

Sought, Struck, and Destroyed

"Our motto was 'Seek, Strike, and Destroy,' and all in all, we did pretty good at it."

—Lieutenant Weldon Adams, platoon commander,
813th Tank Destroyer Battalion[1]

A decision that altered the war for the tank killers emerged from the Führerbunker under the ruins of Berlin during February 1945: 1,675 tanks and assault guns (new or repaired) were sent to the Eastern Front, while only sixty-seven went west. Hitler also stripped the Western Front of half its panzer divisions. The Führer was more worried about the Soviet threat to Berlin than the danger that the Western Allies would leap the Rhine.[2] America's tank destroyers would never again encounter the panzers in large numbers.

Western Europe was littered with the hulks of the panzers that had tangled with the tank killers. As of 28 February, the TD battalions in Third Army alone had reported the destruction of six hundred eighty-two tanks and one hundred twenty-five SP guns—more than a third of the roughly twenty-two hundred panzers Third Army claimed to have destroyed. One battalion commander told Army Ground Forces that his men (equipped with M18s) had the panzer's number and considered the highly mobile and easily hidden PAK 75mm antitank gun to be the most dangerous weapon they faced. As for the panzer, "the enemy tank can be easily out-maneuvered and is extremely susceptible to two-way attack."[3] In short, the men had regained confidence in their ability to handle heavy German tanks with their 76mm and 3-inch guns.

On 1 February 1945, ETOUSA caught up with the field expedient adopted in many TD battalions and ordered that supplementary machine gun mounts be installed on the front of all M10 and M36 turrets. The theater headquarters acknowledged that crews generally wanted a hull-mounted or coaxial machine gun but observed that this was the best available solution.[4]

Surge to the Rhine

Hitler may have decided to stop worrying so much about his Western Front, but the Americans—having eliminated the vestiges of the Ardennes offensives and stopped Nordwind in its tracks—were preparing to take a wrecking ball to the West Wall. On 2 February, the Combined Chiefs of Staff approved Eisenhower's plan to advance to the Rhine along its length and cross in strength in Montgomery's sector north of the Ruhr at the earliest opportunity. Most of Bradley's and Devers's troops were to halt offensive operations in February while Ninth Army (under Monty's operational control) crossed the Roer plain in support of British and Canadian operations to the north.[5]

American forces finally seized the Schwammenauel Dam near Schmidt on 10 February, but the Germans jammed open a release gate, and the Roer River quickly became a temporarily uncrossable barrier. By the time Ninth Army could get going, the American advance would resemble a broad-front offensive.

*   *   *

In the meantime, troops all along the line probed and gathered intelligence they would need when they headed for the Rhine.

The 614th Tank Destroyer Battalion was deployed east of the Vosges Mountains near Prinzheim, France, in early February. Lieutenant Joseph Keeby, a Chicago man in command of the 1st Reconnaissance Platoon, had orders to capture some prisoners for intelligence purposes. The infantry had tried several times without success because of extensive mine fields along the German line. Keeby gathered the thirty-one men of his raiding party three days before the operation. They went over sketches, drawings, and maps of the route to a mill the Germans were using, probably as a command post. Keeby divided his team into an assault group and a security group to provide cover.[6]

The night of 4 February, Keeby led the assault team through the freezing darkness in a cautious approach to the objective. As the men neared the first German outposts, a machine gun opened fire. Keeby and his team dropped to the ground. The security group returned fire immediately, and the machine gun fell silent. One man spotted a second German MG preparing to open fire and killed the crew. The assault group moved forward again.

The men crept closer to the mill. Suddenly, automatic rifle fire snapped through the air. Private First Class Henry Weaver, close behind Keeby, spotted the German and shot back. His aim was true.

Surprise lost, six men stormed through the door of the mill. Private George Bass raked the first room with submachine-gun fire while Keeby tossed hand grenades. When the smoke cleared, eight German soldiers lay dead on the floor. Six others surrendered. The recon men took them back to the battalion's position. Mission accomplished.

*   *   *

Along most of the front, the halt in offensive operations was strategic, not tactical, and the Americans continued to batter away at the West Wall. The doughs, tanks, and TDs were working together better than ever. AARs indicate that provisional platoons combining the two types of armor were occasionally created for some small missions. Captain Duchossois, commanding Company B, 610th Tank Destroyer Battalion (M36), described combined armed operations at Brandscheid at the stump of the Bulge in early February:

> We moved across the line of departure as a tank destroyer, tank, infantry team—infantry, a tank, and a tank destroyer followed by more infantry, another tank, and a tank destroyer. We used this formation because of the poor visibility, the limited routes of approach, and uncertainty of the definite location of all fortifications.

The infantry advanced until they were held up by a fortification. When this happened, the tankers "closed up" the aperture with machine gun fire followed by the tank destroyers firing several rounds of 90mm.

Usually, the Jerries would put some white article out of the embrasure, but they would not come out to surrender until the infantry moved in and brought them out. . . .

We found we had to keep a tank destroyer right behind the lead tank because our routes of approach were such that unless a tank destroyer was up there initially, it would be impossible to pass the tanks in order to fire on the pillbox. As a result, the leading tank destroyer and tank did the majority of the firing.

It is absolutely necessary to have communications with not only the infantry, but the tankers also. One of the simplest ways to accomplish this is to have both tank destroyer and tank platoon leaders equipped with SCR-300 radio sets on the infantry frequency.[7]

*   *   *

Ninth Army crossed the Roer River on 23 February. Tank destroyer battalions played a secondary role, firing direct (typically at ranges between two and three thousand yards) in support of the assault infantry, and reinforced division artillery units. Battalion recon companies crossed the river with the assault wave to provide radio links back to the destroyers.[8]

The AAR of the 821st Tank Destroyer Battalion for February offered the following description of the now-standard operating procedure, in this case during fighting on the east bank of the Roer River near Jülich with the 29th Infantry Division and 747th Tank Battalion: "As the infantry and tanks pushed forward, 821st destroyers provided close-in direct support for the infantry and mutual support for the tanks. As the infantry, tank, and tank destroyer teams approached a town that proved to be an enemy strongpoint, destroyer guns would fire direct covering fire at buildings. This fire neutralized enemy machine gun positions and denied snipers the use of the buildings. When enemy armor or emplaced antitank guns held up the advance of the infantry, destroyer guns were called upon to neutralize the enemy positions. Tanks and tank destroyers were called upon in accordance with the type of mission to be performed and worked together to outflank enemy strongpoints in and around towns. When enemy resistance was neutralized, tank destroyers immediately assumed defensive anti-mechanized positions against possible enemy counter-attacks, while the infantry consolidated their positions and prepared to move on to the next objective."

During the three-day operation described, the TDs killed seven panzers, two SP guns, six AT guns, and two halftracks.

The AAR of the 656th Tank Destroyer Battalion, a newly arrived outfit operating with both the 9th Armored and 78th Infantry divisions, noted, "Resistance, mostly from the German 3d Parachute Division, was determined. . . . Tactics employed were those of tanks rather than tank destroyers. The destroyers followed behind the assaulting wave of infantry. When an obstacle, an enemy machine gun or strongpoint, interfered with the infantry advance, the destroyers [opened fire]. Upon approaching a town, it was customary for the supporting destroyers to fire a preparation. First, destroyers fired on the upper stories of buildings, forcing the enemy into the cellars. The fire was shifted to lower floors and cellars."

The 3d Armored Division broke out of the Roer bridgehead on 26 February. The date was another fateful one for the Tank Destroyer Force, because the tankers were using several of the new M26 Pershings in combat for the first time.[9] The Pershing was more heavily armored than the Sherman and carried the same 90mm gun as the M36 in a fully protected turret. One of the Pershings during the day destroyed two Tigers and a Mark IV at a thousand yards. The tank destroyer once again had no edge in killing power over the American tank.

*   *   *

Bradley launched Operation Lumberjack—a massive pincer operation with First Army attacking east and southeast and Third Army northeast—on 3 March while Ninth Army was still grinding through stubborn German resistance on the Roer plain. Bradley later crowed, "Lumberjack was very nearly flawless, the kind of campaign generals dream about but seldom see. All five corps of both armies advanced according to plan, with dazzling speed and élan. The German armies opposing us were utterly routed, the men falling back in confusion and disarray, leaving a trail of weapons and equipment behind."[10]

By 5 March, Ninth Army had cleared the west side of the Rhine from Düsseldorf to Mörs, First Army troops had entered Cologne, and Third Army had reached the Rhine near Koblenz.[11]

On 7 March—the same day that the First and Third armies' spearheads closed the pincer jaws—a 9th Armored Division task force from First Army captured the only standing bridge across the Rhine that the Allies would take, the Ludendorff railroad bridge at Remagen. The M18s from C/656th Tank Destroyer Battalion formed part of the column that reached Remagen at 0330 hours. Company CO Capt Richard Tuggle was ordered to push his destroyers across the Rhine to support the 14th Tank Battalion. The TDs rolled through the streets of Remagen, following the Shermans under constant artillery fire. The first TD, commanded by Sgt John Jaroscak, had made it two-thirds of the way across the bridge when a track slipped from the planking laid across the railroad tracks. The crew and engineers worked furiously to get the destroyer, which had blocked the entire U.S. Army advance across the Rhine, under way. By 0600 hours, Jaroscak was on the east bank of the river.[12]

When Hodges called Bradley with the news of the bridge's capture, Bradley responded, "Hot dog, Courtney, this will bust him wide open. . . . Shove everything you can across it."

Eisenhower's operations chief, MajGen Harold "Pink" Bull happened to be at Bradley's HQ and was less enthusiastic because the crossing did not conform to the plan. "What in the hell do you want us to do," asked an irritated Bradley, "pull back and blow it up?"[13]

Although still committed to making the main effort in the north, Eisenhower authorized Bradley to push five divisions into the bridgehead.[14] The North Africa veterans from the 899th Tank Destroyer Battalion—the first TDs ashore at Normandy—crossed the Rhine the next day.

*   *   *

Because TD battalion commanders had little or no control over their widely scattered outfits, they were available for other duties—such as running a task force. On 14 March, the Third Army's 90th Infantry Division conducted an assault crossing of the Moselle River near Hatzenport. The following evening, LtCol Frank Spiess—commanding the 773d Tank Destroyer Battalion—was placed in charge of TF Spiess. The command consisted of recon and headquarters companies and Company C from the 773d; Company D of the 712th Tank Battalion; and the 90th Reconnaissance Troop. The task force set off on 16 March, its initial mission to screen the division's southern flank and to clear the enemy all the way to the Rhine at Boppard. By 1430 hours, Spiess had "washed his hands" in the Rhine River per orders from the assistant division commander.

The task force, however, encountered dug-in troops from the 6th SS Mountain Division south of Boppard. A bitter fight ensued, and the task force lost two men killed, one officer and six enlisted men wounded, and two M10s knocked out before it evicted the Germans. At 0900 on 17 March, the M10s of 3d Platoon entered Boppard without much resistance. The gunners then destroyed three vehicles on the far side of the Rhine to kill time while waiting for relief by the 2d Cavalry Group.

On 20 March, Spiess was ordered to lead the division advance on Mainz, for which Company A's TDs had replaced those of Company C. Although the troops were exhausted from the fast movement so far and the lack of sleep, they pushed ahead with lightning speed. By 1200 they had cleared sixteen towns, three minefields, and two roadblocks, and were only three miles from the city limits.

Here they encountered dug-in infantry supported by AT and flak guns and heavy mortar fire. Two M10s were struck and ground to a halt. Spiess personally flushed a German soldier holding a panzerfaust from cover beside the road. Spiess called in a time-on-target (TOT) artillery strike, and the infantry tried to clear the roadblock. They were driven back, and only another artillery preparation enabled them to bull though.

Task Force Spiess was able to rest the next day guarding the flank while three infantry regiments cleared Mainz.[15]

Charging with the Cavalry

Captain Charles Seitz, commanding Company A of the 808th Tank Destroyer Battalion, described how tank destroyers operated with the fast-moving armored cavalry during operations to clear the west bank of the Rhine River during late March. One M36 platoon worked with each squadron. Seitz reported, "The cavalry's mission was to exploit the

Moselle bridgehead in the north of the Moselle triangle and push as quickly as possible to the Rhine and then sweep to the south along the Rhine as fast as possible. This meant rapid movement, so we found it necessary to place the M36s in the support section of the cavalry teams' columns, following a reconnaissance troop and a platoon of light tanks. Each team moved along a different route to the objective. The lighter vehicles could move as fast as the situation allowed without being held back by the slower M36s [the M18 could keep up!]. Then, if something were hit, the destroyer would have time to move up to it and size it up.

"In this type of movement, good liaison was important. This was achieved in one of two ways depending on the situation. One was that the platoon leader rode behind the team commander, and the other was that the team commander had a radio vehicle accompany the platoon leader [the price of having incompatible radio gear].

"When the cavalry did find opposition—chiefly in towns—the destroyers moved into position to supply assault fire. In one instance, the combination of the cavalry's speed and the assault fire of the destroyers persuaded approximately seven hundred fifty Germans in the Bingen area to give up to our much smaller force."[16]

*   *   *

Seventh Army, meanwhile, on 15 March launched Operation Undertone, which aimed at retaking the ground lost during Nordwind and clearing the southern Saar. On 16 March 1945, the men of the 776th Tank Destroyer Battalion were attached to the 63d Infantry Division, which was trying to crack the Siegfried Line defenses near Ensheim, just south of Saarbrücken. Advances in the north might be unfolding with accelerating speed, but here the Germans still fought tenaciously.

In the early dawn hours, company and platoon leaders conducted a foot reconnaissance under small-arms and mortar fire to survey possible firing positions. They then met with infantry commanders to coordinate team play. That night, as the men tried to get some rest in the assembly area, they were subjected to artillery and rocket fire.

The next day at 0500 hours, the M36s of Companies A and C moved forward over sloped terrain under enemy observation in support of the doughs of the 254th and 255th Infantry regiments. Ahead lay three belts of mutually supporting fortifications, the first cleverly concealed along a ridgeline running between two heavily wooded ravines. Minefields and dragons teeth protected the approaches. Antitank ditches further restricted the movement of armor. The defenses included pillboxes, covered trenches, and turrets mounting 75mm guns. Substantial artillery, mortar, and Nebelwerfer rocket launcher units backed the defenders.

As the first M36s advanced, the sound of their engines provoked a heavy barrage of artillery and rocket fire. Fragments whistled over the heads of the crewman crouching in their open-topped turrets, passing close enough to knock off two radio antennae in Company C. Staff Sergeant Oliver Stevens dismounted and ran through the incoming fire to the infantry observation post to make final arrangements about targets. For the rest of the day, he would race between the infantry and the TDs to coordinate action.

The TDs maneuvered into exposed firing positions as close to the pillboxes as possible while German artillery fire began to crash into the assault force. The infantry was forced back initially under the withering fire, but the TDs remained forward, pounding the German lines. Gunners maintained such a high rate of fire that crews had to periodically cease fire to allow their guns to cool. When that happened, a crewman would mount the exposed rear deck and continue to hit the enemy with the .50-caliber antiaircraft machine gun. As TDs ran through their ammunition, they would back to a covered position, reload, and advance again.

The Germans tried to drive the Americans back with infantry counterattacks. Crewmen grabbed their carbines, tommyguns, and fragmentation grenades to beat the assaults back. A bazooka round destroyed one M36, and several others were damaged by artillery and bazooka rounds. One shell blew Private First Class Canterbury's hatch off where he sat in his radio operator's seat. He climbed out, recovered the hatch, and put it back on. Fragments from exploding shells, meanwhile, were raining into the turrets of the forward platoons, and more radio aerials, guns sights, periscopes, and even .50-cals were lost.

Strongpoint by strongpoint, the return fire ceased under pounding from the TDs. The battalion noted that its 90mm fire destroyed embrasures and in many cases pulverized the pillboxes. The doughs were able to advance by the afternoon, and engineers blew gaps in the dragon's teeth. German prisoners were shell-shocked.

The TDs passed through the dragon's teeth, and they were able to engage some emplacements from a distance of only seventy-five to one hundred yards. As Staff Sergeant Stevens moved his platoon forward in one sector, the lead TD broke through a temporary bridge the engineers had established across an antitank ditch. Under heavy fire, Stevens tried to pull the TD out of the way but could not. Stevens drove back to the CP, where the infantry regimental and battalion commanders were anxious to speak with him because enemy fire had knocked out all of their communications with the infantry. He collected bridging material and some engineers and returned to the ditch. The engineer officer asked as they came under renewed machine-gun and artillery fire, "Nothing can live down there! Shouldn't we go back?" In the end, the fire was too heavy, and the effort was abandoned.

The TDs supported the assault for sixty straight hours under constant fire, using the darkness to refuel, rearm, and perform critical maintenance. During the engagement, they fired 2,450 rounds of 90mm ammunition at the fortifications. Every M36 suffered damage, and three were total losses. Two men were killed and eleven wounded, many of whom refused evacuation and stayed with their under-manned destroyers.

And the infantry won through. Stevens commented, "In this operation, the enemy artillery and rocket fire, direct AT fire, and all types of small arms fire exceeded any I have experienced in all the other assaults that I have been in, which include the crossings of the Volturno River, the assault on Cassino, the Gothic Line breakthrough, and the operations around Mateur in Africa."[17]

* * *

On 19 March, Seventh Army finally took Saarbrücken. The next day, German resistance collapsed along the West Wall, and troops swarmed across the Saar-Palatinate triangle to link up with Patton's forces, which had been driving south across the German rear. By 21 March, the Allies held the Rhine's west bank from Arnhem to Switzerland.[18]

Across the Rhine

Montgomery's operatic assault across the Rhine on 23 March was to have been the first Allied crossing, but it was almost the last. Not only had First Army jumped the river at Remagen, Patton sneaked the 5th Infantry Division across the night of 22 March, then quickly carved out two more bridgeheads on the east bank at Boppard and St. Goar on 24 and 25 March. Seventh Army crossed at Worms on 27 March.[19] It was time for the Reich to experience American blitzkrieg.

On 25 March, Bradley told First Army to break out of the Remagen bridgehead. Seventh Corps struck eastward before turning north to isolate the Ruhr. The history of the 3d Armored Division recorded, "At 0400 hours on 25 March the combat commands were rumbling out of bivouac. They went out along the dawn-dim roads in multiple columns of spearheads, 32d and 33d Armored regiment tanks leading, squat and black in the gloom, with blue flame spitting from their exhausts. Tank destroyers of the 703d TD Battalion followed, clacking rapidly over the cobbles, their long 90mm guns perfectly balanced in heavy steel turrets. Armored infantrymen of the 36th, the 'Blitz Doughs,' rode in personnel halftracks."[20]

Mobile warfare was back. The semi-official history of the 628th Tank Destroyer Battalion—which was operating again with the 5th Armored Division—observed, "After being penned for so many months by terrain and prepared defensive positions. . . the only limit on the armored forces was one of resupply of rations and gas. Reminiscent of the hard driving, fast moving armored slashes following the breakthrough at Avranches, France, last August, once again the 5th Armored Division and the tank destroyers were on the loose, deep in enemy territory." Resistance was so fragmented that the battalion would lose only one TD east of the Rhine River.[21]

Ninety Allied divisions—twenty-five of them armored—began slicing through the Reich's heartland.[22]

*   *   *

German tank strength in the West was dwindling toward the vanishing point. When news of Patton's crossing at Oppenheim had reached Hitler, he had called for immediate countermeasures, but

German commanders had nothing with which to respond. The only "reserve" was an assortment of five panzers under repair at a tank depot one hundred miles away. The bottom of the barrel had been scraped.[23] As of 31 March, the entire force of panzers and assault guns in Third Army's sector was estimated at only forty-five vehicles.[24] German Army Group B in the Ruhr had only sixty-five tanks left.[25]

Still, panzers appeared now and again. On 30 March, 3d Armored Division relayed orders to the 703d Tank Destroyer Battalion to support the attack by the division on the road junction at Paderborn, the Fort Knox of the panzer arm. German instructors, officer cadets, and trainees drove their remaining tanks—including some sixty Tigers and Panthers from an SS replacement battalion—out to contest the American advance, and battle flared across the training grounds for two days.[26]

Task Force Welborn formed one of the division's two prongs and was advancing near Etteln at dusk. The column had identified four Royal Tigers ahead, but they had been struck by fighter-bombers, and Col John Welborn had been assured that the panzers had been knocked out. The column advanced, and the very functional Tigers opened fire with their deadly 88s. Seven Shermans were soon burning.[27] The TDs of 2d Platoon, Company B, returned fire and knocked out two Royal Tigers—a job that required thirty-five rounds of AP and five of HE. One 703d recon jeep was destroyed by return fire.[28] During this action, division CG MajGen Maurice Rose was killed when he was cut off by four Royal Tigers. A panzer commander, misinterpreting the general's action, shot him when he reached to drop his holster.[29]

Belton Cooper, in his history of the 3d Armored Division, reports that Royal Tigers destroyed an entire company of Shermans from an unidentified task force and that one M36 was lost during the debacle.[30] The incident is not mentioned in the division's own history. Several sources concur that one M36 was destroyed that day, but the exact circumstances remain unclear.

* * *

The German resistance was brave but futile. On 1 April, Paderborn fell, and the 3d Armored Division linked up at Lippstadt with Ninth Army's 2d Armored Division—which had swung around the Ruhr industrial basin on the north. The Ruhr was cut off from the rest of Germany, trapping more than three hundred thousand German troops.

The 644th Tank Destroyer Battalion, operating with its old partners in the 8th Infantry Division, supported the First Army push from the south to eliminate the pocket. The outfit's informal history recorded, "At first the going was as rough as any we'd had. The TDs operated as tanks, assault guns, personnel carriers, recon vehicles, and anything else that occurred to those minds at higher headquarters. Recon Company showed the division how cavalry troops ought to do it, capturing towns, leading the infantry, poking up side roads to tell the doughs if there were enemy SPs waiting for them, operating twenty-four hours a day." The TDs worked closely in combat teams with the 740th Tank Battalion.[31]

Ninth Army troops, meanwhile, compressed the pocket from the north. On 17 April while the jaws closed tight, the 8th Infantry Division took a record 50,192 prisoners, and organized resistance collapsed. Four days later, Generalfeldmarshall Walter Model, alone but for his intelligence chief, shot himself rather than surrender.[32]

*   *   *

While the battle to reduce the Ruhr Pocket raged, columns fanned deeper into Germany all along the front. The history of the 817th Tank Destroyer Battalion—recently re-equipped with M18s and now supporting the 104th Infantry Division—recorded:

> The Germans were disorganized and scattered. Constant pressure had to be put on them to keep them from being able to reorganize. Daily, the battalion advanced from twenty-five to forty miles, and the supply sections of Headquarters Company were working twenty-four hours a day to fill the seemingly limitless thirst of the Hellcats for gasoline. The Weser had been crossed, and then there was a mad dash for Warburg; then the Leine River and Göttingen. The Leine River crossed, we pushed onward, ever eastward into the heart of the black Reich.
>
> Along the highways of battle, the townspeople and farmers gaped in amazement out of the windows of their white-flag-bedecked houses at the equipment and material of this great American Army. They forgot the advances of their own blitz of '39 and '40 and marveled at ours. They were being conquered and overrun, and they knew it.

Each day, every installation of the battalion moved. The name of last night's town was soon forgotten, and all eyes turned eastward. "Onward! Onward!" was the cry, and the 817th rolled onward, sometimes carrying the doughboys with them. Soon, perhaps, it would be "finis la guerre."[33]

Odd situations cropped up as operations sometimes looked more and more like a somewhat violent installation of a military government than a war. On 5 April, for example, the CP group of 823d Tank Destroyer Battalion—which was sweeping toward Magdeburg on the Elbe River with the 30th Infantry and 2d Armored divisions—entered Lage about noon. The men discovered a state of anarchy, with Russian slave laborers battling the locals in fierce rioting. The Americans spent the rest of the day restoring order. The 823d's AAR noted caustically, "The entire battalion's heart bleeds for the German storekeepers who were so thoroughly looted."

A week later, CP personnel had to disperse slave laborers and Germans who were looting a sugar warehouse at the outfit's temporary home in Braunschweig. The next day, the CP had just set up in Farsleben when it was swarmed by refugees from a train that had been hauling nearly three thousand people to a concentration camp. They were in bad shape and had not eaten in four days, and some had died of starvation. Battalion CO LtCol Stanley Dettmar ordered the bürgermeister to get the bakeries operating and feed the people. Meanwhile, rioting broke out back at the sugar warehouse.[34]

*   *   *

The Germans resisted fiercely in a few cities where they could scrape together some infantry, a few tanks, and 88mm antiaircraft guns. The 3d and 45th Infantry divisions on 16 April encountered one such frustrating situation at Nürnberg, the scene of so many Nazi pageants but now a heap of ruins. The men of the 601st Tank Destroyer Battalion fought their way into a city with the doughs, their first experience with urban fighting. The outfit's informal history reports, "The enemy was in the cellars and on the rooftops and in every window and on all sides. The battalion took some casualties, but it inflicted tenfold and more upon the Kraut. Those '90s' were everywhere, and in several instances the tubes were literally inside the windows of the Kraut strongpoints."[35]

On 17 April, SSgt Bill Harper, who had battled panzers since the swirling dust at El Guettar, dismounted from his M36 and hunted down a troublesome sniper with his pistol.

Nürnberg fell on 20 April, Hitler's birthday.

*   *   *

As always, TD recon men were in the van. The 355th Infantry Regiment, 89th Infantry Division, and C/602d Tank Destroyer Battalion attacked Zwickau on 17 April, because the city had refused to surrender. Lieutenant Kilbourn's reconnaissance platoon, with the help of an escaped British prisoner of war, made a bold dash through the streets in a bid to seize a bridge across the Mulde River. German riflemen and bazooka teams commanded the approach, but the platoon raced past the surprised defenders. The men dismounted and began cutting demolition wires under a hail of rifle and machine-gun fire. One man fell dead, and another was wounded. The platoon saved the bridge.[36]

Queried by 12th Army Group about reports that the long-serving M10s were in bad shape and breaking down in combat, the hard-charging Third Army reported that all of its M10s were in such bad shape they should be replaced by M18s or M36s. First Army indicated that one-third of its M10s were sidelined. Ninth Army, however, said it could squeeze another half year out of its equipment.[37]

The Fat Lady Sings

Way down south in Italy, the crews of the 804th Tank Destroyer Battalion pulled into firing positions behind the doughs of the 88th Infantry Division in early April 1945. Major General Geoffrey Keyes and other brass visited the battalion on 15 April, and Keyes fired the battalion's 200,000th round at the enemy from a Company B M10.

The next day, the American line surged into motion. After cracking through the initial crust of resistance, American forces swept into the Po River Valley and crossed the river itself within ten days. There was resistance here and there, but German troops began to surrender en masse.[38]

The integration of TDs and tanks was nearly complete by now. The 701st Tank Destroyer Battalion was attached to the 10th Mountain Division, for example, as was the 751st Tank Battalion. Force Madden fell under the control of the 751st Tank Battalion and included the TDs of B/701st. Headquarters, 701st Tank Destroyer Battalion, commanded Force Redding, which included Companies B, C, and D of the 751st Tank Battalion. Furthermore, each tank destroyer company swapped one platoon with its correspondingly lettered tank company. Company A of the tank battalion, for example, had two tank platoons and one TD platoon, while the ratio was reversed in the tank destroyer company. The units also exchanged radios and aligned crystals to ensure perfect communications. The mixed companies combined the armor-piercing fire power of the 3-inch guns and the better HE and automatic weapons capabilities of the Sherman.

One mixed company supported each of the six assault infantry battalions. The TDs provided a base of fire while the tanks advanced in direct support of the doughs. Despite the installation of SCR-300 radios in many infantry support tanks in northwestern Europe, the armor and infantry components in Italy still could not communicate by radio at the tactical level.[39]

Life was still plenty dangerous. John Hudson recalled:

> On or about April 13, 1945, C/701st was the first to cut the northwest highway going out of Bologna. . . . Out in front of my TDs, I was suddenly hit and knocked to the ground as I heard a German machine gun fire. The blow was as if somebody hit me with a baseball bat. . . . I took off my helmet (which I almost never wore) to discover three parallel tracks on the top right side, where three shots had hit just above the angle causing them to ricochet off after fracturing the steel and leaving three tracks in my skull!
>
> As we drove fast northwest of Bologna, an artillery shell landed just behind my jeep. A fragment as big as your fist went through the steel spare wheel; the jeep body; the chain locker over the right wheel holding tire chains, wheel jacks, and other tools; the command radio behind my seat; the steel back to my seat; my tanker's jacket; and my clothing. I could feel the hit and asked my driver to get me to the first aid station we came to. There's where we discovered all this damage, plus a big blister on my back where the fragment had burned. Some burn stuff was applied with another band-aid, and we were on our way. . . .

[That evening, battalion executive officer] Bob Childs arrived. He had come from promoting Jack Wright to major, and he brought me Jack's old helmet, with the captain's bars welded onto the front, to announce my own promotion to captain, after nearly a year off and on as CO, Company C. He said, "I just can't have my officers going around without a bath, and your helmet with those three holes won't let you bathe in it!"[40]

By late April, the 701st Tank Destroyer Battalion's AAR reflected a hope that cheered many a weary warrior:

A great valley had been crossed as the Fifth Army advanced from the Apennines to the Alps. A major water obstacle had been crossed, and the German armies in Italy had been virtually destroyed. The spring offensive had been a gratifying success.

For the officers and men of the 701st Tank Destroyer Battalion, this month meant the completion of thirty-five long, arduous months of overseas service. This was perhaps the most singly important month of them all to us, for at long last the end of the European war seemed in sight. Elements of this battalion were among the first American ground forces to engage the Nazi enemy in this war. It was a gratifying thought that the end was so near. . . .

In the closing days of the month, some of the 701st men who came ashore in the first landing at Oran saw their last action supporting the 10th Mountain Division advance along Lake Garda in the Alps. The Americans mounted small amphibious operations to bypass roadblocks and AT guns hidden in tunnels on the east side of the lake. Newly minted Capt John Hudson, now commanding C/701st Tank Destroyer Battalion, mounted two M10s on an old freight boat. When his guns fired on some German activity on the far side of the lake, the vessels jumped six feet sideways and dumped an unsecured jeep into ninety feet of cold water.[41]

*   *   *

North of the Alps, the S-3 for the 818th Tank Destroyer Battalion, which was approaching the German-Austrian border with the 26th Infantry Division, recorded the following notation for 2230 hours on 1 May in his journal: "Radio announcement unofficial that Hitler was dead (good riddance)." By that day, the Germans were estimated to have no more than two hundred tanks or assault guns along the entire Western

Front, half of them in front of Third Army, where remnants of the Sixth Panzer Army had reappeared from the Eastern Front.[42]

But men continued to die until the very end. On 2 May, Lt Joseph Keeby, the reconnaissance officer in the 614th Tank Destroyer Battalion who had led the raid near Prinzheim three months earlier, died with five of his men in a fight on the outskirts of Scharnitz, Austria.[43]

*   *   *

On 5 May, M10s of 3d Platoon, C/804th Tank Destroyer Battalion, advanced up the winding Italian alpine road into the Brenner Pass with doughs of 1/339th Infantry Regiment, 85th Infantry Division. About the same time, two platoons of Shermans from C/781st Tank Battalion, a platoon from C/614th Tank Destroyer Battalion, and doughs from the 103d Infantry Division, entered the pass from the German side. A German guard, complete with burp gun and potato mashers, halted the column at a bridge with a red lantern to warn them that the heavy tracked vehicles could make it across only if they drove slowly. They drove slowly. At 1615 hours, the two columns encountered one another eight miles inside Italy. Fifth and Seventh armies had joined forces.[44]

*   *   *

German representatives signed documents of capitulation in the wee hours of 7 May. To the world, General of the Army Dwight Eisenhower declared simply, "The mission of this Allied Force was fulfilled at 0241, local time, May 7, 1945." At midnight on 8 May, the war in Europe was over for everyone. The AAR of the 645th Tank Destroyer Battalion, whose men had seen and done much since landing in southern Italy so long before, recorded:

> May 8th, the long awaited day for the 645th TD Bn. (VE Day). Most of the men in the battalion could hardly believe it was true. With over five hundred fifteen days in direct contact with the enemy to our credit, a great proud feeling is felt within us. We have made our contribution to this hard-won victory. First thoughts went to the folks back home, and each man wrote that letter that their loved ones were waiting for. "The war is over," and I am healthy and sound. Second thoughts went to our comrades who have fallen in

battle. We had become like brothers, and their absence has made our joy subdued.[45]

The end of the war found the men of the 601st Tank Destroyer Battalion, some of whom had come all the way from Oran, drinking champagne liberated from Hitler's cellars in Berchtesgaden. "For a teetotaler," noted the battalion history, "der Führer carried a wicked supply of everything good to drink."[46]

Mission Accomplished

The TD battalions had racked up some astonishing accomplishments. The first outfit to enter combat, the 701st Tank Destroyer Battalion, had knocked out eighty-seven armored fighting vehicles—or nearly three times its own strength in tank destroyers. This was actually a fairly low total, however, because the battalion had fought in Italy, where panzers were scarce. The other battalion in action since Operation Torch, the 601st Tank Destroyer Battalion, claimed one hundred fifty-five tanks and SP guns.

The tank killers had fought the greatest number of panzers after busting into Fortress Europa at Normandy.

The 823d claimed to have won the kill title out of all fifty-six TD battalions in the ETO—one hundred thirteen tanks, including sixty-eight Mark IVs, twenty-seven Panthers, and eighteen Tigers—as well as the First and Ninth armies' records for tanks destroyed in a single day. The battalion accomplished this feat despite landing at Normandy with towed guns. The outfit fired 4,193 rounds of 3-inch ammunition directly and 33,486 rounds indirectly during the campaign.[47]

But who really knows who was champ? The 773d Tank Destroyer Battalion also claimed one hundred thirteen panzers destroyed, plus twenty-five SP guns.[48] After landing on D+3, the 702d Tank Destroyer Battalion claimed to have destroyed one hundred three panzers, fifty-one SP and AT guns, and one hundred twenty vehicles.[49]

In general, the towed battalions had not proved as valuable as the self-propelled units. The 635th Tank Destroyer Battalion made it past VE Day before receiving orders to convert to M18s. It had engaged a total of only eleven German tanks after D+2. The towed battalion's limited ability to contribute to American combat might was a testament to the regrettable tendency of the generals to prepare to fight the last conflict. Western Europe had not been North Africa.[50]

A U.S. Army study of thirty-nine TD battalions of all types indicated that they, on average, destroyed thirty-four tanks, seventeen towed guns, and sixteen pillboxes. In aggregate, the TDs' contribution was huge. Tank destroyer battalions in Third Army alone claimed the destruction of six hundred eighty-six tanks and two hundred thirty-nine SP guns (as of 28 April 1945). Total TD losses (as measured by replacements) in the entire ETO were five hundred thirty-nine M10s, two hundred fifteen M18s, one hundred fifty-one M36s, and two hundred twenty-eight towed guns.[51]

The kill/loss ratio for the tank destroyer arm was extremely favorable, particularly considering that American forces were usually on the attack. At one extreme, the 703d Tank Destroyer Battalion destroyed ten tanks or SP guns for every TD it lost in action.[52] More typical numbers were good but lower. The 634th Tank Destroyer Battalion between 29 June 1944 and 8 May 1945 destroyed sixty-eight tanks and SP guns in exchange for twenty-eight M10s and one M8.[53] The 628th eliminated fifty-six panzers for the loss of eighteen TDs.[54]

Overall, the tank destroyer battalions in the ETO had suffered far lower human casualties proportionately than other front-line units. One study indicated that on average a TD battalion could expect monthly losses of 6 percent of T/O strength. One out of four battle casualties did not require evacuation, according to the study, while one out of three men evacuated returned within sixty days.[55] To give an idea of absolute numbers, the 634th Tank Destroyer Battalion between 29 June 1944 and 8 May 1945 lost seventy-six men killed and one hundred seventy-five wounded.[56] From D+3 to VE Day, the 702d Tank Destroyer Battalion lost sixty men killed in action.[57] The 601st Tank Destroyer Battalion, which had been in actual combat five hundred forty-six days from North Africa to Bavaria, suffered six hundred eighty-three casualties, including one hundred ten men killed.[58]

*   *   *

But tanks had done well, too. Patton noted in a 19 March 1945 letter that tanks had destroyed the majority of the 2,287 panzers his men had knocked out after becoming operational on 1 August 1944.[59] Moreover, the line between the tank and the destroyer in combat had become so blurry as to be nearly impossible to see. Patton had been right when he predicted the TD would become just another tank.

The ETO's General Board studying tank destroyers concluded that the trend toward tanks with the same fire power and mobility as the TDs, and the incorporation of adequate antitank defenses in the infantry divisions, rendered the tank destroyer superfluous. The board recommended that the Tank Destroyer Force be dissolved.[60]

And so it was done.

Appendix A

Tank Destroyer Battalions by Campaign[1]

North African Theater of Operations

Algeria/French Morocco (8–11 November 1942)

601st, 701st

Tunisia (17 November 1942–13 May 1943

601st, 701st, 776th, 805th, 813th, 894th, 899th

Mediterranean Theater of Operations

Sicily (9 June 1943–17 August 1943)

601st (the 636th and 813th also sent elements but
were not officially credited)

Naples-Foggia (9 September 1943–21 January 1944)

601st, 636th, 645th, 701st, 776th, 805th, 894th

Rome-Arno (22 January 1944–9 September 1944)

601st, 636th, 645th, 701st, 776th, 804th, 805th, 813th, 894th, 899th

North Apennines (10 September 1944–4 April 1945)

679th, 701st, 804th, 805th, 894th

Po Valley (5 April 1945–8 May 1945)

679th, 701st, 804th, 805th, 894th

European Theater of Operations

Normandy (6 June–24 July 1944)

603d, 607th, 612th, 629th, 630th, 634th, 635th, 644th, 654th, 702d,
703d, 704th, 705th, 774th, 801st, 802d, 803d, 813th, 818th, 821st,
823d, 893d, 899th, (1st Tank Destroyer Brigade)

Northern France (25 July–14 September 1944)

602d, 603d, 607th, 609th, 610th, 612th, 614th, 628th, 629th, 630th,
631st, 634th, 635th, 638th, 644th, 654th, 691st, 702d, 703d, 704th,

705th, 773d, 774th, 801st, 802d, 803d, 813th, 814th, 817th, 818th, 821st, 823d, 825th, 893d, 899th, (1st Tank Destroyer Brigade)

Southern France (15 August–14 September 1944)

601st, 636th, 645th

Rhineland (15 September–21 March 1945)

601st, 602d, 603d, 605th, 607th, 609th, 610th, 612th, 614th, 628th, 629th, 630th, 631st, 634th, 635th, 636th, 638th, 643d, 644th, 645th, 648th, 654th, 656th, 661st, 691st, 692d, 702d, 703d, 704th, 705th, 771st, 772d, 773d, 774th, 776th, 801st, 802d, 803d, 807th, 808th, 811th, 813th, 814th, 817th, 818th, 820th, 821st, 822d, 823d, 824th, 825th, 827th, 893d, 899th, (1st Tank Destroyer Brigade)

Ardennes-Alsace (16 December 1944–25 January 1945)

601st, 602d, 603d, 607th, 609th, 610th, 612th, 614th, 628th, 629th, 630th, 631st, 634th, 635th, 636th, 638th, 643d, 644th, 645th, 654th, 691st, 692d, 702d, 703d, 704th, 705th, 772d, 773d, 774th, 801st, 802d, 803d, 807th, 808th, 809th, 811th, 813th, 814th, 818th, 820th, 823d, 824th, 827th, 893d, 899th, (1st Tank Destroyer Brigade)

Central Europe (22 March–11 May 1945)

601st, 602d, 603d, 605th, 607th, 609th, 610th, 612th, 614th, 628th, 629th, 630th, 631st, 633d, 634th, 635th, 636th, 638th, 643d, 644th, 645th, 648th, 654th, 656th, 661st, 691st, 692d, 702d, 703d, 704th, 705th, 771st, 772d, 773d, 774th, 776th, 801st, 802d, 803d, 807th, 808th, 809th, 811th, 813th, 814th, 817th, 818th, 820th, 821st, 822d, 823d, 824th, 825th, 827th, 893d, 899th, (1st Tank Destroyer Brigade)

Appendix B

Battalion Profiles

601st Tank Destroyer Battalion[1]

1st Infantry Division Provisional Antitank Battalion converted to 601st Tank Destroyer Battalion on 15 December 1941. Company C of the original battalion consisted mainly of Battery D, 5th Field Artillery, the only Army unit with a continuous history from the Revolutionary War. Arrived at Gourock, Scotland, on 9 April 1942. Reconnaissance Company landed at Oran, Algeria, on 8 November as part of Operation Torch, and rest of battalion arrived in December. Fought in Battle of Kasserine Pass in February 1943 and at El Guettar in March. Converted to the M10 at end of North Africa campaign. Participated in invasion landings at Salerno, Italy, on 9 September. Made third D-day assault at Anzio on 22 January 1944 and entered Rome in June. Conducted fourth assault landing in southern France on 15 August. Advanced to German border in the Vosges region. Participated in reduction of Colmar Pocket in February 1945, then converted to the M36. Battled along the Siegfried Line until crossing the Rhine on 22 March. Helped capture Nürnberg in April and ended the war occupying Hitler's retreat at Berchtesgaden in Bavaria. Attached to: 1st Armored Division; 1st, 3d, 9th, 34th, 36th, 45th, 103d Infantry divisions.

602d Tank Destroyer Battalion[2]

2d Infantry Division Provisional Antitank Battalion converted to 602d Tank Destroyer Battalion on 15 December 1941. Equipped with M10s, then M18s before leaving the States. Arrived in Scotland on 29 July 1944 and at Omaha Beach on 26 August. Committed to battle along Moselle River on 9 September. Supported operations leading to capture of Metz, France, in November. Transferred to Belgium during Ardennes Offensive, arriving at Neufchateau on 21 December. Supported operations against the Bulge in January 1945. Fought through Siegfried Line in February. Returned to Moselle River area in March, crossed Rhine River at Boppard on 26 March. Advanced through Gotha, Eisenach, and Zwickau in April. Attached to: 17th Airborne Division; 4th and 11th Armored divisions; 26th, 28th, 80th, 87th, 89th, and 90th Infantry divisions; 2d and 6th Cavalry groups.

603d Tank Destroyer Battalion[3]

Activated on 15 December 1941 at Fort Lewis, Washington, from the antitank platoons of the 3d Infantry Division. Issued T70s (M18s) in October 1943, arrived at Cannock, England, on 18 April 1944. Landed at Utah Beach on 21–22 July. Committed to battle on 28 July during Cobra breakout. Advanced through Brittany to Brest and then Lorient in August, and raced east to the Moselle River sector in September. Fought east of Nancy, France, in October and supported push to the Saar River in November. Battled to Sarreguemines in December, shifted to Bastogne area to support counterattack against the Bulge. Crossed Our River and fought through Siegfried Line in February 1945. Moved to Seventh Army sector in March, reached Rhine River at Rhine-Durkheim on 21 March. Reassigned to Third Army, crossed river at Oppenheim on 25 March. Attacked through Fulda Gap toward Erfurt in late March and

April. Helped liberate Buchenwald on 11 April. Reached advance limit line at Mittweida circa 15 April. Attached to: 17th Airborne Division; 4th, 6th Armored divisions; 3d Cavalry Group.

6o5th Tank Destroyer Battalion[4]

Reorganized from the 5th Antitank Battalion (Provisional), 5th Infantry Division, on 16 December 1941 at Fort Custer, Michigan. Arrived at Clyde, Scotland, on 16 December 1944. Landed at Le Havre, France, on 26 January 1945 equipped with towed guns. Entered battle on 16 February near Tevern, Germany. Crossed Roer River on 24 February and joined drive to the Rhine. Deployed to Remagen bridgehead on 12 March. Withdrawn on 17 March and sent to Belgium to support British armored forces, but almost immediately attached to 17th Airborne Division. Crossed Rhine beginning 25 March at Xanten. Participated in reduction of the Ruhr Pocket in April. Crossed Elbe River on 30 April–1 May at Bleckede. Attached to: 17th, 82d Airborne divisions; 79th, 84th, 102d Infantry Division; 11th Cavalry Group; British 33d Armored Brigade.

6o7th Tank Destroyer Battalion[5]

Activated on 15 December 1941 at Fort Ord, California, from the 7th Infantry Division Provisional Antitank Battalion. Converted to a towed battalion in May 1943. Arrived at Liverpool, England, on 21 April 1944. Disembarked at Utah Beach 17–23 June. Supported advance on Cherbourg, fought along Seves River in July. Participated in drive to Le Mans and envelopment of the Falaise Pocket in August. Advanced to Moselle River in September and supported operations against Metz through November. Converted to a self-propelled battalion equipped with M36s in time for final assaut. Joined drive toward Saar River, capture of Saarlautern, and subsequent fight against Siegfried Line in December. Deployed to the Ardennes sector in January 1945. Committed against Siegfried Line again in February in the Schnee Eifel. Supported the capture of Koblenz in mid-March. Crossed the Rhine River at Boppard on 25 March. Sliced through Hessen and Thüringen during

April and reached the Czechoslovak border near Plauen by mid-April. Thereafter remained in defensive positions. Attached to: 82d Airborne Division; 9th, 28th, 87th, 90th, 95th Infantry divisions; 6th Cavalry Group.

609th Tank Destroyer Battalion[6]

Activated on 15 December 1941 at Fort Bragg, North Carolina. Landed at Utah Beach on 20 September 1944 equipped with M18s. Went into corps reserve beginning 28 September east of Moutier, France, where crews fired artillery missions through October. Joined operations against Siegfried Line in November and early December. Most of Company C moved to Bastogne on 18 December with 10th Armored Division; remainder of battalion fought along Sauer River. Entire battalion fought to eliminate the Bulge in January 1945. Deployed to Saar-Moselle triangle in February. Participated in capture of Trier in March. Supported attack south and east out of Mannheim bridgehead across the Rhine in late March and April and reached southern Bavaria near Füssen by the end of the month. Attached to: 101st Airborne Division; 10th Armored Division; 90th, 94th Infantry divisions.

610th Tank Destroyer Battalion[7]

Activated on 11 April 1942 at Camp Barkeley, Texas, as a towed battalion. Arrived Greenock, Scotland, on 11 June 1944. Landed at Utah Beach on 31 July. Committed to action 10 August near Craon, France, and participated in elimination of Falaise Pocket. Raced east to the Moselle River by September. Converted to the M36 in September–October. Helped clear Maginot Line fortifications in November. Ordered to the Ardennes on 21 December. Helped eliminate the Bulge in January 1945. Battled through Siegfried Line in February near Brandscheid. Transferred back south in March. Crossed the Rhine at Worms on 29 March. Raced through central and southern Germany in April and reached the vicinity of Munich by month's end. Ended war in Ingolstadt. Attached to: 4th, 26th, 35th, 42d, 80th, 87th Infantry divisions; 101st Cavalry Group.

612th Tank Destroyer Battalion[8]

Activated on 25 June 1942 at Camp Swift, Texas, as a towed battalion. Arrived at Greenock, Scotland, on 15 April 1944. Landed in France beginning 14 June and committed in the vicinity of Cerisy. Fought at Vire during breakout in July and early August. Moved to Brittany and supported siege and capture of Brest in late August and September. Shifted to Belgium in October and supported operations against the Siegfried Line until December. Engaged Germans in Honsfeld, Belgium, area at outbreak of Battle of the Bulge. Converted to self-propelled battalion (M18s) beginning 29 December 1944. Joined attack through Monschau Forest in February 1945. Crossed Rhine River in March, participated in race through central Germany to Leipzig in April. Attached to: 9th Armored Division; 1st, 2d, 9th, 99th Infantry divisions.

614th Tank Destroyer Battalion[9]

Activated on 25 July 1942 at Camp Carson, Colorado. Reorganized as a towed battalion in May 1943. Arrived in England on 7 September 1944, landed at Utah beachhead beginning 8 October. Deployed to Metz and supported operations against the Siegfried Line nearby in November and December. Shifted to Hagenau Forest area. Continued to support operations against Siegfried Line fortifications until late March 1945. Performed occupation duties in early April, then joined race to Innsbruck, Austria, and Brenner Pass. Attached to: 95th, 103d Infantry divisions.

628th Tank Destroyer Battalion[10]

Established 15 December 1941 from the 28th Infantry Division Antitank Battalion (Provisional). Arrived at Greenock, Scotland on 6 February 1944, disembarked at Utah Beach on 30 July equipped with M10s. Committed to battle on 2 August near Perier, France. Participated in envelopment of Falaise Pocket. Dashed east to the Belgian border, arriving on 2 September. Helped liberate Luxembourg, began assault on the Siegfried Line on 13 September. Conducted artillery missions in October. Converted to M36s in November, then committed to fighting in the Hürtgen Forest in December. Shifted to Aachen sector on 8 December only to be ordered to the Ardennes during the Battle of the Bulge. Fought to eliminate Bulge in January 1945. Crossed Roer River beginning 25 February and reached the Rhine on 10 March. Crossed the Rhine on 31 March at Wessel. Slashed through Germany to the Elbe River by 11 April. Attacked back *west* to eliminate German pockets. Took up occupation duties on 26 April near Peine. Attached to: 82d Airborne Division; 3d, 5th Armored divisions; 75th Infantry Division.

629th Tank Destroyer Battalion[11]

Established 15 December 1941 at Fort Meade, Maryland. Arrived in Dorset, England, in January 1944 and disembarked at Omaha Beach on 2 July with M10s. Performed artillery missions in Caumont sector. Joined 30th Infantry Division in fighting at Mortain in early August, then supported reduction of the Falaise Pocket. Participated in V Corps parade through Paris on 29 August. Advanced to Luxembourg by early September and then supported operations in the Hürtgen Forest and against the Siegfried Line. Shifted to Ardennes sector on 24 December. Fought to eliminate the Bulge in January 1945. Joined renewed assault on Siegfried Line in February. Crossed Rhine River into Remagen bridgehead on 11 March and converted to the M36 that same month. Participated in operations against the Ruhr Pocket in April, then conducted road march south to Bavaria and reached the Isar River before ending offensive operations. Attached to: 82d Airborne Division; 5th Armored Division; 1st, 2d, 5th, 9th, 28th, 30th, 75th, 83d, 99th Infantry divisions.

630th Tank Destroyer Battalion[12]

Activated 15 December 1941 at Ft. Jackson, South Carolina. Disembarked in France from England on 24 July 1944 with towed guns and entered the line near Colombieres. Advanced across France with the 28th Infantry Division to Luxembourg. Supported operations against the

Siegfried Line in September–October. Operated in the Hürtgen Forest in November. Shifted to the Ardennes sector with the 28th Infantry Division in late November, where located at start of German offensive in December. Shifted south to Colmar area in January 1945, where the 28th Infantry Division operated under French control. Returned north in mid-February only to redeploy south to the Saar region in mid-March, after which the battalion converted to the M36. Participated in the elimination of the Ruhr Pocket in April. Took up occupation duties at Zweibrücken on 28 April. Attached to: 17th Airborne Division; 13th Armored Division; 28th Infantry Division.

631st Tank Destroyer Battalion[13]

Activated 15 December 1941 at Camp Blanding, Florida. Reorganized as a towed battalion in December 1943. Arrived at Gourock, Scotland, on 5 August 1944 and at Utah Beach on 31 August. Performed rear-area duties in France, Luxembourg, and Germany for the duration of the campaign as part of Third Army.

633d Tank Destroyer Battalion[14]

Activated 16 December 1941 at Camp Forrest, Tennessee. Arrived at Le Havre, France, on 13 April 1945 equipped with M18s. Moved to Nürnberg, Germany, arriving on 3 May. Advanced to Pilsen, Czechoslovakia. Attached to 16th Armored Division.

634th Tank Destroyer Battalion[15]

Activated at Camp Claiborne, Louisiana, on 16 December 1941. Arrived in England on 10 January 1944. Landed at Utah Beach on 30 June equipped with M10s. Committed to battle on 10 July near Carentan. Participated in Cobra breakout in late July; widely separated elements helped capture Mayenne and defeat Mortain counteroffensive in early August. Raced east to Mons, Belgium. Supported operations against Siegfried Line and capture of Aachen, Germany, in October. Fought in

Hürtgen Forest in November. Moved to Belgium in December, only to race south to Ardennes in late December. Crossed Roer River on 25 February 1945. Pushed to Rhine River at Bonn by 9 March. Crossed river at Remagen on 15 March and supported envelopment of the Ruhr Pocket. Drove east to Harz Mountains in early April. Drove 200 miles to Czechoslovak border by 28 April. Attached to: 1st, 4th, 83d Infantry divisions.

635th Tank Destroyer Battalion[16]

Established 15 December 1941 at Camp Robertson, Arkansas, from the 35th Infantry Division Antitank Battalion (Provisional). Arrived Liverpool, England, on 9 February 1944. Landed at Omaha Beach on 8 June. Advanced through northern France and Belgium. Operated in Roetgen-Aachen sector and Hürtgen Forest during autumn. Transferred to Belgium on 22 December during Battle of the Bulge. Returned to Aachen area in January and supported drive toward Rhine River near Cologne. Transferred to Seventh Army and again almost immediately to Third Army on 1 April 1945. Crossed Rhine at Mannheim and advanced through central Germany to Austria. Supported: 1st, 71st Infantry divisions; 4th Cavalry Group.

636th Tank Destroyer Battalion[17]

Activated on 15 December 1941 at Camp Bowie, Texas. Arrived at Oran, Algeria, on 13 April 1943. Landed at Paestum, Italy, beginning 13 September 1943. Elements performed artillery missions, guarded Fifth Army CP, and trained British troops on M10 and TD doctrine in October and November. Reentered line in Mignano sector in late November, where supported assault on San Pietro. Supported Rapido River crossing in January 1944. Entered Cassino sector in February. Transferred to Anzio beachhead in May. Entered Rome on 4 June. Landed in southern France on 15 August. First unit to enter Lyon and to reach the Moselle River in September. Engaged in the Vosges Mountain region beginning in October. Relieved 601st TD Battalion in Strasbourg in December. Battled German Northwind offensive in January and February 1945.

Converted to M36 beginning late February. Struck Siegfried Line near Wissembourg in late March. Crossed Rhine with 14th Armored Division in April, dashed toward Nürnberg. Ended war in southern Bavaria near Tegernsee. Attached to: 14th Armored Division; 36th Infantry Division.

638th Tank Destroyer Battalion[18]

Established 15 December 1941 at Camp Shelby, Mississippi. Arrived at Cherbourg, France, 7 September 1944 equipped with M18s. Entered the line near Prummern on 20 November and supported operations against the Siegfried Line. Shifted to the Ardennes sector around Rochefort, Belgium, on 22 December. Fought to reduce the Bulge during January 1945. Supported Roer River crossing in February. Crossed the Rhine River on 1 April. Advanced across Germany and reached the Elbe River near Wittenberg on 24 April. Attached to: 84th Infantry Division.

643d Tank Destroyer Battalion[19]

Redesignated from the 44th Antitank Battalion (Provisional) at Fort Dix, New Jersey, on 15 December 1941. Arrived at Gourock, Scotland, in January 1944. Landed at Utah Beach on 11 and 12 July equipped with M10s. Committed to battle south of Le Haye Du Puits with the 8th Infantry Division on 15 July. Participated in Cobra breakout beginning 26 July. Advanced into Brittany in August and helped capture Brest in early September. Moved to Luxembourg in late September. Fought in the Hürtgen Forest in November. Companies A and C moved to the northern Ardennes sector by early December and participated in the Battle of the Bulge, with Company B arriving late in the game. Joined in elimination of the Bulge in early 1945 and the Roer River offensive in February. Reached the Rhine south of Cologne in March. Crossed river at Remagen and supported the reduction of the Ruhr Pocket in April. Swung eastward to the Elbe River and rolled toward the Baltic coast with the 82d Airborne Division, stopping in Schwerin. Attached to: 82d Airborne Division; 3d Armored Division; 1st, 2d, 8th, 9th, 86th, 99th, 104th Infantry divisions; 102d Cavalry Group.

645th Tank Destroyer Battalion[20]

Activated on 15 December 1941 at Camp Barkely, Texas. Battalion arrived in Algeria on 27 May 1943. Landed at Paestum, Italy, on 9 September 1943. Participated in drive up the Italian peninsula, then shifted to Anzio beachhead in February 1944. Withdrawn for training in June 1944 to participate in Operation Dragoon. Landed on 15 August in southern France. Advanced to Vosges Mountains near Grandvillers by October. Joined assault on Siegfried Line in December near Bobenthal, Germany. Fought German Nordwind offensive in January 1945. Converted to M36 beginning late January. Attacked Siegfried Line again south of Sarreguemines in March, crossed the Rhine at Worms on 25 March. Helped reduce Nazi stand at Aschaffenburg at month's end and capture Nürnberg in mid-April. Reached Munich on 29 April. Attached to: 36th, 45th Infantry divisions.

648th Tank Destroyer Battalion[21]

Activated on 6 March 1943 at Camp Bowie, Texas. Converted to a towed battalion in March 1944. Arrived in the United Kingdom by 19 December 1944. Committed to battle near Luneville, France, in February 1945. Began conversion to M18s in early April while near Landstuhl, Germany. Ended war in vicinity of Ingolstadt. Attached to: 36th, 70th, 86th Infantry divisions.

654th Tank Destroyer Battalion[22]

Activated on 15 December 1941 at Fort Benning, Georgia. Disembarked at Omaha Beach on 11 July 1944 with M10s. Committed to battle on 12 July near Fallot, France. Fought at Mortain in August, then advanced across France toward Nancy. Fought along border and crossed the Saar River in early December. Deployed to the Ardennes sector on 21 December. Shifted back south to Metz region in January 1945. Returned to Belgium in February and converted to the M36. Participated in the offensive across the Roer River and then across the Rhine on 24 March. Advanced to Tangerhutte and remained there until taking on military government duties in early May. Attached to: 5th, 30th, 35th, 75th Infantry divisions.

656th Tank Destroyer Battalion[23]

Activated on 3 April 1943 at Camp Bowie, Texas. Arrived in England in December 1944. Disembarked at Le Havre, France, on 6 February 1945 equipped with M18s. Entered the line near Friesenrath, Germany, on 28 February. Pushed toward Rhine River at Remagen and crossed into bridgehead beginning 7 March. Converted to the M36 late that month. Supported 9th Armored Division sweep to help encircle the Ruhr in early April and then dashed eastward to the Mulde River. Turned south and entered Czechoslovakia near St. Sedlo on 6 May. Attached to: 9th Armored Division; 78th Infantry Division.

661st Tank Destroyer Battalion[24]

Activated on 17 April 1943 at Camp Bowie, Texas. Arrived at Le Havre, France, on 21 January 1945 equipped with M18s. Committed to battle at Rocherath-Krinkelt, Belgium, on 16 February 1945. Fought along the Siegfried Line near Helenthal, Germany, in March. Crossed the Rhine on 27 March and advanced across Germany to Leipzig by 17 April, where the men saw their last fighting. Attached to: 28th, 69th, 106th Infantry divisions.

679th Tank Destroyer Battalion[25]

Activated on 26 June 1943 at Camp Hood, Texas, as one of several battalions with black enlisted personnel and mostly white officers. Converted to a towed battalion on 14 July. Disembarked at Le Havre, France, on 21 January 1945, then re-embarked at Marseilles on 1 March for transfer to Italy. Entered the line in IV Corps sector on 17 March. Supported assault on La Spezia in April and advanced to Genoa by early May. Attached to: 92d Infantry Division.

691st Tank Destroyer Battalion[26]

Activated on 15 December 1941 at Fort Bliss, Texas. Entered combat in September 1944 in Lorraine equipped with towed guns. Transferred to Ardennes sector in December. Shifted south again and joined operations in the Saar region in February and March 1945. Converted to the M36 beginning late that month. Advanced across Germany and reached Limbach on 24 April, where action all but ceased. Attached to: 17th Airborne Division; 6th Armored Division; 5th, 26th, 35th, 44th, 65th, 76th, 80th, 87th Infantry divisions; 2d Cavalry Group.

692d Tank Destroyer Battalion[27]

Activated on 10 April 1942 at Camp Gordon, Georgia. Converted to a towed battalion in March 1944. Arrived at Cherbourg, France, on 23 September 1944. Entered the line near Wustwezel, Belgium, circa 28 October. Fought along the Siegfried Line in the vicinity of Stolberg beginning in November. Occupied defensive positions along the Roer River during the Battle of the Bulge. Converted to the M36 in February 1945, supported the drive from the Roer to the Rhine River in late February and early March, and helped capture Cologne. After clearing more Siegfried Line fortifications, crossed the Rhine at Worms on 31 March. Raced across Germany in April and participated in the capture of Furth. Advanced to Munich by 30 April. Attached to: 42d, 63d, 104th Infantry divisions.

701st Tank Destroyer Battalion[28]

Activated on 15 December 1941 at Fort Knox, Kentucky. Attached to 1st Armored Division, which had provided most of cadre personnel. Arrived at Belfast, Northern Ireland, on 11 June 1942. Companies B and C and one platoon of Recon Company participated in Operation Torch landings 8 November near Oran. Advanced toward Tunisia beginning 16 November. Rest of battalion reached North Africa on 10 December. Actions in Tunisia, usually attached to the 1st Armored or 1st Infantry Division, included El Guettar, Faid Pass, Sidi Bou Zid, Sbeitla, Hill 609, and Mateur. Shipped to Italy in October 1943 and entered the line in the Pagnataro area. TDs operated largely as artillery. For much of early 1944, the battalion was attached to II or VI Corps in Cassino sector. Shipped to Anzio beachhead in February 1944. Supported 1st Armored Division during breakout in late May, entered Rome on 4 June. Pushed north to the Arno River, crossed river on 1 September, and reached Florence area. Spent winter training and firing artillery missions. Supported 10th Mountain Division drive into the Po River valley in April 1945. Entered Verona on 26 April. Attached to: 1st Armored Division; 1st, 3d, 9th, 34th, 45th, 88th, 92d Infantry divisions; 10th Mountain Division; British 78th Infantry Division; Brazilian Expeditionary Force.

702d Tank Destroyer Battalion[29]

The "Seven O Deuce" was activated 15 December 1941 at Fort Benning, Georgia. Equipped with T70s (M18s) before shipping to the United Kingdom, where the battalion arrived on 25 February 1944 only to be issued M10s. Landed at Omaha Beach on 11 June. Entered line at Livry on 2 July. Formed part of 2d Armored Division's spearhead during Cobra breakout in late July. Fought at Mortain, established first contact with Canadians during encirclement of Falaise Pocket. Entered Belgium on 5 September and crossed German border near Gangelt. Fought against Siegfried Line along Wurm River in October and November. Re-equipped with M36s in late November. Supported drive on Roer River. Moved to Ardennes in December. Crossed Roer River on 28 February 1945 and Rhine on 28 March. Participated in encirclement of Ruhr Pocket, reached Weser River on 4 April. Reached Elbe River near Magdeburg, after which took on occupation duties. Attached to: 2d Armored Division.

703d Tank Destroyer Battalion[30]

Activated on 15 December at Camp Polk, Louisiana. Landed in France on 1 July 1944. Saw first action near Hautes Vents on 13 July. Participated in Cobra breakout at end of month. Held in reserve during Mortain battle in August. Crossed the River Seine on 26 August, reached the Siegfried Line in the vicinity of Eschweiler, Germany, by 12 September. First battalion converted to M36s beginning 30 September. Fought along West Wall until mid-December, when transferred to Ardennes after launch of German offensive. Fought to reduce the Bulge in January 1945 and joined drive to Cologne in February and early March. Crossed Rhine River on 23 March near Honnef and participated in envelopment of the Ruhr. Slashed east to stop line at Dessau by 14 April. Attached to: 82d Airborne Division; 3d Armored Division; 1st Infantry Division.

704th Tank Destroyer Battalion[31]

Activated on 15 December 1941 at Camp Pine, New York. Arrived in the United Kingdom by April 1944. First battalion in the ETO to receive M18s, which occurred in May. Landed at Utah Beach on 13 July. Participated in Cobra breakout at end of month, advanced into Brittany. Raced east across France, passing north of Orleans, and crossed the Moselle River to Luneville in early September and remained in the general area through October. Fought in Morhange region in November and crossed the Saar River by month's end. Deployed to Ardennes on 19 December. Fought around Bastogne in January 1945, then moved back south. Advanced into Germany near Sinz in February, fighting through Siegfried Line and into the Saar-Moselle triangle. Supported drive to Bitburg in March and reached Rhine by mid-month. Crossed the river on 24 March at Nierstein. Roared east to Gotha by 4 April, passed through Harz Mountains to Bayreuth in late April. Entered Czechoslovakia at Volyne on 6 May. Attached to: 101st Airborne Division; 4th Armored Division; 26th, 87th, 94th Infantry divisions; 6th Cavalry Group.

705th Tank Destroyer Battalion[32]

Activated on 15 December 1941 at Fort Knox, Kentucky. Arrived at Gourock, Scotland, on 27 April 1944. Landed at Utah Beach on 18 July equipped with M10s. Joined Cobra breakout and swept through Brittany to Brest in late July and early August. Helped clear Crozon Peninsula into September. Moved across France in October to Moselle River. Advanced to German border at Kitzing in mid-November. Shifted north to Aachen area in early December. Moved to Bastogne, where TDs participated in famous defense by 101st Airborne Division. Supported drive to Rhine River in March 1945. Crossed river on 29 March at Oppenheim. Conducted drive across Germany through Bayreuth in April, arriving in Neukirchen, Austria, by 6 May. Attached to: Task Force A; 101st Airborne Division; 11th Armored Division; 29th, 83d, 95th Infantry divisions.

771st Tank Destroyer Battalion[33]

Activated on 15 December 1941 at Ft. Ethan Allen, Vermont. Arrived at Glamorganshire, Wales, on 1 January 1944 and shipped to France in late September equipped with M10s. Entered combat with the 102d Infantry Division against the Siegfried Line defenses along the Würm River on 3 November. Participated in the drive to the Roer River and held defensive positions there during December. Converted to the M36 in January 1945. Supported drive toward Rhine River in February. Crossed the Rhine beginning 31 March and joined the 102d Infantry Division's drive across Germany to the Elbe River, reaching same on 14 April. Spent remainder of the war helping to mop up bypassed pockets of resistance between the Rhine and the Elbe. Attached to: 5th Armored Division; 102d Infantry Division; 11th Cavalry Group.

772d Tank Destroyer Battalion[34]

Activated on 16 December 1941. Entered the line near Birgel, Germany, on 22 December 1944. Fought in Belgium in January 1945, then shifted south to Seventh Army's sector along the Rhine in February. Converted to the M36 beginning in late March. Supported operations against the Ruhr Pocket in April and then took on military government duties. Attached to: 30th, 75th, 83d, 106th Infantry divisions.

773d Tank Destroyer Battalion[35]

. Activated on 15 December 1941 from the 73d Provisional Antitank Battalion, which had been formed from Louisiana and Pennsylvania National Guard units in July. Arrived at Gourock, Scotland, on 7 February 1944. Landed at Utah and Omaha beaches on 8 August equipped with M10s. Caught up with spearheads and saw first real action at Le Bourg St. Leonard beginning 17 August during envelopment of Falaise Pocket. Advanced to Moselle River sector via Paris. Fought at Luneville and the Foret de Parroy. Supported capture of Metz in November. Joined operations against Siegfried Line along the Saar in December, ordered to the Ardennes on 6 January 1945. Fought through Siegfried Line in February. Reached the Rhine at Koblenz on 16 March. Crossed the Rhine 23–24 March at Oppenheim. Helped capture Darmstadt and Frankfurt before driving across Germany to Czechoslovakia beginning 1 April. Cleared Czechoslovak-German border area southward and ended war near Petrovice. Attached to: 6th Armored Division; 79th, 90th, 95th Infantry divisions.

774th Tank Destroyer Battalion[36]

Activated on 15 December 1941 at Camp Blanding, Florida. Converted to a towed battalion before arriving at Gourock, Scotland, on 12 June 1944. Debarked at Utah Beach on 7 August. Joined fighting around Argentan. Ran eastward across France to Lorraine as part of a cavalry screen and the 7th Armored Division. Participated in fighting around Metz starting in September. Fought along the Saar in December and then joined rush north to the Ardennes. Converted to the M36 in late February 1945. Drove to the Rhine in March. Held Rhine west of the Ruhr Pocket in April, then took on military government duties. Attached to: 7th Armored Division; 5th, 80th, 90th, 94th, 95th Infantry divisions; 43d Cavalry Group.

776th Tank Destroyer Battalion[37]

On 21 December 1941, a provisional antitank battalion of the 76th Field Artillery Brigade was activated as the 776th Tank Destroyer Battalion. Issued M10s while still in the States. Arrived Casablanca, Morocco, 25 January 1943. Fought in area of Maknassy and Ferryville, Tunisia. Eighteen enlisted men participated in Sicily campaign as radio operators and military police. Debarked vicinity of Cappaci, Italy, beginning 19 September 1943. Main body committed near Rotondi 10 October 1943, where it supported the Volturno River crossing. Supported Rapido River crossing and fought near Cassino and in January–March 1944. Joined breakthrough of Hitler Line May 1944, entered Rome 4 June, and joined drive to Arno River. Transferred to southern France in September–October 1944, during which drew M36s. Moved into line near Luneville on 30 October 1944. Supported French 2d Armored Division advance to Strasbourg in November. Battled German Nordwind offensive around Rimling, France, in January 1945, where claimed first Jagdtiger destroyed on Western front. Attacked Siegfried Line near Omersheim, Germany, and crossed Rhine River near Worms in March 1945. Aided capture of Mannheim, Heidelberg, and Ulm, Germany, and crossed Danube in April 1945. Ended war in Ehrwald, Austria. Attached to: 1st Armored Division; 4th, 34th, 44th, 63d, 85th, 100th Infantry divisions.

801st Tank Destroyer Battalion[38]

As 101st New York National Guard Antitank Battalion was federalized on 6 January 1941 and redesignated 801st Tank Destroyer Battalion on 15 December. Arrived in England as a towed battalion 11 March 1944. Landed at Utah Beach on 13 June and participated in capture of Cherbourg. Fought at Mortain in early August, reached outskirts of Paris on 25 August. Entered Belgium on 8 September and Germany on 12 September. Supported operations in Hürtgen Forest beginning late November. On the line in Ardennes when German offensive struck on 16 December. Moved to Aachen, Germany, in February 1945. Crossed Roer River on 25 February and reached Rhine south of Düsseldorf. Crossed Rhine near Wessel on 29 March and supported drive to the Ruhr and then east to the Elbe River. Transferred south and supported operations in Harz Mountains in late April. Converted to M18s in late April. Crossed Danube and reached Inn River outside Hitler's birthplace—Brunnau, Austria—by VE Day. Attached to: 2d, 13th Armored divisions; 2d, 4th, 9th, 83d, 99th Infantry divisions.

802d Tank Destroyer Battalion[39]

The New York National Guard's 102d Antitank Battalion was federalized on 13 January 1941 and converted into the 802d Tank Destroyer Battalion on 15 December at Camp Shelby, Mississippi. Disembarked in France on 1 July 1944 as a towed battalion. Entered battle near Carentan on 4 July. Advanced into Brittany in August and supported attack on St. Malo in August. Crossed France and entered Luxembourg on 23 September. Supported operations against Siegfried Line through November. Participated in Battle of the Bulge in Luxembourg in late December. Converted to M36s in February–March 1945. Crossed Rhine River at Wessel on 2 April. Joined elimination of Ruhr Pocket, after which took on occupation duties. Attached to: 4th, 80th, 83d, 95th Infantry divisions.

803d Tank Destroyer Battalion[40]

Initially activated as the 103d Antitank Battalion on 30 September 1940 from Washington National Guard troops, federalized on 10 February 1941, and redesignated 803d Tank Destroyer Battalion on 12 December 1941. Departed for England on 24 June 1943. Landed at Omaha Beach on 13 June 1944 equipped with M10s. Helped capture St. Lô in July. Raced across northern France in August and passed through Belgium and Holland before reaching the Siegfried Line in September. Supported operations north of Aachen in October, transferred to Hürtgen Forest. Shifted to Ardennes just before German offensive began in December. Committed against Siegfried Line again in early 1945. Converted to the M36 in February. Participated in capture of Trier, crossed Rhine River on 23 March at Oppenheim. Joined elimination of Ruhr Pocket in April, then pivoted and marched southeast through

Austria and into Czechoslovakia. Attached to: 82d Airborne Division; 3d Armored Division; 2d, 5th, 8th, 29th, 30th Infantry divisions; 1st Belgian Brigade.

804th Tank Destroyer Battalion[41]

Converted in January from the 104th Infantry Antitank Battalion, 45th Infantry Division, at Camp San Luis Obispo, California. Arrived Belfast, Ireland, on 17 August 1942 and at Oran, Algeria, on 1 February 1943. Trained French troops on M10s in North Africa; only battalion observers went to front. Landed at Naples, Italy, on 8 February 1944, and moved Gustav Line along Garigliano River by 9 March. Entered Rome on 4 June. Carried doughs into Livorno on 18 July. Crossed Arno River in September, then supported attack on Gothic Line through October. Broke into Po River Valley in April 1945, crossed Po River on 27 April. Company C part of column that linked up with U.S. Seventh Army troops in Brenner Pass on 5 May. Attached to: 34th, 85th, 88th, 91st Infantry divisions.

805th Tank Destroyer Battalion[42]

105th Antitank Battalion redesignated 805th Tank Destroyer Battalion on 15 December 1941. Arrived in England 18 August 1942. Landed at Algiers 17 January 1943. Actions included Kasserine Pass and Gafsa. Converted to towed 3-inch gun battalion in October 1943. Debarked in Italy 28 October 1943 at Bagnoli. Shipped to Anzio beachhead 12 March 1944. Served largely as artillery even after re-equipped with M18s in June–August. TDs were part of advance guard at capture of Bologna and Brenner Pass. Attached to: 34th, 85th, 91st Infantry divisions.

807th Tank Destroyer Battalion[43]

Activated 1 March 1942 at Camp Cooke, California. Arrived Liverpool, England, on 23 August 1944 and at Utah Beach on 18

September. Fought in Metz sector from September to November. Attacked toward Saarlautern in November and December. Battled German Nordwind offensive in January 1945. Shifted north for offensive to the Rhine in March. Defended Rhine River bridges in April and converted to the M18 in time to join the drive through Bavaria late in the month. Reached vicinity of Salzburg, Austria, in early May. Attached to: 101st Airborne Division; 5th, 30th, 35th, 75th, 83d, 86th, 90th, 95th, 100th Infantry divisions; 3d Cavalry Group.

8o8th Tank Destroyer Battalion[44]

Activated 27 March 1942 at Camp Joseph T. Robinson, Arkansas. Reorganized as a towed battalion in May 1943. Disembarked at Utah Beach on 19 September 1944. Entered the line east of the Moselle River six days later, where it remained until transferring to the Ardennes on 21 December. Protected XII Corps flank through January 1945. Converted to the M36 in February. Supported drive to the Rhine in March and the river crossings south of Boppard late in the month. Joined Third Army's drive through Erfurt, Nürnberg, and south into Bavaria. Advanced to Linz, Austria, in early May. Attached to: 5th, 65th, 76th, 80th Infantry divisions; 2d, 6th Cavalry groups.

8o9th Tank Destroyer Battalion[45]

Activated 18 March 1942 at Camp Forrest, Tennessee. Arrived at Liverpool, England, on 8 December 1944 and Le Havre, France, on 20 January 1945 equipped with M18s. Supported Roer River crossing in late February 1945. Crossed the Rhine on 27 March. Supported operations against the Ruhr Pocket in April and converted to the M36 that same month. Helped clear the Harz mountains in late April. Attached to: 8th Armored Division; 79th, 95th Infantry divisions.

811th Tank Destroyer Battalion[46]

Activated 10 April 1942 at Camp Gordon, Georgia. Arrived at Cherbourg, France, on 15 September 1944 equipped with M18s. Moved to Luxembourg in November and participated in the Battle of the Bulge in December. The battalion was scattered widely and pieces attached to many divisions into January 1945. Supported operations against the Siegfried Line in February and early March. Advanced to the Rhine in late March and crossed river on 30 March. Supported 80th Infantry Division in capture of Kassel and advance to Erfurt and Chemnitz in April. Moved south and crossed Danube River to Regensburg. Entered Austria on 5 May. Attached to: 17th, 101st Airborne divisions; 4th, 9th, 11th Armored divisions; 28th, 78th, 80th, 87th, 89th Infantry divisions; 3d Cavalry Group.

813th Tank Destroyer Battalion[47]

Activated 15 December 1941 at Fort Bragg, North Carolina. Arrived in North Africa on 17 January 1943, where it supported British, French, and American troops in Tunisia. Re-equipped with M10s after end of hostilities. The battalion sent six officers and 400 men to Sicily to handle POWs. Two platoons served briefly in southern Italy before battalion sailed to the United Kingdom in November 1943. Disembarked at Utah Beach on 27 June 1944. Joined drive to Le Mans and then north to Alencon at Falaise Gap. Was first armored unit to cross the Seine River. Entered Belgium 2 September 1944. Moved south and fought around the Foret de Parroy in October. Supported advance to Strasbourg in November, where Recon Company actually preceded 2d French Armored Division to within one mile of Rhine. Battled German Nordwind offensive in January 1945, partially re-equipped with M18s after heavy losses. Shifted to Belgium in February, re-equipped again with M36s. Crossed Rhine River 24 March, participated in reduction of Ruhr Pocket. Conducted long roadmarch south to Ulm. Took on military government duties in early May. Attached to: 44th, 79th, 84th Infantry divisions; 106th Cavalry Group.

814th Tank Destroyer Battalion[48]

Activated by 1 May 1942 at Camp Polk, Louisiana. Arrived at Greenock, Scotland, in February 1944. Landed at Utah Beach beginning 8 August equipped with M10s. Raced across France in August and participated in fighting around Metz in September. Transferred to Peel Marshes in Holland in late September. Began re-equipping with M36s in October, then supported Ninth Army's drive toward the Roer River in November. Transferred with 7th Armored Division to the Ardennes on 17 December and participated in the defense of St. Vith. Supported operations against the West Wall in February 1945. Crossed the Rhine River at Remagen on 23 March. Helped reduce the Ruhr Pocket in April. Drove east to the Elbe River and crossed, reaching the Baltic coast on 3 May. Attached: 7th Armored Division; 113th Cavalry Group.

817th Tank Destroyer Battalion[49]

Activated on 1 June 1942 at Camp Chaffee, Arkansas. Converted to a towed battalion in June 1943. Arrived at Greenock, Scotland, on 31 July 1944 and landed at Utah Beach on 25 August. Took up rear-area security duties in France and Belgium. Entered battle in the Hürtgen Forest with the 8th Infantry Division on 9 December. Shifted to Ardennes in February 1945 and then back to Roer River sector to fire as artillery. Participated in advance to Rhine River with the cavalry. Crossed river at Remagen on 15 March—the only towed TD battalion to enter the bridgehead. Began conversion to M18s on 26 March. Joined the 104th Infantry Division at the Ruhr Pocket in April. Two companies joined the drive eastward from Marburg in mid-April, fighting in the Harz Mountains. Helped capture Halle and advanced to the Mulde River, where offensive operations ceased. Attached to: 8th, 9th, 78th, 99th, 104th Infantry divisions; 4th, 14th Cavalry groups.

818th Tank Destroyer Battalion[50]

Activated on 15 December 1941 at Fort Sill, Oklahoma. Arrived in North Ireland on 1 November 1943. Landed in France on D+36 with towed guns. Advanced across France during August and September to the area of Metz. Supported operations along the Saar until December, when transferred to the Ardennes sector. Participated in race across Germany beginning in March 1945. Converted to M36s prior to mid-April. Ended the war in Kienberg, Czechoslovakia. Attached to: 5th, 26th Infantry divisions.

820th Tank Destroyer Battalion[51]

Activated on 25 June 1942 at Camp Swift, Texas. Arrived Liverpool, England, on 15 October 1944 and at Omaha Beach with towed guns two days later. Moved to the Ardennes sector in early December, where the battalion was deployed with the 106th Infantry Division in the path of the German offensive. Converted to M18s in early 1945. Supported operations in the Ruhr Pocket in April 1945. Crossed Germany to Mesto Touskov area in Czechoslovakia by early May. Attached to: 13th Armored Division; 97th, 106th Infantry divisions.

821st Tank Destroyer Battalion[52]

Activated on 25 July 1942 at Camp Carson, Colorado. Arrived in England 17 April 1944. Disembarked at Omaha Beach 26 June with towed 3-inch guns. Supported capture of St. Lô and subsequent breakout. Entered Brittany in August, supported capture of Brest by 18 September. Moved east in late September to Holland. Conducted operations against Siegfried Line in October near Aachen, Germany. Transferred to Ubach, Germany, in November and supported drive toward Roer River. Converted to M10s beginning in December. Crossed Roer beginning 23 February 1945. Withdrawn from line during March. Company B supported operations against Ruhr Pocket in April. Battalion then marched east to Elbe River. Took up occupation duties on 27 April. Attached to: 29th, 35th Infantry divisions.

822d Tank Destroyer Battalion[53]

Activated on 25 July 1942 at Camp Carson, Colorado. Arrived at Le Havre, France, on 23 January 1945 with towed guns. Entered line with 63d Infantry Division near Sarreguemines on 7 February. Crossed Rhine River on 27 March and reached Heidelberg on 1 April. Reorganized as self-propelled battalion in mid-April, although the battalion possessed some M18s by late March. Advanced across Germany, reached Munsterhausen on 27 April, and took up occupation duties. Attached to: 36th, 63d Infantry divisions.

823d Tank Destroyer Battalion[54]

Activated on 25 July 1942 at Camp Carson, Colorado. Arrived in England in April 1944. Landed at Omaha beach on 24 June with towed 3-inch guns. Supported drive on St. Lô. Fought at Mortain in August. Passed through Belgium and Holland, and entered Germany on 17 September. Fought along Siegfried Line in October, including encirclement of Aachen. Converted to M10s beginning in November. Shifted to the Ardennes in late December and fought to eliminate the Bulge in January 1945. Crossed Roer River on 24 February and Rhine on 24 March. Raced eastward to Elbe River at Magdeburg in April. Began military occupation duties on 21 April. Attached to: 29th, 30th Infantry divisions.

824th Tank Destroyer Battalion[55]

Activated on 10 August 1942 at Camp Gruber, Oklahoma. Reorganized as a towed battalion in May 1943. Arrived at Marseilles, France, on 29 October 1944. Deployed near Sarrebourg on 27 November. Fought around Bitche and against Siegfried Line in December. Battled German Nordwind offensive in January 1945. Converted to M18s in March and crossed the Rhine on the last day of the month. Joined the stiff fight at Heilbronn on 8 April and then advanced to the Austrian border by month's end. Cleared the Bavarian mountains and took Innsbruck in early May. Attached to: 45th, 100th, 103d Infantry divisions; 106th Cavalry Group.

825th Tank Destroyer Battalion[56]

Activated on 10 August 1942 at Camp Gruber, Oklahoma. Reorganized as a towed battalion in July 1943. Assigned to Communications Zone and 12th Army Group security duties between August and December 1944. On 17 December, the battalion entered combat near Malmedy, Belgium. Returned to security duties on 16 January 1945. Attached to: 30th Infantry Division.

827th Tank Destroyer Battalion[57]

Activated on 20 April 1942 at Camp Forrest, Tennessee. One of several battalions with black enlisted personnel and largely white officers. Reorganized as a towed battalion in June 1943. Arrived in Seventh Army's sector east of the Vosges at the height of the German Nordwind offensive in January 1945, equipped with M18s. Fought to eliminate the Colmar Pocket in late January and early February. Transferred to Communications Zone for security duties in March and subsequently undertook other rear-area functions. Attached to: 12th Armored Division; 79th Infantry Division.

893d Tank Destroyer Battalion[58]

93d Infantry Division Antitank Battalion redesignated on 15 December 1941 at Fort Benning, Georgia. Arrived at Liverpool, England, on 20 January 1944. Landed at Omaha beachhead on 1 July equipped with M10s. Committed to battle in the vicinity of St. Jean de Daye. Advanced to Paris by 25 August and thence to the Siegfried Line in the Schnee Eifel. Fought in the Hürtgen Forest in November, supporting the 28th Infantry Division's disastrous assault on Schmidt, and remained there when the division was replaced. Held defensive positions in January 1945. Supported 78th Infantry Division capture of the Roer

River dams in February 1945, then participated an offensive across the Roer toward the Rhine River. Crossed the Rhine at Remagen on 7 March and supported attack northward to Sieg River and subsequent operations against the Ruhr Pocket in April. Attached to: 2d, 4th, 8th, 28th, 78th, 80th, 90th Infantry divisions; 14th, 102d Cavalry groups.

894th Tank Destroyer Battalion[59]

The 94th Antitank Battalion was redesignated the 894th Tank Destroyer Battalion on 15 December 1941. Committed to battle 20 February 1943 at Kasserine Pass in Tunisia. Supported capture of Bizerte. Landed in Italy in late October 1943, located in vicinity of Pignataro in the Migniano sector as of December. Transferred to Anzio beachhead on 25 January 1944, where battalion supported mainly British troops. Entered Rome in June. Crossed Arno River at Pisa in September. Mired at Porretta Terme late 1944–early 1945. Entered Genoa on 27 April. Attached to: 1st Armored Division; 34th, 45th, 85th, and 92d Infantry divisions; 10th Mountain Division; British 1st and 5th Infantry divisions; French Expeditionary Corps; Brazilian Expeditionary Force.

899th Tank Destroyer Battalion[60]

The 99th Antitank Battalion was redesignated the 899th Tank Destroyer Battalion on 15 December 1941. Arrived Casablanca 26 January 1943, where issued new M10s. Deployed to Gafsa-El Guettar sector, Tunisia, on 16 March 1943. Established first American contact with British Eighth Army on 7 April 1943. Arrived Naples area, Italy, on 10 November 1943. Almost immediately shifted to United Kingdom. Liaison personnel accompanied second glider lift of 82d Airborne Division during invasion of Normandy. Battalion proper landed at Utah Beach on D-Day. Helped capture Cherbourg late June. Supported Cobra breakout late July, advance through Mayenne. Entered Belgium 2 September, backed 9th Infantry Division operations in vicinity of Monschau and Hofen, Germany. Fought in Rötgen/Hürtgen Forest region in October. Elements deployed in first days of Battle of the Bulge to stop German advance, others remained in VII Corps area. Supported attack to capture Roer River dams in February 1945. Largely converted to M36s that same month. Crossed Roer River 28 February. Advanced to Rhine near Bad Godesberg, and first elements crossed to Remagen bridgehead on 8 March. Joined attack on Ruhr Pocket in April, then moved east into Harz Mountains. Moved to Mulde River for link-up with Soviet forces, achieved 27 April. Began occupation duty in Bernburg 3 May 1945. Attached to: 82d Airborne Division; 1st Armored Division; 1st, 4th, 9th Infantry divisions.

Note: Some small additions have been made on the basis of attachments as reported by divisions as compiled at the Center for Military History Online, http://www.army.mil/cmh-pg/documents.

Glossary

AA	Antiaircraft
AAR	After-action report
AP	Armor-piercing
AT	Antitank
BrigGen	Brigadier General
Capt	Captain
CG	Commanding General
CO	Commanding officer
Col	Colonel
Cpl	Corporal
ETO	European Theater of Operations
ETOUSA	European Theater of Operations, U.S. Army
Gen	General
HE	High-explosive
HVAP	Hyper-velocity armor-piercing

Jeep	1/4-ton truck
KIA	Killed in action
KO	Knock out, destroy
Lt	Lieutenant
LtCol	Lieutenant Colonel
LtGen	Lieutenant General
M3	TD armed with 75mm gun mounted on a halftrack, or Lee medium tank, or early Stuart light tank
M4	Sherman medium tank
M5	Stuart light tank
M6	TD with a 37mm gun mounted on a weapon carrier
M8	Six-wheeled armored car, armed with 37mm gun
M10	TD with a 3-inch gun mounted on a tracked chassis
M18	TD with a 76mm gun mounted on a tracked chassis
M20	Six-wheeled utility armored car
M36	TD with a 90mm gun mounted on a tracked chassis
Maj	Major
MajGen	Major General
MG	Machine gun
MIA	Missing in action
MLR	Main line of resistance
OP	Observation Post
Pfc	Private First Class
Pvt	Private
RCT	Regimental Combat Team, an infantry regiment with attachments
S-2	Intelligence staff
S-3	Operations staff
Sgt	Sergeant
SSgt	Staff Sergeant
SHAEF	Supreme Headquarters Allied Expeditionary Force
SP	Self-propelled
TD	Tank destroyer
TF	Task Force
WIA	Wounded in action

Notes

Chapter 1: Seek, Strike, and Destroy

1. Dr. Christopher R. Gabel, *Seek, Strike, and Destroy: U.S. Army Tank Destroyer Doctrine in World War II* (Fort Leavenworth, Kansas: U.S. Army Command and General Staff College, 1985), 5. (Hereinafter Gabel.)

2. Kent Roberts Greenfield, Robert R. Palmer, and Bell I. Wiley, *United States Army in World War II, The Organization of Ground Combat Troops* (Washington, DC: Historical Division, Department of the Army, 1947), 74. (Hereinafter Greenfield, et al.)

3. Gabel, 5-7.

4. Greenfield, et al, 74.

5. Christopher J. Anderson, *Hell on Wheels, The Men of the U.S. Armored Forces, 1918 to the Present* (London: Greenhill Books and Mechanicsburg, Pennsylvania: Stackpole Books, 1999), 6. (Hereinafter Christopher Anderson.)

6. Gabel, 8-9.

7. Greenfield, et al, 75.

8. Brigadier General Lesley J. McNair to Adjutant General, AG 320.2 (7-3-40) M-C, 29 July 1940, McNair Files, Box 8, RG 337, National Archives and Records Administration (NARA), quoted in David E. Johnson, *Fast Tanks and Heavy Bombers, Innovation in the U.S. Army 1917-1945* (Ithaca, NY: Cornell University Press, 1998), 150. (Hereinafter Johnson.)

9. Greenfield, et al, 75.

10. Gabel, 14.

11. Greenfield, et al, 76.

12. Gabel, 12-13.

13. Robert Capistrano and Dave Kaufman, "Tank Destroyer Forces," http://www.naples.net/clubs/asmic/TD-Forces.htm, 1998. (Hereinafter Capistrano and Kaufman.)

14. Johnson, 148.

15. History of the 628th Tank Destroyer Battalion.

16. Greenfield, et al, 79.

17. Gabel, 14.

18. Greenfield, et al, 74.

19. Ibid., 81-82.

20. Bertrand J. Oliver, *History, 602d Tank Destroyer Battalion, March 1941 to November 1945* (Lansing, Michigan: 602d Tank Destroyer Battalion Association, Inc., 1990), 1. (Hereinafter Oliver.)

21. Lonnie Gill, *Tank Destroyer Forces, WWII* (Paducah, Kentucky: Turner Publishing Company, 1992), 11. (Hereinafter Gill.)

22. Gabel, 14-15.

23. Ibid., 17.

24. Edward L. Josowitz, *An Informal History of the 601st Tank Destroyer Battalion* (Salzburg: Pustet, 1945), 4. (Hereinafter Josowitz.)

25. Johnson, 148-149. Greenfield, et al, 81. Gabel, 15 ff.

26. Gabel, 17.

27. Capistrano and Kaufman.

28. Gabel, 18 ff. "The Tank Killers," *Fortune*, November 1942, 116. (Hereinafter "The Tank Killers".)

29. Greenfield, et al, 396 ff.

30. Ibid., 403-404.

31. "The Tank Killers," 117.

32. Gabel, 22 ff.

33. "The Tank Killers," 116.

34. Gabel, 22 ff.

35. Ibid.

36. "Tank Destroyers: They Are the Army's Answer to the Tank Menace," *Life*, 26 October 1942, 87.

37. "The Tank Killers," 181.

38. *Study of Organization, Equipment, and Tactical Employment of Tank Destroyer Units* (U.S. Army, US Forces in the European Theater, the General Board, 1946), 10. (Hereinafter *Study of Organization, Equipment, and Tactical Employment of Tank Destroyer Units.*)

39. "The Tank Killers," 118.

40. *Study of Organization, Equipment, and Tactical Employment of Tank Destroyer Units*, 9.

41. Gabel, 20. Gill, 14.

42. Gabel, 27.

43. "The Tank Killers," 116-118.

44. John Weeks, *Men Against Tanks, A History of Anti-Tank Warfare* (New York, New York: Mason/Charter Publishers, Inc., 1975), 96-97.

45. Harry D. Dunnagan, *A War to Win, Company "B" – 813th Tank Destroyers* (Myrtle Beach, South Carolina: Royall Dutton Books, 1992), 79. (Hereinafter Dunnagan.)

46. *The American Arsenal* (London: Greenhill Books, 2001), 44. The Greenhill volume is essentially a reprint of the U.S. Army's *Catalog of Standard Ordnance Items* of 1944. (Hereinafter *The American Arsenal*.)

47. Diary, 701st Tank Destroyer Battalion.

48. Jim Mesko, *U.S. Tank Destroyers in Action* (Carrollton, Texas: Squadron/Signal Publications, Inc., 1998), 8. (Hereinafter Mesko.)

49. *The American Arsenal*, 45.

50. "The Tank Killers," 118.

51. *The American Arsenal*, 51.

52. Telephone interview with John Hudson, May 2002. Gill, 17.

53. Mesko, 13.

54. *Study of Organization, Equipment, and Tactical Employment of Tank Destroyer Units*, 9.

55. *The Story of the 1st Armored Division* (1st Armored Division, 1945), 60.

56. Gabel, 29.

57. Ibid., 29-30. "The Tank Killers, " 181.

58. *An Informal History of the 776th Tank Destroyer Battalion*. Salzburg, Austria: Anton Pustet, 1945?, 13. (Hereinafter *An Informal History of the 776th Tank Destroyer Battalion*.)

59. Ibid., 10.

60. History of the 628th Tank Destroyer Battalion.

61. Diary, 701st Tank Battalion.

62. Gill, 13.

63. Thomas M. Sherman, *Seek, Strike, Destroy! The History of the 636th Tank Destroyer Battalion* (Published by author: 1986), 6. (Hereinafter Sherman.)

64. "The Tank Killers, " 181. Gill, 13.

65. Greenfield, et al, 416-417.

Chapter 2: North Africa: Seeing the Elephant

1. Unless otherwise noted, the material on the activities of the 601st and 701st Tank Destroyer battalions in North Africa is drawn from the operational records of those units.

2. Loading records incorporating unit subordination, records of the 1st Infantry Division.

3. The unit diary records the date as 7 November, when the convoy was actually sailing past Oran in a maneuver to deceive anyone tracking the ships as to their final destination.

4. Gerald Astor, *The Greatest War: From Pearl Harbor to the Kasserine Pass* (New York, NY: Warner Books, Inc., 1999), 400-401. (Hereinafter Astor.)

5.Donald E. Houston, *Hell on Wheels, The 2d Armored Division* (Novato, California: Presidio Press, 1977), 101. (Hereinafter Houston.)

6. Dwight D. Eisenhower, *Crusade in Europe* (Garden City, NY: Doubleday and Company, Inc., 1948), 81-83. (Hereinafter Eisenhower.)

7. George F. Howe, *Northwest Africa: Seizing the Initiative in the West: United States Army in World War II, The Mediterranean Theater of Operations*. Washington, DC: Office of the Chief of Military History, Department of the Army, 1957, 21. (Hereinafter Howe.)

8. Eisenhower, 86-93.

9. B. H. Liddell Hart, *History of the Second World War* (New York, NY: G. Putnam's Sons, 1970), 311-313. (Hereinafter Liddell Hart.)

10. Eisenhower, 85.

11. Howe, 47-48.

12. Ibid., 48, 192.

13. Liddell Hart, 324.

14. AAR, 1st Infantry Division. "Summary of Lessons Derived from Amphibious Operations, November 8-11 1942, at Casablanca and Oran," 25 February 1943.

15. "Observer Report," 5 March 1943. Included in "Report of Observers: Mediterranean Theater of Operations," Volume 1, 22 December 1942-23 March 1943.

16. Josowitz, 7.

17. Gill, 20.

18. Operations report, 1st Armored Division.

19. Operations report, Company B. 701st Tank Destroyer Battalion. Astor, 406-407.

20. Operations report, Company B. 701st Tank Destroyer Battalion. "History of the 1st Armored Regiment," http://macspics. homestead.com/history.html. (Hereinafter "History of the 1st Armored Regiment".) "Interview with LtCol John K. Waters, Commander of 1st Battalion, 1st Armored Regiment (Light Tanks), 1st Armored Division, CP, 24 Miles SE of Oran, December 29, 1942." Included in "Report of Observers: Mediterranean Theater of Operations," Volume 1, 22 December 1942-23 March 1943. Gill, 20.

21. Operations report, 1st Armored Division. Operations report, Company B. 701st Tan22. k Destroyer Battalion.

22. Gabel, 20.

23. Operations report, Company B. 701st Tank Destroyer Battalion. Telephone interview with Arthur Edson, April 2002. John Hudson, letter to author, 8 February 2003.

24. Gill, 21.

25. Telephone interview with Rudolph Mojsl, April 2002.

26. Josowitz, 7.

27. Operations report, 1st Armored Division.

28. H. R. Knickerbocker, et al, *Danger Forward* (Atlanta, Georgia: Albert Love Enterprises, 1947), 5. (Hereinafter Knickerbocker.)

29. "Remarks of Special Service Officer, Central Task Force, Oran, Algeria, December 29, 1942." Included in "Report of Observers: Mediterranean Theater of Operations," Volume 1, 22 December 1942-23 March 1943.

30. Josowitz, 7.

31. Operations report, Company B. 701st Tank Destroyer Battalion. Astor, 451.

32. "Narrative of Observer's Tour with W. T. F., French Morocco," not dated.

33. Operations report, 1st Armored Division.

34. Josowitz, 3. Telephone interview with Bill Harper, April 2002.

35. Josowitz, 7.

36. Letter from Major General Orlando Ward to Lieutenant General Jacob Devers, 1 March 1943. Records of the 1st Armored Division.

37. Liddell Hart, 329, 335.

38. Thomas E. Griess, ed., *The West Point Military History Series, The Second World War, Europe and the Mediterranean* (Wayne, NJ: Avery Publishing Group Inc., 1984), p.173. (Hereinafter Griess.)

39. LtCol F. J. Redding, "The Operations of 'C' Company, 701st Tank Destroyer Battalion (with the British First Army), Vicinity of Medjez-El-Bab – Beja, Tunisia, 24 November-11 December 1942, Tunisian Campaign (Personal Experience of a Company Commander)," unpublished manuscript prepared for the Advanced Infantry Officers Course, 1948-1949. (Hereinafter Redding.)

40. Ibid. Operations report, 701st Tank Destroyer Battalion.

41. "Narrative Report of Antiaircraft Observer in North African Theatre, LtCol Arthur L. Fuller, 27 December 1942 to 13 January 1943."

42. Memo recording the observations of Lt Col W. H. Schaefer and Major Franklin T. Gardner in Algeria and Tunisia, 26 December 1942-20 January 1943, dated 10 February 1943.

43. *Tunisia*, CMH Pub 72-12 (Washington, DC: U.S. Army Center of Military History, not dated), 7-8. (Hereinafter *Tunisia*.) Redding.

44. Redding.

45. *Tunisia*, 11.

46. Redding.

47. *Tunisia*, 8. Liddell Hart, 338. Operations report, 701st Tank Destroyer Battalion. Redding.

48. "Observer Report," 5 March 1943. Included in "Report of Observers: Mediterranean Theater of Operations," Volume 1, 22 December 1942-23 March 1943.

49. Operations report, 701st Tank Destroyer Battalion. Redding.

50. Redding.

51. History, 705th Tank Destroyer Battalion.

52. Redding.

53. Ibid. Operations report, 701st Tank Destroyer Battalion.

54. Liddell Hart, 340. Operations report, 701st Tank Destroyer Battalion.

55. Dr. F. M. Von Senger und Etterlin, *German Tanks of World War II* (New York, NY: Galahad Books, 1969), 46-47, 196-199. (Hereinafter Von Senger und Etterlin.)

56. Ibid., 200-201.

57. Peter Chamberlain, *Pictorial History of Tanks of the World, 1915-1945* (Harrisburg, PA: Stackpole Books, 1972), 129. (Hereinafter Chamberlain.)

58. *The American Arsenal*, 44, 51, 137.

59. Operations report, 701st Tank Destroyer Battalion. Redding. General Order Number 1, Headquarters Combat Command B, 3 January 1943.

60. Liddell Hart, 340. Operations report, 701st Tank Destroyer Battalion. Redding.

61. "Observer Report," 5 March 1943. Included in "Report of Observers: Mediterranean Theater of Operations," Volume 1, 22 December 1942-23 March 1943.

62. Martin Blumenson, *Kasserine Pass* (New York, NY: Jove Books, 1983), 74-75. (Hereinafter Blumenson, *Kasserine Pass*.)

63. Linwood W. Billings, *The Tunisian Taskforce*, http://historical textarchive.com/ww2/tunisian.html. (Hereinafter Billings.)

64. Billings. Blumenson, *Kasserine Pass*, 75.

65. Billings. Operations report, Company B. 701st Tank Destroyer Battalion.

66. Billings. Operations report, Company B. 701st Tank Destroyer Battalion.

67. Billings.

68. Telephone interview with Randolph Mojsl, April 2002.

69. Gill, 23.

70. Operations report, 701st Tank Destroyer Battalion. Telephone interview with Arthur Edson, April 2002.

71. Maj Gilbert A. Ellmann, "Gafsa and Sbeitla," *TD Combat in Tunisia* (Tank Destroyer School, 1944), 13. (Hereinafter Ellmann.) Telephone interview with Arthur Edson, April 2002.

72. Billings. Operations report, Company B. 701st Tank Destroyer Battalion. Ellmann, 14. Telephone interview with Arthur Edson, April 2002.

73. *Tunisia*, 11.

74. Eisenhower, 124-124.

75. *Tunisia*, 14.

76. Josowitz, 8.

77. Blumenson, *Kasserine Pass*, 93-94.

78. Gill, 25. S-3 Journal, 13th Armored Regiment.

79. Josowitz, 10.

80. Operations reports, 1st Armored Division, 601st Tank Destroyer Battalion.

81. Operations report, 1st Armored Division.

82. Ibid.

83. "Observer Report," 5 March 1943. Included in "Report of Observers: Mediterranean Theater of Operations," Volume 1, 22 December 1942-23 March 1943.

84. Unit history, 899th Tank Destroyer Battalion, 1 January-31 December 1943.

85. Untitled document fragment included in "Report of Observers: Mediterranean Theater of Operations," Volume 1, 22 December 1942-23 March 1943.

86. "Observer Report," 5 March 1943. Included in "Report of Observers: Mediterranean Theater of Operations," Volume 1, 22 December 1942-23 March 1943.

87. "Comments of Executive Officer, CCB, 1st Armored Division, Teboursouk, January, 1943." Included in "Report of Observers: Mediterranean Theater of Operations," Volume 1, 22 December 1942-23 March 1943.

Chapter 3: From Gloom to Glory

1. Omar N. Bradley and Clay Blair, *A General's Life* (New York, NY: Simon and Schuster, 1983), 128. (Hereinafter Bradley and Blair.)

2. Eisenhower, 141.

3. Bradley and Blair, 128.

4. Eisenhower, 125-127. Blumenson, *Kasserine Pass*, 115.

5. Blumenson, *Kasserine Pass*, 97-99, 130-132.

6. Bradley and Blair, 127.

7. Blumenson, *Kasserine Pass*, 120-121.

8. Eisenhower, 141-142.

9. Blumenson, *Kasserine Pass*, 121-123, 137. Operations report, 701st Tank Destroyer Battalion.

10. Blumenson, *Kasserine Pass*, 138. Operations report, 701st Tank Destroyer Battalion.

11. Charles Whiting, *First Blood: The Battle of Kasserine Pass 1943* (London: Grafton Books, 1984), 138. (Hereinafter Whiting, *First Blood: The Battle of Kasserine Pass 1943*.)

12. Whiting, *First Blood*, 177. Operations report, 701st Destroyer Battalion. History of the 168th Infantry for Period November 12, 1942 to May 15, 1943.

13. Blumenson, *Kasserine Pass*, 141-143.

14. Operations reports, 701st Destroyer Battalion and 1st Armored Division.

15. History of the 168th Infantry for Period November 12, 1942 to May 15, 1943.

16. Notes of Major General Omar Bradley on visit to the 1st Armored Division, 1 March 1943. Records of the 1st Armored Division.

17. Gill, 26.

18. Blumenson, *Kasserine Pass*, 151. Whiting, *First Blood, The Battle of Kasserine Pass 1943*, 181. Operations report, 701st Destroyer Battalion.

19. Operations report, 1st Armored Division.

20. Operations report, 805th Tank Destroyer Battalion. Howe, 413.

21. Operations report, 1st Armored Division.

22. Operations report, 805th Tank Destroyer Battalion. Howe, 414, 417.

23. The account of CCC's attack is based on Howe, 418 ff; the operations report of the 701st Tank Destroyer Battalion; an undated memo describing the 701st's operations at Sidi bou Zid; and a telephone interview with Arthur Edson, April 2002.

24. Notes of Major General Omar Bradley on visit to the 1st Armored Division, 1 March 1943. Records of the 1st Armored Division.

25. Howe, 423.

26. Operations report, 1st Armored Division.

27. Howe, 430-431. Operations report, 701st Tank Destroyer Battalion.

28. Undated memo describing the 701st Tank Destroyer Battalion's operations at Sidi bou Zid.

29. S-3 Journal, 13th Armored Regiment.

30. Operations report, 1st Armored Division. Howe, 428.

31. Howe, 433.

32. Gill, 27.

33. Operations report, Combat Command B, 1st Armored Division.

34. Howe, 434.

35. Josowitz, 10.

36. Operations report, Combat Command B, 1st Armored Division.

37. Operations report, 1st Armored Division. Operations report, Combat Command B, 1st Armored Division. Josowitz, 10.

38. Unless otherwise noted, the following account is derived from the operations report, 805th Tank Destroyer Battalion.

39. Telephone interview with William Zierdt, April 2002.

40. Telephone interview with John Spence, April 2002.

41. Howe, 433.

42. Telephone interview with John Spence, April 2002.

43. Ibid.

44. Ibid.

45. Howe, 438-441.

46. Regimental history, 26th Infantry Regiment.

47. Unit journal, 26th Infantry Regiment. Operations report, 805th Tank Destroyer Battalion. Gill, 29.

48. Regimental history, 26th Infantry Regiment.

49. Howe, 455.

50. Operations report, 1st Armored Division.

51. Unit journal, 26th Infantry Regiment.

52. Operations report, 1st Armored Division. Howe, 462.

53. *Tunisia*, 17.

54. Operations report, 1st Armored Division.

55. "Commander-in-Chief's Dispatch, North African Campaign, 1942-43."

56. *A Brief History of the U.S. Army in World War II* (Center of Military History, United States Army, Washington, D.C., 1992). (Hereinafter *A Brief History of the U.S. Army in World War II*.)

57. Operations report, 701st Tank Destroyer Battalion.

58. Letter from Major General Orlando Ward to Lieutenant General Jacob Devers, 1 March 1943. Records of the 1st Armored Division.

59. Josowitz, 11.

60. Telephone interview with John Spence, April 2002.

61. Notes of Major General Omar Bradley on visit to the 1st Armored Division, 1 March 1943. Records of the 1st Armored Division.

62. Unit history, 899th Tank Destroyer Battalion, 1 January-31 December 1943.

63. Untitled document fragment included in "Report of Observers: Mediterranean Theater of Operations," Volume 1, 22 December 1942-23 March 1943.

64. Gill, 29.

65. *Tunisia*, 17-18.

66. Operations report, 1st Armored Division.

67. Account of Col J. Barney Jr., undated, records of the 776th Tank Destroyer Battalion.

68. This description is based on several accounts: LtCol Herschel D. Baker, "El Guettar," *TD Combat in Tunisia* (Tank Destroyer School, 1944), 17 ff (Hereinafter Baker); Howe, 560-562; Presidential unit citation, 601st Tank Destroyer Battalion, quoted in Josowitz, 12-14; telephone interview with Bill

Harper, April 2002; operations report and medal citations, 899th Tank Destroyer Battalion; Gill, 31-33; and Rick Atkinson, *An Army at Dawn, The War in North Africa, 1942-1943* (New York, NY: Henry Holt and Company, LLC, 2002), 439-441 (Hereinafter Atkinson).

69. Operations report, 1st Armored Division. Gabel, 37-38.

70. Account of Col J. Barney Jr., undated, records of the 776th Tank Destroyer Battalion.

71. Unit history, 899th Tank Destroyer Battalion.

72. Gill, 34.

73. Greenfield, et al, 425.

74. "Report on OPERATION AVALANCHE," 601st Tank Destroyer Battalion, 25 September 1943.

75. Greenfield, et al, 426.

76. Account of Col J. Barney Jr., undated, records of the 776th Tank Destroyer Battalion.

77. Notes of Major General Omar Bradley on visit to the 1st Armored Division, 1 March 1943. Records of the 1st Armored Division.

78. Greenfield, et al, 427.

79. Lessons learned, 1st Armored Division. The document is undated.

80. Notes of Major General Omar Bradley on visit to the 1st Armored Division, 1 March 1943. Records of the 1st Armored Division.

81. "Observer Report," 13 March 1943. Included in "Report of Observers: Mediterranean Theater of Operations," Volume 1, 22 December 1942-23 March 1943.

82. Bradley and Blair, 159.

83. Greenfield, et al, 428.

84. Rich Anderson, "The United States Army in World War II." Military History Online. http://www.militaryhistoryonline.com/wwii/usarmy, 2000. (Hereinafter Rich Anderson.)

85. *Tunisia*, 29.

86. *Study of Organization, Equipment, and Tactical Employment of Tank Destroyer Units*, 23.

87. *An Informal History of the 776th Tank Destroyer Battalion*, 31.

88. AAR, 701st Tank Destroyer Battalion, May 1944.

89. Greenfield, et al, 430-431. *Study of Organization, Equipment, and Tactical Employment of Tank Destroyer Units*, 23.

90. *An Informal History of the 776th Tank Destroyer Battalion*, 31.

91. AAR, 813th Tank Destroyer Battalion.

92. Gill, 44.

93. Unit history, 645th Tank Destroyer Battalion.

94. Journal, 636th Tank Destroyer Battalion.

Chapter 4: The Tough Underbelly

1. Martin Blumenson, *Salerno to Cassino* (Washington, DC: Office of the Chief of Military History, 1969), 73-77. (Hereinafter Blumenson, *Salerno to Cassino*.)

2. Ibid., 80-82.

3. Ibid., 86.

4. Operations report, 601st Tank Destroyer Battalion.

5. AAR, 645th Tank Destroyer Battalion. Blumenson, *Salerno to Cassino*, 89 ff.

6. Griess, 234. Blumenson, *Salerno to Cassino*, 97.

7. Operations report, 601st Tank Destroyer Battalion. Blumenson, *Salerno to Cassino*, 100.

8. AAR, 645th Tank Destroyer Battalion. Blumenson, *Salerno to Cassino*, 104ff.

9. S-1 logs, 179th Infantry Regiment, 45th Infantry Division.

10. Griess, 234.

11. S-1 logs, 179th Infantry Regiment, 45th Infantry Division.

12. Flint Whitlock, *The Rock of Anzio, From Sicily to Dachau: A History of the 45th Infantry Division* (Boulder, Colorado: Westview Press, 1998), 87-88. (Hereinafter Whitlock.)

13. Blumenson, *Salerno to Cassino*, 108.

14. Journal, 636th Tank Destroyer Battalion.

15. Sherman, 16.

16. Gill, 45.

17. Blumenson, *Salerno to Cassino*, 114-115.

18. Gill, 45.

19. Liddell Hart, 463.

20. *Combat Lessons Learned Number 2*. (U.S. War Department, 1944), 22.

21. Blumenson, *Salerno to Cassino*, 115.

22. Ibid., 118.

23. Journal, 636th Tank Destroyer Battalion.

24. Journal, 636th Tank Destroyer Battalion.

25. Recommendation for Silver Star, 24 September 1943, records of the 636th Tank Destroyer Battalion. Gill, 45.

26. Journal, 636th Tank Destroyer Battalion.

27. Blumenson, *Salerno to Cassino*, 129.

28. AAR, 645th Tank Destroyer Battalion.

29. Liddell Hart, 464.

30. AAR, 601st Tank Destroyer Battalion.

31. John Hudson, letter to author, 8 February 2003.

32. *An Informal History of the 776th Tank Destroyer Battalion*, 34-35.

33. Account of Col J.Barney Jr., undated, records of the 776th Tank Destroyer Battalion.

34. Liddell Hart, 465.

35. Griess, 234-235. Whitlock, 99-100. Blumenson, *Salerno to Cassino*, 183.

36. Quoted in Whitlock, 98.

37. Liddell Hart, 469.

38. *Combat Lessons Learned Number 2*, 53.

39. Military Attache Report 284, "Tank Destroyer Operations," 13 October 1944, 1-4.284/44 (7316 1/2), records of the Adjutant General's Office, National Archives.

40. Generalmajor Martin Schmidt, "Panzer Units, Employment in Central Italy, 1944." MS # D-204. Historical Division, Headquarters United States Army, Europe, 1947. National Archives. (Hereinafter Schmidt.)

41. Josowitz, 19.

42. Blumenson, *Salerno to Cassino*, 159.

43. "Organization and Employment of a Tank Destroyer Battalion," HQS 701st Tank Destroyer Battalion, 11 October 1943.

44. *An Informal History of the 776th Tank Destroyer Battalion*, 37. Telephone interview with Randolph Mojsl, April 2002. AARs, 636th Tank Destroyer Battalion.

45. Account of Col J.Barney Jr., undated, records of the 776th Tank Destroyer Battalion.

46. *An Informal History of the 776th Tank Destroyer Battalion*, 35-36.

47. Josowitz, 19. AAR, 601st Tank Destroyer Battalion.

48. Blumenson, *Salerno to Cassino*, 185.

49. Griess, 236. Liddell Hart, 469.

50. Blumenson, *Salerno to Cassino*, 194 ff.

51. Josowitz, 20. AAR, 601st Tank Destroyer Battalion. Blumenson, *Salerno to Cassino*, 199.

52. Blumenson, *Salerno to Cassino*, 201.

53. Liddell Hart, 469.

54. Blumenson, *Salerno to Cassino*, 181. Griess, 236.

55. Griess, 236-237.

56. AAR, 645th Tank Destroyer Battalion.

57. AAR, 601st Tank Destroyer Battalion.

58. Calvin C. Boykin, Jr., *General A.D. Bruce: Father of Fort Hood* (College Station, Texas: C&R Publications, 2002), 33. (Hereinafter Boykin, *General A.D. Bruce*.)

59. *Combat Lessons Learned Number 1*. (U.S. War Department, 1944), 55.

60. Schmidt.

61. AAR, 601st Tank Destroyer Battalion.

62. AAR, 601st Tank Destroyer Battalion.

63. AAR, 645th Tank Destroyer Battalion.

64. Griess, 238.

65. *Combat Lessons*, 701st Tank Destroyer Battalion, 1 June 1944.

66. AAR, 645th Tank Destroyer Battalion.

67. *An Informal History of the 776th Tank Destroyer Battalion*, 37. Account of Col J.Barney Jr., undated, records of the 776th Tank Destroyer Battalion.

68. Account of Col J.Barney Jr., undated, records of the 776th Tank Destroyer Battalion.

69. John Hudson, letter to author, 8 February 2003.

70. Sherman, 30.

71. AAR, 601st Tank Destroyer Battalion.

72. Dunnagan, 161.

73. AAR, 645th Tank Destroyer Battalion.

74. Blumenson, *Salerno to Cassino*, 249.

75. *The American Arsenal*, 140.

76. History, 805th Tank Destroyer Battalion.

77. Blumenson, *Salerno to Cassino*, 252-253.

78. John Hudson, letter to author, 8 February 2003.

79. Gill, 47-48.

80. AAR, 645th Tank Destroyer Battalion. John Hudson, letter to author, 8 February 2003.

81. AAR, 645th Tank Destroyer Battalion.

82. History, 805th Tank Destroyer Battalion.

83. George Smith, Jack Hallowell, Joe F. Meis, Robert LeMense, Al Morgan, and Irving Kintisch, *History of the 157th Infantry Regiment (Rifle), 4 June '43-8 May '45* (Baton Rouge, LA: Army & Navy Publishing Company, 1946), 48. (Hereinafter Smith, et al.)

84. Sherman, 35.

85. John Hudson, letter to author, 8 February 2003.

86. Blumenson, *Salerno to Cassino*, 269.

87. *An Informal History of the 776th Tank Destroyer Battalion*, 41.

88. Griess, 238.

89. Liddell Hart, 473.

Chapter 5: Anzio and Two Roads to Rome

1. Martin Blumenson, *Anzio: The Gamble That Failed* (New York, NY: Cooper Square Press, 2001), 73-74. (Hereinafter Blumenson, *Anzio: The Gamble That Failed.*)

2. Blumenson, *Salerno to Cassino*, 359.

3. Telephone interview with John Hudson, May 2002.

4. AAR, 601st Tank Destroyer Battalion. Josowitz, 22.

5. History, 894th Tank Destroyer Battalion. Telephone interview with Rudolph Mojsl, April 2002.

6. *The American Arsenal*, 66.

7. Blumenson, *Anzio: The Gamble That Failed*, 75-76.

8. Ibid., 33-40.

9. Ibid., 43 ff.

10. Ibid., 56.

11. Ibid., 61-63.

12. Griess, 239.

13. AAR, 601st Tank Destroyer Battalion.

14. Smith, et al, 52.

15. Battalion history, 894th Tank Destroyer Battalion.

16. Blumenson, *Anzio: The Gamble That Failed*, 85-92.

17. AAR, 601st Tank Destroyer Battalion.

18. Blumenson, *Anzio: The Gamble That Failed*, 85-97.

19. *Lessons from the Italian Campaign, Training Memorandum Number 2*, Headquarters, Mediterranean Theater of Operations, 15 March 1944. *The Story of the 1st Armored Division*, 33.

20. S-3 Journal, 894th Tank Destroyer Battalion.

21. AAR, 601st Tank Destroyer Battalion. *Combat Lessons*, 701st Tank Destroyer Battalion, 19 March 1944 and 1 June 1944.

22. Patrick J. Chase, *Seek, Strike, Destroy, The History of the 894th Tank Destroyer Battalion in World War II* (Baltimore, MD: Gateway Press, Inc., 1995), 32-33. (Hereinafter Chase.)

23. Ibid., 33-34.

24. AAR, 894th Tank Destroyer Battalion.

25. Blumenson, *Anzio: The Gamble That Failed*, 105-117. Gill, 49.

26. AAR, 701st Tank Destroyer Battalion.

27. Smith, et al, 57.

28. Smith, et al, 58ff. Schmidt.

29. Von Senger und Etterlin, 198-199.

30. Smith, et al, 58ff. Gill, 49.

31. Gill, 50.

32. Blumenson, *Anzio: The Gamble That Failed*, 125.

33. See Wehrtechnik.net, http://www.wehrtechnik.net/wehrtechnik/index. (Hereafter Wehrtechnik.)

34. Von Senger und Etterlin, 53,65,202-203.

35. Chris Bishop and Adam Warner, editors, *German Weapons of World War II* (Edison, NJ: Chartwell Books, Inc., 2001), 121.

36. Horst Scheibert, *Kampf und Untergang der Deutschen Panzertruppe, 1939-1945* (Dorheim, Germany: Podzun Verlag, not dated), 9.

37. Smith, et al, 58ff. Blumenson, *Anzio: The Gamble That Failed*, 132.

38. Blumenson, *Anzio: The Gamble That Failed*, 134-135.

39. Gill, 50.

40. Blumenson, *Anzio: The Gamble That Failed*, 134-135.

41. Gill, 50-51.

42. AAR, 894th Tank Destroyer Battalion.

43. AAR, 701st Tank Destroyer Battalion. Telephone interview with John Hudson, May 2002. John Hudson, letter to author, 8 February 2003. Gill, 50.

44. Chase, 42.

45. Smith, et al, 69. John Hudson, letter to author, 8 February 2003.

46. General der Panzertruppen a.d. Walter Fries, "29th Panzergrenadier Division (Feb. 1944)," MS # D-141. Historical Division, Headquarters United States Army, Europe, not dated. National Archives. (Hereinafter Fries.)

47. AAR, 701st Tank Destroyer Battalion.

48. Fries.

49. Gill, 51.

50. John Hudson, letter to author, 8 February 2003.

51. AAR, 894th Tank Destroyer Battalion.

52. Note to author from Bill Harper, 2002.

53. Telephone interview with Rudolph Mojsl, April 2002. Josowitz, 25.

54. AAR, 601st Tank Destroyer Battalion, for April 1944.

55. Military Attache Report 284.

56. AAR, 601st Tank Destroyer Battalion, for April 1944. *Combat Lessons,* 701st Tank Destroyer Battalion, 19 March 1944. AAR, 821st Tank Destroyer Battalion, February 1945.

57. AAR, 894th Tank Destroyer Battalion.

58. Blumenson, *Salerno to Cassino,* 366.

59. Blumenson, *Salerno to Cassino,* 378.

60. Blumenson, *Salerno to Cassino,* 381-382.

61. *An Informal History of the 776th Tank Destroyer Battalion,* 43. Account of Col J.Barney Jr., undated, records of the 776th Tank Destroyer Battalion.

62. Blumenson, *Salerno to Cassino,* 397ff.

63. AAR, 636th Tank Destroyer Battalion.

64. AAR, 636th Tank Destroyer Battalion.

65. AAR, 636th Tank Destroyer Battalion.

66. Blumenson, *Salerno to Cassino,* 444.

67. AAR, 636th Tank Destroyer Battalion.

68. AAR, 636th Tank Destroyer Battalion.

69. Sherman, 75.

70. Maj Wallace L. Clement, Lt Bruce A. Berlin, Lt James D. Freed, and Lt John B. Gregg, *Eight Hundred and Fourth Tank Destroyer Battalion, 1941-1945, A History* (Camp Hood, Texas: 804th Tank Destroyer Battalion, 1945), 12-13. (Hereinafter Clement, et al.) AAR, 804th Tank Destroyer Battalion.

71. AAR, 636th Tank Destroyer Battalion.

72. Smith, et al, 84.

73. Ernest J. Fisher Jr., *Cassino to the Alps: The United States Army in World War II, The Mediterranean Theater of Operations* (Washington, DC: Center of Military History, 1977), 137. (Hereinafter Fisher.) Whitlock, 296. Liddell-Hart, 535.

74. AAR, 601st Tank Destroyer Battalion.

75. AAR, 601st Tank Destroyer Battalion.

76. AAR, 701st Tank Destroyer Battalion.

77. Fisher, 123, 126. AAR, 701st Tank Destroyer Battalion. John Hudson, letter to author, 8 February 2003.

78. Smith, et al, 87-88.

79. John Hudson, letter to author, 8 February 2003.

80. AAR, 701st Tank Destroyer Battalion.

81. S-3 Journal, 805th Tank Destroyer Battalion.

82. Congressional Medal of Honor citation, Capt William Wylie Galt Headquarters, 34th Infantry Division. *Lessons Learned in Combat, November 7/8 1942-September 1944*. September 1944.

83. Josowitz, 29.

84. Sherman, 88.

85. AAR, 636th Tank Destroyer Battalion.

86. AAR, 636th Tank Destroyer Battalion. Sherman, 81.

87. Josowitz, 30.

88. John Hudson, letter to author, 8 February 2003.

89. AAR, 804th Tank Destroyer Battalion.

90. AAR, 636th Tank Destroyer Battalion. *Combat Lessons*, 701st Tank Destroyer Battalion, 1 June 1944.

91. AAR, 636th Tank Destroyer Battalion.

92. Headquarters, Mediterranean Theater of Operations, U.S. Army. Training Memorandum Number 2, *Lessons From the Italian Campaign*. 15 March 1945.

93. Headquarters, Mediterranean Theater of Operations, U.S. Army. Training Memorandum Number 2, *Lessons From the Italian Campaign*. 15 March 1945. AAR, 636th Tank Destroyer Battalion. *Combat Lessons*, 701st Tank Destroyer Battalion, 1 June 1944.

94. Headquarters, 34th Infantry Division. *Lessons Learned in Combat, November 7/8 1942-September 1944*. September 1944.

95. AAR, 636th Tank Destroyer Battalion. *Combat Lessons*, 701st Tank Destroyer Battalion, 1 June 1944.

96. Headquarters, Mediterranean Theater of Operations, U.S. Army. Training Memorandum Number 2, *Lessons From the Italian Campaign*. 15 March 1945.

97. AAR, 601st Tank Destroyer Battalion.

98. *The American Arsenal*, 58.

99. Richard R. Buchanan, Richard D. Wissolik, David Wilmes, and Gary E.J. Smith, general editors, *Men of the 704th: A Pictorial and Spoken History of the 704th Tank Destroyer Battalion in World War II* (Latrobe, PA: Saint Vincent College Center for Northern Appalachian Studies, 1998), 25. (Hereinafter Buchanan, et al.)

100. Oliver, 8.

101. Buick advertisement reproduced in Gill, 81.

102. AARs, 813th Tank Destroyer Battalion.

103. Oliver, 10.

104. AAR, 636th Tank Destroyer Battalion.

105. Sherman, 91.

Chapter 6: Storming Fortress Europe

1. Buchanan, et al, 9.

2. *Normandy*, CMH Pub72-18 (Washington, DC: U.S. Army Center of Military History, not dated), 21. (Hereinafter *Normandy*.)

3. *Normandy*, 26-32. Griess, et al, 295.

4. History, 899th Tank Destroyer Battalion.

5. *Study of Organization, Equipment, and Tactical Employment of Tank Destroyer Units*, 1-2.

6. Ibid., 24.

7. Ibid., 1-2.

8. Ibid., 2.

9. Ibid., 2, 13, 15.

10. History, 702d Tank Destroyer Battalion.

11. Griess, 318.

12. AAR, 899th Tank Destroyer Battalion.

13. *Normandy*, 36.

14. Battle honors memo, 899th Tank Destroyer Battalion, 6 September 1944.

15. Ibid. AAR, 801st Tank Destroyer Battalion.

16. *Normandy*, 36.

17. Griess, 316.

18. Griess, 256.

19. *Combat Lessons Learned Number 4*. U.S. War Department pamphlet, 1944.

20. *Normandy*, 34.

21. *Study of Organization, Equipment, and Tactical Employment of Tank Destroyer Units*, 13.

22. "Panzer Tactics in Normandy," Historical Division, Headquarters United States Army, Europe, 11 December 1947. This is a record of an interview conducted with General der Panzertruppen Leo Freiherr Geyr von Schweppenburg, who was commander of Panzer Gruppe West from 1943 to 5 July 1944 and Inspector of Panzer Troops from August 1944 to May 1945. National Archives. (Hereinafter "Panzer Tactics in Normandy".)

23. AAR, 803d Tank Destroyer Battalion, July 1944.

24. "Panzer Tactics in Normandy," 3.

25. *Study of Organization, Equipment, and Tactical Employment of Tank Destroyer Units*, 13.

26. 746th Tank Battalion Report, 10 July, 83d Div G-2, G-3 Journal File, cited by Martin Blumenson, *Breakout and Pursuit: United States Army In World War Ii, The European Theater Of Operations* (Washington, DC: Center of Military History, 1993), 132. (Hereinafter Blumenso, *Breakout and Pursuit*.)

27. AAR, 6th Armored Group.

28. AARs, 743d Tank Battalion.

29. "Report of the 803d Tank Destroyer Battalion," memo to the First Army antitank officer, 6 July 1944.

30. Ibid.

31. *St. LÔ,* facsimile reprint of CMH Pub 100-13 (Washington, DC: U.S. Army Center of Military History, 1983), 36ff. (Hereinafter *St. LÔ.*) Battle Honors Citations of Companies A and C, 899th Tank Destroyer Battalion, 11 December 1944.

32. Battle Honors Citations of Companies A and C, 899th Tank Destroyer Battalion, 11 December 1944. Medal citations, 899th Tank Destroyer Battalion. Gill, 57. *St. LÔ,* 38.

33. *St. LÔ,* 36ff. Battle Honors Citations of Companies A and C, 899th Tank Destroyer Battalion, 11 December 1944.

34. Medal citations, 899th Tank Destroyer Battalion. Gill, 57.

35. Medal citations, 899th Tank Destroyer Battalion. Gill, 58.

36. *St. LÔ,* 40.

37. *Study of Organization, Equipment, and Tactical Employment of Tank Destroyer Units*, 17.

38. Ibid., 14.

39. Bronze star citation for Lt Wilfred C. Ford. S-3 journal, 899th Tank Destroyer Battalion.

40. AAR, 635th Tank Destroyer Battalion.

41. History, 801st Tank Destroyer Battalion. AARs, 801st Tank Destroyer Battalion.

42. AAR, 802d Tank Destroyer Battalion.

43. AAR, 635th Tank Destroyer Battalion.

44. AARs, 801st Tank Destroyer Battalion.

45. AAR, 821st Tank Destroyer Battalion, July 1944.

46. *Study of Organization, Equipment, and Tactical Employment of Tank Destroyer Units*, 2, 10, 15.

47. AAR, 802d Tank Destroyer Battalion.

48. Michael Green, *M4 Sherman*. Osceola (WI: Motorbooks International Publishers & Wholesalers, 1993), 102. (Hereinafter Green.)

49. *Study of Organization, Equipment, and Tactical Employment of Tank Destroyer Units*, 2.

50. S-3 journal, 899th Tank Destroyer Battalion, 16 July 1944.

Chapter 7: Armored Thunder

1. Col Robert S. Allen, *Patton's Third Army: Lucky Forward* (New York: Manor Books Inc., 1965), 70-71. (Hereinafter Allen.)

2. Edward Jablonski, *Wings of Fire*. Garden City (NY: Doubleday & Company, 1971), 97-98. Griess, 330.

3. Blumenson, *Breakout and Pursuit*, 181.

4. Heinz Guderian, *Panzer Leader* (New York, NY: Ballentine Books, 1972), 265. (Hereinafter Guderian.)

5. Griess, 328.

6. Ibid., 331.

7. Houston, 215.

8. AAR, 702d Tank Destroyer Battalion.

9. AAR, 703d Tank Destroyer Battalion.

10. Houston, 219-221.

11. Ibid., 222.

12. Gill, 59.

13. Griess, 317.

14. See the S-3 Journal, 745th Tank Battalion, which records an order to this effect from Headquarters 1st Army, as does the S-3 Journal of the 747th Tank Battalion.

15. Allen, 71.

16. Houston, 226.

17. Richard D. Wissolik and Gary E.J. Smith, general editors, *Reluctant Valor, The Oral History of Captain Thomas J. Evans* (Latrobe, PA: Saint Vincent College Center for Northern Appalachian Studies, 1995), 3-4. (Hereinafter Wissolik and Smith.)

18. Buchanan, et al, 19.

19. Allen, 72-74.

20. *Study of Organization, Equipment, and Tactical Employment of Tank Destroyer Units*, 5.

21. Oliver, 16.

22. History, 705th Tank Destroyer Battalion.

23. History, 603d Tank Destroyer Battalion, August 1944.

24. Capt Elmer V. Sparks, editor-in-chief, *Victory TD* (Göttingen, Germany: 628th Tank Destroyer Battalion, 1945), 35. (Hereinafter Sparks, *Victory TD*.)

25. Wissilok and Smith, 20.

26. AAR, 703d Tank Destroyer Battalion, 30 July 1944.

27. *Spearhead in the West* (Frankfurt, Germany: 3d Armored Division, 1945), 28. (Hereinafter *Spearhead in the West*.)

28. Wissilok and Smith, 20-23.

29. Ibid., 22. Nat Frankel and Larry Smith, *Patton's Best, An Informal History of the 4th Armored Division* (New York, NY: The Berkley Publishing Group, 1984), 27. (Hereinafter Frankel and Smith.)

30. Buchanan, et al, 23-24.

31. History, 603d Tank Destroyer Battalion, September 1944.

32. *644th Tank Destroyer Battalion* (Göttingen, Germany: Muster-Schmidt, 1945), 22.

33. Houston, 232.

34. AAR, 702d Tank Destroyer Battalion.

35. History, 612th Tank Destroyer Battalion.

36. *Spearhead in the West*, 73.

37. Allen, 78.

38. History, 823d Tank Destroyer Battalion.

39. Griess, 334-335.

40. Mark J. Reardon, *Victory at Mortain, Stopping Hitler's Panzer Counteroffensive* (Lawrence, Kansas: University Press of Kansas, 2002), 46-64. (Hereinafter Reardon.)

41. Guderian, 273.

42. Griess, 335.

43. Michael Reynolds, *Steel Inferno: 1st SS Panzer Corps in Normandy* (New York: Dell Publishing, 1997), 260.

44. History, 823d Tank Destroyer Battalion.

45. History, 823d Tank Destroyer Battalion. "30th Inf Division, Mortain Counterattack, 6-12 Aug 1944," combat interviews, NARA, box 24038.

46. History, AAR, 823d Tank Destroyer Battalion. Reardon, 126. Interview with Lt Leon Neel, "30th Inf Division, Mortain Counterattack, 6-12 Aug 1944."

47. General Freiherr Von Gersdorff, "The German Counterattack Against Avranches," MS # B-725, Historical Division, Headquarters United States Army, Europe, 1946. National Archives. (Hereinafter Von Gersdorff.)

48. History, AAR, 823d Tank Destroyer Battalion.

49. Reardon, 132.

50. History, 823d Tank Destroyer Battalion. Interview with Lt Leon Neel, "30th Inf Division, Mortain Counterattack, 6-12 Aug 1944." Reardon, 128 ff.

51. "30th Inf Division, Mortain Counterattack, 6-12 Aug 1944."

52. Interview with Lt Francis J. Conners, "30th Inf Division, Mortain Counterattack, 6-12 Aug 1944."

53. *Northern France*, CMH Pub72-30 (Washington, DC: U.S. Army Center of Military History, not dated), 15. (Hereinafter *Northern France*.)

54. "30th Inf Division, Mortain Counterattack, 6-12 Aug 1944."

55. General der Panzertruppe Freiherr Heinrich Von Lütwitz, "Questions for Heinrich von Lüttwitz, Commanding General of the 2d Panzer Division Until September 1944," MS # A-904, Historical Division, Headquarters United States Army, Europe, October 1945. National Archives.

56. Von Gersdorff, 42.

57. Gill, 157.

58. Chester Wilmot, *The Struggle for Europe* (Ware, England: Wordsworth Editions Limited, 1997), 401-402. Griess, 335. (Hereinafter Wilmot.)

59. Sparks, *Victory TD*, 36-37.

60. Allen, 83ff. Griess, 336.

61. Griess, 337.

62. Gill, 62. Medal of Honor citation, Sgt. John D. Hawk.

63. AAR, S-3 journal, 773d Tank Destroyer Battalion. Hand-written account of the actions of Company C, contained in the records of the 773d Tank Destroyer Battalion. Medal citations for Lt Delbert G. Reck and S/Sgt. Edward J. Land.

64. Lt Harold H. Eby, *Tank Busters, 607 Tank Destroyer Battalion "Battle with the Jerries"* (Munich, Germany: 607th Tank Destroyer Battalion, 1945?), 17-18. (Hereinafter Eby.)

65. *Spearhead in the West*, 76ff. AAR, S-3 Journal, 703d Tank Destroyer Battalion.

66. Wilmot, 424.

67. Guderian, 299.

68. *Spearhead in the West*, 81.

69. Calvin C. Boykin, Jr., *Gare La Bête* (College Station, Texas: C&R Publications, 1995), 35. (Hereinafter Boykin, *Gare La Bête*.)

70. Capt Roy T. McGrann, *The 610th Tank Destroyer Battalion* (No publication information provided), 48. (Hereinafter McGrann.)

71. Boykin, *Gare La Bête*, 39-40.

72. Dunnagan, 171.

73. AAR, 635th Tank Destroyer Battalion.

74. Frankel and Smith, 39-40. Wissilok and Smith, 3.

75. Wissilok and Smith, 25.

76. History, 702d Tank Destroyer Battalion.

77. Griess, 342.

78. *Southern France*, CMH Pub72-31 (Washington, DC: U.S. Army Center of Military History, not dated), 12-15. (Hereinafter *Southern France*.)

79. Ibid., 7.

80. Josowitz, 34.

81. AAR, 645th Tank Destroyer Battalion. *Southern France*, 14.

82. AAR, 636th Tank Destroyer Battalion.

83. Ibid. *Southern France*, 17.

84. *Southern France*, 9.

85. Ibid., 16.

86. AAR, 636th Tank Destroyer Battalion. Sherman, 98-99. *Southern France*, 22-23. Von Wietersheim, "The 11th Panzer Division in Southern France (15 August – 14 September 1944)," MS # A-880, Historical Division, Headquarters United States Army, Europe, 1946. National Archives, 9.

87. AAR, 645th Tank Destroyer Battalion.

88. *Southern France*, 25.

89. AAR, 645th Tank Destroyer Battalion. Jeffrey J. Clarke and Robert Ross Smith, *Riviera to the Rhine: United States Army in World War II, The European Theater of Operations* (Washington, DC: Office of the Chief of Military History, Department of the Army, 1993), 177. (Hereinafter Clarke and Smith.)

90. AAR, 636th Tank Destroyer Battalion.

91. Ibid.

92. AAR, Company C, 753d Tank Battalion.

93. Sherman, 113.

94. AAR, 645th Tank Destroyer Battalion. *Southern France*, 29.

95. Smith, et al, 105.

96. *Southern France*, 30.

97. *Spearhead in the West*, 86-87. Griess, 351. Blumenson, *Breakout and Pursuit*, 682-684.

98. Griess, 352.

99. *Northern France*, 25.

100. Boykin, *Gare La Bête*, 43-44.

101. *Northern France*, 25. McGrann, 51.

102. *Spearhead in the West*, 95-96.

103. AAR, 703d Tank Destroyer Battalion. Charles B. MacDonald, *The Siegfried Line Campaign: United States Army in World War II, The European Theater of Operations* (Washington, DC: Office of the Chief of Military History, Department of the Army, 1993), 74. (Hereinafter Blumenson, *The Siegfried Line Campaign*.)

104. MacDonald, *The Siegfried Line Campaign*, 76 ff.

105. AAR, 636th Tank Destroyer Battalion.

106. Josowitz, 36.

107. Hugh M. Cole, *The Lorraine Campaign: United States Army in World War II, The European Theater of Operations* (Washington, DC: Historical Division, Department of the Army, 1950), 211-212. (Hereinafter Cole, *The Lorraine Campaign*.)

108. Oberst iG Von Kahlden, Chief of Staff, Fifth Panzer Army. "Fifth Pz Army (15 Sep – 15 Oct 44)," MS # B-472, Historical Division, Headquarters United States Army, Europe, not dated. National Archives, i-ii, 4ff. Cole, *The Lorraine Campaign*, 214. (Hereinafter Von Kahlden.)

109. Von Kahlden, 8, 18. Cole, *The Lorraine Campaign*, 201.

110. Cole, *The Lorraine Campaign*, 221.

111. History, 704th Tank Destroyer Battalion.

112. Cole, *The Lorraine Campaign*, 221.

113. Buchanan, et al, 43.

114. Capt Kenneth Koyen, *The Fourth Armored Division: From the Beach to Bavaria* (Munich, Germany: Herder Druck, 1946), 56. Interview with Lt Jerome J. Sacks, "4th Armd Div, Crossing of the Moselle Near Nancy, 12-22 Sep," combat interviews, NARA, box 24092.

115. History, 603d Tank Destroyer Battalion.

116. Wissolik and Smith, 84. Cole, *The Lorraine Campaign*, 223.

117. Von Kahlden, 18.

118. Cole, *The Lorraine Campaign*, 224. Wissolik and Smith, 31. AAR, CCA, 4th Armored Division. Interview with LtCol Hal Pattison, "4th Armd Div, Crossing of the Moselle Near Nancy, 12-22 Sep," combat interviews, NARA, box 24092.

119. Wissolik and Smith, 83. Interviews with Lt Edwin T. Leiper and Capt William A. Dwight, "4th Armd Div, Crossing of the Moselle Near Nancy, 12-22 Sep," combat interviews, NARA, box 24092.

120. Gill, 70-71.

121. Buchanan, et al, 46.

122. Wissolik and Smith, 83. AAR, CCA, 4th Armored Division. "4th Armd Div, Crossing of the Moselle Near Nancy, 12-22 Sep," combat interviews, NARA, box 24092.

123. Buchanan, et al, 46.

124. AAR, CCA, 4th Armored Division.

125. Interview with Lt Marvin E. Evans, "4th Armd Div, Crossing of the Moselle Near Nancy, 12-22 Sep," combat interviews, NARA, box 24092.

126. AAR, CCA, 4th Armored Division.

127. AAR, CCA, 4th Armored Division.

128. AAR, CCA, 4th Armored Division. Buchanan, et al, 46.

129. Von Kahlden, 22ff. Generalleutnant Wend Von Wietersheim, "The 11th Panzer Division in Southern France (15 August – 14 September 1944)," MS # A-880, National Archives, 1946, 2-3.

130. Generalleutnant Wend Von Wietersheim, "The Employment of the 11th Panzer Division in Lorraine," MS # B-364, Historical Division, Headquarters United States Army, Europe, 10 January 1947. National Archives, 12. (Hereinafter "The Employment of the 11th Panzer Division in Lorraine".)

131. Oliver, 11.

132. Von Wietersheim, "The Employment of the 11th Panzer Division in Lorraine," 14-15.

133. Von Kahlden, 24. Von Wietersheim, "The Employment of the 11th Panzer Division in Lorraine," 13.

134. Cole, *The Lorraine Campaign*, 241. AAR, 602d Tank Destroyer Battalion. Oliver, 12.

135. AAR, 813th Tank Destroyer Battalion, 29 September 1944.

136. Cole, *The Lorraine Campaign*, 242. Griess, 361-362.

137. *Study of Organization, Equipment, and Tactical Employment of Tank Destroyer Units*, 2. AG 322 x 475 OpCG, 29 September 1944.

138. McGrann, 65, 116.

139. *The American Arsenal*, 60. Mesko, 17. "90mm Firing Tests." Memo from HQ, 703d Tank Destroyer Battalion to Commanding General, First Army. 15 December 1944.

140. McGrann, 55.

141. Gabel, 53. Gill, 74. AAR, 703d Tank Destroyer Battalion.

Chapter 8: The Battle for the Border

1. "Defense of the West Wall." ETHINT-37. Historical Division, Headquarters United States Army, Europe. This is an interview with Major Herbert Büchs, aide to Generaloberst Alfred Jodl, 28 September 1945. National Archives.

2. Charles B. MacDonald, *The Battle of the Bulge* (London: Guild Publishing, 1984), 62.

3. Wilmot, 478-9. MacDonald, *The Siegfried Line Campaign*, 31 ff. Griess, 355.

4. MacDonald, *The Siegfried Line Campaign* , 34-5.

5. AAR, 702d Tank Destroyer Battalion, October 1944.

6. History, 823d Tank Destroyer Battalion.

7. Macdonald, *The Siegfried Line Campaign*, xi.

8. "Documentation of Siegfried Line," memo in records of 803d Tank Destroyer Battalion, 12 October 1944.

9. AAR, 803d Tank Destroyer Battalion.

10. AARs, 803d Tank Destroyer Battalion.

11. Griess, 362. Stephen E. Ambrose, *Citizen Soldiers* (New York, NY: Touchstone, 1997), 153.

12. Macdonald, *The Siegfried Line Campaign*, 263ff.

13. *Rhineland*, CMH Pub72-25 (Washington, DC: U.S. Army Center of Military History, not dated), 15. (Hereinafter *Rhineland*.)

14. History, AAR, summaries of medal citations, 823d Tank Destroyer Battalion.

15. Macdonald, *The Siegfried Line Campaign*, 291-292.

16. "1st Inf Div, Battle of Aachen, 8-22 Oct 44," combat interviews, NARA, box 24012.

17. "1st Inf Div, Battle of Aachen, 8-22 Oct 44."

18. "1st Inf Div, Battle of Aachen, 8-22 Oct 44." G-3 Report of Operations, 1st Infantry Division. MacDonald, *The Siegfried Line Campaign* , 310.

19. *Combat Lessons Learned Number 6*. (U.S. War Department, 1945), 18-19.

20. "1st Inf Div, Battle of Aachen, 8-22 Oct 44." AAR, 634th Tank Destroyer Battalion.

21. "1st Inf Div, Battle of Aachen, 8-22 Oct 44." *Rhineland*. 15.

22. AAR, 635th Tank Destroyer Battalion.

23. AAR, 821st Tank Destroyer Battalion, October 1944.

24. Ibid.

25. AAR, 773d Tank Destroyer Battalion.

26. Dunnagan, 81, 147.

27. Ibid., 147-148.

28. AARs, 645th and 636th Tank Destroyer battalions.

29. Commendation, from 183d Field Artillery Group to Commanding General, XII Corps Artillery, 29 October 1944.

30. S-3 Journal, 899th Tank Destroyer Battalion.

31. AAR, 601st Tank Destroyer Battalion.

32. Macdonald, *The Siegfried Line Campaign*, 381-389.

33. Clarke and Smith, 351, 361.

34. Ibid., 368ff. AAR, 813th Tank Destroyer Battalion.

35. Clarke and Smith, 371ff.

36. *An Informal History of the 776th Tank Destroyer Battalion*, 54. AAR, 813th Tank Destroyer Battalion.

37. AAR, 601st Tank Destroyer Battalion. Josowitz, 36.

38. Sherman, 139.

39. Cole, *The Lorraine Campaign*, 373.

40. Ibid., 266.

41. AAR, 773d Tank Destroyer Battalion.

42. Allen, 136. Cole, *The Lorraine Campaign*, 410-412.

43. Cole, *The Lorraine Campaign*, 468.

44. MacDonald, *The Battle of the Bulge*, 64-65.

45. Eby, 32-33. Cole, *The Lorraine Campaign*, 581.

46. *Rhineland*, 17. Bradley and Blair, 343.

47. *Rhineland*, 18-19.

48. Sparks, *Victory TD*, 47-49.

49. *Rhineland*, 21.

50. Macdonald, *The Siegfried Line Campaign*, 497.

51. *Rhineland*, 20.

52. Macdonald, *The Siegfried Line Campaign*, 530.

53. Von Senger und Etterlin, 200-201.

54. Houston, 310-313. Macdonald, *The Siegfried Line Campaign*, 531.

55. Houston, 314-316. AAR, 702d Tank Destroyer Battalion.

56. History, AAR, 771st Tank Destroyer Battalion. Medal citations for Lt George F. Killmer Jr. and Sgt. Walter F. Nedza.

57. Houston, 314-316. AAR, 702d Tank Destroyer Battalion.

58. GNMAR 321, 19 November 1944.

59. MacDonald, *The Siegfried Line Campaign*, 577.

60. Drawn from *614 Tank Destroyers WWII* (no publisher listed), which describes the battle by quoting medal citations and commendations.

61. Wilmot, 621.

Chapter 9: The Battle of the Bulge

1. MacDonald, *The Battle of the Bulge*, 21ff.

2. Wilmot, 577.

3. Allen, 163, 165.

4. Griess, 371-372.

5. MacDonald, *The Battle of the Bulge*, 64-65.

6. Wilmot, 576.

7. Hugh M. Cole, *Battle of the Bulge: United States Army in World War II, The European Theater of Operations* (Washington, DC: Center of Military History, 1993), 98. (Hereinafter *Battle of the Bulge*.)

8. "801st Has Early Origin," undated manuscript in the records of the 801st Tank Destroyer Battalion.

9. AAR, 820th Tank Destroyer Battalion.

10. Griess, 379.

11. AAR, 630th Tank Destroyer Battalion.

12. AAR, 803d Tank Destroyer Battalion.

13. Wilmot, 583-584.

14. Cole, *Battle of the Bulge*, 90-91.

15. AAR and S-3 journal, 801st Tank Destroyer Battalion.

16. Cole, *Battle of the Bulge*, 91.

17. AAR and S-3 journal, 801st Tank Destroyer Battalion. Cole, *Battle of the Bulge*, 94.

18. AAR and S-3 journal, 801st Tank Destroyer Battalion.

19. AAR, 630th Tank Destroyer Battalion.

20. AAR, 820th Tank Destroyer Battalion.

21. Recommendation for Unit Citation, Company C, 811th Tank Destroyer Battalion. History, 811th Tank Destroyer Battalion.

22. Cole, *Battle of the Bulge*, 104. History, 644th Tank Destroyer Battalion.

23. Cole, *Battle of the Bulge*, 109ff. *644th Tank Destroyer Battalion*, 28. History, 644th Tank Destroyer Battalion.

24. Cole, *Battle of the Bulge*, 115.

25. History, 644th Tank Destroyer Battalion.

26. DSC citation, Lt Robert A. Parker. *644th Tank Destroyer Battalion*, 28.

27. Interview with Capt Ralph H. Stallworth, "2d Inf Div, Battle of the Bulge, 16 Dec 44-16 Jan 45," combat interviews, NARA, box 24017. Medal citation, Cpl. Henry J. McVeigh.

28. Cole, *Battle of the Bulge*, 120.

29. Ibid., 109ff. *644th Tank Destroyer Battalion*, 28. History, 644th Tank Destroyer Battalion.

30. History, 644th Tank Destroyer Battalion.

31. "Sixth Pz Army (16 Nov 44 – 4 Jan 45)," ETHINT-21. Historical Division, Headquarters United States Army, Europe, 1945. This is an interview with Generalmajor (Waffen SS) Fritz Kraemer, 8–9 August 1945.

32. "Sixth Pz Army in the Ardennes Offensive," ETHINT-16. Historical Division, Headquarters United States Army, Europe, 1945. This is an interview with Generaloberst (Waffen SS) Josef "Sepp" Dietrich, 8-9 August 1945. National Archives.

33. Wilmot, 580.

34. Griess, 380.

35. Boykin, *Gare La Bête*, 71.

36. MacDonald, *The Battle of the Bulge*, 327, 468. Griess, 380.

37. MacDonald, *The Battle of the Bulge*, 466, 469-470. Boykin, *Gare La Bête*, 78.

38. MacDonald, *The Battle of the Bulge*, 479-480.

39. Cole, *Battle of the Bulge*, 402.

40. MacDonald, *The Battle of the Bulge*, 470-472. Boykin, *Gare La Bête*, 79.

41. AAR, 814th Tank Destroyer Battalion. Cole, *Battle of the Bulge*, 405.

42. MacDonald, *The Battle of the Bulge*, 472-475.

43. Boykin, *Gare La Bête*, 80-81.

44. MacDonald, *The Battle of the Bulge*, 478-479.

45. Ibid., 482-483.

46. Boykin, *Gare La Bête*, 83.

47. AAR, 814th Tank Destroyer Battalion.

48. MacDonald, *The Battle of the Bulge*, 483.

49. Ibid., 485.

50. Boykin, *Gare La Bête*, 101-102.

51. Wilmot, 584-585.

52. Boykin, *Gare La Bête*, 105.

53. Wilmot, 592.

54. History, AAR, 823d Tank Destroyer Battalion.

55. "Operations with 82d Airborne Division, 20 Dec 44-1 Jan 45," attached to AAR, 703d Tank Destroyer Battalion, for February 1945.

56. *Study of Organization, Equipment, and Tactical Employment of Tank Destroyer Units*, 19.

57. AAR, 609th Tank Destroyer Battalion. Telephone interview with John Pilon, September 2002.

58. AAR, 705th Tank Destroyer Battalion.

59. Recommendation for distinguished unit citation, 705th Tank Destroyer Battalion.

60. AAR, 609th Tank Destroyer Battalion. Telephone interview with John Pilon, September 2002. Gill, 96. MacDonald, *The Battle of the Bulge*, 490.

61. MacDonald, *The Battle of the Bulge*, 490-491. Telephone interview with John Pilon. AAR, 609th Tank Destroyer Battalion. Gill, 96.

62. Cole, *Battle of the Bulge*, 452-453.

63. Ibid., 453-454.

64. S-3 journal, 705th Tank Destroyer Battalion. MacDonald, *The Battle of the Bulge*, 498.

65. Cole, *Battle of the Bulge*, 455. MacDonald, *The Battle of the Bulge*, 499. Telephone interview with John Pilon.

66. MacDonald, *The Battle of the Bulge*, 500.

67. AAR, 609th Tank Destroyer Battalion. Recommendation for Unit Citation, Company C, 811th Tank Destroyer Battalion.

68. S-3 journal, 705th Tank Destroyer Battalion.

69. AAR, 705th Tank Destroyer Battalion.

70. AAR, S-3 journal, 705th Tank Destroyer Battalion.

71. Cole, *Battle of the Bulge*, 466.

72. AARs, 609th and 705th Tank Destroyer battalions. S-3 journal, 705th Tank Destroyer Battalion.

73. Cole, *Battle of the Bulge*, 468.

74. Ibid., 470. AAR, 705th Tank Destroyer Battalion.

75. Cole, *Battle of the Bulge*, 472-474.

76. AAR, 705th Tank Destroyer Battalion.

77. S-3 journal, 705th Tank Destroyer Battalion.

78. Memorandum dated 18 February 1945, "4th Armd Div, Defense of Bastogne, 17 to 26 December 44," combat interviews, NARA, box 24102.

79. "Employment of Panzer Forces on the Western Front." ETHINT-39. Historical Division, Headquarters United States Army, Europe, 1945. This is an interview with Generaloberst Heinz Guderian, 16 August 1945. National Archives.

80. AAR, S-3 journal, 705th Tank Destroyer Battalion.

81. AAR, 705th Tank Destroyer Battalion. Unit citation.

82. AAR, 609th Tank Destroyer Battalion.

83. Allen, 174-179.

84. Wilmot, 599.

85. Wissolik and Smith, 33-34.

86. Cole, *Battle of the Bulge*, 513.

87. Ibid., 525.

88. Ibid., 475, 527-529.

89. Wissolik and Smith, 39.

90. Cole, *Battle of the Bulge*, 480.

91. Buchanan, et al, 56.

92. Houston, 333-335.

93. Ibid., 339.

94. MacDonald, *The Battle of the Bulge*, 590.

95. Josowitz, 38.

96. Charles Whiting, *The Other Battle of the Bulge, Operation Northwind* (Chelsea, Michigan: Scarborough House, 1990), 18. *Rhineland*, 25.

97. Sherman, 159.

98. AAR, 813th Tank Destroyer Battalion.

99. "Outnumbered 'Armored Devils' Blast Seven Enemy Tanks." *T-Patch*, 18 February 1945. Reproduced in Sherman, 163-164.

100. Sherman, 165. AAR, 813th Tank Destroyer Battalion.

101. Griess, 385.

102. Gill, 103.

103. *Study of Organization, Equipment, and Tactical Employment of Tank Destroyer Units*, 2.

104. AAR, 811th Tank Destroyer Battalion.

105. George S. Patton Jr., *War As I Knew It* (New York, NY: Bantam Books, 1980), 209. (Hereinafter Patton.)

106. Army Ground Forces Report #700, "ETO—Tank Destroyer Information Ltr No 5," 1 March 1945.

107. AAR, 803d Tank Destroyer Battalion.

108. Boykin, *General A.D. Bruce*, 29.

Chapter 10: Sought, Struck, and Destroyed

1. Dunnagan, 181.

2. Wilmot, 663-664.

3. Army Ground Forces Report #700. Patton, 242.

4. Army Ground Forces Board Report, ETO, No. 777, "Armored Officers Circular Letter No. 6," 28 March 1945.

5. Griess, 394.

6. Drawn from *614 Tank Destroyers WWII*.

7. Army Ground Forces Report #700.

8. Army Ground Forces Report No 808, "Tank Destroyer Information Letter No 8," 4 April 1945.

9. Belton Y. Cooper, *Death Traps, The Survival of an American Armored Division in World War II* (Novato, CA: Presidio Press, Inc., 2000), 226-227. (Hereinafter Cooper.)

10. Bradley and Blair, 401.

11. *Rhineland*, 28-30.

12. History, 656th Tank Destroyer Battalion.

13. Omar N. Bradley, *A Soldier's Story* (New York NY: The Modern Library, 1999), 511.

14. Griess, 398.

15. AAR, 773d Tank Destroyer Battalion.

16. Army Ground Forces Report No 808.

17. *An Informal History of the 776th Tank Destroyer Battalion*, 60-63. Operations report, 776th Tank Destroyer Battalion.

18. *Rhineland*, 33.

19. Griess, 400.

20. *Spearhead in the West*, 131.

21. Sparks, *Victory TD*, 56-57.

22. Charles B. MacDonald, *The Last Offensive: United States Army in World War II, The European Theater of Operations* (Washington, DC: Office of the Chief of Military History, Department of the Army, 1993), 322. (Hereinafter MacDonald, *The Last Offensive*.)

23. Liddell Hart, 678.

24. Army Ground Forces Report No 808.

25. MacDonald, *The Last Offensive*, 345.

26. Ibid., 352. Wilmot, 684.

27. Charles Whiting, *The Battle of the Ruhr Pocket* (New York, NY: Ballentine Books Inc, 1970), 62-63. (Hereinafter Whiting, *The Battle of the Ruhr Pocket*.)

28. S-3 Journal, 703d Tank Destroyer Battalion.

29. MacDonald, *The Last Offensive*, 352.

30. Cooper, 254-256.

31. *644th Tank Destroyer Battalion*, 31-32.

32. Whiting, *The Battle of the Ruhr Pocket*, 140-146.

33. History, 817th Tank Destroyer Battalion.

34. AAR, 823d Tank Destroyer Battalion.

35. Josowitz, 44.

36. AAR, 602d Tank Destroyer Battalion.

37. CX-3620, 30 April 1945. F-4774, 27 April 1945. K-21657, 27 April 1945.

38. Clement, et al, 22-24. AAR, 804th Tank Destroyer Battalion.

39. AAR, 701st Tank Destroyer Battalion.

40. John Hudson, letter to author, 8 February 2003.

41. John Hudson, letter to author, 8 February 2003.

42. Army Ground Forces Report No. 944, "Tank Destroyer Information Letter No. 7," 12 May 1945.

43. AAR, 614th Tank Destroyer Battalion.

44. Clement, et al, 24-26. AAR, 804th Tank Destroyer Battalion. *Up From Marseille, 781st Tank Battalion* (Camp Campbell, KY: The Battalion, 1945), 25.

45. AAR, 645th Tank Destroyer Battalion.

46. Josowitz, 45.

47. "Enemy Material Destroyed," memo, records of the 823d Tank Destroyer Battalion.

48. History, 773d Tank Destroyer Battalion.

49. History, 702d Tank Destroyer Battalion.

50. AAR, 635th Tank Destroyer Battalion.

51. *Study of Organization, Equipment, and Tactical Employment of Tank Destroyer Units*, 25, 28. Army Ground Forces Report No. 944.

52. *Spearhead in the West*, 28.

53. AAR, 634th Tank Destroyer Battalion, May 1945.

54. Sparks, *Victory TD*, 36-38.

55. Captain Elmer V. Sparks. "Analysis of Personnel Losses and Reinforcements for Separate TD Battalion Under Combat Conditions," Memorandum, March 1945.

56. AAR, 634th Tank Destroyer Battalion, May 1945.

57. History, 702d Tank Destroyer Battalion.

58. Josowitz, 45.

59. Green, 35.

60. *Study of Organization, Equipment, and Tactical Employment of Tank Destroyer Units*, 29.

Appendix A

1. Gill.

Appendix B

1. Josowitz. AARs, 601st Tank Destroyer Battalion.

2. Oliver. AARs, 602d Tank Destroyer Battalion.

3. AARs, 603d Tank Destroyer Battalion.

4. History, AARs, 605th Tank Destroyer Battalion. "History of the 605th TD Battalion," pamphlet, 1945.

5. Eby. History, AARs, 607th Tank Destroyer Battalion.

6. History, AARs, 609th Tank Destroyer Battalion.

7. McGrann.

8. History, AARs, 612th Tank Destroyer Battalion.

9. *614 Tank Destroyers WWII.*

10. Sparks, *Victory TD.*

11. History, AARs, 629th Tank Destroyer Battalion.

12. History, journal, AARs 630th Tank Destroyer Battalion.

13. History, 631st Tank Destroyer Battalion.

14. History, AARs, 633d Tank Destroyer Battalion.

15. History, 634th Tank Destroyer Battalion.

16. History of the 635th Tank Destroyer Battalion contained in the battalion's periodic report on medical department activities, 30 June 19.

17. Sherman. AARs, 636th Tank Destroyer Battalion.

18. History, AARs, 638th Tank Destroyer Battalion.

19. *644th Tank Destroyer Battalion.*

20. Operations reports, unit history, 645th Tank Destroyer Battalion.

21. History, AARs, 648th Tank Destroyer Battalion. The records contain major gaps.

22. AARs, 654th Tank Destroyer Battalion. James A. Sawicki, *Tank Battalions of the U.S. Army* (Dumfries, Va.: Wyvern Publications, 1983), 285.

23. History, 656th Tank Destroyer Battalion.

24. See, for example, History, 661st Tank Destroyer Battalion. http://www.69th-Infantry-Division.com/histories/661.html.

25. Diary, AARs, 679th Tank Destroyer Battalion.

26. History, 691st Tank Destroyer Battalion. Sawicki, 290. There are major gaps in the battalion records.

27. History, 692d Tank Destroyer Battalion.

28. Records of 701st Tank Destroyer Battalion.

29. History, 702d Tank Destroyer Battalion.

30. History, AARs, S-3 Journal, 703d Tank Destroyer Battalion. *Spearhead in the West.*

31. History, AARs, 704th Tank Destroyer Battalion.

32. History, AARs, 705th Tank Destroyer Battalion.

33. History, AARs, 771st Tank Destroyer Battalion.

34. AARs, 772d Tank Destroyer Battalion.

35. History, 773d Tank Destroyer Battalion.

36. *774th Tank Destroyer Battalion* (Nürnberg, Germany, 1945).

37. *An Informal History of the 776th Tank Destroyer Battalion.*

38. History, 801st Tank Destroyer Battalion.

39. Reconnaissance Company and battalion histories, AARs, 802d Tank Destroyer Battalion.

40. History, 803d Tank Destroyer Battalion.

41. Clement, et al.

42. Records of 805th Tank Destroyer Battalion.

43. *807th Tank Destroyer Battalion* (Published by unit, 1945?).

44. History, AARs, 808th Tank Destroyer Battalion.

45. History, AARs, 809th Tank Destroyer Battalion.

46. History, AARs, 811th Tank Destroyer Battalion.

47. AARs, Short History of the 813th Tank Destroyer Battalion.

48. Boykin, *Gare La Bête.* AARs, Short History of the 814th Tank Destroyer Battalion.

49. History, 817th Tank Destroyer Battalion.

50. The 818th Tank Destroyer Battalion left almost no records behind. Bits and pieces are available in the unit's medical detachment history, general orders, and S-3 journals for the last few weeks of the war.

51. History, 820th Tank Destroyer Battalion. Battalion records are missing for January-March 1945.

52. History, AARs, 821st Tank Destroyer Battalion.

53. History, AARs, 822d Tank Destroyer Battalion. Sawicki.

54. History, 823d Tank Destroyer Battalion.

55. History, 824th Tank Destroyer Battalion.

56. History, AARs, 825th Tank Destroyer Battalion.

57. History, AARs, 827th Tank Destroyer Battalion.

58. History, AARs, 893d Tank Destroyer Battalion. Sawacki.

59. Records of 894th Tank Destroyer Battalion. Gill, 47. Chase.

60. Records of 899th Tank Destroyer Battalion.

Bibliography

Books and Booklets

614 Tank Destroyers WWII. No publisher listed, 1946?

644th Tank Destroyer Battalion. Göttingen, Germany: Muster-Schmidt, 1945.

774th Tank Destroyer Battalion. Nürnberg, Germany: Zimmermann, 1945.

807th Tank Destroyer Battalion. Published by unit, 1945.

Allen, Col Robert S. *Patton's Third Army: Lucky Forward*. New York: Manor Books Inc., 1965.

Ambrose, Stephen E. *Citizen Soldiers*. New York, NY: Touchstone, 1997.

The American Arsenal. London: Greenhill Books, 2001. The Greenhill volume is essentially a reprint of the U.S. Army's *Catalog of Standard Ordnance Items* of 1944.

Anderson, Christopher J. *Hell on Wheels: The Men of the U.S. Armored Forces, 1918 to the Present*. London: Greenhill Books and Mechanicsburg, Pennsylvania: Stackpole Books, 1999.

Astor, Gerald. *The Greatest War: From Pearl Harbor to the Kasserine Pass*. New York, NY: Warner Books, Inc., 1999.

Atkinson, Rick. *An Army at Dawn: The War in North Africa, 1942–1943*. New York, NY: Henry Holt and Company, LLC, 2002.

Bishop, Chris, and Adam Warner, editors. *German Weapons of World War II*. Edison, NJ: Chartwell Books, Inc., 2001.

Blumenson, Martin. *Anzio: The Gamble That Failed*. New York, NY: Cooper Square Press, 2001.

Breakout and Pursuit: United States Army In World War II, The European Theater Of Operations. Washington, DC: Center of Military History, 1993.

Kasserine Pass. New York, NY: Jove Books, 1983.

Salerno to Cassino. Washington, DC: Office of the Chief of Military History, 1969.

Boykin, Calvin C., Jr. *Gare La Bête*. College Station, Texas: C&R Publications, 1995.

General A.D. Bruce: Father of Fort Hood. College Station, Texas: C&R Publications, 2002.

Bradley, Omar N. *A Soldier's Story*. New York NY: The Modern Library, 1999.

Bradley, Omar N., and Clay Blair. *A General's Life*. New York, NY: Simon and Schuster, 1983.

A Brief History of the U.S. Army in World War II. Center of Military History, United States Army, Washington, D.C., 1992.

Buchanan, Richard R., Richard D. Wissolik, David Wilmes, and Gary E.J. Smith, general editors. *Men of the 704th: A Pictorial and Spoken History of the 704th Tank Destroyer Battalion in World War II*. Latrobe, PA: Saint Vincent College Center for Northern Appalachian Studies, 1998.

Chamberlain, Peter. *Pictorial History of Tanks of the World, 1915–1945*. Harrisburg, PA: Stackpole Books, 1972.

Chase, Patrick J. *Seek, Strike, Destroy: The History of the 894th Tank Destroyer Battalion in World War II*. Baltimore, MD: Gateway Press, Inc., 1995.

Clarke, Jeffrey J., and Robert Ross Smith. *Riviera to the Rhine: United States Army in World War II, The European Theater of Operations*. Washington, DC: Office of the Chief of Military History, Department of the Army, 1993.

Clement, Maj Wallace L., Lt Bruce A. Berlin, Lt James D. Freed, and Lt John B. Gregg. *Eight Hundred and Fourth Tank Destroyer Battalion, 1941–1945, A History*. Camp Hood, Texas: 804th Tank Destroyer Battalion, 1945.

Cole, Hugh M. *Battle of the Bulge: United States Army in World War II, The European Theater of Operations*. Washington, DC: Center of Military History, 1993.

The Lorraine Campaign: United States Army in World War II, The European Theater of Operations. Washington, DC: Historical Division, Department of the Army, 1950.

Cooper, Belton Y. *Death Traps: The Survival of an American Armored Division in World War II*. Novato, CA: Presidio Press, Inc., 2000.

Dunnagan, Harry D. *A War to Win: Company "B"–813th Tank Destroyers*. Myrtle Beach, South Carolina: Royall Dutton Books, 1992.

Eby, Lt Harold H. *Tank Busters: 607 Tank Destroyer Battalion "Battle with the Jerries"*. Munich, Germany: 607th Tank Destroyer Battalion, 1945?

Eisenhower, Dwight D. *Crusade in Europe*. Garden City, NY: Doubleday and Company, Inc., 1948.

Fisher, Ernest J., Jr. *Cassino to the Alps: The United States Army in World War II, The Mediterranean Theater of Operations*. Washington, DC: Center of Military History, 1977.

Frankel, Nat, and Larry Smith. *Patton's Best: An Informal History of the 4th Armored Division*. New York, NY: The Berkley Publishing Group, 1984.

Gabel, Dr. Christopher R. *Seek, Strike, and Destroy: U.S. Army Tank Destroyer Doctrine in World War II*. Fort Leavenworth, Kansas: U.S. Army Command and General Staff College, 1985.

Gill, Lonnie. *Tank Destroyer Forces, WWII*. Paducah, Kentucky: Turner Publishing Company, 1992.

Green, Michael. *M4 Sherman*. Osceola, WI: Motorbooks International Publishers & Wholesalers, 1993.

Greenfield, Kent Roberts; Robert R. Palmer; and Bell I. Wiley. *The Organization of Ground Combat Troops: United States Army in World War II*. Washington, DC: Historical Division, Department of the Army, 1947.

Griess, Thomas E., ed. *The West Point Military History Series, The Second World War, Europe and the Mediterranean*. Wayne, NJ: Avery Publishing Group Inc., 1984.

Guderian, Heinz. *Panzer Leader*. New York, NY: Ballentine Books, 1972.

Houston, Donald E. *Hell on Wheels: The 2d Armored Division*. Novato, California: Presidio Press, 1977.

Howe, George F. *Northwest Africa: Seizing the Initiative in the West: United States Army in World War II, The Mediterranean Theater of Operations*. Washington, DC: Office of the Chief of Military History, Department of the Army, 1957.

An Informal History of the 776th Tank Destroyer Battalion. Salzburg, Austria: Anton Pustet, 1945?

Jablonski, Edward. *Wings of Fire*. Garden City, NY: Doubleday & Company, 1971.

Johnson, David E. *Fast Tanks and Heavy Bombers: Innovation in the U.S. Army 1917–1945*. Ithaca, NY: Cornell University Press, 1998.

Josowitz, Edward L. *An Informal History of the 601st Tank Destroyer Battalion*. Salzburg: Pustet, 1945.

Koyen, Capt Kenneth. *The Fourth Armored Division: From the Beach to Bavaria*. Munich, Germany: Herder Druck, 1946.

Knickerbocker, H. R., et al. *Danger Forward*. Atlanta, Georgia: Albert Love Enterprises, 1947.

Liddell Hart, B. H. *History of the Second World War*. New York, NY: G. Putnam's Sons, 1970.

MacDonald, Charles B. *The Battle of the Bulge*. London: Guild Publishing, 1984.

The Last Offensive: United States Army in World War II, The European Theater of Operations. Washington, DC: Office of the Chief of Military History, Department of the Army, 1993.

The Siegfried Line Campaign: United States Army in World War II, The European Theater of Operations. Washington, DC: Office of the Chief of Military History, Department of the Army, 1993.

McGrann, Capt Roy T. *The 610th Tank Destroyer Battalion*. No publication information provided.

Mesko, Jim. *U.S. Tank Destroyers in Action*. Carrollton, Texas: Squadron/Signal Publications, Inc., 1998.

Normandy. CMH Pub72-18. Washington, DC: U.S. Army Center of Military History, not dated.

Northern France. CMH Pub72-30. Washington, DC: U.S. Army Center of Military History, not dated.

Oliver, Bertrand J. *History, 602d Tank Destroyer Battalion, March 1941 to November 1945*. Lansing, Michigan: 602d Tank Destroyer Battalion Association, Inc., 1990.

Patton, George S., Jr. *War As I Knew It*. New York, NY: Bantam Books, 1980.

Reardon, Mark J. *Victory at Mortain: Stopping Hitler's Panzer Counteroffensive*. Lawrence, Kansas: University Press of Kansas, 2002.

Reynolds, Michael. *Steel Inferno: 1st SS Panzer Corps in Normandy*. New York: Dell Publishing, 1997.

Rhineland. CMH Pub72-25. Washington, DC: U.S. Army Center of Military History, not dated.

Sawicki, James A. T*ank Battalions of the U.S. Army*. Dumfries, Va.: Wyvern Publications, 1983.

Scheibert, Horst. *Kampf und Untergang der Deutschen Panzertruppe, 1939-1945*. Dorheim, Germany: Podzun Verlag, not dated.

Sherman, Thomas M. *Seek, Strike, Destroy! The History of the 636th Tank Destroyer Battalion*. Published by author: 1986.

Smith, George, Jack Hallowell, Joe F. Meis, Robert LeMense, Al Morgan, Irving Kintisch. *History of the 157th Infantry Regiment (Rifle), 4 June '43–8 May '45*. Baton Rouge, LA: Army & Navy Publishing Company, 1946.

Sparks, Capt Elmer V., editor-in-chief. *Victory TD*. Göttingen, Germany: 628th Tank Destroyer Battalion, 1945.

Spearhead in the West. Frankfurt, Germany: 3d Armored Division, 1945.

Southern France. CMH Pub72-31. Washington, DC: U.S. Army Center of Military History, not dated.

St. Lô, facsimile reprint of CMH Pub 100-13. Washington, DC: U.S. Army Center of Military History, 1983.

Tunisia. CMH Pub 72-12. Washington, DC: U.S. Army Center of Military History, not dated.

Up From Marseille, 781st Tank Battalion. Camp Campbell, KY: The Battalion, 1945.

Von Senger und Etterlin, Dr. F. M. *German Tanks of World War II*. New York, NY: Galahad Books, 1969.

Weeks, John. *Men Against Tanks: A History of Anti-Tank Warfare*. New York, New York: Mason/Charter Publishers, Inc., 1975.

Whiting, Charles. *The Battle of the Ruhr Pocket*. New York, NY: Ballentine Books Inc, 1970.

First Blood: The Battle of Kasserine Pass 1943. London: Grafton Books, 1984.

The Other Battle of the Bulge: Operation Northwind. Chelsea, Michigan: Scarborough House, 1990.

Whitlock, Flint. *The Rock of Anzio, From Sicily to Dachau: A History of the 45th Infantry Division*. Boulder, Colorado: Westview Press, 1998.

Wilmot, Chester. *The Struggle for Europe*. Ware, England: Wordsworth Editions Limited, 1997.

Wissolik, Richard D., and Gary E.J. Smith, general editors. *Reluctant Valor: The Oral History of Captain Thomas J. Evans*. Latrobe, PA: Saint Vincent College Center for Northern Appalachian Studies, 1995.

Articles

"Tank Destroyers: They Are the Army's Answer to the Tank Menace." *Life*, 26 October 1942.

"The Tank Killers." *Fortune*, November 1942.

Unpublished Special Studies

Baker, LtCol Herschel D. "El Guettar," *TD Combat in Tunisia*. Tank Destroyer School, 1944.

"Defense of the West Wall." ETHINT-37. Historical Division, Headquarters United States Army, Europe. This is an interview with Major Herbert Büchs, aide to Generaloberst Alfred Jodl, 28 September 1945. National Archives.

Ellmann, Maj Gilbert A. "Gafsa and Sbeitla," *TD Combat in Tunisia*. Tank Destroyer School, 1944.

"Employment of Panzer Forces on the Western Front." ETHINT-39. Historical Division, Headquarters United States Army, Europe, 1945. This is an interview with Generaloberst Heinz Guderian, 16 August 1945. National Archives.

Fries, General der Panzertruppen a.d. Walter. "29th Panzergrenadier Division (Feb. 1944)," MS # D-141. Historical Division, Headquarters United States Army, Europe, not dated. National Archives.

"Panzer Tactics in Normandy". ETHINT-13. Historical Division, Headquarters United States Army, Europe, 11 December 1947. This is a record of an interview conducted with General der Panzertruppen Leo Freiherr Geyr von Schweppenburg, who was commander of Panzer Gruppe West from 1943 to 5 July 1944 and Inspector of Panzer Troops from August 1944 to May 1945. National Archives.

Redding, LtCol F. J. "The Operations of 'C' Company, 701st Tank Destroyer Battalion (with the British First Army), Vicinity of Medjez el Bab–Beja, Tunisia, 24 November–11 December 1942, Tunisian Campaign (Personal Experience of a Company Commander)." Unpublished manuscript prepared for the Advanced Infantry Officers Course, 1948–1949.

Schmidt, Generalmajor Martin. "Panzer Units, Employment in Central Italy, 1944." MS # D-204. Historical Division, Headquarters United States Army, Europe, 1947. National Archives.

"Sixth Pz Army (16 Nov 44–4 Jan 45)." ETHINT-21. Historical Division, Headquarters United States Army, Europe, 1945. This is an interview with Generalmajor (Waffen SS) Fritz Kraemer, 8–9 August 1945.

"Sixth Pz Army in the Ardennes Offensive." ETHINT-16. Historical Division, Headquarters United States Army, Europe, 1945. This is an interview with Generaloberst (Waffen SS) Josef "Sepp" Dietrich, 8-9 August 1945. National Archives.

Study of Organization, Equipment, and Tactical Employment of Tank Destroyer Units. U.S. Army, US Forces in the European Theater, the General Board, 1946.

Von Gersdorff, General Freiherr. "The German Counterattack Against Avranches." MS # B-725, Historical Division, Headquarters United States Army, Europe, 1946. National Archives.

Von Kahlden, Oberst iG, Chief of Staff, Fifth Panzer Army. "Fifth Pz Army (15 Sep–15 Oct 44)." MS # B-472, Historical Division, Headquarters United States Army, Europe, not dated. National Archives.

Von Lütwitz, General der Panzertruppe Freiherr Heinrich. "Questions for Heinrich von Lüttwitz, Commanding General of the 2d Panzer Division Until September 1944." MS # A-904, Historical Division, Headquarters United States Army, Europe, October 1945. National Archives.

Von Wietersheim, Generalleutnant Wend. "The 11th Panzer Division in Southern France (15 August–14 September 1944)," MS # A-880, Historical Division, Headquarters United States Army, Europe, 1946. National Archives.

"The Employment of the 11th Panzer Division in Lorraine." MS # B-364, Historical Division, Headquarters United States Army, Europe, 10 January 1947. National Archives.

On-Line Resources

Anderson, Rich. "The United States Army in World War II." Military History Online. http://www.militaryhistoryonline.com/wwii/usarmy, 2000.

Billings, Linwood W. *The Tunisian Taskforce.* See website: http://historicaltextarchive.com/ww2/tunisian.html.

"History of the 1st Armored Regiment." See website Http:// macspics. Homestead.com/history.html.

Wehrtechnik.net. http://www.wehrtechnik.net/wehrtechnik/index.

Index[*]

[*] (FNU)=First name unknown